The Operational Auditing Handbook

The Operational Auditing Handbook

Auditing Business Processes

**Andrew Chambers
and Graham Rand**

JOHN WILEY & SONS

Chichester • New York • Weinheim • Brisbane • Singapore • Toronto

Other Wiley Editorial Offices

John Wiley & Sons, Inc., 605 Third Avenue,
New York, NY 10158-0012, USA

Wiley-VCH Verlag GmbH,
Pappellalee 3, D-69469, Weinheim, Germany

Jacaranda Wiley Ltd, 33 Park Road, Milton,
Queensland 4064, Australia

John Wiley & Sons (Asia) Pte Ltd, 2 Clementi Loop #02-01,
Jin Xing Distripark, Singapore 129809

John Wiley & Sons (Canada) Ltd, 22 Worcester Road,
Rexdale, Ontario M9W 1L1, Canada

Library of Congress Cataloging-in-Publication Data

Chambers, Andrew D.
    The operational auditing handbook : auditing business processes /
Andrew Chambers and Graham Rand.
        p.   cm.
    Includes bibliographical references and index.
    ISBN 0-471-97060-3
    1. Management audit.   I. Rand, G. V. (Graham V.)   II. Title.
HD58.95.C48   1997
658.4—dc20   96–41459
                                                                                    CIP
British Library Cataloguing in Publication Data

A catalogue record for this book is available from the British Library

ISBN 0-471-97060-3

Typeset in 10/12pt Times from the author's disks by Dobbie Typesetting Ltd, Tavistock, Devon
Printed and bound by Antony Rowe Ltd, Eastbourne

Contents

Preface

This book is designed to fill a gap by providing an up-to-date guide to operational auditing. The format makes the book friendly as a practical handbook.

It is intended as a companion for those who design self-assessment programmes of business processes to be undertaken by management and staff. Likewise it is a mentor for internal auditors and consultants who conduct audits on behalf of others. We have developed the book to cater for both private and public sectors and to be a basis for designing value-for-money audit approaches. We also believe that external auditors dealing with financial and accounting systems and often engaged in management audits will find the book of value and should have it in their libraries.

At the same time we have had in mind the professional qualification requirements in this subject area of the Institute of Internal Auditors, with the intention that this book will be a suitable standard text. Particularly with the student in mind we have where appropriate supported specific points with cross referenced notes which appear at the end of each chapter, and there is a comprehensive bibliography.

The book's timeliness comes partly from the mix of business processes included, and the contemporary treatment given to each. In part it comes from the ways we have attempted to weave in the contemporary approaches and issues of, for instance, business process re-engineering, just-in-time management, downsizing, delayering, empowerment, environment, ethics, control self-assessment and IT. In part it is a matter of the risk evaluation techniques which we describe as often being appropriate aids for those who must review and evaluate business processes.

This is not intended to be the complete "how to audit" book; rather, its aim is to raise the consciousness of the underlying issues, risks and objectives for a wide range of operations and activities. In other words, it aims to stimulate creative thought about the business context of operational audit reviews. In practice, it would be an extremely difficult task to define a set of universal panacea approaches to the audit of the various operational areas of any organisation, as the driving motivations and the contexts into which they are set would vary between entities. In adopting a business-oriented stance supported by practical examples of the key questions to resolve, we hope that audit creativity will be encouraged rather than stifled by over-prescriptive programmes and routines. Readers will need to take account of their own experiences and the relevant aspects of the cultures prevailing within their organisations, and bring these to bear on the contents of this book, so that a suitably tailored approach to auditing operations emerges.

Much of what is here is a distillation in book form of some of the best expertise contained within certain of Management Audit's software products—notably the *Standard Audit Programme Guides* and the control risk matrices of the *Control.IT MINPLAN* software applications. Those products in turn were produced in response to client demand and with major inputs from both public and private sector clients. Other content of this book is the result of specific assignments completed for clients, who have in the main been internal auditors and the audit committees of boards.

So, we are confident that this "real world" pedigree of this book will make it eminently useful for practising auditors, line managers, consultants, and those who intend to become qualified as operational auditors.

We would appreciate readers' comments and advice for future editions.

Andrew Chambers
Managing Director
Management Audit Limited
The Water Mill
Moat lane
Old Bolingbroke
Spilsby
Lincolnshire
PE23 4EU
England

Tel.: +44 (0)1790 763350
Fax: +44 (0)1790 763253
E-mail: 100713.2663@compuserve.com

Acknowledgements

We thank the many clients and friends of Management Audit who have been the stimulus for much of the content and approach of this book. In particular, Andrew Steet, Group Audit Director of Corange has stimulated many insights and provided many opportunities for us to work in this area. We are also indebted to Dr Ian Black, Group Chief Internal Auditor of ICI.

The authors are particularly appreciative of Spencer Pickett and Professor Georges Selim. Both past students of Andrew Chambers, they are now serving their own internal auditing students with distinction at the Civil Service College in England and City University Business School in London. They kindly read through the full manuscript with care, making many useful suggestions which we believe have led to a better book.

We have quoted from sources published by The American Institute of Certified Public Accountants, The British Standards Institute, The Chartered Institute of Public Finance & Accountancy, The City University Business School, The Consultative Committee of Accounting Bodies, The Data Protection Registrar, The Department of Trade & Industry, Frederick A. Prager, The Institute of Internal Auditors, The International Chamber of Commerce, McGraw-Hill, Pitman, and Stanley Thornes. In every case we have endeavoured to provide full attribution for the material we have used and to obtain the appropriate permissions. If there has been any oversight on our part we apologise and would like to correct it at our first opportunity.

The authors are particularly grateful to Jackie Badley of Management Audit for her essential, careful, professional and laborious work on the manuscript; and to Richard Baggaley of Wiley for his friendly and wise support, encouragement and advice at all times both over this project and with respect to the General Editorship of the new Wiley journal *International Journal of Auditing*.

Andrew Chambers
Graham Rand

1

Approaches to Operational Auditing

DEFINITIONS OF "OPERATIONAL AUDITING"

The term "operational auditing" conjures up different images for internal auditors. It may be used to mean any of the following:

The audit of *operating units* such as factories, subsidiary companies, overseas operations. With this meaning the scope of the audit may be limited to accounting and financial controls or it may be given a wider scope.

The audit of accounting and financial control in *the functional areas of a business*, as distinct from the controls that are exercised within the accounting and financial functions of the business. These functional areas might be marketing, sales, distribution, production, and so on, depending on the nature of the business. This use of the expression operational auditing stresses that internal audit has a mission to review all operational areas of the business; it also implies, not necessarily correctly, that internal audit is an agent of the finance director or chief accountant who needs reassurance that appropriate financial and accounting controls are being applied in the operational areas of the business.

The audit of *any part of the business* (operating unit, functional area, department, accounting department, treasury department, etc.) where the audit objective corresponds to a review of the effectiveness and efficiency with which management is achieving its own objectives. This style of operational auditing may go beyond a review of internal control issues since management does not achieve its objectives simply by adhering to satisfactory systems of internal control. Alternatively the scope of the audit may be restricted to the internal control issues (financial and accounting controls and, often more significantly, operational controls) which contribute to the achievement of management's objectives in the operational area subject to review by internal audit.

Support for this style of auditing is given by leading management thinkers, for example:

> An effective tool of managerial control is the internal audit, or, as it is now coming to be called, the operational audit...Although often limited to the auditing of accounts, in its most useful aspect operational auditing involves appraisal of operations generally...Thus operational auditors, in addition to assuring themselves that accounts properly reflect the facts, also appraise policies, procedures, use of authority, quality of management, effectiveness of methods, special problems, and other phases of operations.
>
>   There is no persuasive reason why the concept of internal auditing should not be broadened in practice. Perhaps the only limiting factors are the ability of an enterprise to afford so broad an audit, the difficulty of obtaining people who can do a broad type of audit, and the very practical consideration that individuals may not like to be reported upon. While persons responsible for accounts and for the safeguarding of company assets have learned to accept audit, those who are responsible for far more valuable things—the execution of the plans, policies and procedures of a company—have not so readily learned to accept the idea."[1]

SCOPE

A key issue for a business and its internal audit function to decide upon is whether the scope of internal audit work in an operational area of the business should be restricted to internal control issues or should be a comprehensive, general review of the operation.

The Committee of Sponsoring Organizations (COSO) view of internal control rightly sees one of the three objectives of internal control as being to give "reasonable assurance" of "effectiveness and efficiency of operations". But internal control (i.e. management control) is only one of a number of facets of management—among others being planning, organising, staffing and leading. It is true that these facets overlap and an internal audit which is restricted to internal control issues may need to address planning, organising, staffing and/or leadership issues, since deficiencies in these may weaken control. But there will be many aspects of planning, organising, staffing and leading which are neutral in their control effect but which contribute to the achievement of efficient and effective operations.

The key issue is whether internal audit may legitimately draw management's attention to deficiencies in planning, organising, staffing and leading which, while not weakening control nevertheless impede the achievement of objectives. Internal audit is often defined as *the independent appraisal of the effectiveness of internal control*: control is not the whole of the management process. Should an enlightened enterprise restrict internal audit to internal control matters, or should internal audit be encouraged to review and report on *any matters* which may be commercially unsound? The jury is out on this! Differing positions are adopted in different enterprises. The middle-of-the-road enlightened approach is to encourage internal audit to interpret its mission as being the *appraisal of internal control* only (in all its component parts,[2] in all operational areas of the business and at all levels of management) and not deliberately to broaden its scope beyond this. However, if during the course of audit work, other matters are noted incidentally which should be of management concern but do not directly have a control dimension, internal audit should be encouraged to report them to management.

Beyond the consideration of the point of focus for audit reviews of operational areas, the audit function will have to define those aspects of the organisation which are to be subject to review. In practice, of course, this will vary considerably between organisations, and directly be related to the nature of the business and the way the organisation is structured. For example, a multinational pharmaceutical company may have its principal manufacturing bases and research and development activities in only those few countries where the economic and commercial environments are most suitable, whereas sales and marketing operations (of varying scale) may exist in every country where there is a proven market for the products.

Although the focus of operational auditing is likely to be on those activities which are most strongly associated with the main commercial markets of the organisation (for example, production, sales, after sales support, service provision, etc.), it is likely that the supporting or infrastructure operations will also need to be reviewed on the basis that they too contribute to the well-being of the organisation as a whole. At the top level, one possible categorisation of all these areas could be as follows (although this classification will not fit every business or service-provision scenario):

- management and administration
- financial and accounting
- personnel
- procurement
- stock and materials handling
- production/manufacturing
- marketing and sales
- after sales support
- research and development
- information technology.

This particular top-level classification would be appropriate for a large organisation involved in product development, manufacturing and sales activities. A different type of model would emerge for an organisation (public or private) associated with providing a service (for example, a public health authority or a roadside vehicle repair service).

Below this level of categorisation, there would be specific or discrete activities or systems, each of which may be the subject of a separate operational audit review. The subsequent chapters of this book will predominantly examine operational areas from this systems/activities orientation. For each of the above classifications there will be a number of discrete functions, systems or activities which may be defined within a particular organisation and be subject to examination by the internal auditors. This breakdown of the organisation into a set of separate audit reviews could be said to form the *audit universe* of potential audit projects. For example, the top-level classifications noted above could be broken into the constituent systems or activities listed below, each of which could be the subject of an audit review. In some cases the noted subjects may readily align with a department within the organisation (i.e. payroll, human resources, purchasing, etc.). Alternatively, the activities may require co-ordination between a number of departments or functions (for example, the development of a new product may involve, *inter alia*, the marketing, accounting and research functions). Each organisation will be different and the internal audit function will need to adopt the most suitable definition of their *universe* of potential review assignments in order to match the prevailing structure and style.

Management and administration:

- the control environment
- organisation (i.e. structure)
- management information
- planning
- risk management
- legal department
- quality management
- estates management and facilities
- environmental issues
- insurance
- security
- capital projects
- industry regulation and compliance
- media, public and external relations
- company secretarial department

Financial and accounting:

- treasury
- payroll
- accounts payable
- accounts receivable
- general ledger/management accounts
- fixed assets (and capital charges)
- budgeting and monitoring
- bank accounts and banking arrangements
- sales tax (i.e. VAT) accounting
- taxation
- inventories
- product/project accounting
- petty cash and expenses
- financial information and reporting
- investments

Personnel:

- human resources department (including policies)
- recruitment
- manpower and succession planning
- staff training and development
- welfare
- pension scheme (and other benefits)
- health insurance
- staff appraisal and disciplinary matters
- health and safety
- labour relations
- company vehicles

Procurement:

- purchasing
- contracting (NB: this subject may be further broken down into a number of discrete sub-systems, such as tendering, controlling interim and final payments, etc.)

Stock and materials handling:

- stock control
- warehousing and storage
- distribution, transport and logistics

Production/manufacturing:

- planning and production control
- facilities, plant and equipment
- personnel
- materials and energy
- quality control
- safety
- environmental issues
- law and regulatory compliance
- maintenance

Marketing and sales:

- product development
- market research
- promotion and advertising
- pricing and discount policies
- sales management
- sales performance and monitoring
- distribution
- relationship with parent company (for overseas or subsidiary operations)
- agents
- order processing

After sales support:

- warranty arrangements
- maintenance and servicing
- spare parts and supply

Research and development:

- product development
- project appraisal and monitoring
- plant and equipment
- development project management
- legal and regulatory issues

Information Technology (IT):

- IT Strategic Planning
- IT Organisation
- IT Sites
- processing operations
- back-up and media
- systems/operating software
- system access control
- personal computers
- software maintenance
- local area networks (LANs)
- databases
- data protection
- facilities management
- system development
- software selection
- contingency planning
- electronic data interchange (EDI)
- viruses
- electronic office
- user support
- spreadsheet design
- expert systems
- IT Accounting

It is unwise to restrict one's thinking of these systems or activities as either existing or operating in isolation. This is rarely true. Any organisation will be formed from a number of interacting activities with points of interface. For example, in the case of ordering and receiving goods from external suppliers, where there needs to be a flow of accurate information between the purchasing department, the stock warehouse, and the accounts payable section. Whereas the control processes operating within a function or department may be well defined and applied, there is the potential for control weaknesses at the point of interface with other related functions. There are alternative ways of dividing up the *audit universe* of activities within an organisation and Chapter 16 examines such approaches in some detail.

It is important to stress that the listing of possible systems and activities noted above is but one example of the way in which an organisation can be defined for audit or review purposes. Not all the items will be appropriate in every organisation. Additionally, although a listed activity may be relevant to a particular scenario, the scale and significance of it will vary between organisations. This matter of degree should be taken into account when the audit function is determining its priorities for planning purposes.

When approaching the review of operational areas of the organisation, it is important that the auditor has an accurate appreciation of the related key issues. If necessary, prior research should be conducted in order to provide the auditor with an acceptable level of understanding. Beyond the auditor's self-interest in being able to tackle confidently the review project, there is also the matter of the auditor's credibility in the eyes of operational management. Unless the auditor can readily demonstrate a pragmatic awareness of the critical issues and set these against the objectives set by senior management for the area under review, any subsequent work and findings may be in danger of not being treated seriously by management due to inaccuracies and misinterpretations. The auditing approach to be adopted during operational reviews needs to be both professional and practical, and these elements will need to be set into the context of the formal auditing procedures. The practical and behavioural aspects of auditing are beyond the scope of this book. However, unless management can be suitably assured that the reviews conducted by internal audit are objective, professional and based upon an accurate understanding of the issues, they may question the worth of such activities to the organisation.

AUDIT APPROACH TO OPERATIONAL AUDITS

Adopting the middle-of-the-road orientation to operational auditing, the following is an effective approach, which has the merit that it strikes a chord with management as management's objectives are central to the audit throughout. It can be irksome to line management if the internal auditor seems to be asking only the question "What might go wrong?" and rarely the question "Is management going to achieve their objectives?". Motivated line management are not just charged with the responsibility to prevent unwanted exposures materialising—they have a mission to achieve objectives. An audit approach which acknowledges this will be both more useful and more acceptable. In this context, *some but not all* of management's objectives will relate to the prevention of unwanted outcomes.

Example of the objectives-oriented audit approach

An internal audit team based at Group HQ in New York is commencing an audit of an operating unit which is in Tokyo. As a fundamental part of their preparation for the fieldwork of this audit they meet with senior management who have overall responsibility for the Tokyo operation. There may be several senior managers, perhaps at director level, who share this responsibility for differing aspects of the Tokyo operation but, to simplify this example, let us assume that there is just one Group Production Director in New York to whom the head of the Tokyo operating unit reports for all purposes.

The audit team commences by establishing with the Group Production Director *(1) "what are his or her objectives for the Tokyo operation?"*. Right away the audit team may have significant findings for later inclusion in their audit report if it is apparent that the Director is unclear as to what the objectives are. Nevertheless, it is necessary for the audit team to establish what the objectives must be as the rest of the audit flows from this.

Having established the Director's objectives for the Tokyo operation, the audit team then determines, in consultation with the Director, *(2) "What information does the Director need to receive so as to be in a position to know whether the operation is on course to achieve its set objectives?"*. Here again, the audit team may come up with findings for later inclusion in their audit report as audit investigation may reveal that the director is unclear as to what information he or she needs.

The audit team then checks on the available information at the director's disposal. This may lead to the following audit findings:

- the needed information *is not* being received
  - at all;
  - in time;
  - in a helpful, useful format; etc.
- the director is not making use of some of the needed information which he or she is receiving.

- some unnecessary information *is* being prepared and received.

All of the above is done by the audit team *before* they leave their New York HQ to visit the Tokyo operation. Their approach in Tokyo is to confirm the validity of the information sent from Tokyo to New York and to determine whether there is any other information which New York should be receiving (but are not) in the light of:

- what is actually happening in Tokyo.

- where it has a potential impact on the achievement of management's objectives for the Tokyo operation.

THE "3 E'S" OR THE "6 E'S"

Internal auditors of operations need to understand the distinctive meanings of effectiveness, efficiency and economy.

Effectiveness means "doing the right things"—i.e. achieving objectives.

Efficiency means "doing them well"—for instance with good systems which avoid waste and rework.

Economy means "doing them cheap"—with, for instance, unit costs for labour, materials, etc. being under control.

These three E's can be related to each other as shown in the model in Figure 1.1:

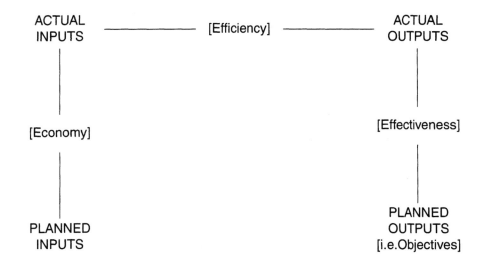

ACTUAL
INPUTS ——————— [Efficiency] ——————— ACTUAL
OUTPUTS

[Economy]

[Effectiveness]

PLANNED
INPUTS

PLANNED
OUTPUTS
[i.e.Objectives]

> *Economy*—the ratio between planned inputs and actual inputs in terms of unit costs.
> *Efficiency*—the ratio of actual inputs to actual outputs.
> *Effectiveness*—the ratio of actual outputs to planned outputs.

Figure 1.1   The three E's

Internal auditors are now adding further E's to their portfolio of matters of audit interest:

Equity—avoidance of discrimination and unfairness.

Environment—acting in an environmentally responsible way.

Ethics—legal and moral conduct by management and staff.

VALUE FOR MONEY (VFM) AUDITING

Value for money auditing is auditing which takes account of the 3 E's. It frequently makes extensive use of performance indicators in the form of ratios and other statistics to give an indication of value for money—especially when trends are explored in these performance indicators over time, or variations in performance are identified and explained between different operating units. This subject is more fully explored in Chapter 2.

ENVIRONMENTAL AUDITING

Environmental auditing has been defined as:

"A management tool comprising a systematic, documented, periodic and objective evaluation of how well environmental organisation, management and equipment are performing with the aim of helping to safeguard the environment by:

- facilitating management control of environmental practices;
- assessing compliance with company policies, which would include meeting regulatory requirements."[3]

Where an enterprise has environmental considerations as some of their objectives it is entirely necessary and appropriate that internal controls should facilitate the assured achievement of those objectives. Hence environmental auditing becomes something that concerns internal auditors. Businesses may choose to have separate environmental audits conducted by someone other than internal audit; but internal audit should be in a position to provide this service to the business, and to take account of work done by others that contributes to meeting this objective.

As with other issues that are subject to internal audits, the establishment of management's objectives (in this case relating to environmental responsibility) is not so much the remit of internal audit as is the appraisal of the extent to which internal controls provide management with an assurance of meeting those objectives. Specialist environmental auditors may take more naturally to commending to management what their environmental objectives should be. Nevertheless it is wise that internal auditors should be willing to give this advice to managements who seek it from them.

Internal audit has long been concerned to advise management when regulatory requirements in general are not being met—one of the accepted (COSO) objectives of internal control is "to provide reasonable assurance regarding the achievement of . . . compliance with applicable laws and regulations". Where there are applicable laws and regulations relating to environmental matters, a scope for internal audit work which includes environmental considerations becomes mainstream for internal auditors, unless explicitly excluded by management and the board.

Auditing environmental responsibility is further examined in Chapter 15, and a sample Code of Ethical Conduct covering scientific and environmental matters is given in Appendix 9.

QUALITY AUDIT

Enterprises that have adopted total quality management (TQM) principles and have sought to develop (and perhaps to register) so-called quality systems (QS) under ISO, British or other similar standards, may entrust to specialist quality auditors the task of reviewing the enterprise's performance with respect to TQM and QS. As with environmental auditing, it is not inappropriate for internal audit to take on this responsibility: if the organisation has objectives relating to TQM and QS it is appropriate for internal audit to review the internal controls that contribute to the achievement of those objectives.

The concepts of TQM and the implications for internal audit are further discussed in Chapter 17.

NOTES

1. Koontz H., O'Donnell, C. and Weihrich, H. (1976) *Management*, 8th edn. McGraw-Hill, Singapore, pp. 670–1.
2. The COSO *Internal Control—Integrated Framework* study (September 1992) identified the five components of internal control as being (1) control environment, (2) risk assessment, (3) control activities, (4) information and communication and (5) monitoring.
3. The International Chamber of Commerce (1989) *Environmental Auditing*. ICC Publishing SA, Paris.

2

Evaluating Operational Performance

INTRODUCTION

In Chapter 1, we introduced the concept of the 3 Es of effectiveness, efficiency and economy using the model and definitions shown in Figure 2.1.

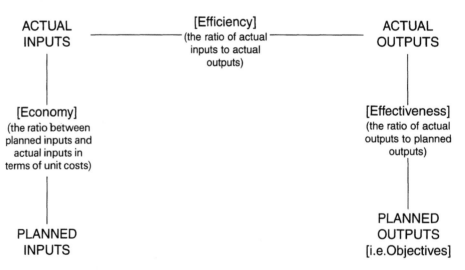

Effectiveness means "doing the right things" — i.e. achieving objectives.
Efficiency means "doing them well" — for instance with good systems which avoid waste and rework.
Economy means "doing them cheaply" — with, for instance, unit costs for labour, materials, etc. being under control.

Figure 2.1 The three E's of effectiveness, efficiency and economy

In this chapter we build on this premise and explore the related subjects of measuring operational performance and value for money auditing.

In order to bring all the relevant issues closer to home, we conclude this chapter by applying the principles of performance measurement to the internal auditing function itself.

PRODUCTIVITY AND PERFORMANCE MEASUREMENT SYSTEMS

Overview

Organisations are likely to have in place a number of key performance measures, so as to, among other things, assess the achievement of their objectives and goals, assess their progress, and compare relative performance (for example, over time). The nature and form of such measures will, of course, vary between types of organisation and indeed specific specialised forms of measurement may apply in certain industries or sectors. However, there are a number of general measures of effectiveness, efficiency and economy which usually apply universally and we shall look at some examples later in this chapter.

Measurement methods can be applied in order to identify whether there is any initial potential for improvement, and then subsequently used to monitor that the required levels of performance are maintained. The need to apply effective and realistic performance measurement methods is often generated as a by-product of fundamental change processes where, for example, an organisation is re-focusing its strategy and position.

The Audit Implications for Measurement

During the course of a review of an operational area, the auditor is often faced with the need either to set the review findings into an appropriate context, or to indicate the performance of the area under review against the criteria previously established by management.

In most cases, it is preferable to utilise the measurement standards and criteria put in place by management as this results in the auditor using a common and compatible language when communicating results and points of concern. Conversely, if the auditor chooses to use a new, alternative or perhaps radical form of performance measure, this may influence or jeopardise management's view of the auditor's findings. This is not to say that auditors should only adopt the prevailing measurement criteria established by management, as there may be a compelling reason for introducing another objective form of performance assessment in some cases. Whatever the form of measurement applied, its use must be founded on both accurate and reliable data and a proven method, otherwise the credibility of internal audit will suffer.

Although it is important to establish a reliable and meaningful vocabulary for the measurement of performance in key operations, auditors must not lose sight of the fact that such measures can only point to potential areas of improvement and do not of themselves offer solutions.[1] Assuming that the conclusions drawn from the review of such criteria are accurate and relative, they can then be used to frame and support audit recommendations and the appropriate corrective action(s).

In their use of performance measurement, auditors should be careful not to supplant management's use and interpretation of the same criteria. On the one hand, it may be legitimate for an auditor to investigate further the lack of management response to an adverse measurement indicator, but this does not necessarily mean that management has abdicated their basic responsibility for monitoring and control. This underlines a basic truism, in that measurement data is provided for interpretation and unless there is a formal measurement protocol in place, there may be the potential for differing conclusions to be drawn from the same data. This stresses the importance of formally establishing, for the organisation, a performance measurement policy and framework so that all concerned are clear about the nature of the data and how to use it in practice. Additionally, the creation and communication of corporate targets and goals can remove (or at least contain) some of the ambiguity associated with the required level of performance and expected level of associated achievement.

Each operational audit review project will present the auditor with a challenge to identify the most appropriate and meaningful performance measures to utilise, whether or not such criteria are already applied within the organisation.

Example Performance Measures

When establishing performance measures, it is logical to structure them on a hierarchal basis with the macro-level indicators being broken into more detailed (micro-level) measures relative to specific areas or subdivisions of either the operations or organisation. This should be borne in mind when considering the following example performance measures. The examples in this section were drawn from *Internal Auditing* by Chambers, Selim and Vinten (1987), pages 361–2.

Workload/Demand Performance Measures

Indicate the volume of output, whether services, products or other, and when linked to measures of input of resources, give useful information on quality or quantity matters.

Examples:

- Number of users.
- Number of units produced.
- Number of books in a library.
- Percentage of first class degrees in a university.

Economy Performance Measures

These may highlight waste in the provision of resources indicating that the same resources may be provided more cheaply or that more enterprise may be conducted at the same cost.

Examples:

- Cost of actual input in comparison with planned input.
- Cleaning costs per hour worked.
- Maintenance costs per unit area.
- Cost of the finance function per 100 staff.
- Cost of the chief executive's department per 1000 clients.

Efficiency Performance Measures

These may highlight potential opportunities to convert given resources to end product with less waste. Many performance measures will point to either uneconomic or inefficient practices, or both. It is often not possible to distinguish between one and the other.

Examples:

- Ratio of actual input to actual output.
- Breakdown per production day.
- Accidents at work per 1000 personnel.
- Degree success in comparison to school examination grades.

Effectiveness Performance Measures

These performance measures focus on how objectives are being achieved— regardless of economy, efficiency or equity (except where the objectives relate specifically to economy, efficiency and equity).

Examples:

- Actual output in comparison to planned output.
- Degree success (in a college or university).
- Research output per 100 research staff.
- Ratio of customer complaints to sales.

Equity Performance Measures

These performance measures draw attention to unfairness or potential social irresponsibility in terms of corporate policy and practice.

Examples:

- Departmental grant per member of staff.
- Number of library books per category of user.
- Proportion of female employees.
- Proportion of disabled employees.

VALUE FOR MONEY (VFM) AUDITING

Value for money auditing takes account of the 3 Es. It frequently makes extensive use of performance indicators in the form of ratios and other statistics to give an indication of value for money—especially when trends are explored in these performance indicators over time, or variations in performance are identified and explained between different operating units.

The term value for money is often applied to public sector spending in the UK, where there is an implied obligation placed on public bodies to ensure that they obtain and provide services on the most economic grounds. This process invariably involves elements of competition where cost comparisons are made between parties being invited to supply goods and services. For example, many services within UK local government have been put out to tender in order to obtain the "best deal", and very often this tendering process has also included the internal department or function that had previously been supplying the service.

This striving for procurement on a *least cost* basis appears to be very logical and represent common sense, especially where the expenditure of public funds is involved. However, it is equally important to consider whether the potential service provider (or supplier or contractor) can meet the required quality and performance standards as well. Therefore, any consideration of value for money must take in quality and performance achievement factors as well, as there may be serious commercial or operational implications if the relevant services/goods are not up to a given standard.

Value for money auditing will involve the assessment of an appropriate range of performance measurement criteria. It could be asked that unless management have clearly established their own basis for measuring and assessing the supply of goods and the provision of services, why did they embark on the process in first place? In other words, what was their driving motivation in either fulfilling the requirements or seeking alternatives?

In both the management and audit assessment of matters of value for money, the usual approach is to make comparisons with a range of options or possible solutions to the principal problem. These comparisons should be conducted as scientifically and objectively as possible and utilise appropriate measurement means. This part of the process begins with realistically identifying all the practical options and alternatives (perhaps including doing nothing at all).

In a more formal environment (for example, where acquiring new computing facilities) it may be necessary and desirable to go through a detailed feasibility study as part of an overall project appraisal process. This can then incorporate the appropriate cost and performance comparisons which underline the determination of value for money. In such scenarios, it is important that the auditor is content with the chosen assessment mechanism and measurement criteria so that, taken together, the appropriate reassurance can be derived that the process is sound and accurate. In some instances it may be necessary for the auditors to recommend improvements in these areas to add value to the process, whilst avoiding usurping management's ultimate responsibility for their system.

Whether or not a formal procedure is in place to determine generally the achievement of value for money, the internal audit function may be required (or indeed obliged) independently to assess such matters on behalf of management. Auditors should always avoid taking on activities which should, in the first place, be the responsibility of management. However, where internal audit has a legitimate role to play, auditors should endeavour to identify all the probable options and the most suitable basis on which they should be measured and assessed in value terms.

In order to avoid any potential problems at the conclusion of their assessment, auditors should consider discussing their proposed assessment and measurement criteria with management at the outset, and furthermore to obtain the agreement of management on the applied methodology. In certain sectors and industries, recognised criteria may already exist and so it may not be necessary for auditors to develop their own process.

BENCHMARKING

Benchmarking can be defined simply as a comparison of one's own performance in a specific area with that applied by others in compatible circumstances. As a technique it is founded on the premise that there may be viable alternative ways of performing a process and fulfilling a requirement.

For a benchmarking exercise to be meaningful, it is necessary to understand fully the existing processes, systems and activities as a firm basis for subsequent comparison with external points of reference (such as industry or professional standards). This process of realisation often incorporates the establishment of critical success factors for an operation (or part thereof). The principal objectives of benchmarking are likely to include

- maintaining a competitive advantage in the appropriate market
- establishing current methods, best practice and related trends
- ensuring the future survival of the organisation
- maintaining an awareness of customer expectations (and being able to address them)
- ensuring that the organisation has the appropriate approach to quality issues.

The focus of a benchmarking exercise can be varied in relation to the fundamental justification and objectives of the process. For example, if the objective was primarily to examine the existing processes within the organisation as a means of identifying common factors and best practices to apply throughout the company, the focus could be said to be downward and inward. Alternatively, if the organisation was seeking views on the strengths and weaknesses of competitors this is outward looking in nature, and could involve one-to-one competitor benchmarking, industry benchmarking, or best-in-class benchmarking methods.

Internal audit departments can often benefit from participating in benchmark comparisons with other audit functions; such involvement can contribute to their understanding of:

- the internal auditing trends and practices as applied by the companies surveyed
- the implications and potential of the findings for the participant's own organisation
- the validity of the participant's own stance on internal auditing in relation to that apparent from the survey data.

Involvement in such exercises will enable participants to take a view of the need for change or review of their own organisation's approach to internal auditing in light of the survey data.

Of course, benchmarking is not an end in itself, but rather one platform used to identify and subsequently launch the required or necessary processes of change within a department, function, activity, process or organisation.

EFFECTIVE MEASURING OF INTERNAL AUDITING'S CONTRIBUTION TO THE ENTERPRISE'S PROFITABILITY

Introduction

At a time when internal auditing is being challenged by outsourcing alternatives and by other methods of reviewing managerial effectiveness, it is particularly important to be able to measure its contribution to the enterprise's profitability.

In this section we take a look at performance measures for internal auditing— measures of inputs (*economy*), process (*efficiency*) and especially outputs (*effectiveness*). Appropriate specific measures are recommended. In doing this we will be identifying the key aspects of internal auditing which need to be focused upon in order to improve internal auditing's contribution to the enterprise's profitability. We consider the difficulties of reaching reliable measures of internal audit performance, and distinguish between qualitative and quantitative measures. We suggest a value-for-money approach to assessing internal audit performance.

It will be necessary to identify the categories of performance measures which may be used to evaluate internal audit performance and the strengths and weaknesses of each. We give advice on their interpretation. We place the measurement of internal audit in context with: (a) the general business environment, (b) professional standards for internal auditing, and (c) good management practice on planning and control. Lastly, we present a particular approach to the use of performance measures in value for money auditing which may be applied to assessing internal auditing performance.

The General Business Environment—The Recession

Historically the growth of internal auditing as a business service has been "counter cyclical", though there are indications that this may not be so during the present recession. By this we mean that in the past internal auditing has developed most strongly during times of economic constraint. It may be that directors and managements consider that investment in internal auditing is particularly important in constrained times as an antidote to the control risks sometimes associated with stringent cost cutting. Or it may be that managements have turned their attention away from financial, accounting and operational control (to which internal audit can contribute) when extra profits have been more easily secured by burgeoning sales.

Whether or not internal audit prospers in constrained times, it certainly behoves internal audit to be able to demonstrate that its function is cost-effective and is managed so as to maximise its cost-effectiveness. Where internal auditing is not a mandatory requirement by statute law or by regulation, there is added pressure for audit to be able to demonstrate its worth.[2]

There are indications that managements are now placing internal auditing under a microscope with the intention of determining whether it pays its way. Internal auditing is a costly service to run. Each productive day of internal auditor time may cost typically some £400—clearly sizable amounts of profits from sales are needed to resource an internal audit function.

Competitive Tendering

Even where internal auditing is a mandatory requirement the current vogue for competitive tendering makes internal auditing a prime candidate for market testing and contracting out.[3] Established in-house internal auditing functions find they are tendering competitively against firms of public accountants, consultants specialising in internal auditing and other in-house internal auditing functions who have been given the freedom to tender for external work. To win the contract, these outside parties may be willing to bid at marginal cost—especially if they have surplus capacity. Bids at £150 (compared with the £400 quoted above) per day are not unknown.

The many arguments for and against an enterprise contracting out its internal auditing are summarised below. An aspect that has been largely overlooked is that performance measures for internal audit are particularly important for providing the means of establishing performance-related contracts for internal audit provision, and for monitoring its ongoing provision after the contract has been let.

With the bias being towards accepting lowest cost bids, it is particularly important to devise and use internal audit performance measures which focus upon *outputs* first, *process* second and *inputs* last—this categorisation is followed in this discussion. Each of these three is, of course, important. Senior general management and the board responsible for contracting out decisions should ensure that this sort of internal audit performance monitoring is in place. In-house heads of internal audit can influence management and the board towards this and, in so doing, should be maximising their own opportunities for securing into the future the internal audit work for their in-house internal audit departments.

If management and the board allow decisions on letting contracts for internal audit work to be made on price alone, rather than value for money, they are acting irresponsibly. Decisions on price alone betray a lack of commitment to the value of internal auditing—perhaps merely a resignation to the provision of a skeletal internal audit service due to statutory or regulatory obligations. Even in enterprises with acute cash flow problems, decisions on price alone are unjustified as it is especially important that such businesses maximise value.

Since (a) mandatory obligation to have internal auditing and (b) cash flow difficulties often come together within the public sector, it is within that sector that we are currently experiencing most pressure to contract out internal auditing on price grounds alone.

Potential advantages of contracting out internal auditing

1. The business can more readily vary its spend on internal auditing, according to what it can afford, from time to time.
2. The contractor is motivated to perform well and can be held to account for that performance.
3. The provider can be changed more easily.
4. The service may be provided at a lower price.
5. An external provider may have a wider understanding as to how other enterprises tackle similar business issues.
6. An external provider may have more extensive audit support resources to draw upon.
7. An external provider may be able to develop the enterprise's own staff.
8. The actual and perceived independence of an external provider may be greater—leading to more confidence in the results of the audit work.

Potential advantages of in-house internal audit provision

1. A deeper grasp of the enterprise's affairs.
2. A finer adjustment of internal audit emphasis to the enterprise's needs.
3. "On the spot" responsiveness to management and the board; better able to take on unplanned work.
4. A training ground for the future senior executives.
5. Confidentiality.
6. More likely to have a genuine internal audit orientation as distinct from an exernal orientation.
7. Unable to "walk away".

Professional Standards for Internal Auditing

The Standards of The Institute of Internal Auditors[4] have a specific standard that "the chief internal auditor should establish plans to carry out the responsibilities of the internal auditing department". Supporting guidelines require that "these plans should be consistent with the internal auditing department's charter and with the goals of the organisation", and that "the goals of the internal auditing department should be capable of being established within specified operating plans and budgets and, to the extent possible should be measurable. They should be accompanied by measurement criteria and targeted dates of accomplishment." These Standards also require that "The chief internal auditor should establish and maintain a quality assurance programme to evaluate the operations of the internal auditing department", and this is elaborated in, *inter alia*, the statement that "A key criterion against which an internal auditing department should be measured is its charter". Quality assurance is seen as being preserved by means of supervision, internal reviews and external reviews. These reviews are "performed to appraise the quality of the department's operations" and should be "structured to evaluate the degree of compliance with the Standards" themselves.

So it is clear that the Institute of Internal Auditors considers that there should be performance measures of an internal auditing department and that these should include an evaluation of compliance with the Charter of the department and also with the Standards of the Institute; they should also include a measurement of the achievement of target dates.

The UK's Consultative Committee of Accountancy Bodies (CCAB) is less forthcoming. Their guidance to their members[5] merely says: "The head of internal audit should establish arrangements to evaluate the performance of the internal audit unit. He [*sic*] may also prepare an annual report to management on the activity of the internal audit unit in which he [*sic*] gives an assessment of how effectively the objectives of the function have been met."

Categories of Performance Measures

Measures of internal audit performance have tended to focus upon *input* and *process* rather than upon *output*. Auditors will understand the association between these three and *economy*, *efficiency* and *effectiveness*, respectively, as illustrated in Figure 2.1. The greatest challenge is now to develop a range of measures which throw light upon internal audit effectiveness (i.e. output measures).

Quantitative, Quasi-quantitative and Qualitative Measures

Another way to categorise performance measures is according to whether they are quantitative or qualitative. In reality each performance measure can be conceived as being somewhere on a gradation between the extremes of objective (quantitative) and subjective (qualitative). An important characteristic of quantitative performance measures is that their measurement is objectively determined. Yet even in a very clear-cut case of a quantitative performance measure[6] subjectivity is not avoided as the selection and design of that performance measure will have been based upon a judgement that it provided relevant guidance on relative internal audit performance, and the interpretation of the resulting data also will be very subjective. Soft, subjective measures are often given an aura of objectivity, so that they may be termed *quasi-quantitative*.

For instance, a satisfaction survey of internal audit clients, asking questions similar to those suggested in Figure 2.2 may be analysed numerically and trends compared over time or between different audit sections. The numeric presentation of the data tends to mask the high degree of subjectivity inherent within this performance measure. The client satisfaction survey is discussed further below.

Client satisfaction survey

Please answer each of the following questions with a score 1–5 on the following scale:
1 = not at all; 2 = barely; 3 = adequately; 4 = very; 5 = excellently.

1. How useful do you find internal audit?

2. How appropriate have been the objectives and scope of internal audit's work in your area?

3. How useful have been your discussions with audit *at the commencement* of the audit?

4. How useful have been your discussions with internal audit *during* the audit?

5. How open and communicative were the auditors with you and your staff?

6. How satisfactory was the timing of the audit fieldwork?

7. How satisfactory was the duration of the audit?

8. How satisfied were you with the time it took for internal audit to issue an agreed audit report?

9. How fair and balanced do you consider the audit report to have been?

10. How fully do you consider you were consulted on matters which were included within the audit report?

11. How useful did you find the audit report?

Figure 2.2   Client/management satisfaction survey

Performance measures with a higher degree of objectivity than others are not necessarily the preferred ones to use: the criteria for selection of a performance measure should include a matching to the aspects of internal audit performance which are most important and which need to be monitored most.

Of crucial importance is to determine which aspects of internal audit performance are most important and which need to be monitored most. Strictly speaking, an aspect of internal audit performance could be of first importance while not needing to be monitored so closely as other aspects—*if* its achievement were assured *or*, occasionally, if it were outside the scope of management to regulate its achievement.

Using our model of *input*, *process* and *output*, we now consider for each of these categories the most important aspects of performance as they relate to internal audit. Some measures of performance inform about more than one of these categories. For instance, the success of the internal auditing function in completing its planned programme of audits relates closely to whether the function has achieved its objectives (planned outputs) but it also gives potential insights as to whether the function has approached its work efficiently (process).

Another example of this overlap between categories of performance measure is the *client satisfaction survey* (see Figure 2.2 for an example) which provides data on the reputation of audit. To some extent this will result from the judgement that management has made about the professionalism of internal auditors they have observed in action (audit process); to some extent the answers will depend on management's experience of the value of audit findings and recommendations (audit output). Some of the questions put to management in the survey will be targeted more to process than to output, and vice versa; but the impressions that management have about the professionalism of the audit process are likely to colour their answers to questions targeted at audit output; and their satisfaction with the audit output is likely to colour their impression of the audit process.

Input Measures

These performance measures throw light upon the economy with which the internal auditing activity is provided—whether by in-house provision or by external providers. Possible candidates for use as economy measures are:

- Numbers of auditors per 1000 staff compared to sector average.
- Levels of expenditure:

  - budget: actual
  - cost per auditor day
  - ratio of payroll to other costs
  - comparison between audit sections
  - comparison with previous periods.

- Allocation of productive time according to type of work (audit type; audit and non-audit work [such as firefighting] etc.)
- Extent audit staff are stretched.

Those measures selected may need to be adapted if internal auditing is contracted out. For instance the "number of auditors per 1000 staff compared to the sector average" would require a conversion to full-time staff equivalents based on the time that the outside consultants were spending in performing internal audit work. Data on the norms for each business sector are available from the impressive surveys of internal auditing conducted by the Institute of Internal Auditors.[7] A ratio of one internal auditor to every 50 or 100 total staff employed by the enterprise might be typical of financial institutions where tight control is an absolute priority, whereas 1:1000 or 1:2000 is more typical of civil engineering constructing firms—probably on account of other personnel, such as quantity surveyors, being engaged in quasi-internal auditing tasks.

As a bald measure of economy, the number of auditors employed is useful, but there may still be diseconomies to be identified. Audit expenditure may be out of control—either audit payroll expenditure or non-payroll costs. Some sections of the audit department may be more costly than others, perhaps without justification. Even where there is justification for differential costs between audit sections, this is useful information for management as it may point to possible opportunities to obtain better value for money in certain parts of the total audit programme than in other parts. Whether or not this is so will depend not just on cost considerations, but also on the potential for audit effectiveness in the various parts of the total audit programme. So measures of economy must be interpreted together with measures of effectiveness (outputs) and efficiency (process) before appropriate management action can be determined.

We suggest among our input measures a measure of the extent to which audit staff are stretched. It is arguable that this should be categorised as an efficiency (process) measure. If audit staff are not being extended it is likely that the staff input is unduly costly. Ensuring that audit staff are extended is a matter of managing the audit function efficiently. If staff are extended they are likely to perform better and the effectiveness (outputs) of the audit function may be improved.

Audit departments are now frequently calculating the cost of each audit. Audit reports often highlight this figure. An increasing number of audit functions are charging out the cost of the audit to the activity which has been audited. This practice encourages auditors to perform well in order to keep clients satisfied, and encourages clients to take the audit process more seriously as they are paying for it. It also more accurately reflects the total costs of running the different parts of the business. On the other hand, since line management should not determine whether or not an audit is conducted, nor what resources are allocated to it, it is arguable that those costs should not be charged against their budgets.

Process Measures

The emphasis with respect to *process* measures is the *efficiency* with which the internal audit activity functions. The *efficiency* analogy with an automobile is whether it runs as a well-oiled, well-maintained machine. This is distinct from the costs associated with running the automobile, which are matters of *economy*. It is also distinct from whether or not the automobile achieves the objectives set for it—such as luxury, prestige, timeliness, etc.—which is a matter of *effectiveness*. Of course, these three overlap, as we have said before: a poorly maintained automobile is less likely to be effective, for instance.

See Figure 2.3 for a breakdown of process performance measures.

Process performance measures

- **Training**
- **Professional activities**
- **Rotation of audit staff**
- **Extent of real responsibility—or is audit work specified in detail?**
- **Compliance with Standards**
- **Proportion of time which is productive**
- **Categorisation of productive time according to the stages of audit**
- **Target dates for various stages of an audit**
- **Time delay between end of fieldwork and issuance of final audit report**
- **Time spent on individual audits in comparison with planned time**
- **Comparison of time with results**
- **Time spent on total audits – in comparison with planned time**
- **Rate of completion of audits on schedule**
- **Reputation of internal audit (client satisfaction survey results)**

Figure 2.3 Process performance measures

Our model in Figure 2.1 shows that *efficiency* links *economy* with *effectiveness*. Perhaps a good overall measure of audit efficiency is therefore the average cost of each implemented audit recommendation.

Insight into the audit function's overall efficiency will come from exploring the achievement of target dates and the extent that audit management has been successful in maximising auditors' time actually spent conducting audits and, within that productive time, the way it has been allocated and supervised.

The audit client may also have some useful impressions about the professionalism of the audit approach which can be explored in a survey—see Figure 2.2. The main measure of professionalism of internal auditing is generally held to be *The Standards for The Professional Practice of Internal Auditing* of the

Institute of Internal Auditors: performance measures can be devised to assess the extent to which an internal auditing function complies with these Standards. It should be pointed out that compliance with them requires commitment to them by the internal auditing function, but also needs support by senior general management and the board.

Output Measures

Here we are considering (a) whether or not internal audit achieves its objectives, and (b) indeed, even *whether it achieves the right objectives.*

The Charter of the internal auditing function, as a statement of the distinctive rights and obligations of the audit function, is an important yardstick against which audit effectiveness or output should be measured. Certain elements of the Standards also relate to audit effectiveness as distinct from audit process.

Audit output is hard to measure. Internal auditors are knowledge workers whose output is not always tangible. Knowledge workers conventionally issue reports and internal auditors are no exception. Internal audit reports are a repository of information on audit output. Perhaps the principal objectives of internal auditors is to reassure management that their systems of internal control are sound and, where they are not, to persuade management to implement their recommendations. Figure 2.4 summarises the implicit or explicit objectives of internal auditing.

The implicit and explicit objectives of internal auditing:

1. To reassure managment that internal control is sound.

2. To identify non-compliance and urge future compliance.

3. To identify system weaknesses and make recommendations for improvement.

4. To persuading managment to accept and implement successfully the audit recommendations for improvement.

Figure 2.4   The objectives of internal auditing

Figure 2.5 outlines output performance measures.

The existence of an audit function with broad coverage provides a measure of reassurance to management and the board with respect to point 1 in Figure 2.4 and discourages future abuse due to the deterrent effect of audit. Perhaps the nearest we can get to measuring this type of audit effectiveness is to measure the planned coverage of internal audit and the extent to which internal audit succeeds in completing its planned programme of work.

Output performance measures

- **Reporting success**
- **Cost savings achieved**
- **Increased opportunities identified by audit**
- **Completion of audit plan**
- **Client satisfaction**
- **Compliance with internal audit charter**
- **Audit staff advancement**
- **Occasions on which internal audit is consulted on systems changes**
- **Level of requests for special audit assignments**

Figure 2.5 Output performance measures

An analysis of the findings in audit reports can measure the success of the department in identifying non-compliance with essential controls—perhaps comparing with the previous year, or comparing the success of different audit teams, or comparing the success of the audit function in certain areas of audit work compared to other areas.

With regard to points (3) and (4) in figure 2.5, a similar analysis of (a) past audit reports and (b) audit records of audit follow-up should allow a measurement similar to the example in Table 2.1. Admittedly this is an inexact set of measures—it presumes, for instance, that success can be assessed. Even where it can be assessed, the time delay is likely to be too great to make it a useful measure of internal audit performance. So it might be more practical to measure in accordance with Table 2.1 but stopping short of trying to evaluate whether or not an implemented audit recommendation was successful.

It may be possible to attach money values to cost savings which follow management's acceptance and subsequent correction/implementation of audit findings and recommendations in points (2), (3) and (4) of Figure 2.4. It will,

Table 2.1 Example of internal audit reporting success

	Recommendations		Acceptances		Implementations		Successes
Number	1000		800		700		650
Losses	200		100		50		
Loss rate (%)		20		12.5		7.1	

however, never be possible to account for the total value of the audit function to the business as a whole in terms of cost savings. The impact on costs of many accepted and implemented audit recommendations is indeterminable, as usually we will never know what would have happened if management had not so acted. Nevertheless, a historical record of known cost savings which have followed from audit work can give *one* indication of audit value for money. It is, however, human nature to overlook the additional costs which are often associated with points (2), (3) and (4) Internal audit also tends to take credit for good suggestions from line staff. Certainly, management and staff should be given credit for successful implementation of audit recommendations. In measuring cost savings it is difficult to determine the length of time into the future that the audit department should compute the saving: the decision is arbitrary. For instance, if the audit department takes credit for savings over a twelve-month period, this overlooks that the business may continue to benefit from that audit finding indefinitely. Despite these objections, measuring cost savings does have a place in the assessment of audit effectiveness.

Interpretation of Performance Measures

Any performance measure may mislead if it is interpreted on its own. For instance, the number of internal auditors per 1000 staff employed may show a very economic approach to internal auditing, but other measures may indicate that internal auditing is not very effective. Completion of all audits and reports by their target dates may be at the expense of useful findings and recommendations being made. Measures of reporting success should be linked with measures of cost savings, time utilisation and the achievement of audit plan.

We also need to be cautious about placing too much confidence in our performance measures. It might be that they indicate a high degree of audit success and yet overlook important issues which bear upon internal audit effectiveness. Here we highlight just two possible issues of this sort.

First, *audit independence*. This is a prerequisite of successful internal auditing. Secondly, the *scope* of internal auditing work. Two quotations are helpful here:

Whether or not audit is able to perform the full range of audit functions effectively and efficiently largely depends upon management attitude and support which is itself largely influenced by status and independence. The real sign of independence is that auditors are not impeded in their efforts to examine any area within the organisation whereas status often determines the significance attached to audit findings by management.[8]

There is no persuasive reason why ... internal auditing should not [appraise operations generally, weighing actual results in the light of planned results]. Perhaps the only limiting factors are the ability to afford so broad an audit, the difficulty of obtaining people who can do a broad type of audit, and the very practical consideration that individuals may not like to be reported upon. While persons responsible for accounts and for the safeguarding of company assets have learnt to accept audit, those responsible for far more valuable things—the execution of plans, policies and procedures of a company—have not so readily learnt to accept the idea.[9]

Figure 2.6 highlights some of the issues which affect audit independence.

Internal audit independence

1. Is internal audit organisationally distinct from any part of the enterprise in which it conducts audits?

2. Does internal audit derive its authority from the board?

3. Does internal audit have a direct working relationship with the audit committee of the board, and does the head of internal audit have a right of access to the chair of that committee?

4. Does the head of audit have direct access to the chief executive, and does the chief executive receive reports on audit assignments from the head of audit?

5. Does the head of audit have unrestricted access to the organisation's external auditors and to relevant regulatory authorities?

6. Is the recognised scope of internal audit consistent with the resources allocated to it?

7. Are there no operational areas or levels which are precluded from internal audit review?

8. Does internal audit have unrestricted access to personnel and information?

9. Is internal audit free of any responsibilities for conducting any operations other than independent reviews of internal control, and does internal audit avoid detailed involvement in systems design?

10. Is it clearly *management's* as distinct from *Audit's* responsibility to accept and implement audit recommendations?

11. Are the audit assignments conducted, and their timing, consistent with the assessment of the head of audit as to relative audit need?

12. Is the content of audit reports entirely at the discretion of the head of audit?

13. Is the organisational status of the audit department, and the executive seniority of the head of the audit and its staff, sufficient to underwrite the above requirements?

14. Is it policy to staff the audit function with professionally competent and qualified personnel, and to require observance of the Code of Ethics and compliance with the standards of the Institute of Internal Auditors?

15. Is the assignment of auditors to particular audit assignments done with due regard to the need to maintain effective independence?

16. Is there a charter which sets out the distinctive rights and obligations of the audit function which is consistent with the above needs and is generally understood throughout the enterprise?

Figure 2.6 Factors affecting internal audit independence

Integrating Performance Measures with Good Management Practice

The performance measures we use to evaluate internal audit should harmonise with those applicable to the enterprise as a whole:

The importance of the objectives identified for audit is that these should underpin an organisation's overall aims and objectives, so that audit's achievements aid the development of the organisation as a whole.[10]

Top management and the board should take the trouble to satisfy themselves that this is so. The Chartered Institute of Public Finance and Accountancy (CIPFA) suggests there are four fundamental questions to be asked of internal auditing, without which performance measures for internal audit have little meaning:

1. Does internal audit have agreed and established goals?
2. Is the work planned and resourced in such a way as to make achievement a realistic possibility?
3. Does the achievement of these goals contribute to the attainment of the corporate objectives, i.e. establishing and maintaining internal control?
4. Does internal audit achieve its defined goals?[11]

These questions should be addressed by the audit committee, by management, by the head of internal audit, and by external audit. The charter of the internal auditing department should ensure positive answers to these four questions.

A Value for Money Approach to Evaluating Internal Audit, Using Performance Measures

In essence, value for money auditing endeavours to assess economy, efficiency and effectiveness, making use of carefully chosen and carefully interpreted performance measures. So the approach we have taken is a value for money approach to evaluating the internal auditing function.

A refinement of the value for money audit approach is to organise the chosen performance measures into three hierarchies, where the more junior levels of performance measures are intended to interpret the measurement of the more senior ones. The most senior measure in each hierarchy is intended to most accurately reflect the most important measure of economy (or efficiency, or effectiveness). Examples of these structures are given in Figures 2.7, 2.8 and 2.9.

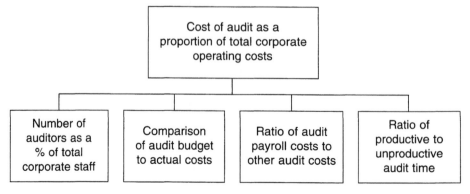

Figure 2.7 Economy (*inputs*) measures in the context of a value for money approach

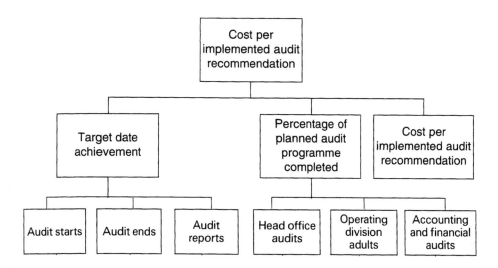

Figure 2.8   Efficiency (*process*) measures in the context of a value for money approach

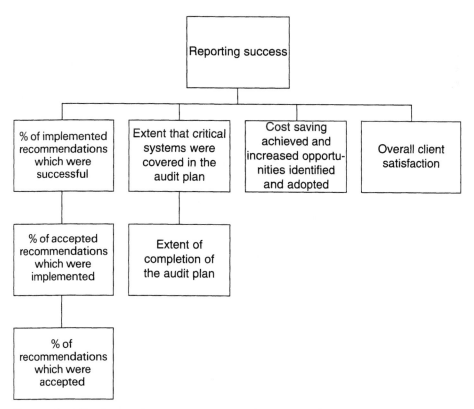

Figure 2.9   Effectiveness (*outputs*) measures in the context of a value for money approach

It is no longer sufficient for audit to view the historic reasons for its establishment as justification for its continued existence. Audit must and should be prepared to provide proof of its worth and value for money to the organisation as part of the organisation's continual growth.[12]

NOTES

1. Chambers, A. D., Selim, G. M. and Vinten, G. (1987) *Internal Auditing* 2nd edn. Pitman, London, p. 86.
2. CIPFA (Chartered Institute of Public Finance and Accountancy) (January 1992) *Measuring the Performance of Internal Audit.* Page 3.
3. The UK expression *contracting out* is the equivalent to the US expression *outsourcing,*
4. The fifth Standard of the Institute of Internal Auditors is on "Management of Internal Auditing Department", and in this paragraph we have quoted specific standards 520 and 560, together with reference to supporting guidelines 520.01, 520.03 and 560.01. We have also used material from "The Institute of Internal Auditors' *Statement on Internal Auditing Standards [SIAS] No 4* on "Quality Assurance" (December 1986).
5. Consultative Committee of Accounting Bodies, (June 1990) *Guidance for Internal Auditors,* Auditing Guideline 308. London.
6. Such as, for instance, *the elapsed time between ending audit fieldwork and issuing the audit report.* The decision to include this as one of the performance measures would be bound to be a matter of judgement; similarly there may be judgement involved in deciding the start and end points of the elapse time which is being measured. Judgement also has to be exercised in interpreting the resultant data—for instance, what elapse time is acceptable?
7. See for example, *Survey of Internal Auditing in the United Kingdom & Eire, 1985* (Research Report No. 15, The Institute of Internal Auditors—UK) and similar international surveys with a US bias by IIA Inc.
8. Chartered Institute of Public Finance and Accountancy (1981) *An Approach to the Measurement of the Performance of Internal Audit,* Audit Occasional Paper No. 3.
9. Koontz, Harold and O'Donnell, Cyril (1976) *Management—A Systems and Contingency Analysis of Managerial Functions,* 6th edn (International Student Edition). McGraw-Hill, Tokyo, pp. 670–1.
10. CIPFA (1981) *An Approach to the Measurement of the Performance of Internal Audit,* Audit Occasional Paper No. 3, p. 2.
11. Ibid., p. 6.
12. Ibid., p. 1.

3

Developing Operational Review Programmes for Managerial and Audit Use

SCOPE

In this chapter we will introduce a practical method of documenting all the elements of an operational audit review in a form which resembles the traditional internal control questionnaire (ICQ). We have called this method **Standard Audit Programme Guides (SAPG)**.

The original concept of SAPGs was built around their use within word processing software, where each discrete programme was a separate document file that could easily be updated and maintained using the facilities of the word processing environment. This form of usage had the principal advantage of being a familiar software environment supported by extensive functionality. However, printed blank proformas can be used as an alternative.

In this chapter we shall discuss the format of the SAPG and how to use it. The landscape format of the SAPG illustrated in this chapter is, of course, but one possible layout, and users of this technique can create their own design within the word processing system of their choice.

To save space, we will in subsequent chapters give listings of relevant control objective and risk/control issues taken from SAPG documents, but not in the full SAPG landscape format. Our general aim is to highlight the salient points of audit concern for the functions and activities rather than to emphasise any particular SAPG document layout.

This chapter concludes with a discussion on the subject of risk in operational auditing and features a control matrix approach to assessing risk and control effectiveness.

PRACTICAL USE OF SAPGs

SAPGs are intended for use during management and audit reviews of activities within an organisation.

Today an increasing amount of auditing is done in a self-audit context where management, together with their staff, consider in quite a formalised though participative way (a) the risks of not achieving their objectives now and into the future, and (b) whether internal control is equal to the task of giving reasonable assurance of achievement of objectives. We discuss control self-assessment (or control risk self-assessment as it is often called) fully in Chapter 17. SAPG documents offer an ideal basis for control self-assessment. They raise the right questions and encourage management and staff to consider whether controls are satisfactory to address the issues raised. They provide a self-documenting record of the progress of the control self-assessment which is available for subsequent audit or senior management review. The classification of SAPGs into a wide variety of business activities means that a suitable SAPG is likely to be available for most functional areas. Where the scope of the self-assessment is a complete operating unit, a high level review programme, which we discuss later in this chapter, is likely to be appropriate. In the following chapters we provide checklists of control issues which are as relevant to managers for self-audits as for auditors to use during their audits.

In the auditing context, there are obviously a number of ways that the organisation can be divided for the purposes of reviewing the effectiveness of internal controls. For example, *functionally* based on the organisational structure, or *operationally* based on the prime activities of organisation. SAPGs can be used a variety of ways, and each SAPG can be suitably scoped to meet the method of defining the discrete audit review projects. For example, an audit department could choose to view the organisation as noted in the following listing, and accordingly create a separate SAPG for each activity or system. This example structure is based on the division of the audit universe of potential review projects into eleven main areas.

1.   **Management and administration**

   - The control environment
   - Organisation (i.e. structure)
   - Management information
   - Planning
   - Risk management
   - Legal department
   - Quality management
   - Estates management and facilities
   - Environmental issues
   - Insurance
   - Security
   - Capital projects
   - Industry regulation and compliance

- Media, public and external relations
- Company secretarial department

2.   Financial and accounting

- Treasury
- Payroll
- Accounts payable
- Accounts receivable
- General ledger/management accounts
- Fixed assets (and capital charges)
- Budgeting and monitoring
- Bank accounts and banking arrangements
- Sales tax (i.e. VAT) accounting
- Taxation
- Inventories
- Product/project accounting
- Petty cash and expenses
- Financial information and reporting
- Investments

3.   Personnel

- Human resources department (including policies)
- Recruitment
- Manpower and succession planning
- Staff training and development
- Welfare
- Pension scheme (and other benefits)
- Health insurance
- Staff appraisal and disciplinary matters
- Health and safety
- Labour relations
- Company vehicles

4.   Procurement

- Purchasing

5.   Stock and materials handling

- Stock control
- Warehousing and storage
- Distribution, transport and logistics

6.   Production/manufacturing

- Planning and production control
- Facilities, plant and equipment
- Personnel

- Materials and energy
- Quality control
- Safety
- Environmental issues
- Law and regulatory compliance
- Maintenance

7. Marketing and sales

- Product development
- Market research
- Promotion and advertising
- Pricing and discount policies
- Sales management
- Sales performance and monitoring
- Distribution
- Relationship with parent company (for overseas or subsidiary operations)
- Agents
- Order processing

8. After sales support

- Warranty arrangements
- Maintenance and servicing
- Spare parts and supply

9. Research and development

- Product development
- Project appraisal and monitoring
- Plant and equipment
- Development project management
- Legal and regulatory issues

10. Information technology

- IT strategic planning
- IT organisation
- IT sites
- Processing operations
- Back-up and media
- Systems/operating software
- System access control
- Personal computers
- Software maintenance
- Local area networks (LANs)
- Databases
- Data protection
- Facilities management

- System development
- Software selection
- Contingency planning
- Electronic data interchange (EDI)
- Viruses
- Electronic office
- User support
- Spreadsheet design
- Expert systems
- IT accounting

11. Contracting

- Contract management environment
- Project management framework
- Project assessment and approval
- Engaging, monitoring and paying consultants
- Design
- Assessing viability/competence of contractors
- Maintaining an approved list of contractors
- Tendering procedures
- Contract and tender documentation
- Insurance and bonding
- Selection and letting of contracts
- Management information and reporting
- Performance monitoring
- Sub-Contractors and suppliers
- Materials, plant and project assets
- Valuing work for interim payments
- Controlling price fluctuations
- Monitoring and controlling variations
- Extensions of time
- Controlling contractual claims
- Liquidations and bankruptcies
- Contractor's final account
- Recovery of damages
- Review of project outturn and performance
- Maintenance obligations

During the course of an audit review there will be a number of common factors to record and evaluate. For example, the control objectives for the activity being reviewed, the risks or operational issues, the controls and measures in place to address the risks and issues, the results of audit testing, and the conclusions drawn. The SAPG format illustrated later in this chapter will cater for all these factors and we will subsequently describe how the SAPG can be completed and used to document these key review elements.

Once they have been developed for use, the SAPGs can be used either singly or in various combinations to provide detailed guidance and direction during audit projects and field visits. They should aim to define the key and essential knowledge about a given subject, and thus form a key part of the audit documentation.

The scope and nature of each audit project may be different. This variability is driven by such practical aspects as availability of audit resources, the relative scale of the target business operations, logistical considerations, areas of specific management concern, etc. SAPGs can be used in combinations to match the audit coverage to the specified business systems and activities. Although each SAPG can be used in a "free-standing" context, they can also be linked in a number of ways to support the objectives established by audit management:

- Most SAPGs will be designed to cover systems which have interfaces with other systems (for example, there are logical linkages between purchasing, accounts payable and stock control). It follows, therefore, that perceived weaknesses in one system/activity may have implications for issues in another related system or activity. Each SAPG can be provided with a table of such interrelationships so that the user can promptly determine the knock-on effects of any noted concerns.
- The principal activities of an operating unit or overseas subsidiary can also be flexibly related to a number of individual activity or system-based SAPGs.
- Away from the use of individual SAPGs to support the examination of discrete activities, there is the alternative view of a business expressed in terms of business processes (or alternatively cycles, although not every process is actually cyclic in form). These business processes can be described as being a series of related or interlinked economic events. The structure of individual SAPGs can also be used as the basis of using them in combinations supporting auditing on a business process basis. (See Chapter 16 for an exploration of alternative views of the business.)

In any event, it is likely that most audit visits will be the subject of some prior research and preparation so that the audit time spent on site is optimised for efficiency and direction, and that the auditors are focused on the most worthwhile investigations. In order to assist with such deliberations, special forms of SAPG can be developed which support the gathering of such research information. For example, users of the SAPG approach may choose to develop a "fact finding programme" or a "high level review programme" to meet such requirements. (Refer to Chapter 5, which discusses the use of such programmes in the context of auditing subsidiaries and remote operating units.)

FORMAT OF SAPGs

In our proposed SAPG format, the critical contents of each SAPG are a number of **risk or control issues** relevant to the specific system. These are expressed in the form of questions which raise the issues in the context of what is being done either to achieve a desired outcome or to avoid an unwanted one. Examples of such questions would be:

- How does management ensure that the business activities of the organisation are conducted in accordance with all the prevailing and relevant legislation and regulations?
- What processes would ensure that any failures to fully comply with current legal requirements were promptly identified and resolved?

This form of question structure supports the use of the format in either the traditional audit situation where the direction is set by "What can go wrong?", or where a management orientation is adopted where the emphasis is placed on "What do we need to achieve?"

The risk and control issues are further divided into two groups, namely **key issues** and **detailed issues**. The former are the more significant and crucial points about the system under review and the aim should be always to take them into account during the audit. The latter category of issues take the user into more of the underlying system considerations, and would be utilised only if there was a potential weakness revealed as a consequence of considering the key issues. We will return to the context of this division of issues later in this chapter.

The purpose of the SAPG is to guide the auditor through an examination of the issues specific to the system or activity with the intention of recording the nature of measures and controls in place to ensure either that business objectives are achieved, or that risks and exposures are successfully avoided. The auditor will need not only to record the nature of measures and controls in place, but also to consider their effectiveness, and dependent upon that interpretation record the nature and results of any audit testing applied to determine whether the situation needs to be reported to management.

The suggested form of the SAPG is divided into three distinct sections:

- a title page
- the risk/control issues
- system interfaces.

The format and use of each of these are described in following sections.

Note that in all the examples that follow, the text in *italics* relates to that entered by the user during the course of the audit review, whereas the normal text relates to the information entered at the initial design stage.

SAPG Title Page

The title page has three separate areas:

- an area which records the details of the subject matter covered by the SAPG and a reference number (see Figure 3.1).
- an area used to record details about the specific audit project (see Figure 3.2).
- a section which describes the control objectives for the relevant system (see Figure 3.3). In practical usage, the text in this last section of the page can be edited and updated whenever necessary by the user.

SAPG Ref.: *0102*	Function: *Management & Administration*	Activity/System: *Organisation*

Figure 3.1 SAPG title page—subject matter covered

Company: *Acme Corporation*	Division: *Orthopaedics*	Country: *USA*	Site: *New York*
Audit Ref.: *USA01-97*	Date: *3 January 1997*	Completed by: *John Brown*	Reviewed by: *G. V. Rand*

Figure 3.2 SAPG title page—details about audit project

The Risk/Control Issues

This is the main part of the SAPG and consists of a table based on the headings noted in Figure 3.4. If the table facilities within a word processor have been used to develop this format, it should be possible for all the cells to expand down the page as text is entered. On this and subsequent pages, the use of each column is discussed.

The **Seq.** column contains a sequential number used to identify each risk/control issue. These issues are divided into two groups, **Key Issues** which are

---

Control Objectives:

(a) To ensure that the organisational structure is appropriate to the business and the achievement of strategic objectives; (b) To ensure that the organisational structure is determined by the business and operational needs and avoids needless sub-divisions and excessive levels; (c) To ensure that the structure enables the flow of key information upwards and outwards within the orgnisation and across all the business activities; (d) To ensure that relevant responsibilities, authorities and functional terms of reference are defined and in place; (e) To ensure that responsibilities and authorities are adequately segregated in order to avoid conflicts of interest and the potential for fraudulent practices; (f) to ensure that the structure is periodically reviewed and any changes are agreed and authorised at a senior level; (g) To ensure that each manager's span of control is optimised and avoids either over or under-utilisation; (h) To ensure that adequate staff resources are determined, authorised and provided in order to achieve the functional and business objectives; (i) To ensure that the prevailing organisational structure is suitably documented and communicated to all relevant staff; and (j) To ensure that the organisational structure and the related functional divisions of responsibility are accurately and adequately reflected in the accounting and management information systems.

Figure 3.3 SAPG title page—control objectives

Seq.	Risk/Control Issue	Current Control/Measure	WP Ref.	Effec-tive Yes/No	Compliance Testing	Substantive Testing	Weakness to Report
1	**Key Issues**						
1.1	**What measures are in place to ensure that management are kept informed of production activities as the basis for their decision making?**						
2	**Detailed Issues**						
2.1	How can management be assured that production downtime caused by plant breakdown is minimised?						

Figure 3.4   SAPG—outline of risk/control issues

identified by being both in the sequence starting **1.1** and printed in **bold** text, and **Detailed Issues** which are in the sequence starting at 2.1. (Refer to Figure 3.4). The Key Issues reflect the top-level and critical aspects of the system/activity under review and should always be considered by the auditor. There are normally between six and ten key issues noted on each system/activity SAPG. The detailed issues examine the relevant subject in greater elemental detail and should be addressed by the auditor only if the responses obtained in relation to the key issues suggest that there could be further inherent weaknesses in control. There can be any number of detailed issues recorded within an SAPG dependent on the complexity and relevance of the system/activity.

The **Current Control/Measure** column is used by the auditor to record a brief description of any controls or measures that are in place to address the issues raised in the Risk/Control Issue column. (Refer to Figure 3.5). Try to avoid going into too much detail in this column. This type of information can be obtained in a number of ways, for example, as a result of discussion with departmental staff, from a review of documented procedures, or from previous audit working papers. In practice there may be more than one control or measure in place which has an effect on the issue raised; any number of these can be noted in the Current Control/Measure cell.

The **WP Ref.** column can be used to note any working paper cross reference, such as a system flowchart or procedure manual.

The **Effective Yes/No** column is used to note whether the recorded current control or measure is likely to be effective in either supporting the required objective or counteracting any underlying risk posed by the issue. This judgement, which may need to be applied by the audit manager or supervisor, is an opinion on likely effectiveness. The responses recorded in this column can be used to determine those areas which should be subject to audit testing. The decision

Seq.	Risk/Control Issue	Current Control/Measure	WP Ref.	Effec-tive Yes/No	Compliance Testing	Substantive Testing	Weakness to Report
1	Key Issues						
1.1	What measures are in place to ensure that management are kept informed of production activities as the basis for their decision making?	Regular manage-ment report (type PRO78X) produced and circulated to unit managers. Contents are reviewed, discussed, and signed off at weekly team meetings.	Flow chart PRD04 page 8	YES			

Figure 3.5   SAPG—example of a partly completed risk/control issues

whether or not to apply audit testing will, of course, be relative to the user's own auditing standards, but a number of logical tactics could apply. For example, the consideration that a particular control or measure would be effective (i.e. a YES response), may obviate the need for any testing; however, at this stage, the auditor does not know whether the control is actually being applied correctly and/or consistently. This suggests that some limited compliance testing is desirable to ascertain if the control is actually being applied appropriately in every instance. In order to contain the amount of audit time spent on compliance testing, it is often desirable to identify the key controls and measures which represent the greatest potential and target these for compliance tests. The **Compliance Testing** column can be used to record the test applied and a summary outcome. (Refer to Figure 3.6.) Because space is limited, the user can elect just to record a working paper cross-reference to the detailed testing schedules rather than a full explanation.

In instances where either the compliance testing revealed an inadequate application of the measure or the control/measure was judged unlikely to be effective, further substantive testing may be justified to evaluate if a potential weakness has been exploited. Summary details of such substantive testing can be noted in the **Substantive Testing** column. By way of illustration, Figure 3.6 incorporates example entries in the **Compliance** and **Substantive Testing** columns.

The last column (**Weakness to Report**) can be used to note any points of audit concern arising from the audit review and testing which should either be discussed further with management or formally reported to them as a recommendation for action. The contents of this column can be interfaced with the reporting processes used by the audit function.

The completed SAPG file can be saved as a word processing document file and printed out to form part of the audit working papers and permanent file.

Seq.	Risk/Control Issue	Current Control/Measure	WP Ref.	Effec-tive Yes/No	Compliance Testing	Substantive Testing	Weakness to Report
1	**Key Issues**						
1.1	**What measures are in place to ensure that management are kept informed of production activities as the basis for their decision making?**	*Regular management report (type PRO78X) produced and circulated to unit managers. Contents are reviewed, discussed, and signed off at weekly team meetings.*	*Flow chart PRD04 page 8*	*YES*	*WP: Test 23 Reports for November 1996 examined— no evidence of examination or review*	*WP: Test 54 November and December 1996 reports examined in detail— 13 instances of production shortfall reported with no apparent follow-up action.*	*Recommend to management that they ensure that this control is applied as defined in the procedures manual and that all reports are monitored for evidence of action taken to address reported problems. Discussed with Production Manager 01.01.97*

Figure 3.6 SAPG—example of a completed risk/control issues

System Interfaces

This page of the SAPG (as illustrated in Figure 3.7) is intended to alert auditors to the likely interfaces between the system or activity being addressed in the SAPG and any others. Where weakness and control problems have been revealed during the system review, there may be consequences or implications for other systems either "downstream" or "upstream" of the system under review. The System Interfaces Table is intended to draw auditors' attention to systems with input or output connections. These connections may be based solely on data flow or have additional operational implications. The example Systems Interface Table featured in Figure 3.7 is provided for illustrative purposes and is related to an accounts receivable system.

RISK IN OPERATIONAL AUDITING

Matters of risk have traditionally been of concern to auditors and although the profession has also embraced other business-oriented approach s, risk is likely to remain a potent determinant in directing audit work.

SYSTEM INTERFACES FOR ACCOUNTS RECEIVABLE

It is unlikely that any activity or system will operate in complete isolation, but will need to interact with other data and systems in order to be fully effective. At a simple level, such interaction could relate to the input of data from a source system and the generation of amended or enhanced data which can be output to the next process. For example, taking coded transactions from an accounts payable system into the general ledger as the basis for subsequently producing management accounts information.

It is often at the point of interaction between systems where controls are critical. Auditors should be satisfied that the data moving between systems is consistent, complete and accurate, in order that the subsequent processes are undertaken upon a reliable basis.

The following table aims to plot, for the subject system of this Standard Audit Programme Guide, the potential interfaces with other systems which may require audit attention. Indicators are provided to differentiate between those interfaces which act as input sources to the subject system and those which are potential output targets. The "SAPG Ref." column records the reference number of the Programme Guide which addresses the issues for the related system

System	SAPG Ref.	Input Source	Output Target	System	SAPG Ref.	Input Source	Output Target
Management Information	0103		✓	Stock Control	0501	✓	
Treasury	0201		✓	Warehousing/Storage	0502	✓	
General Ledger & Management A/Cs	0205		✓	Sales Performance/ Monitoring	0706	✓	✓
Budgeting & Monitoring	0207		✓	Warranty Arrangements	0801	✓	
Bank Accounts/ Arrangements	0208	✓	✓	Maintenance and Servicing	0802	✓	
VAT Accounting (where applicable)	0209		✓	Spare Parts and Supply	0803	✓	
Inventories	0211	✓	✓				
Product/Project Accounts	0212		✓				
Financial Information & Reports	0214		✓				

Figure 3.7   SAPG—System Interfaces page and Systems Interfaces table

The internal auditor's use of risk assessment can operate at different levels of audit planning and activity:

At a **tactical** level the auditor may choose to apply risk assessment techniques to the potential universe of possible audit projects as a means of setting relative priorities, and thus determine those higher risk audit projects for inclusion into the annual audit plan. This approach normally involves the development of an audit risk formula.

At the **operational** level (i.e. during the course of a specific audit project), risk assessment linked to an evaluation of control effectiveness can focus the auditor's attention on aspects of the subject under review which are more deserving of his or her attention. With audit resources under pressure, it is important that auditing efforts are concentrated on the highly risky, poorly controlled aspects where management action may be required.

Two proven risk assessment methods for audit planning, which can be computerised using spreadsheet software, are explored in *Effective Internal Audits*.[1] We shall, later in this section, briefly explore an operational level risk and control assessment technique using a control matrix methodology. However, before doing so, we shall consider (in the next section) general matters of risk and control in operational auditing.

There is now an active market in IT-based risk analysis tools, some of which are specifically designed for use by auditors. The Information Faculty of the Institute of Chartered Accountants in England & Wales has published a report on risk analysis and a survey of the available software products.[2]

The Nature of Risk

In simplistic terms, risk can be defined as a function of *what is at risk* and *how likely is it to be at risk*. In other words, the extent (or size) of the risk and the probability of that risk actually occurring. An alternative term for the size dimension would be *inherent risk*. An alternative term for the probability dimension would be the *control risk* or the *system risk*.[3]

Whereas the size of a given risk may be relatively easy to determine objectively, for example the known value of stock held or the actual level of cash turnover at a retail outlet, the probability element is generally a more subjective dimension. In the auditing context, the probability of a given risk occurring is fundamentally seen as a by-product of the effectiveness of the controls put in place by management. Put simply, the poorer the level of control exercised over a process or function, the greater the probability of risk *exposure* occurring. However, the interpretation of the effectiveness of controls can be subjective and the subject of some debate between auditors and their client managers. In all honesty it is very difficult, if not impossible, to remove totally the subjectivity in risk assessment, especially where matters of effectiveness, quality and opinion are involved. All parties to a risk assessment process should recognise any such limitations and take practical steps towards reducing and/or understanding the potentially subjective aspects of the process.

The term "exposure" in relation to risk could be defined as "an unwanted event or outcome that management would wish to avoid". Although it is perhaps usual for auditors to relate risks primarily to financial values (i.e. value of cash lost, extent of additional costs, etc.), initial exposures can also be non-financial in nature, although most exposures may have a related or ultimate financial impact. An example of a primarily non-financial exposure, would be the loss of reputation and the impact on the corporate image following a well-publicised breach of regulations (such as unauthorised discharge of a harmful substance into the environment). It could be said that any resultant loss of business will have a financial dimension, as will any operational restrictions imposed by the regulatory authorities over and above any fines or penalties. Auditors, when considering risk exposures during a project, should take a broad view of the potential impacts on the organisation and not concentrate solely on financial aspects.

Each organisation may have specific sector or operational aspects which need to be considered in risk terms; for example, the ability of a hospital trust to maintain the required levels of contracted services could be affected by the public reputation of the medical facilities offered, or the continuing operation of a chemical plant will be governed by the continued adherence to the laid-down health, safety and environmental regulations.

Measuring Risk

For any given system, process, activity or function there are likely to be a number of possible risk exposures. However, when these exposure elements are compared with each other, they may exhibit variable degrees of inherent (or size) risk for the organisation, and we should aim to take account of this risk variability in our determination of risk. So we need to identify ways of measuring the various aspects of risk. For instance, in a review of the payroll function, the following two possible risk exposures could, *inter alia*, apply:

1. Errors in the calculation and payment of net salaries due to the incorrect application of annual pay review data to the payroll records
2. Payments made to unauthorised or invalid people set up on the payroll.

It may be considered that the impact of risk (1) might be potentially much greater than that of risk (2). For instance, it is likely to affect a greater number of employees (indeed, possibly all employees' payroll records), whereas risk (2) is more likely to be restricted to a relatively few fraudulent or erroneous payroll records. Clearly risk (1) also has the potential for a wider range of exposure types when compared to risk (2); for instance, beyond the financial impact of such a risk, the following aspects may also apply, each with its own degree of relativity for the organisation beyond the size extent:

- the reaction of the taxation authorities to such a large scale error (i.e. casting doubts over the accuracy and reliability of the other payroll processes)
- the cost and disruption involved in recovering from the error
- the processing of overstated transactions through the company bank account and the attendant effects on cash flow
- the affects on staff morale given the scale of error in salary payments
- the effect of adverse publicity on the organisation's reputation and image.

In the control matrix we discuss later in this chapter, two elements of inherent (or size) risk are accounted for. First, an expression of the type of exposure, on a category scale of likely relative importance to the business; and secondly, the likely extent (or the measure of the size) of the exposure. For example, the first element could be related to a scale of type of effect for the company as follows, using a category scale of 1 to 6, where a score of 6 represents the greater degree of relative risk:

6 (most serious)	Financial impact with implications for the achievement of corporate objectives and financial targets.
5	Loss of cash or other asset, or increase in liability.
4	Political sensitivity or loss of reputation.
3	Loss or exaggeration of profit.
2	Distortion of the balance sheet.
1 (least serious)	Accounting error with no effects on profit and loss or balance sheet.

We could term this measure as a *type* (of risk) score.

If, for instance, we had an exposure which reached point 5 on the above *type* scale because there was a potential loss involved, we then have to give substance to the likely extent of that loss should it occur, and we do this by allocating an additional measure of the likely *size* of that loss. We could relate this *size* element either to a scale of actual loss values or to a summary form of scale such as small, medium and large degrees of actual impact represented on three-point scale, where 3 is the largest potential loss. So, for our example, we could conclude that the likely extent of our loss (*Type* score 5) would be high (*Size* score 3), and these may be combined mathematically to produce a composite measure of the relative inherent risk. One such method would be to multiply the two scores; i.e. $5 \times 3 = 15$ (as a measure of inherent risk).

We shall return to this approach in our subsequent examination of the control matrix method. However, we have dealt with only one part of the risk equation, i.e. that part relating to inherent risk (or *what is at risk*). We will now turn our attention to the measurement of control effectiveness, which is a moderator of the real risk position.

Measuring Control Effectiveness

In the same way that varying degrees of inherent risk will apply to the constituent exposures for a given system, activity, process or function, control effectiveness also has a variability. Overall control effectiveness can be said to be the product of two dimensions, namely:

1.   the potential effectiveness of a control activity[4] assuming that it is applied correctly all the time by staff and management

combined with

2.   the actual extent it is complied with.

This viewpoint supports the premise that however *potentially* effective a control may be, it becomes effective only when it is complied with; and even if a control is complied with all the time it may not be 100% effective in eliminating an exposure. Just as there are varying degrees of inherent risk, there will, in the real world, be differing extents of potential control effectiveness and variations in the way that controls are complied with. Additionally, the effectiveness of a control will vary between the exposures it impacts upon.

It is possible to apply a simple mathematical approach to these related measures of control effectiveness, by expressing each of the two aspects as percentages, i.e.:

- The potential effectiveness of the control (i.e. if applied correctly all the time) can be expressed on a scale of 1 to 5, where a score of 5 equates to 100% effective (4 = 80%, 3 = 60%, 2 = 40%, 1 = 20%, and a score of zero means no effect at all in addressing the related risks).
- The extent to which the control is actually complied with can be determined by the auditor during initial compliance testing and scored using the same five-point scale. For example, if the compliance test examination of a sample of transactions suggested that the control was complied with for only 60% of the time, the score of 3 for compliance would be given.

The two scores can then be combined as a measure of the contribution made by this control for reduction or eradication of the related risk exposures. For example, if a control has an 80% level of potential effectiveness but is only complied with for 60% of the time, this could be expressed as a resultant control contribution of 48% (i.e. 60% of 80).

Using such an approach it is a simple matter for the auditor (and management) to conclude on the type of action required. If the potential effectiveness of a control is high, but compliance is poor, the obvious solution is to improve the level of compliance. Alternatively, if the potential effectiveness level is low, then irrespective of the level of actual compliance, the related risk will remain unaddressed, thus suggesting that alternative control action is required.

It is necessary to be aware of the subjectivity associated with these forms of measurement, especially in respect of potential control effectiveness. It could be said that this method facilitates the painting of a more precise picture of the control situation when compared to the internal control questionnaire (ICQ) approach—in shades of grey (or indeed in colour) as opposed to black and white. But, the down side is that care is required in the determination of the relative scoring, otherwise the conclusions can easily be challenged by auditee management. Although there is no escaping fundamental subjectivity, a great deal can be achieved by prior discussion of the technique with management and getting them to 'buy-into' the method. In any event, the use of any method of risk assessment by the internal audit function should ideally have the sanction of the audit committee.

Earlier in this chapter we considered the traditional use of ICQs by auditors as means of evaluating control effectiveness against predefined control objectives for a given system or function. When using an ICQ, the auditor is expected to evaluate control effectiveness in a fairly restrictive way—i.e. normally by responding *Yes* or *No* to the question "*Is this control effective?*" Presumably behind the answer to this question, are a number of facts and findings which aid the auditor in responding to the rather blunt answering parameters.

ICQs don't cater especially well for the varying extents of inherent risk, potential control effectiveness and control compliance. Additionally, in reality a particular control process may address a number of different risk exposures—to different degrees of effectiveness; and a particular risk exposure may be addressed by a number of controls, all operating at different levels of potential effectiveness and compliance. However, the traditional ICQ format does not readily facilitate the mapping of such interactions.

In the following section we shall introduce a control matrix method which incorporates some of the principles of risk and control measurement we have examined so far.

A Control Matrix Approach to Risk and Control Evaluation

In this section we will outline the mechanics of the control matrix method using a simple example and building up the required data in stages. The processes used are based on the concepts of risk and control measurement noted in the earlier sections. For a more comprehensive exploration of this and other risk-based audit planning methods, see *Effective Internal Audits*.[5] At the end of this section we provide two examples of more realistic and comprehensive matrices.

The control matrix technique is ideally suited to the spreadsheet environment, and the comprehensive examples featured as Figures 3.16 and 3.17 were generated using a software package operating in the Lotus 1-2-3 environment.[6]

The control matrix can be used by auditors during any audit project or review. The aim of the control matrix method is to bring together, in a mathematically sound way, the dimensions of risk and control as a means of calculating a *risk score* for each of the component risk exposures. This risk score can then used to direct the auditor's attention to those aspects of the system under review which may, among other things, require substantive testing, discussion with management, the agreement of the required corrective action, etc.

Although our simple example matrix will focus on the previously discussed risk and control approach to audit review, it should be noted that this method can also equally be applied to reviews using an alternative, positive, approach (i.e. "What do we need to achieve in respect of this system, function or process?", and "What measures have we put in place in order to ensure that achievement?"). This form of the method aligns more readily with the view of the business adopted by management, who see their role as primarily relating to the achievement of objectives and not solely geared to countering risks. The comprehensive example matrix shown in Figure 3.17 uses Objectives (as opposed to exposures) and measures (as opposed to Controls) in order to illustrate this positive orientation of the control matrix method.

The Development of an Example Control Matrix

For the purposes of our simplified example, we will consider a limited number of risks and controls applicable to a management information system (MIS). The items we have selected for our illustration of the method are not intended to be comprehensive, and you will easily be able to define additional and alternative examples that more realistically fit the prevailing scenario in your own organisation.

EXPOSURES:

A Unable to maintain/amend the MIS
B Inaccurate, incomplete, or out-of-date information
C Data corruption
D Inaccurate system parameters, variables and assumptions
E Leak of sensitive company data—competitive disadvantage, malpractice

---

Figure 3.8 Selected *exposures* for a management information system

First, it is necessary to identify the likely risk exposures associated with an MIS. Figure 3.8 lists five possible top-level exposures. In practice there will be others, but this reduced list serves to illustrate the technique.

The process of identifying the possible exposures for the system under review will normally be undertaken early in the audit project as a basis for the work that follows. In doing so, it is important to ensure that the identified items are comprehensive, realistic and pitched at the appropriate level.

It is important when noting exposures that cause and effect are differentiated. For example, a failure to ensure adequate segregation of duties is not essentially an exposure, but the possibility of introducing false accounting transactions by taking advantage of poor segregation is an exposure. Remember the earlier definition of an exposure: an unwanted event or outcome that management would wish to avoid.

Although we have given only one-line descriptions of the exposures, further implications can be assumed; for example, in respect of exposure B (which relates to inaccurate information) we could also assume that the quality of management decisions will be affected by the poor data quality.

The accurate identification of the risk exposures associated with the system under review is a crucial stage as all that follows will be dependent on the foundation of possible risk components. In practical situations, the process of recording the exposures may be undertaken under the auspices of audit management or in a brainstorming session. Furthermore, the auditor may wish to involve management from the area under review, so that the perceptions of inherent risk are accurate, realistic and mutually agreed at the outset of the audit project. The prevailing management culture and the way in which internal audit is perceived will obviously affect the decision to involve auditee managers in the risk assessment process.

The next stage would be to identify the controls in place for the system under review. Details of these controls may be obtained from a number of possible sources, for example:

- previous audit working papers (where they exist), updated with any amended or additional practices
- interviews with staff and management

- a review of official policies, procedures and/or operations manuals (subject to confirmation that they are correctly applied in practice).

Figure 3.9 lists five possible control activities relevant to an MIS. This is an abbreviated listing and many other controls are likely to apply in practice.

We have now gathered the basic elements for the construction of our control matrix for the subject of the MIS. Figure 3.10 depicts the basic form of the matrix incorporating the example exposures and controls taken from Figures 3.8 and 3.9.

Before moving on, we'll look generally at the structure and purpose of the matrix format of Figure 3.10.

The vertical columns of the matrix relate to the exposures. In our example, the five exposures (as noted in Figure 3.8) are represented in the columns labelled **A** to **E**. In the adjacent box at the top of the matrix, the exposure descriptions are repeated.

The horizontal rows of the matrix represent the example controls which should be in place (as noted in Figure 3.9).

There are a number of points of intersection between the vertical (exposures) and horizontal (controls) elements. We will step through the completion of these cells and provide, where necessary, a description of the underlying theory and simple mathematics.

We need to apply the previously discussed measures of inherent risk to each of the five noted exposures as a means of reflecting their relative significance. We do this in the two rows near the top of the matrix columns labelled *Type* and *Size*. First, the *Type* score, which accounts for the degree of significance of the risk to the organisation, needs to be determined. In order to ensure consistency in the application of such scores, an agreed scale is required, such as the six-point scale shown in Figure 3.11.

Each of the noted exposures needs to be considered against this scale, which in nature resembles a ladder to be climbed until the highest relevant point is reached for the exposure under consideration—i.e. the most serious type or category of unwanted outcome which this exposure represents. For example, when considering exposure A (MIS not adequately documented—unable to maintain/ amend) it might be relevant to climb the ladder scale (depicted in Figure 3.11) up

---

CONTROLS
1. System specification is documented and any amendments are updated and verified.
2. 90% of data input is via feeder systems direct interfaces—thus minimising keying errors.
3. System access is controlled by user-ID and password. Access system is maintained by the systems administrator.
4. Standing data and parameters are entered and verified by the financial accountant prior to the use of the MIS.
5. Access to standing data and parameters is further protected by the use of an additional (higher-level) password control system.

Figure 3.9 Limited selection of example controls for a management information system

Management Information System—Abbreviated Example Matrix Exposures: A Unable to maintain/amend the MIS B Inaccurate, incomplete, or out of date information C Data corruption D Inaccurate system parameters, variables and assumptions E Leak of sensitive company data—competitive disadvantage, malpractice		EXPOSURES					
		A	B	C	D	E	
	Calculated Risk Score	Risk						
	Scale 3 (6 is the most serious)	Type						
	Size (3 is the maximum)	Size						
	CONTROLS							
1	**System specification is documented and any amendments are updated and verified**	Best						
		Test						
		Both						
2	**90% of data input is via feeder systems direct interfaces—thus minimising keying errors**	Best						
		Test						
		Both						
3	**System access is controlled by user-ID and password. Access system is maintained by the systems administrator**	Best						
		Test						
		Both						
4	**Standing data and parameters are entered and verified by the financial accountant prior to the use of the MIS**	Best						
		Test						
		Both						
5	**Access to standing data and parameters is further protected by the use of an additional (higher-level) password control system**	Best						
		Test						
		Both						

Figure 3.10   Blank control matrix for a management information system

to position 4; this can then be entered into the *Type* score cell on the matrix corresponding to exposure A. Refer to Figure 3.12, which depicts possible scores for the example exposures A to E.

The second dimension of inherent risk is its *Size* ranking based (in our example) on a simple three-point scale where the value chosen reflects the size extent of the unwanted outcome (i.e. 1 = small, 2 = medium and 3 = large) which we selected from the ladder scale. We have inserted in Figure 3.12 the possible *Size* scores for

Start climbing this ladder scale from the bottom until you reach the highest relevant point for the exposure.

Point of
scale:

6   Failure to achieve business objectives, and/or loss of credibility.

5   Systems failure.

4   Loss of control of the corporate database.

3   Damaging delay.

2   Unnecessary financial costs.

1   Delay of no commercial significance.

Figure 3.11   Example exposures-oriented category scale for determining the *Type* score

our chosen exposures. You will note that values have now appeared in the *Calculated Risk Score* row of the matrix in Figure 3.12. The formula used to generate these scores is discussed later, but this *Risk* score is one of the key outputs of the matrix process as it aims to reflect the residue risk of each exposure taking into account the inherent risk dimensions (i.e. a combination of the *Type* and *Size* scores) and the effects of the controls in place. Of course, at this stage of data entry into our matrix, only the inherent risk values have been entered and the *Risk* score calculation is incomplete. The *Risk* score is generated in the range 1 to 4, where a score of 1 means an insignificantly low degree of residue risk, whereas a score of 4 equates to a high risk exposure which is poorly controlled and which therefore may require additional audit investigation, etc. We shall subsequently return to consider the *Risk* score after we have entered the score data for the controls in place.

We have concluded that control effectiveness consisted of two elements, namely: (1) the potential effectiveness of a control assuming it was being followed by staff and management as intended, and (2) the extent to which the control is actually being complied with. Taken together, these two factors will give an indication of the actual contribution made by the control in addressing the inherent risk. The matrix technique facilitates the recording of these factors.

Figure 3.13 shows some example *Best* scores inserted into the matrix. These relate to a measure of potential control effectiveness based on a scale of 0 to 5, as follows:

5   Would eliminate the risk if followed (i.e. 100% effective)

4   80% effective

3   60% effective

2   40% effective

1   20% effective

0   No effect (or not applicable to this exposure)

Management Information System— Abbreviated Example Matrix			EXPOSURES					
Exposures: A Unable to maintain/amend the MIS B Inaccurate, incomplete, or out of date information C Data corruption D Inaccurate system parameters, variables and assumptions E Leak of sensitive company data—competitive disadvantage, malpractice			A	B	C	D	E	
Calculated Risk Score	Risk		3	4	3	3	3	
Scale 3 (6 is the most serious)	Type		4	6	5	4	6	
Size (3 is the maximum)	Size		3	3	2	2	2	

Figure 3.12 Entry of *Type* and *Size* scores to determine the inherent risks for the noted exposures

Figure 3.13 reveals that a *Best* score of 5 for control 1 in addressing exposure A suggests a very optimistic expectation for its effects, whereas a less optimistic stance is taken with the application of a *Best* score of 2 for control 3 in relation to exposure B. Also by looking at the mapping of the interactions of controls and exposures as represented in Figure 3.13, we can see that:

- one control (i.e. number 3) is capable of addressing (to differing extents) a number of exposures (i.e. references B, C and E)
- one exposure can be addressed by a number of controls to varying degrees of potential effectiveness (i.e. exposure B is targeted by controls 2, 3, 4 and 5).

This mapping also aids the identification of the more significant (or key) controls and their interaction with the underlying (or inherent) risks. If audit time was limited, it may be more practical to concentrate on such key controls. This method also graphically indicates where there may be redundant controls.

Wherever there is an interaction of an exposure with a control a question mark is inserted in the *Test* score cells as a reminder that data concerning control compliance is required. The *Test* score aims to reflect the other dimension of control, namely the degree to which each control is actually complied with, as determined by normal compliance testing methods. The degree of compliance is measured using the following 0 to 5 scale:

5   100% compliance
4   80% compliance
3   60% compliance
2   40% compliance
1   20% compliance
0   No compliance

The degree of compliance for each of the featured controls is determined and then entered into the matrix along the *Test* score row where a *Best* score has been

Management Information System—Abbreviated Example Matrix			EXPOSURES					
Exposures: A Unable to maintain/amend the MIS B Inaccurate, incomplete, or out of date information C Data corruption D Inaccurate system parameters, variables and assumptions E Leak of sensitive company data—competitive disadvantage, malpractice			A	B	C	D	E	
Calculated Risk Score	Risk		3	4	3	3	3	
Scale 3 (6 is the most serious)	Type		4	6	5	4	6	
Size (3 is the maximum)	Size		3	3	2	2	2	
CONTROLS								
1	System specification is documented and any amendments are updated and verified	Best		5					
		Test	?	?					
		Both							
2	90% of data input is via feeder systems direct interfaces—thus minimising keying errors	Best			4				
		Test	?		?				
		Both							
3	System access is controlled by user-ID and password. Access system is maintained by the systems administrator	Best			2	5		3	
		Test	?		?	?		?	
		Both							
4	Standing data and parameters are entered and verified by the financial accountant prior to the use of the MIS	Best			3		4		
		Test	?		?		?		
		Both							
5	Access to standing data and parameters is further protected by the use of an additional (higher-level) password control system	Best			2		3		
		Test	?		?		?		
		Both							

Figure 3.13 Example control potential (*Best*) scores

previously entered. Figure 3.14 shows the matrix after the entry of the required *Test* scores.

  The following important points should be noted from Figure 3.14:

1. The insertion of the *Test* scores has resulted in the calculation of the *Both* scores for each control in the cells below. The *Both* score is a mathematical combination of the *Best* and *Test* scores with the intention of representing

Management Information System—Abbreviated Example Matrix

Exposures:

A   Unable to maintain/amend the MIS
B   Inaccurate, incomplete, or out of date information
C   Data corruption
D   Inaccurate system parameters, variables and assumptions
E   Leak of sensitive company data—competitive disadvantage, malpractice

				EXPOSURES				
				A	B	C	D	E
	Calculated Risk Score	Risk		1	4	2	3	3
	Scale 3 (6 is the most serious)	Type		4	6	5	4	6
	Size (3 is the maximum)	Size		3	3	2	2	2
	CONTROLS							
1	**System specification is documented and any amendments are updated and verified**	Best			5			
		Test		5	5			
		Both			5			
2	**90% of data input is via feeder systems direct interfaces—thus minimising keying errors**	Best			4			
		Test		3	3			
		Both			2			
3	**System access is controlled by user-ID and password. Access system is maintained by the systems administrator**	Best			2	5		3
		Test		4	4	4		4
		Both			1	4		2
4	**Standing data and parameters are entered and verified by the financial accountant prior to the use of the MIS**	Best			3		4	
		Test		2	2		2	
		Both			0		1	
5	**Access to standing data and parameters is further protected by the use of an additional (higher-level) password control system**	Best			2		3	
		Test		4	4		4	
		Both			1		2	

Figure 3.14 Control matrix after inserting the compliance (*Test*) scores

the contribution made by the relevant control in addressing the inherent risk to exposure. The *Both* score is calculated using the following formula where *B* represents the *Best* score and *T* relates to the *Test* score:

$$B - (5 - T) = Both$$

Management Information System—Abbreviated Example Matrix			EXPOSURES					
Exposures: A Unable to maintain/amend the MIS B Inaccurate, incomplete, or out of date information C Data corruption D Inaccurate system parameters, variables and assumptions E Leak of sensitive company data—competitive disadvantage, malpractice			A	B	C	D	E	
	Calculated Risk Score	Risk		1	4	2	3	3	
	Scale 3 (6 is the most serious)	Type		4	6	5	4	6	
	Size (3 is the maximum)	Size		3	3	2	2	2	
	CONTROLS								
1	**System specification is documented and any amendments are updated and verified**	Best		5					
		Test	5	5					
		Both		5					
2	**90% of data input is via feeder systems direct interfaces—thus minimising keying errors**	Best			4				
		Test	3		3				
		Both			2				
3	**System access is controlled by user-ID and password. Access system is maintained by the systems administrator**	Best			2	5		3	
		Test	4		4	4		4	
		Both			1	4		2	
4	**Standing data and parameters are entered and verified by the financial accountant prior to the use of the MIS**	Best			3		4		
		Test	2		2		2		
		Both			0		1		
5	**Access to standing data and parameters is further protected by the use of an additional (higher-level) password control system**	Best			2		3		
		Test	4		4		4		
		Both			1		2		
Inherent Risk (Size) Score [5 is worst risk; 1 best] — 3									
Overall Control Score [5 is worst risk; 1 best] — 3									

Figure 3.15 Completed Control Matrix with Overall *Risk and Control* scores

2. The *Calculated Risk Scores* at the top of each **Exposure** column have also changed and now take into account all the data in the column. The following formula is used to compute the *Risk* scores and it takes account of the *Type*,

Size and all of the *Both* scores in the relevant columns, where *B* is the sum of the cubes of the *Both* scores in the column:

$$Type \times Size \times [125 - B]$$

The output of this calculation is related to a *Risk* score scale of 1 to 4 as follows:

Result	Score
if greater than 1500	4
between 751 and 1500	3
between 1 and 750	2
if less than or equal to 0	1

The *Risk* score is the key output of the matrix technique, in that it indicates those exposure elements (and their related controls) which are more deserving of further audit attention. A *Risk* score of 4 suggests an important exposure (due to its high inherent risk value) and the relative absence of effective control exercised over it. Having completed the control matrix to the point depicted in Figure 3.14, the auditor can allocate the remaining audit time in proportion to the *Risk* scores for the component aspects of the system under review (i.e. more time to those exposures with *Risk* scores of 4 and 3, and less (or none at all) on those with *Risk* scores of 2 and 1).

Figure 3.15 again shows the completed matrix with the addition of some data at the bottom in the form of overall inherent risk (size) and overall control scores. The inherent risk score has been calculated from all the *Type* and *Size* scores in the matrix as an indication of the overall level of risk for the system under review. The overall control score is generated from all the *Both* score data as an indication of the general level of control effectiveness. Both these scores can be useful as overall ratings for the subject under review, especially where there is a requirement to measure the output of the current audit examination against previous reviews.

So far we have deliberately used a limited range of exposures and controls in our examples in order to illustrate the control matrix technique. However, in practical use, the matrices created are likely to be much more comprehensive than the one in Figure 3.15. Figures 3.16 and 3.17 are more typical examples of matrices.

Figure 3.16 is an exposures-oriented matrix which, like our simplified examples above, addresses the subject of a management information system. However, it contains suggested exposures and controls.

Figure 3.17 addresses the subject of planning, and uses the alternative orientation of the matrix method which replaces exposures and controls with objectives and measures. The objectives in the vertical columns relate to *what needs to be achieved* in relation to planning; the measures represent the steps taken to aid the achievement of the given objectives. In this context, the term "measures" is broader in scope than the "controls" used in the former example, in that management will implement a wide range of measures in order to achieve their objectives, which although they may include control activities, are not

Management Information System—EXPOSURES

Exposures:

A	MIS not adequately documented—unable to maintain/amend	H	Unable to recover use of MIS in event of system failure
B	Inadequate operating instructions—error, system failure	I	Inadequae management reporting facilities—additional effort
C	Use of inaccurate, incomplete or out of date information	J	Inaccurate system parameters, variables and assumptions
D	Re-keyed data contains errors—affect on decision making	K	Failure to back-up MIS data—delay, cost, unable to recover
E	Unable to trail/prove data to source(s)—affects decisions	L	Leak of sensitive company data—competitive disadvantage
F	Unauthorised access to/use of MIS—error, leakage, etc.	M	Insecure or poorly designed spreadsheets—logic errors, etc.
G	Inadequate specification & testing of MIS—credibility, etc.	N	Absence of spreadsheet model documentation and/or testing

SCALE 3 (ABRIDGED)

6   Loss of information
5   Loss of cash or other asset, or increase in liability
4   Political sensitivity or loss of reputation
3   Loss or exaggeration of profit
2   Distortion of the balance sheet
1   Accounting error without P & L or balance sheet effect
(Exposures-oriented scale)

Management Information System—   EXPOSURES

			A	B	C	D	E	F	G	H	I	J	K	L	M	N
	Calculated Risk Score	Risk	3	2	4	3	2	3	2	4	3	3	4	3	2	2
	Scale 3 (6 is the most serious)	Type	6	6	6	6	6	6	6	6	6	6	6	6	6	6
	Size (3 is the maximum)	Size	2	1	3	2	1	2	1	3	2	2	3	2	1	1
	CONTROLS															
1	**System specification is documented and any amendments are updated**	Best	4													
		Test	?	?												
		Both															
2	**User & operating manuals have been developed— contents agreed with users & IAD**	Best	4	4												
		Test	?	?	?											
		Both															
3	**Analysis & reporting module handbooks are available**	Best	4	4												
		Test	?	?	?											
		Both															
4	**90% of data input is via feed system direct interfaces— threrefore no keying errors**	Best			4											
		Test	?		?											
5	**Input data is reconciled back to source system(s)**	Best			4											
		Test	?		?											
		Both															

Management Information System—			EXPOSURES													
			A	B	C	D	E	F	G	H	I	J	K	L	M	N
	Calculated Risk Score	Risk	3	2	4	3	2	3	2	4	3	3	4	3	2	2
6	Update file headers validated to prevent incorrect or duplicate loading of data	Best			4											
		Test	?		?											
		Both														
7	Limited re-keying is necessary—all such input is reconciled to source control values	Best				5										
		Test	?			?										
		Both														
8	Operations log maintained for all MIS processing & activity—source file input is recorded	Best				4										
		Test	?			?										
		Both														
9	System reports on "missing" data input files to ensure MIS update is complete	Best			3	3										
		Test	?		?	?										
		Both														
10	System operates on restricted access Novell network located in Executive suite	Best						4						4		
		Test	?					?						?		
		Both														
11	System access is controlled by user-ID and password	Best						5						4		
		Test	?					?						?		
		Both														
12	Network PC based MIS was developed per user management requirements specification	Best							4							
		Test	?						?							
		Both														
13	MIS was tested by users and IT Dept. before live use—all modifications also tested	Best							5							
		Test	?						?							
		Both														

continued

Management Information System—EXPOSURES (*continued*)

Exposures:

A	MIS not adequately documented—unable to maintain/amend
B	Inadequate operating instructions—error, system failure
C	Use of inaccurate, incomplete or out of date information
D	Re-keyed data contains errors—affect on decision making
E	Unable to trail/prove data to source(s)—affects decisions
F	Unauthorised access to/use of MIS—error, leakage, etc.
G	Inadequate specification & testing of MIS—credibility, etc.
H	Unable to recover use of MIS in event of system failure
I	Inadequae management reporting facilities—additional effort
J	Inaccurate system parameters, variables and assumptions
K	Failure to back-up MIS data—delay, cost, unable to recover
L	Leak of sensitive company data—competitive disadvantage
M	Insecure or poorly designed spreadsheets—logic errors, etc.
N	Absence of spreadsheet model documentation and/or testing

SCALE 3 (ABRIDGED)

6	Loss of information
5	Loss of cash or other asset, or increase in liability
4	Political sensitivity or loss of reputation
3	Loss or exaggeration of profit
2	Distortion of the balance sheet
1	Accounting error without P & L or balance sheet effect

(Exposures-oriented scale)

Management Information System— EXPOSURES

			A	B	C	D	E	F	G	H	I	J	K	L	M	N
	Calculated Risk Score	Risk	3	2	4	3	2	3	2	4	3	3	4	3	2	2
	Scale 3 (6 is the most serious)	Type	6	6	6	6	6	6	6	6	6	6	6	6	6	6
	Size (3 is the maximum)	Size	2	1	3	2	1	2	1	3	2	2	3	2	1	1
CONTROLS																
14	**Contingency plan allows for emergency use of alternative network**	Best								4						
		Test	?							?						
		Both														
15	**Source files are backed-up to tape in relevant department**	Best								4		4				
		Test	?							?		?				
		Both														
16	**MIS data backed-up to tape streamer on a daily basis**	Best								4		4				
		Test	?							?		?				
		Both														
17	**Flexible reporting, analysis & query software interfaces have been incorporated into design**	Best									5					
		Test	?								?					
		Both														
18	**Standing data & parameters are verified by Financial Accountant before system use**	Best										4				
		Test	?									?				
		Both														

Management Information System—				EXPOSURES													
				A	B	C	D	E	F	G	H	I	J	K	L	M	N
	Calculated Risk Score		Risk	3	2	4	3	2	3	2	4	3	3	4	3	2	2
19	Access to standing data and parameters is protected by additional password control	Best											4		2		
		Test	?										?		?		
		Both															
20	Use of MIS facilities is restricted on a "need to know" basis	Best							4						4		
		Test	?						?						?		
		Both															
21	Back-up media stored in Financial Accounts Dept. safe	Best													4		
		Test	?												?		
		Both															
22	MIS hard copy circulation is restricted and in sealed confidential packets	Best													3		
		Test	?												?		
		Both															
23	IT Dept develop all criticial company spreadsheets to ICAEW best practice standards	Best														4	
		Test														?	
		Both															
24	User specifications produced for all spreadsheets —delivered systems are signed-off by users	Best														3	4
		Test	?													?	?
		Both															
25	IT Dept and users conduct testing of all spreadsheets— results & admendments documented	Best														4	
		Test	?													?	
		Both															
26	Documentation is incorporated into spreadsheets for ease of use —updated as required	Best															4
		Test	?														?
		Both															

Figure 3.16   Management Information System

Planning—OBJECTIVES

A	Establish a suitable & robust Strategic Planning framework
B	Ensure planning processes & models are rigorously tested
C	Ensure company mission/objectives are clearly communicated
D	Ensure all plans (i.e. IT, Manpower, etc.) are co-ordinated
E	Ensure mechanism addresses sustained competitive advantage
F	Ensure that corporate goals are realistic & measurable
G	Provide accurate/reliable information for planning purposes
H	Ensure action plans & adequate resources are provided
I	Ensure actual progress is monitored against the plan(s)
J	Maintain awareness of organizations' strengths & weaknesses
K	Ensure all planning activity remains realistic/objective
L	Ensure adequate staff involvement in planning process
M	Ensure senior management are committed to planning process
N	Ensure commercially sensitive data remains confidential

SCALE 1 (ABRIDGED)
6   Management must be able to understand what is happening at a strategic level
5   Medium to long term corporate objectives must be achieved
4   Budgets and profit targets must be achieved
3   Management must be taking appropriate action to correct performance
2   Management must understand what is happening at operational level
1   Motivation must be high
(Objectives-oriented scale)

Planning			OBJECTIVES													
			A	B	C	D	E	F	G	H	I	J	K	L	M	N
	Calculated Risk Score	Risk	4	2	4	4	4	4	3	3	2	2	3	3	3	3
	Scale 1 (6 is the most serious)	Type	6	6	5	6	6	5	6	5	2	2	5	3	3	5
	Size (3 is the maximum)	Size	3	1	3	3	3	3	2	2	3	3	2	3	3	2
	MEASURES															
1	**Planning Dept. established with the brief to develop & implement a suitable planning method**	Best		3												
		Test	?	?												
		Both														
2	**External consultants to assist in initial process & provide objectivity during reviews**	Best		4									4			
		Test	?	?									?			
		Both														
3	**Planning method/ procedures are documented in manual—copies supplied to affected staff**	Best		4	3				2							
		Test	?	?	?				?							
		Both														
4	**Initial pilot exercise conducted for subsidiary X— procedure amendments incorporated**	Best		5												
		Test	?		?											
		Both														
5	**Overview mission statement & key objectives circulated to all staff**	Best			5										2	
		Test	?			?									?	
		Both														

Planning			OBJECTIVES													
			A	B	C	D	E	F	G	H	I	J	K	L	M	N
	Calculated Risk Score	Risk	4	2	4	4	4	4	3	3	2	2	3	3	3	3
6	Key senior managers involved in the planning process	Best			4			3		4			3	4	4	
		Test	?		?			?		?			?	?	?	
		Both														
7	Methodology links all aspects of planning & ensures compatibility of goals, etc.	Best				4										
		Test	?			?										
		Both														
8	Divisional plans are subject to review to ensure compliance with Group plan objectives, etc.	Best				4										
		Test	?			?										
		Both														
9	All plans are ratified by the Board	Best				4		3								
		Test	?			?		?								
		Both														
10	Each business activity is analysed in respect of internal & external influences	Best					3									
		Test	?				?									
		Both														
11	All potential projects are subject to feasibility study & assessment	Best					4	3								
		Test	?				?	?								
		Both														
12	Measurable targets are allocated to each goal—monitored for progress, achievement, etc.	Best						4			3					
		Test	?					?			?					
		Both														
13	MIS established as source for company planning data — contents reconciled to source(s)	Best						4								
		Test	?					?								
		Both														

continued

Planning—OBJECTIVES (*continued*)

A Establish a suitable & robust Strategic Planning framework	H Ensure action plans & adequate resources are provided
B Ensure planning processes & models are rigorously tested	I Ensure actual progress is monitored against the plan(s)
C Ensure company mission/objectives are clearly communicated	J Maintain awareness of organizations' strengths & weaknesses
D Ensure all plans (i.e. IT, Manpower, etc.) are co-ordinated	K Ensure all planning activity remains realistic/objective
E Ensure mechanism addresses sustained competitive advantage	L Ensure adequate staff involvement in planning process
F Ensure that corporate goals are realistic & measurable	M Ensure senior management are committed to planning process
G Provide accurate/reliable information for planning purposes	N Ensure commercially sensitive data remains confidential

SCALE 1 (ABRIDGED)
6   Management must be able to understand what is happening at a strategic level
5   Medium to long term corporate objectives must be achieved
4   Budgets and profit targets must be achieved
3   Management must be taking appropriate action to correct performance
2   Management must understand what is happening at operational level
1   Motivation must be high
(Objectives-oriented scale)

Planning			OBJECTIVES													
			A	B	C	D	E	F	G	H	I	J	K	L	M	N
	Calculated Risk Score	Risk	4	2	4	4	4	4	3	3	2	2	3	3	3	3
	Scale 1 (6 is the most serious)	Type	6	6	5	6	6	5	6	5	2	2	5	3	3	5
	Size (3 is the maximum)	Size	3	1	3	3	3	3	2	2	3	3	2	3	3	2
	MEASURES															
14	**External information gathered from documented and reliable official sources**	Best							4							
		Test	?						?							
		Both														
15	**Specific expertise/research data acquired as necessary**	Best							4							
		Test	?						?							
		Both														
16	**Method requires production of action plans & resource requirements for Board approval**	Best								4						
		Test	?							?						
		Both														
17	**Divisional Managers agree action plans & are held responsible for implementation within deadlines**	Best								4				4	4	
		Test	?							?				?	?	
		Both														
18	**Monthly progress reports are presented to Board**	Best									5					
		Test	?								?					
		Both														

Planning			OBJECTIVES													
			A	B	C	D	E	F	G	H	I	J	K	L	M	N
	Calculated Risk Score	Risk	4	2	4	4	4	4	3	3	2	2	3	3	3	3
19	Market Analyst canvasses customers, etc. for external opinion of company/ performance	Best										4				
		Test	?									?				
		Both														
20	Key performance factors are monitored & fed into the planning process	Best										4				
		Test	?									?				
		Both														
21	Cross-functional involvement in the planning process provides broad basis for contents review	Best											3	4	3	
		Test	?										?	?	?	
		Both														
22	Complete copies of interim & final planning reports only circulated to Board members	Best														4
		Test	?													?
		Both														
23	All research data/reports held on secure PC protected by access control system	Best														4
		Test	?													?
		Both														

Figure 3.17 Management Information System

restricted to only controls. For example, staff will need to be trained in preparation for a new business venture or computer software will be acquired/ developed to address an operational requirement.

The objectives are assessed using a type scale which aims to reflect their relative significance to the organisation and the size score reflects the level (or scale) of that contribution (i.e. small, medium or large). Measures are given *Best* scores which reflect the extent of the potential contribution to the achievement of the related objective and the *Test* scores represent the extent to which they are followed and applied. The *Risk* score indicates the extent to which the measures in place address the driving objectives. The higher the generated *Risk* score, the more significant the objective and the less likely it is that it will be achieved. The auditor's attention is therefore focused on those aspects of the subject under review that are worthy of additional audit attention. Management can also use this technique to assess and monitor their progress and the likelihood of achieving their objectives.

NOTES

1. Chambers, A. D. (1992) *Effective Internal Audits*. Pitman, London.
2. Chambers, A. D. and Rand, G. V. (1995) *IT-based Risk Analysis*. ICAEW, London.
3. Some auditors, for some purposes, regard a proportion of the probability dimension as belonging to inherent risk rather than to control risk on the basis that this proportion represents that part of the system which is inherently vulnerable.
4. We use the expression *control activity* loosely here in the sense that it might refer to any element of internal control. The COSO *Internal Control—Integrated Framework* identified five components of internal control of which they called one "control activities". Our use of the term here could refer to a control element in any one of COSO's five components of internal control. Rutteman ((December 1994) *Internal Control and Financial Reporting—Guidance to Directors of Listed Companies Registered in the UK*, report of the ICAEW's Working Group chaired by Paul Rutteman) adopted the UK COSO's five components of internal control but called them criteria and used slightly modified wording:
   1. Control environment
   2. Identification and evaluation of risks and control objectives
   3. Information and communication
   4. Control procedures (COSO's "control activities")
   5. Monitoring and corrective action.
5. Chambers (1992), op. cit.
6. Details of the MINPLAN software package are available from Management Audit Ltd, Water Mill, Moat Lane, Old Bolingbroke, Spilsby, Lincolnshire PE23 4EU, England. Telephone +44 (0) 1790 763350 or fax +44 (0) 1790 763253.

4

Internal Control and the Review of the Control Environment

SCOPE

In this chapter we will briefly examine the meaning of internal control in order to set the scene for conducting a review of the control environment. This part of the chapter will explore the development of the internal control concept up to the current time.

We shall be using the following definition of the term "control environment" provided by the Committee of the Sponsoring Organizations of the Treadway Commission (known generally as COSO) in their publication *Internal Control—Integrated Framework*:

The control environment sets the tone of an organisation influencing the control consciousness of its people. It is the foundation for all other components of internal control, providing discipline and structure. Control environment factors include the integrity, ethical values and competence of the entity's people; management's philosophy and operating style; the way management assigns authority and responsibility, and organises and develops its people; and the attention and direction provided by the board of directors.[1]

INTERNAL CONTROL

Control

"Control" divides into external control by the stakeholders of a business (such as the shareholders, debenture holders, creditors) and internal control by management.

External control is facilitated in part by shareholder election of directors to (a) look after the management of their interests, and (b) to render an account to them: "Without audit, no accountability; without accountability, no control; and if there is no control, where is the seat of power? . . . great issues often come to light only because of scrupulous verification of details."[2]

Internal control is synonymous with *management control*. It is control by management of the internal affairs of the business. The audit committee of the board, on behalf of the board, should conduct overall monitoring of the arrangements for internal control since this is part of the board's stewardship on behalf of the shareholders who appointed them.

In an overall sense the board is responsible for all the affairs of the business including internal control. However, under the direction of the board, management (and principally the chief executive) have responsibility for ensuring that internal control arrangements are effective.

It is difficult to separate out internal control from the other elements or functions of management, namely:

- planning
- organising
- staffing
- directing and leading
- controlling
- co-ordinating.[3]

These functions interact, overlap and coalesce. Control is an important set of threads woven through the tapestry of management. It has been argued that control is virtually *all* of management[4] and it is vital for auditors to have an understanding of this as it bears upon the scope of internal audit. Internal audit may be defined as: **The independent appraisal of the effectiveness of internal control**.

If internal control were all of management, then *internal audit* would be: **The independent appraisal of the management process**.

It would be misleading to suggest that internal control is *all* of management. The arguments in favour can be summed up as follows:

1. Many of the definitions of internal control are very broad so as apparently to leave little space for any other managerial functions. We look at some of these definitions later.
2. Control depends on each of the other functions of management. There is no control without:
- Planning—For instance, design of the right procedures (which is part of planning) is essential for effective control. There has to be a plan against which to exercise control. Without a plan there can be no control.
- Organising—For instance, structuring the business into subdivisions and determining reporting arrangements.[5]
- Directing and leading—Few would question that the quality of leadership impacts upon control.
- Staffing—Too few or too many staff can lead to things getting out of control— as can incompetent, disloyal, dishonest or lazy staff.

- Co-ordinating—Is the art of ensuring that happenings occur in harmony with each other—without which things will be out of control.

Despite these arguments, it is more prudent to acknowledge that while planning, organising and the other functions of management are mechanisms by which management achieves control, managers also achieve other objectives apart from control by the judicious application of these elements of management. For instance, they may develop effective long-term plans; or they may make excellent staffing arrangements so that not only control but other elements of management are better handled.

If internal auditors interpret their mission as to conduct an independent appraisal of the effectiveness of internal control, it is true that they may be drawing management's attention to weaknesses in planning, organising, directing, staffing and co-ordinating which may account for control weaknesses. It would not, therefore, be beyond the scope of internal auditing to raise audit points which relate to weaknesses in planning, staffing, directing and so on. Conventionally this would be done when these weaknesses provide an explanation for actual or potential breakdowns of control. There may be other weaknesses in planning, staffing and so on which do not impinge directly on control and which may therefore be beyond the scope of internal audit to detect or comment upon. On the other hand, the terms of reference of many internal auditing departments require them to draw management's attention to anything they find that is commercially unsound, and so not too much ceremony may be attached to whether an audit finding is, or is not, a control point. Nevertheless, the generally accepted emphasis of internal audit is the review of internal control so it is perhaps less likely that internal audit will detect weaknesses in the other elements of management which do not have a significant control impact.

The Meaning of Internal Control

We have already explored some important concepts which should contribute to our understanding of internal control. We can summarise them as follows:

1. Control consists of external as well as internal control.
2. Internal control is synonymous with management control.
3. Management is responsible for internal control.[6]
4. Internal audit is the independent appraisal of the effectiveness of internal control on behalf of management.
5. Management control is achieved by the judicious application of all the elements of management—planning, organising, directing, staffing, controlling and co-ordinating.

We now move on to explore the meaning of internal control in more detail.

Control in Fayol's terms is analogous to the process of a central heating or air-conditioning thermostat, which:

- has a planned temperature (e.g. 70°F)
- takes measurements of actual performance

- compares actual against plan
- notes the variance between actual and plan
- makes a decision whether to switch on the pump (or fan) to keep actual performance within a tolerable range of planned performance.

With this model of control it is clear that: (1) there is a need for a plan against which to control; (2) control entails monitoring; (3) control requires decision taking: decision taking is usually associated with planning, but it is also right at the heart of controlling—an indication that it is impossible neatly to unravel planning from controlling.

A seminal definition of internal control dates back to 1948 and is only now being replaced by the new COSO definition, which we look at later. In 1948, the American Institute of Certified Public Accountants (AICPA) defined internal control in a way which they acknowledged was "broader than the meaning sometimes attributed to the term", as follows:

Internal control comprises the plan of organisation and the co-ordinate methods and measures adopted within a business to safeguard its assets, check the accuracy and reliability of its accounting data, promote operational efficiency, and encourage adherence to prescribed managerial policies.[7]

The two key points to note about this definition are:

- it identifies planning, organisational arrangements and procedures as being basic to internal control
- it gives four objectives of internal control which are to do with
  - safeguarding assets
  - reliability of accounts
  - operational efficiency
  - effectiveness (achievement of policies).

A significant milestone in the development of conventional wisdom about internal control came in 1958 when AICPA divided internal control into (a) *administrative control*, and (b) *accounting control*.[8] This distinction has been with us ever since.[9] The motivation for the distinction was an awareness on the part of public accountants acting as external auditors that their primary concern is with the controls which contribute to the reliability of the accounts (or published financial statements) and that they as external auditors are not so concerned with administrative controls over operations. Dividing internal control into administrative and accounting controls was intended to allow external auditors largely to restrict their interest in internal control to the accounting controls only.

AICPA make the distinction as follows:

Accounting control comprises the plan of the organisation and the procedures and records that are concerned with the safeguards of assets and the reliability of financial records.[10]

Administrative control includes, but is not limited to, the plan of organization and the procedures and records that are concerned with the decision processes leading to management's authorization of transactions. Such authorization is a management function directly associated with the responsibility for achieving the objectives of the organization and is the starting point for establishing accounting controls of transactions.[11]

In the UK a broadly similar understanding about the nature of internal control has emerged. To date, the generally accepted UK definition of internal control has been that of the Consultative Committee of Accountancy Bodies (CCAB) and the Chartered Institute of Management Accountants (CIMA):

The whole system of controls, financial and otherwise, established by the management in order to carry on the business in an orderly and efficient manner, ensure adherence to management policies, safeguard the assets and secure as far as possible the completeness and accuracy of the records.[12]

An alternative UK definition of internal control (which does not replace the above definition) is:

The regulation of activities in an organisation through systems designed and implemented to facilitate the achievement of management objectives.[13]

We must make reference to the position of the Institute of Internal Auditors (IIA). The IIA has a straightforward definition of internal control which can be reconciled to the definitions we have already used. The IIA identifies five objectives of control, in contrast to the four explicit in the AICPA/CCAB pronouncements we have already considered and the three objectives in the COSO framework to which we turn our attention shortly. The IIA continues to adhere to their position that internal control exists to achieve these five objectives in contrast to COSO's three objectives,[14] notwithstanding that the IIA was one of the five COSO bodies.

The IIA's Definition

The overall system of internal control is conceptual in nature. It is an integrated collection of controlled systems used by an organization to achieve its objectives and goals.[15]

The IIA's Five Objectives of Control

The primary objectives of internal control are to ensure:

> (a)   the reliability and integrity of information;
>
> (b)   compliance with policies, plans, procedures, laws and regulations;
>
> (c)   the safeguarding of assets;
>
> (d)   the economical and efficient use of resources;
>
> (e)   the accomplishment of established objectives and goals for operations or programmes.[16]

Treadway, COSO and the UK Equivalents

During the 1980s five US bodies,[17] known as COSO (Committee of Sponsoring Organizations) invited Treadway to head a commission of enquiry in the wake of concern about fraudulent financial reporting. The so-called Treadway Report[18] was published in 1987. Treadway recommended that management should include a report on internal control with their published financial statements. Adoption of this proposal was deferred pending clarification of the meaning of internal control and the form and process of any such report by management, and it now looks as if it will continue to be a voluntary, though frequently followed, practice in the USA. To provide this clarification, COSO funded a further project, the fieldwork of which was conducted by Cooper & Lybrand, which led to the publication in 1992 of *Internal Control—Integrated Framework*.[19] This gives us a new definition of internal control which is supplanting the 1948 AICPA definition and its derivatives. COSO also gives guidance on how internal control is achieved—by means of five interrelated control components. Finally, COSO gives guidance on the process and form of public reports by management on internal control.

The new US COSO Definition of Internal Control

Internal control is broadly defined as a process, effected by the entity's board of directors, management and other personnel, designed to provide reasonable assurance regarding the achievement of objectives in the following categories:

- Effectiveness and efficiency of operations;
- Reliability of financial reporting
- Compliance with applicable laws and regulations.

COSO recognises that the three objectives of control are "distinct but overlapping categories [which] address different needs and allow a directed focus to meet the separate needs". It is easier to reconcile these three categories of objectives with the four objectives of control in the 1948 definition if one bears in mind that the drafters of the COSO definition intended that "safeguarding of assets" should be regarded as part of the effectiveness and efficiency of operations" objective.

The definition puts stress on process though this is a largely cosmetic change of nomenclature from the earlier uses of the expressions "methods and measures" and "system" which we referred to earlier. (The UK continues to use the expression "system"). The COSO definition also usefully stresses that internal control cannot guarantee the achievement of control objectives—but can give "reasonable assurance" of doing so.

COSO goes on to provide a classification of the ways in which internal control is achieved—which they term the "five interrelated control *components*"—and COSO's extensive discussion of the nature of these components is extremely useful:

Control environment—for instance, the ethical tone set by the board.

Risk assessment—for instance, it is necessary for management to assess relative risk as a prerequisite for developing and maintaining commensurate effective internal control.
Control activities—for instance, segregation of duties.
Information and communication—for instance, exception reports.
Monitoring—for instance, by internal audit.

The New UK Definition of Internal Control

A parallel development has been taking place in the UK. The Cadbury Report on corporate governance[20] recommended that directors of listed companies should report publicly on internal control, and guidance has been prepared on this.[21]

This guidance defines internal control as:

The whole system of controls, financial and otherwise, established in order to provide reasonable assurance of:

1.   effective and efficient operations
2.   internal financial control
3.   compliance with laws and regulations.

The UK is therefore perpetuating the 1972 suggestion that it is possible and helpful to distinguish between financial and other controls, whereas COSO makes the distinction only at the level of the objectives of control, not the process of control. In other words, COSO is saying internal control can give reasonable reassurance of the achievement of three categories of objective, whereas the UK agrees that there are these three aims but suggests further that there are also at least two sub-sets of internal controls (one of which comprises the *internal financial controls*), and that control over the reliability of financial statements is achieved by the internal financial controls subset. COSO does not go so far as to claim there are two sub-sets of internal control. COSO only goes as far as to recognise, with regard to the three categories of objectives of control, that "these distinct but overlapping categories address different needs and allow a directed focus[22] to meet the separate needs".

The UK also places less emphasis upon "process".

The UK replaces the five US components by which control is achieved by five similar "criteria" taking exception to the word "components". The criteria are:

- control environment
- identification and evaluation of risks, and control objectives
- information and communication
- control procedures
- monitoring and corrective action.

Audit Interest in Internal Control

The internal auditor's mission is to review internal control arrangements so as to reassure management as to their adequacy and provide persuasive advice on any improvements. External auditors have a different mission: to assure those to whom they report that the financial statements are true and fair. So, for internal auditors internal control evaluation is the objective of their work. For external auditors it is one means by which they may obtain reassurance; other means are:

- analytical review (especially of accounting data)
- vouching (the reperformance of accounting activity)
- verification (e.g. that assets exist, are owned by the business and are valued correctly)
- subsequent events review.

Internal auditors may also resort to all but the last of these means for determining whether the systems of control are functioning economically, efficiently and effectively.

THE CONTROL ENVIRONMENT

Introduction

We shall now turn to the subject of reviewing the control environment within an organisation. First we shall establish the top-level control objectives for this subject and then examine the relative risk and control issues posed in the form of questions. During the course of their review, auditors will be seeking to answer these questions by, first, determining the controls and measures that are in place in each instance, and secondly to evaluate the effectiveness of these controls/ measures by performing compliance and substantive testing as appropriate.

Remember the COSO definition of the term control environment:

The control environment sets the tone of an organisation influencing the control consciousness of its people. It is the foundation for all other components of internal control, providing discipline and structure. Control environment factors include the integrity, ethical values and competence of the entity's people; management's philosophy and operating style; the way management assigns authority and responsibility, and organises and develops its people; and the attention and direction provided by the board of directors.[23]

Control Objectives for a Review of the Control Environment

The following two objectives are deliberately pitched at a top-level view of the control environment. However, it would be straightforward to break these down to a more detailed set.

1. To ensure that management conveys the message that integrity, ethical values and commitment to competence cannot be compromised, and that employees receive and understand that message.
2. To ensure that management continually demonstrates, by word and action, commitment to high ethical and competence standards.

Risk and Control Issues for a Review of the Control Environment

In order to evaluate whether the two control objectives listed above are being met, the auditor will need to consider the underlying risks and control issues. Noted below are a set of questions related to the risk and control issues that are inherent to the subject of the control environment.

The issue questions have been divided into two sets, namely the key issues (numbered 1.1 to 1.7) and the detailed issues (numbered 2.1 to 2.15). The auditor should always seek to answer the key issue questions, turning to the detailed set either when there is a noted weakness in the controls in place for the key set or whenever time permits.

Key Issues

1.1 Are there in place satisfactory Codes of Conduct and other policies which define acceptable business practice, conflicts of interest and expected standards of integrity and ethical behaviour?

1.2 Do management (from the top of the business downwards to all levels) clearly conduct business on a high ethical plane, and are departures appropriately remedied?

1.3 Is the philosophy and operating style of management consistent with the highest ethical standards?

1.4 Do the human resource policies of the business adequately reinforce its commitment to high standards of business integrity, ethics and competence?

1.5 Has the level of competence needed been specified for particular jobs, and does evidence exist to indicate that employees have the requisite knowledge and skills?

1.6 Are the board and its committees sufficiently informed and independent of management such that necessary, even if difficult and probing, questions can be explored effectively?

1.7 Is the organisation structure such that (a) all fully understand their responsibilities and authorities, and (b) the enterprise's activities can be adequately monitored?

Detailed Issues

2.1 Are Codes of Conduct comprehensive, addressing conflicts of interest, illegal or other improper payments, anti-competitive guidelines and insider trading?

2.2 Are Codes of Conduct understood by and periodically subscribed to by all employees?

2.3 Do senior managers frequently visit outlying locations for which they are responsible?

2.4 Is it the impression that employees feel peer pressure "to do the right thing"

2.5 Is there sufficient evidence that management moves carefully in assessing potential benefits of ventures?

2.6 Does management adequately deal with signs that problems exist (e.g. hazardous by-products) even when the cost of identification and remedy could be high?

2.7 Are sufficient efforts made to deal honestly and fairly with business partners (e.g. employees, suppliers, etc.)?

2.8 Is disciplinary action sufficiently taken and communicated in the case of violations?

2.9 Is management override of controls appropriate when it occurs, and sufficiently authorised, documented and explained?

2.10 Are there job descriptions (which adequately define key managers' responsibilities) and performance appraisals with follow-up action to remedy deficiencies?

2.11 Is management and staff turnover reasonable, i.e. not excessive?

2.12 Are staffing levels adequate but not excessive?

2.13 Do staff recruitment procedures sufficiently enhance the enterprises commitment to high standards of integrity, ethics and competence?

2.14 Do training programmes sufficiently enhance the enterprise's commitment to high standards of integrity, ethics and competence?

2.15 Do sufficient lines of communication exist to obviate the temptation of "whistleblowing"?

When examining questions from both the key issues and the detailed issues you should consider how, as an auditor, you would go about answering them. Additionally, you should also apply some thought as to what sort of controls and measures need to be in place to adequately address the inherent risks.

RISK ASSESSMENT

Risk is present in every activity and we all, to varying degrees, continually evaluate the relative significance of risk in our lives and take appropriate steps to counteract the potential implications.

In a business context, risk can be an inherent feature of the operations of an organisation, especially where there is notable change taking place. The nature of risk may be, on the one hand, critical to the continued survival of the organisation, or a matter of a positive commercial image on the other hand. There are, of course, numerous shades of grey in respect of the relative impact of risks, and each entity will be likely to have a unique mapping of implications and consequences.

In order to plan effectively and economically for the reduction or containment of business-related risks, an organisation will need to identify all the risks that may apply in the course of their operations. In the case of launching new business ventures, an assessment of risk will normally feature as part of the strategic level of planning. Although the risks associated with established business activities may be (or thought to be) well known, there is always the necessity to ensure that changes in business objectives, legislation, and so on are catered for in the organisation's view of relative risks.

The identification of risk within a business should be an ongoing process sensitive to the implications of changed market conditions, operational work-loads, macroeconomic parameters, and so on. Effective management should be able to anticipate the need for change and accordingly evaluate the amendments to the corporate risk profile.

Given that the control awareness and philosophy of an organisation should ideally be driven from the top and have the express commitment of senior management, then it logically follows that the associated assessment of risk should also emanate from a high level within an organisation. This is especially relevant when an organisation is undergoing radical or far-reaching change, perhaps as a matter of continued survival.

Data on risks should be accurate and viewed in the context of likelihood of occurrence. For existing activities there may be historic risk data available based on past achievements to draw upon. Risks can be represented by either quantitative or qualitative factors and will certainly have differing degrees of potential impact.

Identified risks should be prioritised and control objectives established in every case. The objectives can reflect the required performance indicators applicable to each risk as a means of establishing the thresholds of tolerance. Taken collectively the ranking and objectives data will drive the definition and design of the required control systems.

Objectives may be classified in a number of ways, for example:

- operations objectives (e.g. performance/profitability goals)
- financial reporting objectives (e.g. accurate statements prepared in accordance with prevailing requirements)
- compliance objectives (e.g. adherence to relevant sector regulations, legislation, etc.)

In basic terms, one measure of success for any system of internal control is that there is reasonable assurance that the established control objectives have been achieved, and will be in the future.

Business and society are not static entities, they are subject to all manner of changes initiated from both within and outside an entity. The assessment of risks should be an ongoing process with reappraisal of the implications for the business. Changes in the nature or priority of risk should then be carried through to the setting of control objectives and the modification/creation of the system of internal control.

CONTROL ACTIVITIES

The establishment of a system of control benefits from being approached afresh, but it is more likely that, in practice, the mechanisms have evolved progressively over a considerable time. The methods prescribed in both COSO's *Internal Control Framework*[24] and ICAEW's *Internal Control and Financial Reporting*[25] suggest an idealistic "green field" perspective.

The creation of a high-profile control environment, the undertaking of a risk assessment of an entity's operations, and the setting of a range of control objectives will naturally lead to, or flush out, the required control mechanisms. It is too simplistic to say that every exposure and control objective will need to be matched with a control activity, as there may be inevitable overlap with both objectives and control activities, with the potential for varying degrees of significance when viewed in combination.

There are two dimensions to control activities. First there is the establishment of a policy which defines what has to be done to achieve the related business objective. Secondly, a procedure is required which defines the processes necessary to meet the policy requirements. Generally speaking, policies are normally defined at a fairly high level, while procedures have a tendency for a markedly lower or detailed level of definition. The policies may specify the best form of control type to achieve the desired effect, whereas the procedures will be concerned with the elemental mechanism of the preferred approach. Ensuring that the spirit of both these elements remains compatible is therefore essential if the underlying objectives are to be achieved.

Control activities/procedures will need to be accurately defined and effectively communicated to those involved. It is always preferable to establish written procedures which remove the possibility of misinterpretation so often associated with verbal instructions. Control activities may be defined in the form of procedures, user manuals, job descriptions, etc. Any timing requirements, reporting criteria or authority thresholds should be incorporated clearly into such documents. Operational changes should be subject to prompt review so that any required procedural changes can be accommodated and communicated.

The nature and extent of control activities will need to be considered against the balance between the costs of implementing them and the benefits derived. Where there are compensating controls, any redundant processes should be pruned out, but only after achievement of control objectives is assured.

The form of control activities employed will obviously be dependent on the nature of the associated risks and control objectives and there are few hard and fast rules that can be brought to bear. The generic form of controls (i.e. preventive or detective) and their eventual form (i.e. authorisation, reconciliation, segregation of duties, etc.) will need to be matched to both the risks and objectives.

In key areas, it may be essential that some form of trail of control activities is maintained as evidence of appropriate application of the procedure. Such trails can be monitored by management to provide some assurance that the control is being complied with.

Where the control activity requires a specific or specialised skill, there should be a mechanism in place to ensure that the requisite knowledge levels are maintained, perhaps through ongoing training and staff development programmes.

With the increasing influence of information technology on all manner of everyday business activities, it is crucial for the integrity of corporate data and continuation of service provision that specific control objectives and activities are targeted at computer systems. Data is often the lifeblood of an organisation and steps should be taken to ensure that it remains accurate, complete, secure and authorised.

INFORMATION AND COMMUNICATION

In order to function efficiently and successfully, an organisation requires that relevant information is provided to the right people at the right time. It is inconceivable that a modern business could run and achieve its objectives without a flow of relevant information. Additionally, it is essential that such information is reliable in terms of accuracy and completeness. Inaccurate or outdated data will affect management's ability to make the appropriate decisions and control the business. Where necessary data should be authorised and secure, especially where it is commercially sensitive.

In a contemporary business, all manner of data will be gathered, analysed and distributed. It may, for example, relate to operational matters, performance statistics, financial status or matters of control compliance.

Selected staff will require the receipt of information in order to perform their specific tasks. Working with outdated or incomplete data may jeopardise both their performance and the achievement of corporate objectives.

Corporate information should not be considered purely from the internal viewpoint, as relevant data received from, and sent out to, external bodies can also be crucial; for example, order call-off details from a major customer will impact on both production and stock functions, whereas the timely release of invoices will potentially benefit cash flow, etc. Matters such as data accuracy can take on a different significance when there are external dimensions, in that the image and reputation of an organisation can severely be damaged if incomplete or invalid information is distributed to customers or suppliers.

Inevitably in the present business environment, information directly relates to some form of computerised process. Of course, information technology brings great benefits to the business world, but unless carefully controlled and monitored there is the potential for severe adverse impacts. A cynic may be inclined to say that computers have an unnerving knack of generating rubbish a lot faster than human beings can. As a general rule there should be independent proof that a system has generated accurate and complete data, and the fact that "the computer produced this report" should not be taken as positive evidence that the data is reliable.

There is normally a key set of data elements which form the heart of a business, and whereas the systems (or applications) which process and manipulate such data may change over time, the nature of this crucial data is likely to remain fairly consistent. As part of a corporate level information technology strategic plan, a form of data modelling can be undertaken which seeks to identify the required data structure and assign factors such as ownership, access rights and security levels for each element.

In the appropriate circumstances there may be benefits associated with the development of a formal information policy defining the key components of the business information system. Having established a management information system (MIS) or equivalent, it is relatively easy to build in required controls aimed at ensuring the accuracy, integrity and timeliness of data.

In the context of a control environment, information sources may have a discrete control implication in that, for example, they provide the means to operate a control or highlight the failure of a control condition. When defining and building a control environment and associated control activities, the use of key information elements is inevitable. Reconciliation and testing routines can provide management with assurances that systems are operating correctly.

The term "communication" has a broader significance than pure information. For example, communication systems can relate key messages about the culture and control awareness of an enterprise, and engender a collective responsibility for control matters if handled appropriately.

Internal communications can cater for flows in various directions, i.e. up the hierarchy, across functions or down through all layers of management and responsibility. Although any organisation should have a healthy regard for the sensitivity and confidentiality of information flowing through lines of communication, it is as important to ensure that staff do receive the information they require to fulfil their responsibility as it is to prevent unauthorised access to data.

The communication routes to utilise in the event of either a problem or failure occurring should be defined clearly so that the prompt reporting of anomalies is facilitated.

External communication requirements will cater for both inward and outward flows. For example, in a service industry context, it may be crucial to ensure that customer complaints or operational failures are swiftly and accurately routed to the appropriate personnel. Alternatively, periodic performance or compliance reports may have to be sent out to a regulatory body.

We are presented with a variety of means of communication, where speed, accessibility and security will all vary with the method. Defining standards for the use of an appropriate method in specific circumstances can provide greater assurance that communications will be effectively achieved.

MONITORING

Following the publication of the UK Cadbury Report, and after the London Stock Exchange made disclosure of compliance with its Code of Best Practice conditional on listed companies, directors are making public statements on their companies' internal financial control. Similar practice is followed by many companies in the USA and elsewhere—either voluntarily or as a regulatory requirement. Patently, in order to fulfil this obligation, the directors need access to the relevant data that will give them the necessary degree of assurance.

Assurances are required that the proper accounting records have been maintained and that all financial information is reliable. Furthermore, directors should be able to satisfy themselves that they are able to make a public statement on the effectiveness of the internal control system.

We have discussed elsewhere the development of the control environment, the establishment of control activities geared to the risks present in the organisation and the required flow of business-related information. Each organisation will further need to consider how these components contribute to the director's need to obtain the required levels of assurance in order to make the necessary public statements through, for example, the annual accounts and report.

Information systems should provide the principal means of monitoring the effectiveness of internal control systems. Equally important is the establishment of mechanisms which, having identified either a problem or control failure, ensure that management is made aware so that the necessary corrective action can promptly be taken.

As to who should undertake the responsibility for monitoring the internal control system, this should fall ultimately to the board, who in any event have the final responsibility for the operations of the organisation. In practical terms, directors cannot operate all aspects of monitoring on their own. Line management should have defined responsibilities for ongoing or day-to-day monitoring of operations, financial performance, etc. Ideally a degree of independence should be brought to bear on the monitoring process. Non-executive directors can play a vital role in monitoring, for example through an audit committee of the board with specific responsibilities for reviewing financial statements and assessing the effectiveness of the internal control system and the activities of the internal audit function.

The board should further monitor the identification of business risks and the development of control objectives and priorities, although the initial detailed work may be undertaken by more junior management.

The internal audit function has the potential to play a vital role in independently assessing the effectiveness of controls and reporting on them to the board, perhaps through the auspices of the audit committee.

The processes of ongoing and/or periodic review, whoever conducts them, should not only consider the effectiveness of the existing control system, but should also question whether the system itself is still relevant and suitable. Businesses and operations will invariably change and have to adapt to external forces, so that it is probable that practices and therefore control will have to be modified to meet the new demands. Whether the reviewer has detected a failure of the existing control system or the requirement for that system to be updated, there needs to be a defined mechanism and a route that enables prompt and effective reporting of the shortcomings. Management should have in place a system for receiving feedback from a number of sources about control-related problems, etc. These may be formal in nature such as would apply to internal and external auditors' reporting channels, but should also cater for more junior members of staff who may suspect that an improper act has been perpetrated.

A procedure for dealing with reported shortcomings and ensuring that appropriate corrective action is applied by management, will also be necessary to avoid either a recurrence or more significant breach of policy.

Evidence of review of the system of internal control should be available; this may be in the form of internal audit reports, summaries of significant control issues co-ordinated by the audit committee, or minutes of board meetings, etc.

The consolidation and reporting of the conclusions of control self-assessment programmes, especially in the absence of an internal audit function, are likely to have a significant role to play in assessing internal control effectiveness within an enterprise.

After the year end, but shortly before finalising the Annual Report, the audit committee should meet to consider internal control. Their scope may be confined to internal *financial* control, but ideally it should not be so limited. The committee's formal review of internal control should have inputs, process and outputs. Companies have considerable discretion in their approach, which is likely to make use of some of the following:

Inputs (i.e. evidence on internal control for the committee to consider[26]):

- intelligence gathered as board members during the year
- a report from the Executive on the key procedures which are designed to provide effective internal control
- the committee's assessment of the effectiveness of internal audit
- reports from internal audit on scheduled audits performed
- reports on special reviews commissioned by the committee from internal audit or others
- internal audit's overall summary opinion on internal control
- the overall results of a control self-assessment process
- confirmation that key line managers are clear as to their objectives[27]
- letters of representation ("comfort letters") on internal control from line management
- the external auditors' management letter
- a Losses Report from the chief executive officer or financial director

- an Executive report on any material developments between the balance sheet date and the present
- the Executive's proposed wording of the internal control report for publication.

Process:

- ensure adequate committee time (half a day?) and enough advance notice to prepare and study agenda papers
- bring forward to mid-year meetings as much as possible of the committee's consideration of internal control, away from the year end deadlines and allowing more time for remedial action
- review all evidence (inputs, above) in committee
- take oral advice from management, internal and external audit and others in attendance
- draw conclusions as a committee

Outputs
—for transmission to the board prior to going to print with the Annual Report:

- endorsement of the key control procedures (note: Rutteman for the ICAEW says these are for the *directors* to have established) as being satisfactory
- committee opinion on internal (financial) control effectiveness—whether for publication or for internal use only
- committee's proposed draft internal control report for publication
- any committee concerns about internal control of sufficient importance for the board.

—for transmission to senior executive management:

- outstanding committee concerns about internal control
- the committee's required revisions of approach for the future.

FRAUD

Fraud is an intentional, deceitful act for gain with concealment. As such, it is more than theft. Defalcation is theft by a person in a position of trust. Fraud may be perpetrated by one person working on his or her own, but many frauds are able to occur only as a result of collusion—between collateral associates working in different positions within the business, between a manager and someone reporting to that manager, or between an insider and an outsider. There may be mass collusion, for instance between many salespeople and many customers, even to the extent that the fraud tacitly may have become regarded as a regular perk.

It is frequently because of the collusion characteristic that fraud is so difficult to prevent and detect since effective systems of internal control often become ineffective when collusion circumvents the segregation features of a control system. This illustrates that an effective system of internal control requires much more than a good set of control activities such as segregation of duties—it also always requires the other components of internal control as the COSO report called them:—control environment, risk assessment, information and communication, and monitoring.

We may classify fraud as:

- management fraud, for instance fraudulent financial reporting
- employee fraud
- outsider fraud
- collusive fraud.

Some fraud, especially computer program frauds, may be continuous, working for the defrauder indefinitely into the future. Some continuous frauds require no further direct action by the defrauder once they have been set up, as they continue working automatically. Some continuous frauds require constant maintenance by the defrauder, such as teeming and lading frauds. Other frauds are not continuous but have a "smash and grab" character with the defrauder absconding with the gains in a carefully timed way just before the perhaps inevitable detection.

One important deterrent for fraud is for the business to have a good record of detecting fraud. If a prospective defrauder knows there is a high risk of detection and that the consequences upon detection will not be pleasant, then that person will be less likely to engage in the fraud. Given a personal need, an opportunity to perpetrate a fraud and a conviction that detection is most unlikely or that the consequences upon detection would not be too disgraceful, then many ordinary people will be sorely tempted to engage in fraud. It is up to management to make sure that these ingredients are not present in their business.

Difficult though it is to achieve, the most effective antidote to fraud is a strong system internal control in all its component parts. Of course, good internal control also reduces the risk of accidental error or loss. Both fraud and accidental errors and losses share the characteristic of occurring in part due to a breakdown in the system of internal control.

In designing control systems some managers find it helpful to consider that day-to-day control is achieved by a mix of segregation and supervision—each of which may be exercised by people or in an automated way, or a combination of both depending on the circumstances. Segregation controls have the advantage that no specific action may be required in order for them to function, and so no cost is associated with their functioning. Where control is not regarded as effective by virtue of the array of segregation measures in place, management must resort to supervisory controls. Supervisory controls, especially if dependent on individual supervisors, tend to be unreliable, as work pressures make it likely that they are exercised in a token way only. IT-based reporting by exception may be an example of part-automated supervisory control where the computer provides management with the opportunity for them to complete the supervisory task in an efficient way.

There are a number of different types of segregation control, including:

- Segregate knowledge—on a need-to-know basis.
- Segregate operations that are incompatible from a control point of view—such as selling from credit control.

- Segregate duties—so that key control-sensitive tasks are shared by more than one person, who act as cross-checks on each other.
- Segregate staff—so that staff engaged on operations which have been segregated do not work in adjacent areas or substitute for each other.
- Segregate authorisation from accounting from custodianship—so that, for instance, the cashier has custody of cash but cannot authorise its use and does not maintain the control accounts for cash. Similarly, the storekeeper does not maintain the accounts for stock and does not authorise the issue of goods from stock or the replenishment of stock.
- Segregate authorisation from accounting from the operation—such as a purchase is made by a purchasing manager against the budget head's authorisation and neither of these two have any part in updating the accounts relating to the transaction.
- Segregation of time—such as deliberate time delays where time is likely to reveal any undesirable circumstances (time locks on safes, computer terminal log off after time out, etc).
- Segregation of operations from monitoring—such as having an independent internal audit function.

Consult the Internal Control Guides for Management and Staff (see Appendices 4 and 5), which have been drawn up with the fraud risk in mind. Appendix 6 is a suggested Board Policy Statement on Fraud. Having such a statement is one aspect of ensuring that the control environment is appropriate. Further aspects of this might be a Statement of Corporate Principles (see, for example, Appendix 7) and a Code of Business Conduct (see Appendix 8). A letter of Representation on Internal Control (see Appendix 10) can also be helpful.

NOTES

1. COSO (September 1992) *Internal Control—Integrated Framework*. New York AICPA.
2. Mackenzie, W. J. M. (1966) "Foreword". In Normanton, E. L. *The Accountability and Audit of Governments*. Manchester University Press, Manchester, p. vii. Also published by Frederick A. Praeger, New York (1966).
3. Henri Fayol first described the elements or functions of management in 1916 in his classic book *Administration Industrielle et Générale* and he was the first to identify "controlling" as a function of management. Fayol, who then became acknowledged as the father of management theory, described the functions of management in terms which to us now appear dated: planning, organising, commanding, co-ordinating, controlling. Had Fayol been widely read soon after he wrote his book, perhaps the concepts of internal control would have been established much sooner—and perhaps the Institute of Internal Auditors would have been established earlier than 1941.
4. Chambers, A. D., Selim, G. M. and Vinten, G. (1987) *Internal Auditing*, 2nd edn. Pitman, London, see Chapter 4.
5. To illustrate the proximity between *organizing* and *controlling* it is illuminating to remember that Fayol (ibid.) used the label "span of control" to describe the issue of how many subordinates one boss might supervise—yet this is clearly a matter of organisation as well as of control.
6. In the UK, the CCAB: Auditing guideline 308: *Guidance for Internal Auditors* (1990) puts it like this: "It is a management responsibility to determine the extent of internal control in the oganisation's systems which should not depend on internal audit as a

substitute for effective controls. Internal audit, as a service to the organisation, contributes to internal control by examining, evaluating and reporting to management on its adequacy and effectiveness. Internal audit activity may lead to the strengthening of internal control as a result of management response."

7. American Institute of Certified Public Accountants (AICPA) (1948/49) *Internal Control—Elements of a Co-ordinated System and its Importance to Management and the Independent Public Accountant*. AICPA, New York.
8. AICPA (October 1958) *Statement on Auditing Procedure No. 29*. New York, AICPA.
9. See, for example, AICPA (November 1972) *SAP 54 (Statement on Auditing Procedure, No. 54)*; also AICPA: *SAS No. 1 and No. 55 (Statement on Auditing Standards, No. 1 and No. 55*; and more recently the distinction is continued in the US COSO (1992) report (ibid.), and the Uk exposure draft *Internal Control and Financial Reporting* 1993.
10. AICPA, 1972 (ibid.)
11. AICPA (June 1 1988) *Professional Standards, Volume 1*. New York, AICPA.
12. Consultative Committee of Accountancy Bodies (CCAB), Auditing Practices Committee (1980) *Auditing Guideline*, Section 3; Chartered Institute of Management Accountants (CIMA) (1992) *A Framework for Internal Control*.
13. Consultative Committee of Accountancy Bodies (CCAB) (1990) Auditing Guideline 308: *Guidance for Internal Auditors* (Glossary of Terms section).
14. This was discussed and agreed at the mid-year meeting of the Internal Auditing Standards Board of IIA Inc. (December 1993) and is being applied, for instance, in the exposure draft of a new Statement on Internal Auditing Standards (SIAS) on *Summary Reporting on Internal Control*.
15. IIA Inc. (July 1983) *Control: Concepts and Responsibilities* SIAS, No. 1.
16. IIA Inc. *Standard 305*.
17. American Institute of Certified Public Accountants; American Accounting Association; The Institute of Internal Auditors; The Institute of Management Accountants; The Financial Executives Institute.
18. "The Treadway Commission Report" (1987) *Report of the National Commission on Fraudulent Financial Reporting*. National Commission on Fraudulent Financial Reporting, New York.
19. COSO (September 1992) *Internal Control—Integrated Framework*. New York, AICPA.
20. "The Cadbury Report" (December 1992) *Report of the Committee on the Financial Aspects of Corporate Governance*. Gee, London.
21. ICAEW (December 1994) *Internal Control and Financial Reporting*.
22. For example, by auditors.
23. See note 1.
24. COSO (1992) *Internal Control Framework*.
25. See note 21.
26. For the UK, in general these inputs should relate to the period under review. The US guidance envisages that the published report on internal control will relate only to control in place as of the year end date whereas Rutteman of the ICAEW requires (§9) that: "The directors' statement should cover the period of the financial statements and should also take account of material developments between the balance sheet date and the date upon which the financial statements are signed."
27. Contemporary definitions of internal control (COSO and Rutteman) acknowledge that internal control is intended to provide reasonable assurance of the achievement of objectives. It follows that to assess whether internal control has been effective, management should be clear as to their objectives and whether they have been achieved. Failure to achieve objectives might not be a consequence of defective internal control; for instance it may be due to external events. Succeeding in achieving objectives might not be a consequence of effective internal control since control weaknesses might not have been exploited. So it is wise to consider both the extent to which objectives have been achieved as well as the framework of internal

control in coming to an opinion on the effectiveness of internal control. The Rutteman focus is (inappropriately) almost exclusively on the latter—implying that the internal control processes themselves are the criteria for assessing internal control effectiveness with no regard to whether objectives have been achieved. COSO is more balanced.

5

Auditing Subsidiaries and Remote Operating Units

INTRODUCTION

In this chapter we will examine the specific practical considerations that apply in the auditing of subsidiaries or remote operating units (such as those located in other countries).

The modern corporation is increasingly organised into decentralised profit centres, some of which may be located overseas. It is normally the role of the centre to provide leadership, inspiration and direction in order to achieve the necessary performance potential. This presupposes that the required objectives and performance standards have been established, agreed and accurately communicated to those affected.

The degrees to which functions are devolved to the subsidiary and remote units will, of course, vary. Senior management will have to decide what business aspects remain the prerogative of the centre; for example, these could include:

- approving budgets
- setting production schedules
- reviewing divisional strategies
- allocating capital resources
- responsibility for research and development
- defining standards
- appointing divisional managers.

The roles and responsibilities of group and subsidiary management will need to be defined and clear policies generated; for example, on such matters as trading within the group, where the stances on sourcing from within the group and selling on to other subsidiaries will need to be defined.

For the most part, the fundamental audit approach to the bulk of the audit field work will be the same in this type of operational review as it would be for those conducted within the parent company or head office. In other words, the systematic review and assessment of the controls and measures in place both to counteract the inherent risks within the operation(s) being examined and to ensure that the established objectives are achieved. On the ground there may be some potential additional practical matters to address, such as the local language and legislative considerations. However, of prime concern to the audit manager will be how can he/she ensure that the time spent during the audit visit is productive and focused upon the appropriate things. This will be especially true if this is to be the first audit of the operation.

The audit manager may be under pressure to deploy precious resources in a cost-effective manner and in proportion to the perceived level of risks. This may be especially true when the additional costs of travel, accommodation and subsistence have to be added to the fixed payroll costs of the audit function. In the eyes of senior management there can be no justification for wasting audit time on low-risk operations with little overall significance to the organisation.

When contemplating the total audit universe of possible review projects, the audit manager may apply some form of relative risk assessment in order to identify auditing priorities as the basis for forming the audit plan for the coming year. We do not examine such formal risk assessment methods here,[1] but rather suggest two possible techniques for gathering key data about any subsidiary or remote operation as the basis for assessing the audit priorities within an review project.

This chapter mainly concentrates on how auditors can acquire the information necessary to ensure that the field visit is effectively directed towards the key areas of the operations, especially those which represent greater degrees of risk to the organisation as a whole.

First, we consider effective fact finding prior to the main field audit visit as a means to set the scene for the forthcoming operational review. Secondly, we look at the process of conducting a high level review as a means of identifying key operational areas where audit review attention should be concentrated at either a system or activity level. Within these two approaches, we provide comprehensive examples of the types of questions to be posed.

We conclude this chapter with a discussion of joint ventures, and consider the internal audit role in such activities.

FACT FINDING

In the course of preparing for an audit visit, one method of gathering the key background and performance data and environmental facts about a potential audit review target would be to use a fact finding programme. The data collected during this process may be obtained from a number of sources including existing management information and accounting records, senior management representatives and local operating reports.

In sections A to D below, we provide some examples of the sort of questions and subjects that should be considered for inclusion into such a fact finding programme. Our example assumes that the target is located overseas; where this is not the case, some of the supplied questions will not apply. The data is divided into a number of logical categories, namely:

A   nature and scale of business
B   organisation and key contacts

C   economic and political background

D   policies and procedures.

It may be possible to gather the required facts and data without visiting the target operation and thus avoid the costs associated with field visits. Where the required information is only available on-site, a form of brief reconnaissance trip may be justified. In either case, the intelligence obtained should aim to provide a reliable basis for subsequently scoping and focusing the planned audit visit activities on the key areas of the target operations.

The information gathered during this sort of fact-finding exercise can be used to ensure that appropriate arrangements are put in place for the detailed audit review visit and that key circumstances are taken into account during the creation of the detailed audit review programmes. By following this sort of process, the possibility of wasting valuable time during the site visit is potentially reduced (although there is no guarantee that it can be completely eradicated).

Where the data is related to financial or performance matters, care should be taken to ensure that the sources are reliable and the data is both accurate and up to date. Where there is the likelihood of a prolonged delay between the date the data was gathered and the intended date of the audit field visit, the contents may have to be reviewed in the interim so that more current and credible information is made available to support the determination of audit coverage.

Particular attention should be paid to the appropriate interpretation of data trends or performance variances, as these may be influenced by legitimate events, such as seasonal sales patterns or the effects of local fiscal regulations. Where necessary, unusual data or underlying implications should be subject to further validation enquiries.

When the auditor is compiling the fact-finding document, care should be taken to ensure that commercially sensitive and confidential data is adequately protected from unauthorised access and leakage.

One other practical consequence of using the fact-finding approach is that it should ensure that the auditors engaged in the project and the subsequent review visit are suitably aware of the key environmental considerations. This will hopefully demonstrate to local management that the audit function has taken the time and effort to set the operation in context and obtained an accurate impression of the business under review. This sort of informed preparation can enhance the perceived credibility of the auditing function.

Noted below is an example fact finding programme. This is an illustrative example only. In practice, there may be further elements that could legitimately be included in such a programme. Conversely, items currently included may be irrelevant for use within your own organisation.

EXAMPLE FACT-FINDING PROGRAMME

A. Nature and Scale of Business

A.1   What categories of business operation are conducted within this unit (i.e. sales, production, or research and development)?

A.2   List all the relevant types of products and services marketed through this operation.

A.3   Provide an indication of the scale of each operation in terms of turnover, size of expenditure budget, or level of capital invested. *Clearly indicate the currency used.*

A.4   Is this operation solely funded by the parent company? (*If no, see A.5 below.*)

A.5   If external or joint funding applies to this operation, note the names of the other interested parties, their defined role in the relationship, and the level of their investment. Consider the implications for conducting the audit and the possible requirement to access records held by third parties.

A.6   What is the unit's trading and business relationship with the parent company (e.g. marketing outlet for centrally produced products, marketing of locally produced and licensed products, agent, or distributor)?

A.7   Have the taxation implications of the relationship with the parent company been considered, planned for, and authorised? Obtain overview details and consider whether any specific aspect of the operation will need to be reviewed in order to ensure that the taxation objectives are being achieved.

A.8   When was the operation established?

A.9   Note the nature of the significant events in the development and growth of this operation (with approximate dates).

A.10   Has the parent company defined the performance expectations for the business? If so, obtain the details and note any specific sales, turnover or other financial targets for the current accounting year.

A.11   Determine the accounting year dates. (Is this consistent with the parent company, if not, why?) Additionally, have accounting reporting lines been established with the parent company with a defined timetable for submission?

A.12   Obtain a copy of the official trading and management accounts and summarise the key performance figures for a 12-month period. Key data should include (when applicable) sales turnover, profit on sales, total expenditure, inventory values, net profitability, etc.

A.13   Using the data summarised for point A.12 above, highlight any unusual trends or anomalies for investigation and clarification.

A.14   Record details of the banking arrangements including the number and type of accounts, their purpose, and the established authorisations.

A.15   Where applicable, determine the arrangement for reconciling the "payables" to the parent company.

A.16   Determine and note the details of any significant local trading relationships with agents, distributors or major customers. Provide an indication of the relative levels of such key relationships.

A.17   Further to point A.16, determine whether there are legally binding agreements in place for key relationships, and if possible note the main operational elements.

A.18   Is there a local direct sales force? If so, obtain details of the authorised expense rates and the actual travel expenses for marketing and sales staff for the past six months.

A.19   If budget versus actual data is available for key performance factors, obtain a copy and note any major variances. Are local management obliged to report on major variances to the parent company? If so, are explanations of unusual items available centrally?

A.20   Obtain and review any available management information or progress reports, and record summary details of specific and relevant events (noting any action that is planned or being taken).

A.21   Have any specific large-scale investments been made in this operation? Obtain and summarise the key details (e.g. value, commercial objectives, investment period, funding basis, progress against targets).

A.22   If medium and long-term (strategic) plans are available, note the key objectives and their current status.

A.23   Are there warranty implications for the operation? If so, determine what facilities are provided for servicing and maintaining products (including the availability of adequate stocks of spare parts).

A.24   Record when the operation was last audited and note the significant findings and concerns.

A.25   Determine whether there were any major recommendations arising from the last audit visit and their status (i.e. accepted, rejected, actioned, or outstanding).

B. Organisation and Key Contacts

B.1   Obtain current organisation charts and note likely key contacts with their locations and telephone numbers.

B.2   Establish those responsible for key functions and confirm their availability during the planned audit visit.

B.3   Determine whether there have been any recent changes in senior management, and assess whether this is likely to influence the effectiveness of the audit visit.

B.4   Are up-to-date job descriptions available for the key positions? If so, obtain a copy and assess whether the key responsibilities are adequately defined.

B.5   Record overview statistics on the number of staff employed in key operational areas (e.g. sales, administration and accounting, production, development) and the level of staff turnover.

B.6   Determine whether there have been any recent major changes in staffing establishment levels (such as contraction due to poor economic conditions, or expansions due to increased opportunities and demand).

B.7   Determine whether parent company executives have been given responsibilities for the local operations (i.e. note the nature and scope of such involvement). NB Depending on the nature of the responsibility, it may be desirable to arrange a meeting with the relevant executive in order to enhance the understanding of the local trading and fiscal situations.

B.8   Has initial contact been made with key local managers and if so have any potential logistic, operational or practical difficulties been identified?

B.9   Note the location(s) of the operations to be subject to audit review (and consider the implications for travel, accommodation, required audit resources, etc.).

B.10   Note the relevant national language(s) and whether key personnel are fluent in any others. Consider the implications for the audit visit.

B.11   Where external agents, distributors, etc. are involved in the operations, are there agreements in place permitting the parent company auditors to inspect the third party records and documentation? Consider whether any likely restrictions or problems of access will influence the quality and scope of the proposed audit visit.

C. Economic and Political Background

C.1   What is the local trading currency?

C.2   What are the current key business exchange rates? (*Also see C.4.*)

C.3   What are the principal characteristics of the local/national economies (i.e. the basis of national trade, growth, recession, etc.)?

C.4   What has been the nature of currency exchange rates over the previous 12 months and are there any implications for the performance and profitability of the operation? Note any dramatic fluctuations and the nature of any action taken (internally or externally) to stabilise the currency.

C.5   Ascertain the local rate of inflation over the past 12 months and note any apparent trends. When applicable, what is local government apparently doing in relation to inflation, and are their measures showing any signs of success?

C.6 Have any specific plans been established by the company to counteract or reduce the effects of local currency or inflation instability?

C.7 Where relevant, determine the level of local commercial interest rates and their relationship to those applicable to the parent company/country.

C.8 Describe the political nature of the host country, paying particular regard to its fundamental principles (e.g. capitalistic), stability, whether or not a change is imminent/likely, etc. Discuss relevant points with management and note any implications for the business operations and the planned audit visit.

C.9 To what extent are local conditions (economic and political) likely to affect the business operations? (NB: such influences are likely to vary and be dependent on the nature of the business being conducted.)

C.10 Have documented and authorised pricing and discount policies been established? If so, obtain an overview of their main elements, and determine if they are reviewed and adjusted against the background of any local economic and political events.

C.11 Note any specific local accounting requirements and their effect on records and accounting conventions.

C.12 Note the principal elements of those local taxation conditions with implications for the business (e.g. sales taxes, corporation taxes, income or other employment taxes).

C.13 What steps have been taken to optimise the taxation implications for the parent company?

C.14 What are the characteristics of the local employment market and what are the implications for the business operations (e.g. levels of unemployment, available skills in relation to operational skill requirements, effects of local employment legislation, levels of employment related taxation, etc.)?

D. Policies and Procedures

D.1 Are local operations generally governed by the policies and procedures developed by the parent company? If not, are local variants in place? (*Also see D.8.*)

D.2 Determine the operational systems in use and whether documented and authorised procedures are provided.

D.3 Obtain details of the computing arrangements in place and whether the installation conforms to any defined standards established by the parent company.

D.4 Establish the degree of reliance on computer systems as a basis for considering the necessity of computer audit reviews.

D.5   Record details of the main computer application systems in use (e.g. accounting, stock control, customer billing).

D.6   Determine whether the key computer applications are those used or recommended by the parent company. If not, consider whether they are likely to be adequate, stable and obtained from reliable sources.

D.7   Establish if a "control environment" ethic is applied to the operation and if this is supported by the stance of the parent company. Obtain details of any documented requirements.

D.8   Have local policies, procedures or objectives been developed, authorised and implemented for the following areas? (NB Not all those listed below will necessarily apply in every situation):

- general operational and administration procedures
- control environment
- management information
- planning (strategic, tactical, manpower, etc.)
- accounting (including pricing and discount policies)
- financial information and reporting
- staffing and employment
- risk management
- quality management
- capital projects
- legal and industry regulation and compliance
- treasury and investments
- authority procedures
- budgeting and monitoring
- taxation
- stock inventories
- purchasing and procurement
- production and manufacturing operations
- marketing and sales
- after sales support
- research and development
- information technology
- contracting.

D.9   Where necessary and practical (taking into account any language implications) obtain and review key policy and procedure documents in relation to their apparent scope, quality, relevance, etc.

HIGH-LEVEL REVIEW PROGRAMME

Having concluded that a particular subsidiary or operation should be subject to operational audit review, it will be necessary to obtain an accurate impression of the relative risk priorities within the organisation, so that audit review resources can be suitably targeted. In the real world, this may present practical difficulties, especially where the chosen operation is located overseas. In such circumstances, the auditor may have to resort to a range of information sources so that a comprehensive picture of the operations can be formed. These sources may include:

- reviewing and analysing accounting, performance and other data sent to the parent company
- conducting interviews with senior (parent company) executives with line responsibility for the relevant operation
- getting local senior management to complete and return questionnaires covering the key areas of audit interest
- where available, reviewing previous audit working papers and reports.

One possible solution to gathering the relevant data about the prevailing condition of internal controls and management attitudes is to conduct a high-level review of the operation. This can be undertaken either by the audit department as a reconnaissance exercise prior to the main audit visit, or by soliciting the co-operation of local managers to provide the necessary data. This latter option may be more pragmatic in the case of an overseas operation where the associated travelling and accommodation costs may prevent two audit visits, especially where audit management are keen to ensure that any review time spent on site is productive and not used to gather background facts. If the responses were to be completed by local management, they would obviously require some guidance as to the purpose of the process and the type and level of information required.

The following section of this chapter contains a series of example high-level risk and control issues relevant to a subsidiary or remotely located company. The fictitious company depicted is known to be primarily involved in sales and marketing activities, but also has the usual management, accounting, and personnel functions. Accordingly the risk and control issues focus upon these areas at a high level. The responses to the noted questions can be used in variety of ways by the audit department. It primarily provides the basis for a high-level examination of an operating unit from the point of view of the prevailing management and control structure.

Audit management also has the option to use the fact-finding programme to bring together a wide range of relevant facts about the nature and type of business operation being considered for an audit review. The data contained in that programme could, in itself, indicate selected activities which could benefit from a full-scale audit review (for example, by virtue of the level and significance of a particular business activity or trading relationship). However, the additional use of the high-level programme approach can provide yet further insight into the underlying quality and effectiveness of management within the business.

EXAMPLE HIGH-LEVEL REVIEW PROGRAMME

The issues are presented (in this example version) in categories relevant to the key system/activity areas and are structured around the main organisation elements, such as management, finance and accounting, and personnel. Given that every organisation has a specific and often unique business or operational environment, it is highly probable that either additional or alternative key questions could apply. Additionally, the functions and activities addressed in this example programme are likely to be subject to differing scales of relevance within a range of organisations, and this will have a notable bearing on the appropriateness of the questions. When reading through the listed points, consider your own organisation and whether changes are required to adequately reflect its activities and corporate direction.

The questions should be answered by providing details of the controls and measures in place. The questions could be incorporated into a format similar to that used in the Standard Audit Programme Guides (SAPGs) introduced in Chapter 3. Following entry of the current controls and measures, audit management can take a view of their relative or potential effectiveness. In instances where there are concerns about the quality of control, etc., a comprehensive review can then be applied using a more detailed SAPG during the fieldwork visit.

1. Management and Administration

1.1 The Control Environment

Are there in place satisfactory Codes of Conduct and other policies which define acceptable business practice, conflicts of interest and expected standards of integrity and ethical behaviour?

Do senior managers frequently visit outlying locations for which they are responsible?

Is disciplinary action sufficiently taken and communicated in the case of control or ethical violations?

1.2 Organisation

How does management ensure that the organisational structure is optimised and appropriate to the achievement of strategic objectives?

Have documented terms of reference, responsibilities and authorities been agreed, authorised and implemented for all functions and departments, and are they maintained and kept up to date?

1.3 Management Information

Is applicable external information (e.g. about the market) available, as well as internally generated information about business performance?

Has the business considered the scope to develop strategic information systems (targeted at suppliers and/or staff and customers) which achieve a competitive advantage by reducing costs and/or improving service and reliability?

Is information sufficiently timely, complete, and accurate to be used reliably by management?

Are all exception reports followed up?

Is an inventory maintained of confidential and sensitive corporate information, and is the handling and issuance of this information subject to proper authorisation controls?

1.4 Planning

What processes ensure that the organisation will continue to develop in an effective manner?

What mechanisms ensure that the achievement of authorised objectives is adequately planned for?

Are all plans fully assessed, costed and authorised prior to implementation?

Are there mechanisms in place to enable management to measure the success of business operations against defined objectives?

1.5 Risk Management

What steps has management taken to identify accurately potential risks?

Have adequate plans been developed to counteract, reduce or avoid risks to assets, persons and the organisation's reputation?

Where the organisation is heavily dependent on the use of information technology, has specific consideration been given to the effects on the business of a loss (or disruption) of computing facilities?

1.6 Quality Management

Have the objectives of the quality programme been clearly defined (e.g. in terms of potential competitive advantage, improved customer satisfaction)?

What steps have management taken to ensure that the appropriate national or international quality standard accreditation will be achieved and maintained?

Are all the quality initiatives subject to ongoing monitoring in order to ensure that targets and objectives are realised?

1.7 Estates Management and Facilities

How does management accurately identify requirements for buildings and premises in order to address the operational objectives of the organisation?

What measures ensure that all the relevant prevailing building laws and regulations are identified and complied with?

What processes ensure that all property costs are correctly accounted for, authorised and monitored?

How does management ensure that adequate and effective security, fire prevention and protection facilities are provided, maintained, and tested?

1.8 Environmental Issues

Has an approved and documented environmental policy been established that defines the required approach for business operations?
How does management ensure that all the relevant environmental legislation and regulations are fully complied with?
Are measures in place which ensure that all environmental impacts are identified, monitored, and effectively managed (and what is the evidence for this)?

1.9 Insurance

How does management ensure that all insurable risks are identified, assessed and adequately covered?
How does management ensure that insurance costs are competitive and represent value for money?
How does management ensure that all insurance claims are accurately assessed, costed, and eventually settled?

1.10 Security

What measures are in place to prevent the following:

- unauthorised access to company premises
- theft of company property from premises
- damage and disruption caused by vandalism, burglary, and other security threats?

Have potential risks and security threats been adequately defined and assessed, and how can management be assured that security measures are effective?
Have documented procedures and instructions been implemented for emergency drills, building evacuations, and contingency arrangements (and how is their effectiveness assessed)?

1.11 Media, Public and External Relations

Has an agreed and authorised public and media relations policy been implemented, and if so how is management to be assured that the policy is always complied with?
What steps does management take in order to remain aware of local community issues and to foster good relations with the local community?
What action does management take to ensure that the organisation is actively represented within the relevant trade and industry bodies?

2. Financial and Accounting

2.1 Treasury

Has senior management established and issued a written policy governing treasury operations, objectives, authorised transaction types, financial limits, etc?

Are working capital requirements defined, communicated, monitored, and reacted to?

Are all treasury transactions and fund movements accurately accounted for, correctly recorded in the accounting system, and reported to management?

2.2 Payroll

What mechanisms prevent payroll payments being made to invalid or unauthorised persons?

How does management make certain that the amounts paid via the payroll are correctly calculated and that income taxation and other deductions are accurately calculated and disbursed?

How does management ensure that all payroll transactions are correctly reflected in the accounting system in the proper accounting period?

2.3 Accounts Payable

How does management ensure that only valid invoices are paid where the goods and services have been correctly and fully received?

Are all invoices authorised prior to payment and confirmed as being within the agreed budget?

What processes ensure that the values of paid accounts and outstanding invoice liabilities are accurately and completely reflected in the accounting system?

2.4 Accounts Receivable

How is management assured that all goods delivered and services performed are identified and accurately invoiced to customers using the appropriate prices and discounts?

What procedures ensure that all invoices are recorded, despatched and accounted for within the accounting system?

How does management make certain that all customer remittances are correctly identified, recorded, and accounted for?

Are overdue accounts promptly identified and effectively progressed?

2.5 General Ledger and Management Accounts

How is management certain that the general ledger accounting data is accurate, complete and up to date?

How does management ensure that the accounting records and systems comply with the prevailing laws, regulations and recognised accountancy good practice?

How is accuracy of published and statutory accounting statements confirmed?

What prevents the processing of unauthorised or invalid accounting entries?

2.6 Fixed Assets and Capital Charges

Has management implemented an authorised policy governing capital acquisitions and expenditure, depreciation, etc. which conforms with recognised accounting practice?

How does management confirm that all asset acquisitions are authorised, and correctly reflected in the accounts?

Are assets subject to adequate protection and regular verification, with the follow-up of anomalies?

2.7 Budgeting and Monitoring

Has management developed and implemented a documented budgeting process for use throughout the organisation, and does this clearly allocate responsibilities for action and follow up of variances?

How is the budget and actual data reflected by the budget system confirmed as authorised, accurate and complete?

How does management verify that all subsequent amendments to the budget data are justified, authorised and accurately applied?

2.8 Bank Accounts and Banking Arrangements

Are corporate bank accounts established only at the request of senior management for a defined and authorised purpose (and how is this process evidenced)?

Are the prevailing banking terms and conditions optimised in terms of account type, transaction levels, interest payable on balances, levels of charges, etc.?

How is management assured that all banking transactions are accurate, complete and authorised?

2.9 Sales Tax Accounting (Where Applicable)

How does management ensure that all input and output VAT on applicable transactions is accurately identified, accounted for and included on the appropriate returns?

What processes ensure that all the required VAT returns are accurately completed in accordance with the current legislation, and that the correct amount is either paid over or recovered?

Is the current company registration for VAT confirmed as correct and up to date?

2.10 Taxation

How does management verify that all taxation liabilities are correctly calculated and discharged in accordance with the prevailing regulations?

What measures ensure that taxation liabilities are minimised within the prevailing legislation?

How does management ensure that all the regulations are complied with and the underlying accounting data accurately supports the official returns?

2.11 Inventories

How does management verify that the accounting systems and year-end financial statements accurately reflect the values of inventory stocks?

What processes ensure that all processed stock movements are valid, correctly priced, and accurately posted to the relevant stock accounts?

Are stock values adequately and regularly verified, and how is this evidenced?

Are all stock adjustments, write-offs and disposals suitably authorised?

2.12 Petty Cash and Expenses

How does management ensure that only valid, accurate and authorised expenses are processed and correctly reflected in the accounts?

Has management established clear policies and procedures for recording, authorising and processing petty cash and expense claims?

2.13 Financial Information and Reporting

How does management make sure that all the required external and statutory financial reports/returns are accurately generated and released on time?

Has management identified, documented, and addressed all their financial information requirements?

What processes prevent the creation and circulation of inaccurate, invalid or out-of-date financial data?

How does management ascertain that all accounting records are maintained in accordance with the current accounting regulations, standards, and professional good practice?

3. Personnel

3.1 Human Resources Department

Have documented policies been established for staff recruitment, training, remuneration, performance appraisal, and disciplinary matters?

How is ongoing compliance with all the prevailing employment regulation and laws confirmed, and would failure to comply be promptly detected?

How does management ensure that the personnel records are up to date, accurate and adequately protected from unauthorised use and access?

3.2 Recruitment

Have standard remuneration scales and employment conditions been implemented, and would management be made aware of staff engagements which fall out with these standards?

How does management confirm that all staff recruitment and appointments are warranted and authorised?

How does management ensure that the most appropriate and cost-effective method of recruitment is utilised?

What steps are taken to confirm the previous employment record and educational qualifications of candidates, and what prevents the engagement of staff with either an invalid or unsuitable record?

Are all staff engagements supported by an accurate contract of employment?

What measures ensure that new employees are correctly set up on the payroll?

3.3 Manpower and Succession Planning

Has management implemented a structured approach to manpower and succession planning?

Have the implications of the mid to long-term strategic business objectives been taken into consideration (with all the other internal and external influences) when determining the manpower requirements?

Have current and future skill requirements been accurately identified, and what action is being taken to ensure that staff are appropriately developed to meet the requirements?

3.4 Staff Training and Development

How is management assured that all training and staff development activities are justified, authorised and appropriately targeted?

Has management determined the required skill and knowledge base for the workforce and planned to ensure that employees remain competent and able to discharge their duties?

Are training activities monitored for their effectiveness, and how are the most suitable and cost-effective training methods selected?

3.5 Pension Scheme (and other Benefits)

How does management make sure that the pension scheme is correctly established and operated, and that it complies with the current legislation and recognised good practice?

How are management and trustees certain that all pension funds are kept strictly separate from company activities and remain fully accounted for?

What measures ensure that all pension contributions are valid, correctly calculated, deducted, paid over, and fully accounted for?

Is the pension fund subject to regular scrutiny by suitably qualified external auditors (or any regulatory bodies)?

Are there processes in place to ensure that all payments from the fund are valid, authorised, correctly calculated, paid over to bona fide persons, and fully accounted for?

How does management confirm that the operations of any other schemes (e.g. Employee Share, Share Options, Profit Related Pay) fully comply with the current legislation and are fully accounted for?

3.6 Staff Appraisal and Disciplinary Matters

How does management confirm that staff are performing at the appropriate level and standard?

Are staff performances assessed against realistic and measurable factors and objectives, and how are these recorded and monitored?

Are performance shortcomings used as the basis for determining and agreeing the personal training and development needs of staff (and are these subject to justification)?

Do all staff appraisal and disciplinary procedures comply with the current legislation?

Is management confident that cases of persistent absenteeism or serious misconduct would be detected and appropriately dealt with?

3.7 Health and Safety

How does management verify that they have identified and adequately addressed all the health and safety risks and hazards within the organisation?

What processes ensure that staff are fully aware of workplace risks and how to correctly utilise safety equipment and protect themselves?

Has sufficient and appropriate safety equipment been provided and what measures ensure that it all remains in working order and effective?

Have sufficient fire prevention and protection systems been provided and are they regularly tested?

Have adequate first aid, medical, hygiene and cleanliness facilities been provided?

Are all incidents and accidents reported and appropriately dealt with?

How does management ensure that all hazardous materials are safely, correctly and securely stored?

3.8 Labour Relations

Has the basis for communicating with the workforce and their representatives been clearly established, endorsed and communicated?

Have suitably experienced and qualified staff, familiar with negotiation and other relevant techniques, been employed and allocated the responsibility for dealing with labour relations?

4. Procurement

4.1 Purchasing

How does management ensure that all purchase orders are justified, authorised, within budget and accounted for within the correct accounting period?

What measures are in place to ensure that adequate and appropriate supplies (of a suitable quality) are obtained to sustain the required business objectives?

How does management ensure that goods and services are always obtained at the most economic and fair price?

5. Stock

5.1 Stock Control

How does management determine the current and future stock requirements, and how can they be sure that actual stock levels can accurately meet the sales and production demands?

What measures ensure that all stock movements are valid, authorised, correctly processed, and accounted for?

Is management made aware of overstocking or stock shortages, and how is their reaction evidenced?

5.2 Distribution, Transport and Logistics

Is there adequate and timely liaison and information flow between the sales, production, stock control, distribution and transport functions in order to ensure that customer demands are efficiently fulfilled?

How does management make sure that the most appropriate, efficient and cost-effective distribution and transport options are utilised?

How is management certain that all deliveries are undertaken in the required timescale, that they are received in good condition, agreed and signed for?

6. Marketing and Sales

6.1 Product Development

Has management defined and authorised strategic business objectives, and how can they be sure that all product developments comply with these targets?

Has management established, authorised and implemented documented procedures for the development and evolution of all product ranges?

6.2 Market Research

What steps are taken to ensure that customer requirements are identified and effectively addressed?

Are all market research activities accurately costed, justified as being worthwhile and authorised?

How does management identify potential new markets or opportunities to differentiate their products?

6.3 Promotion and Advertising

How is management assured that advertising and promotional expenditure is adequately targeted, budgeted, effectively used, monitored for its effectiveness, and fully accounted for?

What measures ensure that all advertising and promotional activities are lawful, accurate and project a positive corporate image?

6.4 Pricing and Discount Policies

Have documented pricing and discount policies been authorised and implemented?

What steps are taken to ensure that prices remain competitive, profitable and sustainable?

How does management verify that the correct prices and discounts are always applied to invoices?

6.5 Sales Management

What measures are in place to ensure that current and potential customers are identified and that customer data is accurately maintained and kept up to date?

How does management ensure that adequate (and justifiable) sales staff are provided and that they are suitably trained and knowledgeable about the company products?

What measures are applied to ensure that customers are financially stable and reliable (and what prevents the acceptance of unsuitable customers)?

How are individual customer credit limits determined, and are they subject to a higher level of authority prior to orders being accepted?

6.6 Sales Performance and Monitoring

How does management ensure that projected sales targets are accurately and realistically determined?

What steps ensure that management is provided with accurate and timely sales performance statistics, and what action is taken to detect and react to shortfalls, etc.?

How does management determine and justify the staffing establishment of the sales function so as to avoid either under or over-staffing?

6.7 Order Processing

What measures ensure that all orders (from all possible sources) are correctly identified, logged, reviewed, authorised to proceed, and accounted for?
What measures are applied to ensure that orders are accepted only from established, authorised and bona fide customers?
How is management assured that credit limits are strictly observed and only amended when suitably authorised?
What measures ensure that all orders are acknowledged and efficiently fulfilled?
How is management assured that accurate invoices are subsequently raised and accounted for within the accounts receivables systems?

JOINT VENTURES

Any organisation must be alert to commercial opportunities that either support their objectives or have the potential to profitably exploit new areas. The maintenance of strategic and competitive advantage will drive organisations to seek new, improved, alternative and innovative ways of doing business. The search for such expansion opportunities may indeed be driven by the simple and basic expediency of ensuring the continued survival of the entity.

In some instances the cost of entering a new market area can be prohibitive and there may be other entry barriers to surmount (for example, technical and regulatory issues). Where another organisation has developed either a specific area of expertise or a market presence in a particular business operation, it may be more worthwhile considering a formal alliance with them, rather than struggle to enter the same marketplace singlehandedly. For example, a small software development company may enter into a joint marketing arrangement with a larger hardware company, and thereby take advantage of an established infrastructure. However, such concepts presuppose that there can be tangible benefits for both parties, otherwise why should the organisation with the established business or specific knowledge share their crock of gold with others? The business development strategy adopted by an organisation may have been historically cautious in nature, and any move into activities associated with higher risk and potentially high returns can be tempered if additional partners can be found to share the risk load, and of course share the profits if the exercise is successful.

The partners to a joint venture need not be solely restricted to commercial organisations. Financial institutions and government agencies can also be involved. Indeed, any other party with similar or shared objectives and goals could have a legitimate role to play. However, some partners may wish to impose specific conditions which may prove onerous (for instance, government agencies may be in the position to demand that prospective partners conform to their standards and practices). Alternatively, the parties may bring together their own specific, different and possibly specialised attributes, which amalgamate to form an innovative solution.

The nature of joint venture exercises can vary, for example:

- co-operation on a particular development project (e.g. a new computer software system, a new pharmaceutical product, or an oil pipeline)
- the co-ownership of a separate new company, operated and owned by all the parties
- the operation of a business venture by one organisation on behalf of another.

The joint pooling of resources and efforts towards a mutually beneficial goal, may have other potential benefits, such as economies of scale, improved efficiency levels, shared capital investment programmes and gaining access to areas of specialist knowledge. However, there are also attendant disadvantages, for instance only taking a share of the income and profits (if applicable), possible conflicts over the individual partner's strategic direction, onerous levels of communication, the absence of appropriate trust, the threats of competition in other areas of business, a disproportionate amount of time spent on resolving corporate cultural differences, and so on.

Wider economic factors will also have an effect on the market for joint venture exercises. Whenever the general or national economy is under pressure and trading conditions are affected, it may be more prudent for businesses to co-operate on joint ventures.

The nature and form of international trading relationships may become important (or indeed vital) to an organisation's survival strategy; for example, the opening up of the European market will give companies operating in different countries further opportunities for co-operative ventures while drawing on local market know-how and/or familiarity with diverse national business practices. However, involvement in international joint ventures does present additional potential problems, such as:

- localised business practices, laws, ethics, accounting standards, taxation and other regulations (e.g. conforming to local requirements, selecting the appropriate legal jurisdiction for contractual arrangements)
- the prevailing economic and political circumstances (e.g. possible affects on business operations and/or performance expectations)
- problems associated with time zone differences (e.g. disruption and elongation of lines of communications)
- difficulties concerning languages (e.g. clarity of communications, ensuring the uniformity and acceptability of documentation, regular reporting)
- currency and foreign exchange implications
- internal auditors will be particularly interested in the role played by statutory auditors in overseas locations and the extent to which co-operation can be expected.

On the global business stage, there have been significant developments which could influence the general environment for joint venture relationships. The break-up of the former Soviet Union may offer western businesses trading and development opportunities with local partners, who have an appreciation of the emerging economic situation but perhaps lack the necessary skills and leading edge techniques to exploit their potential. The same situation applies to the former eastern bloc countries, who, having shed communism, are now seeking to take their place in a free global marketplace.

When considering joint ventures, managements are faced with fundamental questions about levels of investment, involvement, ownership, responsibility and control. Although all these elements can be defined in contractual terms and agreed procedures, there should always be a balance in allocation of risks, responsibilities, duties, liabilities and obligations.

It is crucial for any organisation to have a defined strategic plan which maps out the future development and growth of the business. All the day-to-day activities of the organisation should be linked to the agreed strategic plan, and this includes the role to be played by joint ventures. Joint ventures may be the only viable option for an organisation to achieve the required diversity and flexible growth within the required timescale; but such important steps should always be driven by sound and stable strategic thinking.

In the establishment of any relationship, it is easy to become distracted from the real issues and to lose a sense of informed realism. This may be because the parties view their contribution as but one part of the whole, and unless the roles and responsibilities of each participant are clearly defined, there is the danger that some issues will fall between the ensuing cracks.

Whenever two (or more) parties come together for a given purpose there is always the possibility that the specified venture may fail (or at least flounder). Very often an absence of clear communication leads to a breakdown fundamentally caused by a lack of accurate appreciation of the other parties' objectives. In the commercial world, joint business ventures are essentially partnerships of effort bound by contractual obligations and rights, but there can be a real chasm of difference between the high-level business objectives and the detailed reality of the situation on the ground. One solution is to define (in the contractual and operating documentation) the requirements for regular meetings and the exchange of significant information about the venture and its progress.

Once the venture is up and running, its day-to-day operations are potentially influenced by all the different factors affecting all the partners. Some of these forces may either have implications for the joint venture (e.g. the need to concentrate resources on a crisis nearer to home) or potentially have simultaneous affects for all the parties to the joint venture. Lines of communication and planning should be flexible enough to enable a prompt response to such events, so as to ensure that the possible effects on the venture are communicated, understood and adequately reacted to.

In common with all business activities, management involved in joint ventures will need to ensure that controls form part of the target environment in order that investments in capital, resources and time are duly protected. The stance taken on internal control within joint ventures will depend, in part, on the attitudes to corporate governance and accountability that prevail in the partners' business environment, especially where they are overseas partners operating in different national arenas. If the basis of the joint venture is predominantly entrepreneurial in nature, there could be implied resistance to the application of too much control (e.g. control processes may be viewed as an unnecessary overhead or as an impediment to progress and growth). The need for incorporating internal control into the joint venture may be seen (especially by internal auditors) as self-evident, however, as in all operations there must be a realistic balance drawn between providing adequate, effective control and avoiding burdensome or suffocating control levels.

Many of the points raised so far in this section will need to be addressed during the period of negotiation prior to the formalisation of the joint venture relationship.

The Internal Audit Role in Joint Ventures

Where both (or all) parties to a joint venture arrangement have their own internal auditing functions, it will, at least, be necessary to ensure adequate co-operation and co-ordination of internal audit review activities. Given the loyalty expected of auditors to their employers, complete frankness and openness with their counterparts in other organisations is unlikely. However, internal auditors in one organisation should have a fundamental right of access to the records, premises and staff of the venture partners. Such access rights should clearly be defined in the contractual agreements and any definitions of auditing scope and timing should also be incorporated. Auditors may also be called upon to assess whether the business objectives established for the venture are likely to be achieved. If the audit review work is to be conducted in accordance with established auditing standards (such as those promoted by the Institute of Internal Auditors), this requirement should also be defined, together with any other qualitative factors, in the agreement documents.

The driving criteria for internal audit assessment of the joint venture operations will be to assure management that appropriate control activities are in place and that they are effective in protecting the organisation's investment and interests.

Internal audit management will need to maintain an up-to-date awareness of the general business plans for their organisation, so that they can anticipate the implications for audit planning and establish the foundation of audit assignments in the future. The chief internal auditor (or director of auditing) will need to consider the risks associated with the proposed joint venture(s) and agree with management the scope, extent and timing of any proposed audit involvement. When assessing the relative significance of the proposed venture, audit management should take into account the following prime factors:

- the financial impacts of the venture (i.e. levels of investment, projected income/benefits, etc.)
- the inherent nature of the venture (i.e. familiar environment or new ground?)
- the extent of possible risks (i.e. external influences such as economic conditions, political stability)
- known control factors (i.e. the experience and ability of management, the stance taken on internal control responsibilities, previous track record, etc.).

It will be necessary to develop an audit strategy and plan for assessing the venture which is linked to the implementation timetable and designed to intermesh with the key stages of the project so that the auditor's contribution and impact are maximised.

It could strongly be argued that internal audit involvement at the inception of a joint venture relationship (i.e. prior to the live implementation of the exercise) should ensure that adequate attention is paid to matters of internal control and accountability. Whereas auditors should always avoid taking over the prime responsibility of management in matters of control, their involvement at this early stage can, at least, ensure that control is considered as an important issue.

As the negotiations progress and policies, responsibilities and procedures start to emerge, it is proper for auditors to review these outputs and comment on them from a control standpoint.

Early involvement in the venture development processes also enables the internal auditors to acquire an appreciation of the key business and operational issues of the proposed association. This is valuable intelligence for application in subsequent audit reviews, and additionally promotes the impression that the auditors are well informed and capable of conducting a targeted review.

Once the venture is implemented, the audit review programme is likely to be divided into two principal areas, namely:

- those aspects which relate generally to all business activities (i.e. the accuracy and timeliness of accounting information, the protection of assets, the banking arrangements, management information arrangements, compliance with regulations, laws, and so on)
- those aspects which are very specific to the nature of the joint venture operations.

In the case of the former category, the auditors can usually rely on the programmes that they apply elsewhere in the organisation, with suitable amendments to take account of any specific local or national conditions. The business issues arising from the latter category may be very specific (perhaps even unique in the organisation), and will therefore require the auditors to develop tailored programmes of work. In order to come up with realistic and high-quality programmes for the venture-specific activities, auditors will need to be fully acquainted with the driving objectives and goals established for the operation. Auditors may be called on to independently assess the progress being made with the venture and in doing so they will need to be familiar with the relevant performance criteria.

It is extremely likely that the audit reviews will involve visits either to the jointly owned site or to the premises of the venture partners. In either case, there is an obvious requirement for the audit staff to project a professional, purposeful and informed image.

If the venture was of a fixed term nature (such as a building development), the auditors may be required to undertake a post-completion and outturn review, where the actual performance achieved at the conclusion of the project is compared to the related objectives established at the outset. Such a review will be of use if the organisation is contemplating similar ventures or wishing generally to improve its procedures for forming and managing other joint schemes as there may be lessons to learn in the handling of particular aspects of the process which can then be incorporated into future procedures.

NOTE

1. Risk analysis techniques for audit planning are explored in Chambers, A. D. (1992) *Effective Internal Audits*. Pitman, London.

6

Auditing the Finance and Accounting Functions

INTRODUCTION

In this chapter we consider the financial and accounting aspects of an organisation. First, we will consider the systems and functions that are likely to constitute this area of activity. Secondly, we shall examine each of these component functions and highlight the relative control objectives and the risk and control issues arising from the various activities.

The finance and accounting areas have long been the traditional domain of the internal auditor, perhaps to the extent that management only thought of internal auditing in terms of conducting reviews of accounting records. As this book seeks to demonstrate, the auditor has a legitimate role to play in all the operational areas of the organisation, but invariably even this broader view of the auditor's universe leads back to the accounting functions and the records they maintain. Most operational areas involve interfaces with the accounts, for example in terms of operating costs, income levels, budget and actual comparisons, and so on.

For discussion of related issues, refer to the Contents pages or to the Index to identify relevant topics. For instance, Electronic Data Interchange (EDI) is discussed in Chapter 13.

Although you may consider this to be familiar ground, this material should hopefully stimulate you into considering the implications from the organisation's standpoint that are inherent within the accounting and finance functions.

SYSTEM/FUNCTION COMPONENTS OF THE FINANCIAL AND ACCOUNTING ENVIRONMENT

Defining the Finance and Accounting Universe

There are a number of ways an auditor can define the constituent elements of finance and accounting within an organisation, for example:

- *functionally*, based upon the discrete accounting departments that are in place (and perhaps as recorded on the internal telephone list); or
- In terms of the *Financial cycles*, such as the revenue cycle, the expenditure cycle or the treasury cycle.

In the latter approach, the term "cycle" can be misleading as the processes are not always cyclic in nature; perhaps the term "process" would be more apt.[1] This approach does have one potential benefit when compared to the functional approach in that it takes account of the inevitable flow of data across functional boundaries where control is often at its weakest. This could be referred to as "a cradle to grave" review. Using the functional approach means that the internal auditor should always be alert to the input and output interfaces that usually exist between the function under review and those which interact with it.

We have chosen to use the *functional* approach to define the financial and accounting audit universe, which gives us the following possible breakdown of the key functions, systems or activities:

- treasury
- payroll
- accounts payable
- accounts receivable
- general ledger/management accounts
- fixed assets (and capital charges)
- budgeting and monitoring
- bank accounts and banking arrangements
- sales tax (VAT) accounting
- taxation
- inventories
- product/project accounting
- petty cash and expenses
- financial information and reporting
- investments.

CONTROL OBJECTIVES AND RISK AND CONTROL ISSUES

We shall now examine the control objectives and the related risk and control issues (divided into key issues and detailed issues) for each of the finance and accounting areas listed above. The data can be used within the format of the Standard Audit Programme Guides (SAPG) looked at in Chapter 3. To save space we have concentrated on the objectives to be set and the questions to be asked and have not presented them within the SAPG format.

The data supplied in the following sections are deliberately general and broad in nature, so that they can be related to a range of possible organisational scenarios. However, in practice, all manner of specific industry or sector factors may apply and these should be suitably incorporated into the data. Conversely, some of the issues raised may not apply (either in organisational or national terms) and these can accordingly be disregarded. The overall aim of the supplied data is to provide a general awareness of the likely elements for each activity.

TREASURY

Here we are primarily concerned with the adequacy of funding and the accountability for transactions, which are normally, by their nature, of high value. Given these two high-profile attributes, it is preferable that treasury operations are driven by authorised policies and procedures.

Control Objectives for Treasury

(a) To ensure that the organisation's funds are appropriately managed with the aim of providing adequate levels of working capital.

(b) To ensure that suitable and secure investments, financial instruments, etc. are utilised to the maximum benefit of the organisation and within the constraints of the prevailing laws and regulations.

(c) To ensure that treasury staff are suitably experienced and qualified, and operate within the limits of established policy and practices.

(d) To ensure that treasury activities are monitored as part of an overall view of risk management.

(e) To prevent the processing of unauthorised and fraudulent transactions.

Risk and Control Issues for Treasury

1 Key Issues

1.1 Has senior management (i.e. the board) established and issued a written policy governing treasury operations, authorised transaction types, financial limits, etc.?

1.2 Has management established and clearly communicated their objectives for the treasury function?

1.3 Have formal written treasury procedures been established which support the aims of the agreed treasury policy?

1.4 Have adequate independent and timely treasury monitoring facilities been established?

1.5 Has management provided suitably trained treasury personnel and the other necessary resources to ensure that their objectives are achieved?

1.6   Are working capital requirements defined, communicated, monitored and reacted to?

1.7   How does management ensure that all the relevant laws and regulations are being complied with?

1.8   Are treasury staff provided with adequate, accurate, relevant and timely data to support their decision making and trading activities?

1.9   Are all treasury transactions supported with accurate documentation, authorisation (if required), and effective audit trails?

1.10   Are all treasury transactions and fund movements accurately accounted for, correctly recorded in the accounting system, and reported to management?

1.11   How does management verify that all treasury transactions are of the approved type and within the established limits for individual transactions?

1.12   Are all maturing funds/investments, income and interest receipts identified, recorded and correctly accounted for?

2 Detailed Issues

2.1   Are the Treasury Policy and operational procedures regularly reviewed, maintained and kept up to date?

2.2   What mechanisms prevent unauthorised treasury transaction types being processed?

2.3   Would unauthorised or fraudulent transactions be highlighted, reported and promptly reacted to?

2.4   How are unauthorised staff prevented from initiating and processing unauthorised treasury transactions?

2.5   What prevents the processing of unauthorised and invalid transaction types?

2.6   What prevents trading with unsuitable, financially unstable, or non-approved counterparties?

2.7   Are all transactions subject to suitable authorisation before processing?

2.8   Are sensitive transactions assessed for inherent risk and subject to additional authorisation?

2.9   Are market trends and fiscal indicators monitored as part of management's ongoing assessment of the most appropriate treasury policy?

2.10   What prevents the payment of invalid or inaccurate fees and commissions?

2.11 How is unauthorised use of all electronic fund transfer facilities prevented?

2.12 Are security and financial instrument documents securely stored and adequately protected from loss, damage or misuse?

2.13 If market or financial conditions change, can the organisation promptly identify the potential exposures and take speedy remedial action?

2.14 How does management confirm that all income from treasury activities is accurately reported and accounted for?

2.15 Are treasury staff suitably aware of their obligations and responsibilities in respect of the prevailing policy, laws and regulations governing their activities?

2.16 How is management sure that non-compliance with current regulations will be detected promptly?

2.17 How is the accuracy of data input from other systems confirmed?

2.18 How is the accuracy of data output to other systems confirmed?

2.19 How does management make sure that payments of interest and dividends are valid, accurate and complete?

2.20 Are all foreign currency transactions suitably authorised?

2.21 Are all "hedging" activities suitably authorised and reported to management?

2.22 Are all funding debts identified, accounted for, and correctly administered/discharged?

2.23 Are changes in the relative values of investments and debts accurately ascertained and reflected in the accounts?

PAYROLL

In most cases it is likely that personnel costs will represent the greatest proportion of total overheads for an organisation. The scope of the following review points incorporates the initial authorised set-up of new employees, the processing of suitably authorised amendments (such as salary increases, holiday payments, bonuses), periodic payroll runs, payment arrangements, the correct accounting for taxation and national insurance deductions, reconciliation of the payroll, and the removal of employees from the payroll.

The payroll function has strong functional links with the human resources (or personnel) department. (Chapter 11 examines related personnel areas, such as recruitment.)

Control Objectives for Payroll

(a) To ensure that only valid employees are paid and at the correct and authorised rate.

(b) To ensure that the calculations of all payments and deductions are correct and in accord with the relevant taxation and other regulations and requirements.

(c) To ensure that all deductions are correctly disbursed.

(d) To ensure that unauthorised access to the payroll system and data is prevented.

(e) To ensure that all payroll transactions are accurately reflected in the accounting system.

(f) To ensure that regular and accurate management and statutory information is produced.

Risk and Control Issues for Payroll

1 Key Issues

1.1 What mechanisms prevent payroll payments being made to invalid or unauthorised persons?

1.2 How does management ensure that amounts paid via the payroll are correctly calculated?

1.3 How does management confirm that income taxation and other deductions are accurately calculated and disbursed?

1.4 Is management provided with accurate payroll cost data on a regular basis to support their decision making, etc.?

1.5 How does management verify that all payroll transactions are correctly reflected in the accounting system in the proper accounting period?

2 Detailed Issues

2.1 Is the payroll system adequately protected from either misuse or unauthorised access?

2.2 What mechanisms prevent the set-up of fictitious employees on the payroll system?

2.3 How does management ensure that only valid employees are being paid via the payroll?

2.4   What prevents the set-up of incorrect or inaccurate payroll data (e.g. salary rates)?

2.5   Are payroll salary rates correct in relation to agreed pay scales/national rates, etc.?

2.6   How does management ensure that employees are not paid for work not done?

2.7   Are payroll payment transactions (overtime, bonus, salary increases, etc.) adequately authorised (prior to data entry) and correctly entered?

2.8   What prevents the entry and processing of duplicated payroll payment data?

2.9   How does management obtain assurance that the payroll system accurately calculates net salary and accounts for all disbursements?

2.10   What mechanisms prevent the incorrect calculation of income tax and any other statutory deductions?

2.11   How is management certain that all the necessary taxation and other deductions are correctly accounted for and paid over to the relevant authorities?

2.12   Are all holiday and sickness payments accurate, valid and within both the company policy and legislative requirements?

2.13   Are all exceptional payments adequately authorised?

2.14   Are pension and any other welfare deductions accurately calculated, deducted from salary and accounted for as inputs to their target systems?

2.15   What mechanisms prevent staff fraud or malpractice in relation to payroll activities?

2.16   Are payroll runs adequately reconciled to the accounting system and anomalies promptly identified and resolved?

2.17   What processes prevent the generation of inaccurate, incomplete or duplicated bank credit data (e.g. for automated fund transfer systems such as BACS in the UK)?

2.18   Are payroll payments, automated fund transfer data or salary cheques subject to adequate levels of authorisation?

2.19   What prevents payroll payments continuing to be made to former staff members who have left the organisation?

2.20   Is sensitive or confidential payroll data adequately protected from unauthorised access?

2.21   Are all the necessary/statutory payroll outputs and forms accurately produced and distributed in accordance with the required timetables?

2.22   Are comprehensive and up-to-date payroll procedures available?

2.23 Have specific responsibilities for the payroll function been suitably defined and allocated?

2.24 If wage/salary payments are made in cash, are the security precautions adequate to prevent theft and/or injury to staff distributing the pay?

ACCOUNTS PAYABLE

In this area, auditors should be taking an overview which incorporates related processes such as linking to the original purchase orders or instructions, confirmation of the receipt of goods/services, confirming the accuracy and validity of invoices, obtaining the authority to pay, maintenance of accurate creditor records, and account settlement. Accordingly there are natural functional linkages with the purchasing function, which is further discussed in Chapter 7.

Control Objectives for Accounts Payable

(a) To ensure that all payments are for valid and suitably approved creditor accounts for goods and services actually received.

(b) To ensure that all payments are correct and accurately reflected in the accounting system.

(c) To ensure that the prevailing sales tax or VAT regulations are correctly complied with.

(d) To ensure that good relationships are maintained with key suppliers.

(e) To prevent the possibility of supplier or staff malpractice.

Risk and Control Issues for Accounts Payable

1 Key Issues

1.1 How does management ensure that only valid invoices are paid where the goods and services have been correctly and fully received?

1.2 What mechanisms prevent the payment of inaccurately priced/calculated or duplicated invoices?

1.3 Are all invoices authorised prior to payment and confirmed as being within the agreed budget?

1.4 How does management ensure that the application and accounting treatment of VAT (or local sales tax) and duty is correct and in accord with the prevailing legislation or requirements?

1.5 What processes ensure that the values of paid accounts and outstanding invoice liabilities are accurately and completely reflected in the accounting system?

2 Detailed Issues

2.1   Is the organisation adequately protected from the payment of invalid or fraudulent invoices?

2.2   What would prevent staff from introducing false invoices into the system and these subsequently being paid?

2.3   Are all invoices identified, recorded, trailed and accounted for?

2.4   How does management ensure that the goods and services being charged for have actually been fully received?

2.5   What prevents payment of invoices where the goods were returned or proved to be unsatisfactory?

2.6   What prevents invoices from being paid more than once?

2.7   What prevents copy invoices from being paid?

2.8   Are invoice payments only made to valid and approved suppliers?

2.9   Would all invoice pricing and calculation errors be detected and resolved prior to payment?

2.10 Are all invoices subject to authorisation at the appropriate management level prior to payment and how is this process evidenced?

2.11 Is there adequate segregation applied between those originating purchase orders and those authorising the relevant invoice for payment?

2.12 Are VAT (or the equivalent sales taxes) and duty charges checked for validity and mathematical accuracy?

2.13 How does management verify that all VAT (or the equivalent sales tax) and duty is being correctly and accurately accounted for and recovered (if applicable)?

2.14 How does management confirm that all invoice transactions are correctly coded and accurately reflected in the financial records?

2.15 Are cheque or other methods of payment confirmed as correct and suitably authorised by an appropriate official before release?

2.16 Are all settlement cheques or payments accurately recorded, confirmed as being promptly despatched and subsequently accounted for through the relevant bank accounts?

2.17 Are individual supplier accounts accurately maintained so as to reflect the current situation?

2.18 Are foreign currency payments accurately calculated using the correct exchange rates?

2.19 Are invoices from overseas suppliers correctly treated in respect of sales tax or VAT recovery, etc.?

2.20 Are staff (and others) prevented from applying unauthorised amendments to the accounts payable system data?

2.21 How is the integrity of the accounts payable system assured?

2.22 Is management provided with accurate and relevant data from the accounts payable system on a timely basis?

2.23 Are credit notes and other adjustments (i.e. balance write-offs) confirmed as being correct and authorised for entry?

2.24 Are all transactions adequately trailed and supported by the relevant documentation?

2.25 Are discounts (including settlement discounts) correctly applied whenever relevant?

2.26 Are invoice payments made at the appropriate time (i.e. avoiding premature or overdue payment)?

2.27 Have comprehensive and up-to-date procedures been produced and circulated governing the accounts payable function?

2.28 Do the current procedures accurately define the requirements for ensuring compliance with any applicable regulatory requirements?

2.29 Are staff aware of their specific obligations and responsibilities?

2.30 How is the accuracy of data input from other systems confirmed?

2.31 How is the accuracy of data output to other systems confirmed?

ACCOUNTS RECEIVABLE

This area of activity has linkages to the vetting of customers for their stability and sales order processing, both of which are further addressed as part of Chapter 9.

The use of electronic data interchange (EDI) between large-scale trading partners is growing. The objectives and issues for EDI are discussed in Chapter 13.

Control Objectives for Accounts Receivable

> (a) To ensure that all income generating activities are identified and accurately invoiced to customers.
>
> (b) To ensure that all invoices are paid and the income is correctly identified and accounted for and reflected in the accounts.

(c) To minimise the extent of debt and provide for the prompt follow-up of overdue accounts.

(d) To maintain the integrity of the accounts receivable system and data.

Risk and Control Issues for Accounts Receivable

1 Key Issues

1.1 How does management ensure that all goods delivered and services performed are identified and duly invoiced to customers?

1.2 What steps are taken to avoid trading involvement with financially unstable or unsuitable customers?

1.3 What procedures ensure all the required invoices are correctly raised using the appropriate prices and discounts, and that they are recorded, despatched, and accounted for within the accounting system?

1.4 How is management certain that all customer remittances are correctly identified, recorded and accounted for?

1.5 Is management provided with adequate, timely and accurate information on potential and actual debt cases to enable prompt reaction?

1.6 Are overdue accounts promptly identified and effectively progressed?

1.7 Is output VAT (or equivalent sales taxes) correctly and consistently applied in accordance with the prevailing legislation?

2 Detailed Issues

2.1 Are all goods and services provided by the organisation accurately identified as the basis for subsequent customer billing?

2.2 How does management verify that all invoices are raised using the correct/ appropriate prices and discounts?

2.3 What processes prevent the generation of duplicate invoices?

2.4 What would prevent the generation and despatch of an incorrectly completed invoice?

2.5 Are all invoices and credit notes identified and accounted for?

2.6 Are all invoices and credit notes correctly posted to an individual customer account?

2.7 What steps are taken to ensure that the correct rate of output VAT (or equivalent sales tax) is applied to all relevant invoices?

2.8   What mechanisms ensure that all the required invoices are printed and promptly despatched to customers?

2.9   Are potential customers appraised for creditworthiness and financial stability prior to trading relations being established?

2.10 What other measures are taken to prevent future bad debt situations?

2.11 Are there adequate procedures for the authorisation and setting of realistic customer credit limits?

2.12 What measures ensure that agreed credit limits are not exceeded?

2.13 What action is taken if an invoice is returned as undelivered by the postal service?

2.14 How does management ensure that all invoice values are posted to the accounts receivable system?

2.15 What prevents staff raising invalid or false credit notes in order to manipulate an account?

2.16 Are all credit notes checked for validity/accuracy and authorised by an appropriate member of staff?

2.17 Are all credit notes accounted for and confirmed as despatched?

2.18 Are all other account adjustments authorised as valid and confirmed as being processed?

2.19 Are all accounts receivable transactions accurately reflected in the general ledger for the appropriate accounting period?

2.20 How does management ensure that all customer remittances are identified, accounted for, correctly entered into the system against the relevant customer, and promptly banked?

2.21 Is someone responsible for reconciling all transactions passing through the accounts receivable system to the relevant source and target systems?

2.22 How does management ensure that the individual customer account balances are correct?

2.23 Are customer remittances banked as soon as possible?

2.24 Are queries raised by customers logged and promptly resolved?

2.25 Are rejected or unidentified payments highlighted and promptly reacted to?

2.26 Are unauthorised members of staff prevented from accessing and amending the accounts receivable system and data?

2.27 Are statements accurately produced for all relevant customers and confirmed as despatched?

2.28 Have specific responsibilities been allocated for the speedy identification and follow-up of overdue accounts?

2.29   Are all overdue accounts (and those approaching being overdue) highlighted for action?

2.30   Is adequate, accurate and timely information produced and circulated for debt follow-up purposes?

2.31   Are all reasonable and permitted courses of action taken to pursue outstanding accounts and how is the action taken evidenced?

2.32   Are levels of bad debt accurately and regularly reported to management?

2.33   Are all bad debt write-offs authorised by an appropriate member of staff or management?

2.34   Can invalid or false write-off entries be processed?

2.35   Are the more serious and significant bad debt cases adequately and cost-effectively pursued?

2.36   Are all transactions adequately trailed and supported by appropriate documentation?

2.37   Have documented operational procedures been provided for the accounts receivable department?

2.38   Have specific responsibilities and authorities been clearly defined and allocated?

2.39   How is the accuracy of data input from other systems confirmed?

2.40   How is the accuracy of data output to other systems confirmed?

GENERAL LEDGER/MANAGEMENT ACCOUNTS

The accounting effects of all the economic events within the organisation are eventually reflected in the general ledger system and therefore both the overall structure and integrity of the system are critical issues. The general ledgering system will be used to generate financial information for both internal (i.e. management accounts) and external (i.e the statutory accounts) consumption, and therefore it must operate in a stable and secure environment.

Control Objectives for General Ledger/Management Accounts

(a)   To ensure that the general ledger and management accounts are accurate, reliable, and appropriately reflect the structure and operations of the organisation.

(b)   To ensure that the accounting data is capable of meaningful and accurate analysis in order to support management decisions and actions.

> (c) To ensure that the accounting records are maintained in accordance with the prevailing laws, regulations and professional good practice.
>
> (d) To ensure that the accounting information can be used to generate all the required statutory published accounting statements.

Risk and Control Issues for General Ledger/Management Accounts

1 Key Issues

1.1 Has the chart of accounts been approved by senior management and does it suitably reflect the organisation and operations of the company?

1.2 How does management ascertain that the general ledger accounting data is accurate, complete and up to date?

1.3 How does management ensure that the accounting records and systems comply with the prevailing laws, regulations and accountancy good practice?

1.4 How does management verify that all summaries and analyses of accounting data are accurate and reliable?

1.5 How is the accuracy of published and statutory accounting statements confirmed?

1.6 What mechanisms protect the organisation's accounting data from loss, unauthorised amendment, or leakage?

1.7 Is management provided with timely, accurate and relevant accounting information to support decisions and actions?

2 Detailed Issues

2.1 How does management make sure that all relevant economic events are identified and correctly reflected in the accounts?

2.2 How is the accuracy of data input from other systems confirmed?

2.3 How is the accuracy of accounting data output to other systems and external sources confirmed?

2.4 What prevents the processing of unauthorised or invalid accounting entries?

2.5 Is someone responsible for the accuracy and completeness of accounting data?

2.6 Are there mechanisms to prevent the unauthorised set up of accounts?

2.7 Has management approved the current chart of accounts and exercised adequate control over subsequent changes?

2.8   How does management ensure that transactions are being correctly posted to the appropriate nominal accounts?

2.9   How does management confirm that the correct and appropriate accounting treatment is being applied (e.g. for fixed assets)?

2.10   Would posting errors be identified and corrected?

2.11   Are key, control and suspense accounts regularly scrutinised and reconciled?

2.12   Are there mechanisms in place to ensure that transactions are correctly posted in the appropriate accounting period?

2.13   Are all source departments aware of the general ledger processing timetable and their specific data submission deadlines?

2.14   How is unauthorised access to the accounting system prevented?

2.15   What measures are taken to prevent the unauthorised production and circulation of accounting system reports and printouts?

2.16   Are journal adjustments subject to a suitable level of authorisation?

2.17   What prevents the processing of unauthorised or invalid journal adjustments?

2.18   What prevents the duplicate processing of accounting entries and journals?

2.19   How does management ensure that all required adjustments have been correctly processed?

2.20   Have written accounting procedures been provided for the guidance of the relevant staff?

2.21   Is management provided with adequate, timely and accurate accounting data to enable it to discharge its responsibilities?

2.22   What processes ensure that all the required published and statutory accounting statements are accurately produced on time?

2.23   Are the accounting records maintained in accordance with the prevailing laws and regulations?

2.24   Is management capable of detecting any material errors in the accounts and published statements?

2.25   Is someone given responsibility for keeping up to date with current accounting and related legislative requirements and ensuring ongoing compliance?

FIXED ASSETS (AND CAPITAL CHARGES)

In this section we are concerned with notable investments in such items as buildings, motor vehicles, plant and machinery, and office and computer equipment.

Initially there should be appropriate authorisation for capital acquisitions, followed by accurate and complete accounting processes covering the purchase, depreciation, verification and eventual disposal of the assets.

Control Objectives for Fixed Assets (and Capital Charges)

(a) To ensure that assets are correctly and accurately reflected in the accounts.

(b) To ensure that all capital expenditure is justified and approved.

(c) To ensure that all assets are identified, recorded and regularly verified.

(d) To ensure that depreciation is appropriate and in accordance with both company policy and the prevailing regulations.

(e) To ensure that all asset disposals and write-offs are valid, authorised and correctly reflected in the accounts.

(f) To ensure that assets are appropriately protected and insured.

Risk and Control Issues for Fixed Assets (and Capital Charges)

1 Key Issues

1.1 Has management implemented an authorised policy governing capital acquisitions and expenditure and is it subject to review and update?

1.2 How is management assured that all capital expenditure and asset acquisitions are authorised?

1.3 How does management confirm that all assets are identified and correctly reflected in the accounts?

1.4 Are assets subject to regular verification, with the follow-up of anomalies?

1.5 Has management established and implemented a depreciation and accounting treatment policy for assets which reflects current and permitted accounting practices?

1.6 What mechanisms ensure that the correct depreciation is being calculated and reflected in the accounts?

1.7 Are fixed assets adequately protected against loss or damage?

1.8 Are asset disposals and write-offs suitably approved and conducted in the best interests of the organisation?

1.9 Where appropriate, are assets adequately insured?

1.10 Does management ensure that suitable reserves are calculated for the replacement of key assets?

2 Detailed Issues

2.1 Are documented procedures available governing all aspects of asset acquisition, accounting treatment, disposal, etc.?

2.2 Has the organisation developed an approved policy affecting assets and their management?

2.3 How are all asset purchases identified?

2.4 Are all asset purchases approved at the appropriate level and how is this evidenced and confirmed?

2.5 Is the correct reflection of assets in the accounts confirmed and how is this evidenced?

2.6 Are adequate and accurate asset registers maintained and subjected to regular reconciliation?

2.7 How does management ensure that the appropriate depreciation charges are being calculated in all cases?

2.8 How does management verify that all the relevant depreciation charges are being accurately reflected in the accounting system?

2.9 Are amendments to the asset or depreciation policies suitably approved and documented?

2.10 What processes are in place to protect the assets records and accounting information from loss or unauthorised access?

2.11 Would management be able to detect promptly the loss or misplacement of an asset item?

2.12 Are the assets values that are contained in published or statutory accounting data confirmed as being accurate and fair representations?

2.13 How is compliance with any prevailing regulations or accounting practice confirmed?

2.14 How is the accuracy of asset data output to other systems confirmed?

2.15 Are asset transfers (i.e. inter-company) suitably approved, documented and trailed?

2.16 Are assets adequately identified and protected from theft, loss, damage, etc.?

2.17 Are all relevant staff made aware of their responsibilities to safeguard and protect asset items?

2.18 Is the existence of assets regularly verified?

2.19 Are apparently missing or unaccounted for assets investigated and resolved?

2.20 Are key assets adequately insured and does management ensure that insurance cover is maintained and at the appropriate level?

2.21 Is sales tax, VAT and/or duty on fixed asset transactions determined and accounted for in accordance with the relevant regulations?

2.22 Are all asset disposals subject to adequate levels of authorisation, and how is this evidenced?

2.23 How is management assured that the best terms and conditions are obtained in respect of asset disposals?

2.24 Are all asset disposal proceeds accounted for and posted to the appropriate accounts?

2.25 Could an asset item be disposed of without the knowledge of management or without the relevant proceeds being accounted for?

2.26 Are the asset records/registers correctly updated on the disposal of an asset item?

2.27 Are all accounting adjustments applied to asset accounts approved at the appropriate level and how is this evidenced?

2.28 If permitted, are all pledges of assets as security suitably authorised, documented and confirmed as allowable under the prevailing regulations?

2.29 Are key assets suitably identified in order to plan for their replacement?

2.30 How does management ensure that future budgets incorporate accurate estimates for replacing key assets?

BUDGETING AND MONITORING

Here we are interested in both the general budgeting framework (i.e. how the budgets are initially generated, authorised and rolled out) and the allocated responsibilities for subsequently monitoring actual performance against budgets (i.e. identifying and reacting to significant variances, authorising budget amendments, etc.).

Control Objectives for Budgeting and Monitoring

(a) To provide an accurate and reliable budgeting system as a means to ensure that agreed financial and business objectives are achieved.

(b) To provide a realistic and accurate budgeting framework and plan which accurately reflects the structure and operations of the organisation.

(c) To provide management with a means to monitor progress against financial targets.

> (d) To ensure that variations, deviations and failures to achieve targets are promptly identified for management action.

Risk and Control Issues for Budgeting and Monitoring

1 Key Issues

1.1 Has management developed and implemented a documented budgeting process for use throughout the organisation and does this clearly allocate responsibilities for action and follow-up of variances, etc.?

1.2 How is management certain that the budgeting model and processes adequately and accurately reflect the structure and operations of the organisation?

1.3 Are the budgeted figures agreed by the relevant members of management and how is this signified?

1.4 How is the accuracy and completeness of data input from other source systems confirmed?

1.5 How is the budget and actual data reflected by the budget system confirmed as accurate and complete?

1.6 Is the budget information produced and circulated on a timely basis?

1.7 How does management ascertain that all subsequent amendments to the budgeted data are justified, authorised and accurately applied?

1.8 Are significant budget versus actual variations identified and promptly acted upon?

1.9 How is the action taken in reaction to variations, shortfalls, etc. verified as complete and effective?

2 Detailed Issues

2.1 What mechanisms ensure that the budget model/system remains up to date with structural and operational changes?

2.2 How does management ensure that the assumptions and factors underlying the budgeting system are relevant and accurate?

2.3 How does management ensure that the data contained in the budgeting system accurately and completely reflects all the processes and events taking place in the business?

2.4 Does the budgeting system underpin the key objectives for the business?

2.5 Does line management have sufficient input into the process of determining accurate and realistic budgets?

2.6   How does management ensure that the system appropriately reflects the agreed financial scenario?

2.7   What prevents the application of unauthorised or invalid adjustments to the budget model data?

2.8   How does management ensure that the budget system data is an accurate reflection of the source systems?

2.9   How are subsequent amendments to the budget figures and targets confirmed as being suitably authorised and correctly applied?

2.10   Is the budget versus actual data circulated on a timely and prompt basis?

2.11   How is commercially sensitive or confidential accounting data protected from unauthorised exposure?

2.12   Has management clearly defined the level of variances that require follow-up action and the nature of the action required?

2.13   Have specific responsibilities been allocated for the monitoring and follow-up of budget versus actual data?

2.14   Are purchase commitments confirmed as being within budget prior to being processed?

2.15   Are all potential budget revisions identified and approved prior to update of the budgeting system?

BANK ACCOUNTS AND BANKING ARRANGEMENTS

This subject area affects all businesses. The variety of account types and the range of other services offered by the wider financial services community makes the selection of the appropriate account arrangements critical. There is a fundamental requirement to consider the type of banking facilities best suited to both the operational and financial needs of the business (for example, in retailing situations where there are likely to be considerable levels of cash lodgements to be made on a daily basis).

Due attention should be paid to the control and monitoring of account usage, especially in terms of devolved authorities for such activities as cheque signatories and fund transfers. Regular, independent and effective account reconciliations to internal records are essential, as they can limit the possibility of defalcation passing undetected.

Control Objectives for Bank Accounts and Banking Arrangements

(a)   To ensure that banking arrangements and facilities are appropriate and adequate for the business.

(b)   To ensure that all banking transactions are bona fide, accurate and authorised whenever necessary.

> (c)   To ensure that overdraft facilities are authorised and correctly operated within the limits defined by management and the organisation's bankers.
>
> (d)   To ensure that fund transfers and automated methods of effecting banking transactions are valid, in the best interests of the organisation, and authorised.
>
> (e)   To ensure that the potential for staff malpractice and fraud are minimised.
>
> (f)   To ensure that all income is banked without delay.
>
> (g)   To ensure that banking charges are effectively monitored and minimised.

Risk and Control Issues for Bank Accounts and Banking Arrangements

1 Key Issues

1.1   Is management aware of all active corporate bank accounts, their purpose, and current status?

1.2   Are corporate bank accounts established only at the request of senior management for a defined and authorised purpose (and how is this process evidenced)?

1.3   What mechanisms prevent the unauthorised set-up and operation of a bank account?

1.4   Are the prevailing banking terms and conditions optimised in terms of account type, transaction levels, interest payable on balances, levels of charges, etc.?

1.5   How is management assured that all banking transactions are accurate, complete, and authorised whenever necessary?

1.6   Have written procedures governing the set-up and use of banking facilities been established and implemented?

1.7   Do the prevailing banking arrangements maximise the return on surplus cash balances?

1.8   Would management be aware of impending overdraft situations and are all overdraft arrangements negotiated and suitably authorised in advance?

1.9   Have suitable and realistic cheque-signing mandates been established and what prevents an unauthorised member of staff from raising and issuing a cheque drawn against a corporate account?

1.10   How does management ensure that all bank account activities and balances are taken into account within the treasury function?

1.11   How does management ensure that only authorised bank loans and financing arrangements are established?

2 Detailed Issues

2.1   Have responsibilities for monitoring bank account balances been defined and allocated?

2.2   Has senior management clearly defined and communicated their objectives in respect of the operation of all bank accounts?

2.3   How does management ensure that the current banking arrangements adequately meet objectives?

2.4   Are bank accounts monitored in order that required changes in terms and conditions can be identified and implemented?

2.5   Are all bank account movements accurately reflected in the accounting system(s)?

2.6   Are bank accounts regularly reconciled and how is this evidenced?

2.7   Are reconciliation anomalies promptly identified, investigated and resolved?

2.8   Are excess balances promptly identified and authorised for transfer?

2.9   Are inter-account movements optimised to the benefit of the organisation or to avoid shortfalls?

2.10   How are unauthorised overdrafts avoided?

2.11   What prevents the processing of a transaction that would place an account in overdraft?

2.12   Are overdraft limits established, and if so what prevents the limit being exceeded?

2.13   How are banking entries input from other source systems confirmed for accuracy and validity?

2.14   How is the validity of direct debit, standing order and other automated transactions verified (for both debits and credits to the corporate accounts)?

2.15   What controls are in place over the storage and usage of blank company cheques, and are all company cheques accounted for?

2.16   Have effective measures been put in place to ensure that all cheques are authorised (before release) by a mandated member of staff?

2.17   Are all defaced and void cheques accounted for?

2.18   Would instances of blank cheques being pre-signed be detected?

2.19   Are cheque-signing mandates in place and applied which define various levels of authority limit?

2.20   Are all cheques raised adequately trailed to the supporting accounting event/transaction (and do cheque signatories know what the cheque is for)?

2.21   Are all customer payments processed directly into a corporate bank promptly identified and allocated to the appropriate debtor account?

2.22   How is the accuracy and completeness of all transaction data relevant to the input to other systems confirmed?

2.23   Have adequate levels of transaction authorisation been defined and applied in practice?

2.24   How is management assured that all income is correctly identified and banked without delay?

2.25   Would management be aware of a missing or significantly delayed bank lodgement?

2.26   What measures are in place to prevent unauthorised use of electronic transaction facilities (such as CHAPS, BACS, and telegraphic transfer)?

2.27   If cheques are signed using a signature printing system, what mechanisms prevent unauthorised use of the plates?

2.28   What action is taken to avoid the issue of incorrectly completed cheques?

2.29   Are cheques rejected as "refer to drawer", etc. promptly identified and effectively dealt with?

2.30   Are adequate precautions taken to protect members of staff involved in making bank lodgements?

2.31   Are banking charges reviewed, authorised, and followed up if in error?

2.32   What processes prevent the establishment of unauthorised or unfavourable bank loan facilities?

2.33   Are all borrowing terms adequately documented?

2.34   How does management ensure that all borrowings are paid at the due time?

2.35   If relevant, how are exposures to interest rate and/or foreign currency exchange rate movements identified and minimised?

SALES TAX (VAT) ACCOUNTING

This section uses the value added tax environment as the standard model; however, the issues raised can easily be modified and applied to other sales taxation regimes. All aspects of mainstream VAT accounting are considered, including registration, the calculation of and accounting for input and output tax, compliance with the regulations, the production and submission of regular VAT returns, and the settlement of any taxes due. There are special VAT schemes (e.g. for retailers) and some activities have specific VAT implications (such as property development), but such considerations are not specifically considered here as we concentrate upon general issues.

The ability of VAT systems to cope with the current demands has also to be balanced against their flexibility to react effectively to, as yet unspecified, future changes (e.g. the introduction of a range of taxation rates for different goods and services). Most (if not all) recognised accounting systems do allow for multiple sales taxation rates, but there is still a necessity to ensure that all the other administrative activities can accordingly respond (perhaps very quickly) to changes.

Control Objectives for Sales Tax (VAT) Accounting

> (a)   To ensure that all valid input and output VAT is accurately identified at the appropriate rate, recorded and reported.
>
> (b)   To ensure that the correct net value of VAT is either reclaimed or paid over and supported by the relevant return.
>
> (c)   To ensure that the prevailing VAT regulations are correctly observed at all times.
>
> (d)   To ensure that the business remains correctly registered for VAT and correctly displays its registration number on all relevant documentation.

Risk and Control Issues for Sales Tax (VAT) Accounting

1 Key Issues

1.1   How does management ensure that all output VAT and duty on applicable sales is accurately identified, accounted for and duly reported?

1.2   How does management ensure that all input VAT and duty on applicable purchases is accurately identified, accounted for and duly reported?

1.3   What processes ensure that all the required VAT returns are accurately prepared in accordance with the current legislation?

1.4   How does management ensure that the correct net value is either reclaimed or paid over to Customs and Excise (C & E) (or equivalent regulatory body)?

1.5°   Is the current company registration for VAT correct and up to date?

1.6   Have contingency plans and practical arrangements been made to cater for implementing variations in VAT rate?

1.7   What mechanisms ensure that all the required VAT returns are correctly completed and despatched on time?

1.8   Does the correct VAT registration number appear on all the relevant company stationery and documentation?

2 Detailed Issues

2.1   Have written procedures been established and implemented covering all VAT matters?

2.2   How does management ensure that exempt and invalid VAT entries are excluded from the accounting records and subsequent VAT returns?

2.3   Would errors in the calculation and accumulation of both input and output VAT be detected and corrected as necessary?

2.4   Is the content of the regular VAT return checked for completeness and accuracy before release (and how is this process evidenced)?

2.5   Would non-completion or non-submission of the VAT return be detected promptly?

2.6   How does management confirm that all company invoices consistently reflect the correct calculation of output VAT?

2.7   Are the company accounting systems capable of coping simultaneously with a number of different VAT rates?

2.8   Has management established contingency plans in the event of a VAT rate change at short notice (e.g. following a government budget)?

2.9   Does the accounting system adequately cater for zero-rated and exempt items?

2.10   Has management confirmed that the current accounting system complies with the requirements of Custom and Excise, and has the C & E formally acknowledged their acceptance of the system?

2.11   What would prevent the incorrect determination of the relevant tax point for a VAT-related transaction?

2.12   Are all imported purchases from other EU states correctly documented and accounted for?

2.13   Are all export sales to other EU states correctly documented and accounted for?

2.14   Are all VAT related transactions adequately trailed (i.e. to facilitate an inspection by the C & E)?

2.15   Has management allocated a responsibility to maintain an accurate awareness of current VAT legislation as a means of ensuring ongoing regulatory
compliance?

TAXATION

This area of accounting practice is potentially very complex and there are no general
panacea solutions available. Therefore it is assumed that each organisation will have
in place a taxation policy which takes into account all the factors relevant to its own
trading and fiscal situation. Many larger organisation will either employ someone
suitably experienced, or use the services of an external taxation specialist to ensure
that they have an appropriate (and legal) taxation strategy.

The subject of taxation management can be viewed simply as a balance between
minimising liabilities and ensuring compliance with often very complex
regulations.

Control Objectives for Taxation

(a)   To ensure that all tax affairs are appropriately planned and managed.

(b)   To ensure that clear objectives are established in relation to taxation
matters with a view to minimising tax liabilities within the confines of
the prevailing legislation and regulations.

(c)   To ensure that all tax liabilities are accurately determined and
supported by accounting data.

(d)   To ensure that all required taxation returns are correctly completed
and filed on time.

(e)   To ensure compliance with all relevant taxation legislation and
regulations.

(f)   To ensure that allowances and concessions are identified, accurately
assessed and accordingly claimed.

(g)   To ensure that all tax payments are suitably authorised.

(h)   To provide management with adequate and accurate information on
taxation matters and liabilities.

Risk and Control Issues for Taxation

1 Key Issues

1.1   Has management identified all the potential taxation liabilities for the
organisation and defined a planned approach to ensuring that the relevant
requirements are correctly met?

1.2 How does management ensure that all taxation liabilities are correctly calculated and discharged?

1.3 What measures ensure that taxation liabilities are minimised within the prevailing regulations?

1.4 How does management ensure that all the required regulations are satisfactorily complied with?

1.5 Is management supplied with regular and accurate data on corporate taxation liabilities as a means to support decision making?

1.6 Are all tax payments subject to suitable authorisation and how is this evidenced?

1.7 What processes prevent the unauthorised or incorrect settlement of taxes?

1.8 Are all taxation returns accurately supported by the underlying accounting system data?

2 Detailed Issues

2.1 Have suitably experienced staff been allocated the responsibilities of preparing and submitting all the necessary taxation returns?

2.2 How does management remain abreast of changing taxation requirements and ensure that the adopted approach is up to date and correct?

2.3 Has management taken adequate account of the taxation implications of the established relationships with either their parent or subsidiary companies?

2.4 Are complex taxation situations referred to independent taxation specialists for advice?

2.5 How is management sure that assessments of taxation liability are accurate and complete?

2.6 Has management issued and implemented a clear policy on taxation matters?

2.7 How is management certain that the correct/current rate of tax is being calculated?

2.8 Are affected staff aware of the required methods to reduce or contain the organisation's taxation liabilities?

2.9 What mechanisms ensure that all the relevant concessions and allowances are identified and taken into account?

2.10 How are breaches of current regulations prevented?

2.11 What prevents the submission of an incorrect taxation return?

2.12   What prevents the late submission of a taxation return?

2.13   How is the accuracy of the underlying accounting information confirmed?

2.14   How does management confirm that all relevant tax credits are correctly identified and reclaimed?

2.15   Would management be made aware of abnormal or significant variations in tax liability (and what action would they take in such instances)?

2.16   What prevents the premature or overdue settlement of taxes?

2.17   Are all new business operations reviewed in respect of their potential taxation implications?

2.18   How is accuracy of taxation payments data output to other systems confirmed?

2.19   How are taxation data, records and documentation protected from loss or damage?

2.20   Are taxation entries and data adequately documented and trailed to facilitate inspections undertaken by the relevant regulatory bodies?

INVENTORIES

In this section we primarily focus on the accounting dimensions of inventories. Chapter 10 includes a specific section on Stock Control in the operational context.

Control Objectives for Inventories

(a) To ensure that the accounting system and statutory accounts accurately reflect the value of current inventory stocks.

(b) To ensure that all stock purchases, issues and other movements are valid and correctly reflected in the inventory accounts.

(c) To ensure that stocks are correctly priced.

(d) To ensure that inventory values are periodically verified as correct.

(e) To ensure that all adjustments to stock valuations are suitably investigated and authorised.

(f) To ensure that inventory items utilised in production and customer sales activities are correctly charged out of the inventory accounts and accounted for in target systems.

(g) To ensure that write-offs of excess, scrap or obsolete stocks are valid and authorised.

(h) To provide adequate, accurate and timely management information.

Risk and Control Issues for Inventories

1 Key Issues

1.1   How does management make sure that the accounting system accurately reflects the values of inventory stocks?

1.2   How does management confirm that the year end and statutory accounts contain accurate stock valuations?

1.3   What processes ensure that all processed stock movements are valid, correctly priced, and accurately posted to the relevant stock accounts?

1.4   Are stock values adequately and regularly verified, and how is this evidenced?

1.5   How does management ensure that all amendments to stock values are valid and correctly applied?

1.6   What measures ensure that all stocks used in production or sold to customers are correctly accounted for?

1.7   What prevents stocks being incorrectly priced?

1.8   Are all stock write-offs, disposals and adjustments suitably authorised and how is this evidenced?

1.9   Is management regularly provided with current and accurate information on stock holdings?

1.10 Does the accounting and management information provide the means to identify anomalies, and if so are such queries actively followed up?

2 Detailed Issues

2.1   What processes ensure that all stock movements are correctly reflected in the relevant stock accounts?

2.2   How is management assured that the stock accounts adequately identify and account for all stocks at all possible locations (e.g. in production, out with subcontractors)?

2.3   What prevents authorised stock entries and movements being processed?

2.4   How is unauthorised access to the stock accounting system prevented?

2.5   How is the accuracy of data input to the stock accounts system from other systems confirmed?

2.6   What prevents stock movements being incorrectly priced, and what prevents the set-up of an invalid or unauthorised stock price?

2.7   Are stock levels regularly and effectively verified by independent staff?

2.8   Is effective and adequate action taken in respect of stock variances revealed during stocktaking exercises?

2.9   Are all stock adjustments authorised and how is this evidenced?

2.10   What prevents the acceptance and processing of invalid, incorrect or unauthorised stock adjustments?

2.11   Is the quality of the underlying stock records assessed and verified?

2.12   Are adequate facilities provided to ensure that levels of stock losses, shrinkage, adjustments, etc. are regularly reported to management for action (and how is their reaction evidenced)?

2.13   Would excessive stock levels be promptly identified and corrective action taken?

2.14   What prevents the unauthorised write-off or disposal of stock items?

2.15   What mechanisms ensure that the income from stock disposals is maximised and fully accounted for?

2.16   What prevents stock items being despatched to customers without an invoice being raised?

2.17   Would processing errors, duplications, etc. be detected and corrected?

PRODUCT/PROJECT ACCOUNTING

The general issues raised in this section can be equally applied to accounting for products or specific projects. Chapter 12 (which addresses subjects relevant to research and development), includes a separate section on product development in the wider context, incorporating the marketing and technical issues.

Control Objectives for Product/Project Accounting

(a) To ensure that all projects and product developments/launches are suitably authorised as part of the strategic direction of the organisation.

(b) To ensure that the appropriate costing method is selected.

(c) To ensure that all the relevant costs are identified and accurately recorded.

(d) To ensure "local" factors are appropriately taken into consideration, such as market share, price sensitivity, price controls, etc.

(e) To establish budgets based on reliable data and assumptions.

(f) To ensure that actual costs and progress are adequately monitored and that variances are identified and acted upon.

> (g) To ensure that actual sales or project outturn performance is monitored and managed.
>
> (h) To ensure that the accounting system accurately reflects all the relevant economic events associated with each product/project.

Risk and Control Issues for Product/Project Accounting

1 Key Issues

1.1 Are all product developments or projects authorised and ratified by senior management as part of the long-term strategic direction of the organisation, and what prevents unauthorised product/project activity?

1.2 Have key objectives been set for the product/project (such as the required rate of return on the investment or target sales income) as the basis for performance and achievement monitoring?

1.3 Has management established the most appropriate costing method for the product/project and ensured that all the relevant cost elements and underlying assumptions have been identified and incorporated?

1.4 How is management certain that all the relevant cost data is accurate, complete, and being correctly accumulated in the accounting system?

1.5 Has management taken adequate account of local factors, such as taxation, pricing controls, competitors' strategies, available subsidies and grants, etc.?

1.6 Have the key project stages, milestones and deliverables been identified and incorporated into a workable progress monitoring system for management review and action?

1.7 How is management certain that cost overruns, failures to achieve target objectives, etc. will be promptly detected and followed up?

1.8 How does management verify that it has accurately identified, and made available, all the required resources?

1.9 Has management defined the break even point for the product/project and established adequate monitoring of actual sales/performance to ensure achievement of their objectives?

2 Detailed Issues

2.1 Does management undertake a full appraisal of all potential products and projects and how is this evidenced?

2.2   Has management developed and agreed an authorised pricing policy based on market share, action by competitors, local pricing considerations, supply and demand, geographic differences, and so on?

2.3   Are all product developments/launches considered in relation to the established pricing policy?

2.4   Has management determined targets and objectives for each product/ project, and established a mechanism to monitor actual performance against the targets?

2.5   How does management confirm that products/projects are achieving the required objectives?

2.6   How does management ensure that it has accurately identified all the direct and indirect costs associated with the product/project?

2.7   How does management confirm that all the resources (labour and material) actually expended are being identified and accurately costed?

2.8   Have all special costs (such as special tooling, capital equipment, employing external consultants, etc.) been taken into account?

2.9   If the product/project involves materials or services provided by external suppliers, has management taken due regard of the consequences of variations in the related costs?

2.10 Has the most relevant and appropriate costing method been applied?

2.11 How does management ensure it has accurately and realistically determined the profit level for the product (and is this linked to a critical and realistic level of sales activity)?

2.12 How is the accuracy of costing data input from other source systems confirmed for completeness and correct coding?

2.13 How is the accuracy of output costing data (budget and actual) confirmed?

2.14 Have all of the discrete production and other stages been identified, and how can management be certain that the associated costs are accurately reflected in the accounting/costing systems?

2.15 What processes prevent the inclusion of invalid or incorrect costs for a product or project?

2.16 Have cost targets been established for all the key stages of the project, and are actual costs monitored against the targets?

2.17 Are all cost overruns or performance shortfalls promptly brought to management's attention?

2.18 Is the impact of standard cost variances considered in relation to the inventory and cost of sales?

2.19 Are significant problems or cost variances recorded together with the proposed courses of management action?

2.20 How does management ensure that all identified problems, shortfalls, overspends, etc. are followed up and resolved?

PETTY CASH AND EXPENSES

Petty cash reviews are generally related to questions of scale. The levels of petty cash and general expense expenditure will vary considerably between organisations. Taking account of the possible low-level scale of petty cash costs, management may feel content with the application of common sense controls and cost containment principles, as it will consider that there are more pressing business issues to address. However, given the relatively simple processes involved and the possible proliferation of an attitude that "everybody fiddles their expenses, don't they?", a lack of basic control can very easily lead to losses and staff behaving unethically.

Control Objectives for Petty Cash and Expenses

> (a) To ensure that all expenses are valid and authorised.
>
> (b) To ensure that all expenses are correctly identified, recorded and accurately reflected in the accounting system.
>
> (c) To ensure that all expense payments are in accord with company policy and any relevant external regulations (e.g. for sales tax or VAT).

Risk and Control Issues for Petty Cash and Expenses

1 Key Issues

1.1 How does management monitor that only valid, accurate and authorised expenses are processed?

1.2 What mechanisms prevent the acceptance and processing of invalid, unauthorised or incorrect expenses?

1.3 Are all petty cash floats identified and accounted for?

1.4 Has management established clear policies and procedures for recording, authorising and processing petty cash and expense claims?

1.5 How does management confirm that all petty cash and expenses are correctly reflected in the accounting system?

1.6 How is compliance with the prevailing VAT (or the equivalent sales tax) regulations for expenses confirmed?

2 Detailed Issues

2.1   Are expenses claims and petty cash returns supported by the relevant receipts?

2.2   Have expense authority levels and mandates been established, and how is their correct application evidenced?

2.3   Are petty cash and personal expense floats accounted for and regularly verified?

2.4   How does management ensure that petty cash/expense floats are appropriately recovered when an employee leaves the organisation?

2.5   Have staff been made aware of their responsibilities in respect of petty cash and expenses, especially their guardianship of floats?

2.6   What prevents the processing of personal cheques, loans and IOUs through the petty cash float?

2.7   Is the VAT or sales tax content being correctly identified and accounted for, and how are errors prevented?

2.8   Are all petty cash/expense claims adequately supported and trailed?

2.9   Are floats accurately determined, and how are excessively large floats avoided?

2.10   Have adequate and secure storage facilities been provided for petty cash and expense floats?

2.11   Has management determined and implemented standard rates for selected expense categories (e.g. meal allowances or mileage rates) and what prevents the processing of a claim for an invalid rate?

2.12   Have procedures been established governing the use of company fuel cards and credit cards?

2.13   What processes prevent the misuse of fuel cards (e.g. to cover private journeys)?

2.14   What processes prevent the misuse or inappropriate use of company credit cards?

FINANCIAL INFORMATION AND REPORTING

The issues raised in this section take account of both internal and external financial reporting requirements. The key concerns relate to accuracy, completeness, timeliness and security of the information.

Control Objectives for Financial Information and Reporting

> (a) To ensure that management (and others within the organisation) are provided with accurate and timely financial information to support their decision making and activities.
>
> (b) To ensure that all the relevant financial reports and returns are accurately prepared and distributed to external bodies in accordance with the prevailing legislation, regulation and contractual obligations.
>
> (c) To ensure that accounting records and statements are correctly maintained and prepared in accordance with the prevailing accounting standards and good practice.
>
> (d) To ensure that all financial information is adequately protected from loss, misuse or unauthorised leakage.
>
> (e) To ensure that sensitive or confidential corporate financial information is adequately protected.

Risk and Control Issues for Financial Information and Reporting

1 Key Issues

1.1 Has management identified and documented all its financial information requirements?

1.2 How is management certain that all the required financial information is accurate and provided on time?

1.3 What processes prevent the creation and circulation of inaccurate, invalid or out-of-date financial data?

1.4 How is management assured that all the required external and statutory financial reports/returns are accurately generated and released on time?

1.5 What mechanisms prevent the release of inaccurate financial data to external bodies?

1.6 How does management monitor that all accounting records are maintained in accordance with the current accounting regulations, standards and professional good practice?

1.7 What measures are in place to ensure that financial data is adequately protected from loss, distortion, misuse or unauthorised leakage?

2 Detailed Issues

2.1 Are internal financial information requirements regularly reviewed and updated so as to ensure that information flows are relevant, current and adequately address the needs of management and staff?

2.2 Are redundant and out-of-date information flows identified and terminated?

2.3 How does management ensure that information is being accessed only by authorised and relevant employees?

2.4 Are those managers responsible for maintaining the corporate financial records kept aware of all current and forthcoming requirements, accounting regulations, etc. in order to ensure ongoing compliance?

2.5 Would the failure to produce and distribute statutory financial information be detected and reacted to?

INVESTMENTS

Given the notable financial and timing implications associated with investment activities, it is crucial that authorised policies are in place and adhered to.

Control Objectives for Investments

(a) To ensure that all investment decisions are adequately researched and authorised in accordance with the established objectives.

(b) To ensure that investment commitments do not interfere with the required cash flow and that sufficient working funds are maintained.

(c) To ensure that the timescale and liquidity implications of investments are adequately considered and catered for.

(d) To ensure that invested funds and the income generated are correctly accounted for.

(e) To ensure that all relevant regulations, exchange controls and accountancy standards are complied with.

(f) To ensure that investment documentation is adequately and securely stored.

Risk and Control Issues for Investments

1 Key Issues

1.1 Has management established an approved investment policy which clearly defines their objectives (i.e. required levels of return, timescale, etc.)?

1.2   How does management ensure that investment income is maximised within the prevailing law and regulations?

1.3   How does management ensure that only suitable and authorised investments are made, which accord with the established objectives?

1.4   What processes prevent investment commitments from adversely interfering with the day-to-day cash requirements of the business?

1.5   Are all invested funds and the income generated from them accurately accounted for?

1.6   How does management confirm that all investments comply with the relevant laws, regulations and accounting standards?

1.7   Is investment documentation securely and adequately stored and protected from loss, misuse or damage?

2 Detailed Issues

2.1   What prevents the set-up of an unauthorised investment?

2.2   What prevents the set-up of an investment that is outwith the defined policy and management objectives?

2.3   How are the cash flow implications of proposed investments assessed so as to avoid shortages of day-to-day funding across the lifetime of the investment?

2.4   How is management authorisation for investments evidenced?

2.5   Are investment considerations adequately assessed for inherent risk?

2.6   Are investments aimed at achieving the highest yield and are they assessed in respect of achieving defined objectives?

2.7   Are all investments correctly recorded in the accounting system?

2.8   How does management ensure that all income due from investments is received in full and at the appropriate time?

2.9   Is investment income correctly identified and appropriately recorded in the accounting system?

2.10   Would investment activities which fail to comply with the prevailing regulations be prevented or promptly detected and reported?

NOTE

1. Chapter 16 examines the alternative review approaches including those using *cycles* and *processes*.

7

Auditing Contracts and the Purchasing Function

INTRODUCTION

In this chapter we look at the purchasing function through an examination of the relative control objectives, and the related risks and control issues.

Purchasing activities can take many forms, ranging from the comparatively straightforward acquisition of the consumable items required for everyday business, through sourcing supplies required to keep a production process running smoothly, to sophisticated procurement contracting processes perhaps involving the selection of appropriate suppliers and tendering procedures.

The first section of this chapter concentrates on the issues related to the simpler forms of general purchasing. In the later sections we suggest a possible universe of contract auditing projects, and then examine in detail some of the more common activities associated with contracting.[1]

Consult other chapters for discussion of related issues (refer to the Contents and the Index). For instance, just in time (JIT) management, which may be applied by management to purchasing, is discussed in Chapter 17.

CONTROL OBJECTIVES AND RISK AND CONTROL ISSUES

For each area, we shall examine the component functions and highlight the relative control objectives and the risk and control issues (divided into key issues and detailed issues) arising from the various constituent activities. This data can be used within the Standard Audit Programme Guides (SAPGs) looked at in Chapter 3. To save space, we have concentrated on the objectives to be stated and the questions to be asked and have not presented them within the SAPG format.

PURCHASING

Control Objectives for Purchasing

(a) To ensure that all purchasing activities are supported by authorised and documented policies and procedures.

(b) To ensure that purchasing appropriately supports the business objectives of the organisation.

(c) To ensure that the appropriate goods/services are obtained at the optimum price and at the relevant time.

(d) To ensure that all purchasing activity is valid, justified, authorised and within the prescribed budgets.

(e) To ensure that suppliers are reliable, financially stable, and able to satisfy the organisation's purchasing demands.

(f) To ensure that all goods and services are of an appropriate quality to satisfy the organisation's objectives.

(g) To ensure that supplier's trading terms and conditions are appropriate.

(h) To ensure that purchasing activities comply with all the prevailing legislation and regulations.

(i) To ensure that all purchasing activity is correctly reflected in the organisation's stock control records and accounts.

(j) To ensure that overdue and late deliveries are progressed.

(k) To ensure that supplier performance is adequately monitored and reacted to.

(l) To provide management with adequate, accurate and timely information on purchasing activities.

These control objectives are deliberately broad in nature. The purchasing motivation and approaches of various organisations will be subject to variation in respect of scale, nature, market pressures and potential operational impacts. For example, there will inevitably be different emphasis placed on the approach adopted for purchasing between the public and private sectors or between a service organisation and an engineering company.

Risk and Control Issues for Purchasing

1 Key Issues

1.1 Have authorised and documented purchasing policies and procedures been developed, implemented, and adequately communicated to all affected parties?

1.2   How does management verify that all purchase orders are justified, authorised, within budget and accounted for within the correct accounting period?

1.3   What mechanisms prevent the invalid, unauthorised and fraudulent use of official orders?

1.4   How does management ensure that adequate and appropriate supplies are obtained to sustain the required business activities?

1.5   How does management ensure that goods and services are always obtained at the most economical and fair price?

1.6   How does management verify that all suppliers are stable, reliable, and capable of meeting the organisation's needs at the optimum price?

1.7   What processes ensure supplies are to the required standard, specification and quality?

1.8   What mechanisms ensure that all goods are received on time and that overdue deliveries are identified and progressed?

1.9   How does management verify that all purchases are correctly reflected in stock control and accounting records?

1.10   What processes ensure that all purchasing activities fully comply with all the relevant legislation and regulations?

2 Detailed Issues

2.1   Have purchasing authority limits (financial and type) been established, and what mechanisms prevent such limits being exceeded?

2.2   Are adequate purchasing procedures in place and what processes ensure that they are kept up to date?

2.3   What measures ensure that purchase orders are issued only from authorised sources?

2.4   What mechanisms prevent the processing of purchase orders outwith the established policy conditions?

2.5   Are all purchase orders formally justified and suitably authorised, and how is this evidenced?

2.6   How is management assured that all purchasing activity across the organisation is suitably co-ordinated in order to avoid waste and maximise purchasing terms, etc.?

2.7   Are purchase orders confirmed to be within the agreed budgets at the point of commitment, and how is an unauthorised commitment prevented?

2.8   How does management verify that the format and content of all official orders conform to the required standards and legislation?

2.9   Are purchase orders adequately supported with sufficient details, descriptions, specifications, prices, delivery location, call-off and freight terms in order to ensure that the precise requirements of the business are met?

2.10   What processes prevent the despatch of inaccurate, incomplete or ambiguous purchase orders?

2.11   What processes prevent the raising and despatch of duplicate purchase orders?

2.12   What mechanisms ensure that the appropriate quantities of goods are ordered to support the operational requirements of the business?

2.13   What mechanisms ensure that all subsequent purchase order amendments are valid, authorised and correctly applied?

2.14   What mechanisms are in place to prevent over-ordering of items?

2.15   How are potential suppliers selected and what prevents the use of unstable or poor quality suppliers?

2.16   How is management certain that the purchasing function fully researches the optimum sources for their requirements?

2.17   Where approved suppliers have been identified, what mechanisms prevent the use of unauthorised sources of supply?

2.18   Are suppliers adequately and independently assessed for "approved" status, and what prevents staff/supplier misuse of the process?

2.19   Are accurate and up-to-date records of approved/suitable suppliers maintained, and what mechanisms prevent unauthorised and invalid access or amendment of such records?

2.20   Is the performance of suppliers monitored against all requirements and expectations so that unsuitable, unreliable or poor quality suppliers can be promptly identified and the appropriate action taken?

2.21   Would management be alerted if there was undue preference being given to a specific supplier, or there was an unreasonable demand being placed on any one supplier, or if there was potential for an unethical relationship being established between a supplier and purchasing management?

2.22   Is there adequate liaison between the purchasing function and all other affected activities (production, sales, stock control, etc.) and how are problems and conflicts avoided?

2.23   How does management verify that delivery requirements and call-offs are accurate, up to date and complied with?

2.24   Does the purchasing function maintain an adequate awareness of market conditions, prices, etc. in order to ensure the placement of orders at the optimum price?

2.25   How does management ensure that all available discounts are suitably exploited?

2.26   Are all relevant purchase versus leasing options adequately appraised to ensure that the most advantageous purchase terms are utilised?

2.27   How does management monitor that all the required quality and standards for supplied goods are achieved?

2.28   Would the supply of substandard, inadequate or poor quality goods be detected?

2.29   Are all rejected and returned goods correctly identified and a suitable credit claimed and accounted for?

2.30   How does management confirm that all the goods ordered and invoiced have in fact been received on time?

2.31   How is accuracy of data input from other systems (e.g. sales or production requirements) confirmed?

2.32   How is the accuracy of data output to other systems (e.g. stock control, warehousing) confirmed?

2.33   What steps are in place to ensure that the value of all order commitments and the associated cash flow impact is accurately calculated and accounted for?

2.34   Are the processes of ordering, accounting and receiving goods adequately segregated to prevent staff malpractice?

2.35   If staff purchase orders are processed, what mechanisms ensure that they are correctly and separately accounted for, and correctly and fully settled by the employee?

2.36   Where goods are obtained from overseas suppliers, how does management ascertain that all the relevant import and foreign exchange regulations have been identified and correctly addressed?

2.37   Is management provided with accurate, timely and relevant information on purchasing activities to support their decision making, etc.?

CONTRACTING

For many organisations in both the private and public sector, contracting activities can represent a significant degree of risk. In this section we will define a comprehensive universe of functions and activities associated with contracting, and from that broad universe make a selection of the more generally applicable processes for further, detailed examination of the related issues.

Contractual relationships can take many forms and indeed relate to a wide range of activities; for example, major civil engineering projects in the public sector or specialised goods and service procurement in the private sector. The contracting approaches applied in these differing scenarios will vary in form and scale, and may be affected by sector-specific regulations and practices. In order to take account of this potentially wide-ranging scope of contracting activities, we offer below a suggested audit universe structure divided into three distinct areas. Not all the activities listed will apply in every organisation.

Suggested Audit Universe

1. Contract management environment and pre-contract processes:

    *   contract management environment (i.e. procedures and methods)*
    *   project management framework
    *   project assessment and approval
    *   engaging, monitoring and paying consultants
    *   design
    *   assessing the viability and competence of contractors*
    *   maintaining an approved list of contractors*
    *   tendering procedures*
    *   contract and tendering documentation*
    *   insurance and bonding
    *   selection and letting of contracts*

2. During the currency of the contract:

    *   management information and reporting
    *   performance monitoring*
    *   arrangements for sub-contractors and suppliers
    *   materials, plant and project assets
    *   valuing work for interim payments*
    *   controlling price fluctuations
    *   monitoring and controlling variations
    *   extensions of time
    *   controlling contractual claims
    *   liquidations and bankruptcies

3. Upon and after contract completion:

    *   contractors final account*
    *   recovery of damages
    *   review of project outturn and performance*
    *   maintenance obligations.

---

*These activities represent the more generally applied contracting processes and will be examined in more detail in the remainder of this chapter.

CONTRACT MANAGEMENT ENVIRONMENT

In situations where the level of contracting activity justifies the establishment of an overall contract management environment, there is a broad range of component issues to take account of. For example, matters of project viability, authority to proceed, contractor competence and reliability, fair tendering processes, regulatory compliance, and so on. Certain sectors have long-established protocols for dealing with contracting, for instance the public sector and the civil engineering industry. However, not all contracting processes are correct for every situation, and some (such as tendering) may not be economically viable options.

Consider the level of contracting prevailing within your own organisation in the context of the potential risks (i.e. what is at stake).

Control Objectives for Contract Management Environment

(a) To ensure that contracting activities support the cost-effective achievement of agreed business objectives.

(b) To provide and maintain suitable documented procedures in order that contracting activities are effectively administered and so that staff malpractice and fraud are prevented.

(c) To ensure that contract requirements are correctly identified, appraised, justified, and documented.

(d) To ensure that the optimum contracting solution is selected.

(e) To ensure that contracts awarded represent value for money and meet the required quality and performance standards.

(f) To ensure that only stable, financially secure, and appropriately qualified contractors are engaged.

(g) To ensure that there is a fair and equitable basis for selecting contractors.

(h) To ensure that all requirements and objectives are identified, documented and met.

(i) To ensure that all payments against the contract are valid, authorised, and correctly accounted for.

(j) To ensure that contracts are completed on time, within budget and to the required standard.

(k) To ensure that responsibilities are identified and allocated.

(l) To ensure that management information is accurate, appropriate, complete and timely.

(m) To ensure that progress is adequately monitored and that problems are promptly reacted to.

(n) To ensure that all statutory and regulatory issues are identified and correctly addressed.

(o) To ensure that the most appropriate form of contract is utilised and that the organisation is adequately protected in the event of contractor default.

(p) To ensure that any design requirements are fully explored and accurately communicated.

(q) To ensure that subsequent design changes are authorised and/or minimised.

(r) To ensure that delays and extensions of time are reported, minimised and authorised where necessary.

(s) To ensure that price fluctuations throughout the course of the contract are justified, authorised and correctly applied.

(t) To ensure that contractual claims are minimised, controlled and satisfactorily resolved.

(u) To ensure that all project assets, plant and materials are adequately protected and correctly accounted for.

(v) To ensure that valid claims for damages are correctly raised, pursued and settled.

Risk and Control Issues for Contract Management Environment

1 Key Issues

1.1 How does management ensure that significant contract activity is in accord with, and supports the achievement of, the business objectives of the organisation?

1.2 What steps ensure that all potential contracts or projects are fully appraised for viability, cost-effectiveness and justification (and how is this evidenced)?

1.3 How is management assured that realistic and accurate contract cost estimates are generated and subject to adequate ongoing monitoring throughout the contract?

1.4 What processes ensure that the most appropriate form of contract/project funding is selected and authorised (and how is this evidenced)?

1.5 How is management assured that the most suitable form of contract is used, and that the clauses represent a fair balance of the risks between the parties?

1.6   How does the organisation avoid the engagement of unstable, financially insecure or inadequately skilled contractors?

1.7   What measures ensure that contractors are selected on a fair and equitable basis (and how is staff malpractice and fraud prevented)?

1.8   How are all the relevant requirements, design, performance and quality criteria accurately identified and reflected in the contracting documentation?

1.9   What measures ensure that contracts are completed on time, within budget, and to the required standards?

1.10   How is management assured that all contract and related management information is accurate, complete, up to date and appropriately routed to all affected parties?

1.11   What steps ensure that all contract payments are for work actually completed and are correctly calculated in accordance with the contract conditions?

1.12   When applicable, what measures are in place to deal effectively with price fluctuations during the course of a contract (and how is the organisation protected from unreasonable amendments to contract costings)?

1.13   Does management take steps to prevent or minimise the effects of potential contractor default?

1.14   Are all extensions of time subject to management authorisation, and what prevents unauthorised extensions?

1.15   What steps are taken to minimise contractual claims and potentially costly disputes?

1.16   What measures ensure that all contractual claims for damages against the contractor are fully assessed, accurately costed, and authorised to proceed (and how is this evidenced)?

1.17   What processes ensure that all valid/authorised damage claims are pursued, settled and correctly paid?

1.18   How does management ascertain that all contractor claims are identified, assessed and authorised (and what prevents the settlement of unauthorised or invalid claims)?

1.19   How does management ensure that all project/contract assets, plant and materials are accounted for and adequately protected from loss or damage?

1.20   How does management confirm that the anticipated benefits arising from contract activities are actually subsequently achieved, and what action is taken to address weaknesses in both the specific and general contract administration processes?

2 Detailed Issues

2.1   What specific measures would prevent any contractual activities which do not comply with the strategic direction of the organisation?

2.2   How are management and staff made aware of their responsibilities with regard to contracting activities, and has a suitable and workable procedural framework been provided for their guidance?

2.3   Are all the potential options and solutions explored as part of the appraisal process (and what prevents options being overlooked)?

2.4   What specific measures are in place to prevent and/or reveal staff mal-practice, bias or fraud?

2.5   What measures ensure that only suitably justified and authorised contracts are progressed (and what specifically prevents the establishment of unauthorised contract relationships)?

2.6   What measures ensure that all the implications and costs are identified and reviewed (i.e. including ongoing running or maintenance costs)?

2.7   How does management ensure that all relevant insurance arrangements are optimised and current throughout the life of the contract?

2.8   How does management ensure that contractors under consideration have adequate and suitably skilled resources to meet the demands of the contract?

2.9   Whenever appropriate (or when required by legislation) are fair and properly controlled tendering procedures applied, and if so, what measures ensure that all the bids are impartially reviewed?

2.10   How does management ensure that the design and specification processes are adequate in order to avoid subsequent (and potentially costly) design changes?

2.11   Are measures in place to review and specify the required design and technical standards?

2.12   What steps are taken to ensure that realistic and workable targets and milestones are established and communicated as the basis for subsequent progress monitoring?

2.13   What measures ensure that contract/project progress and the achievement of contractual obligations are accurately and effectively monitored (and how can management be assured that problems, delays and shortcomings would be promptly identified and dealt with)?

2.14   How does management ensure that adequate and appropriate resources are provided (at the correct time) by the organisation in order to fulfil its obligations?

2.15   What steps are taken to ensure that the organisation's staff resources are adequately skilled and trained to discharge their contractual and administrative obligations?

2.16   What measures ensure that key contract/project activities are adequately documented and trailed?

2.17   What measures prevent the processing of unauthorised, invalid, duplicated or incorrect contract payments (i.e. for work not completed or for goods not supplied)?

2.18   What measures ensure that all contract payments are accurately reflected in the project and main accounting systems?

2.19   What action is taken to provide for adequate and accurate channels of communication and representation (both between the employer and contractor, and between affected areas within the employing organisation)?

2.20   Are actual costs adequately monitored against authorised budgets, and would variances promptly be identified for follow-up?

2.21   If subsequent design changes prove necessary, are they subject to accurate costing and authorisation (and how is this evidenced)?

2.22   What measures are in place to avoid the excessive cost and disruption of litigation for disputed contract claims?

2.23   Whenever necessary, what measures ensure that all statutory and regulatory issues are correctly addressed (and would non-compliance promptly be identified)?

ASSESSING THE VIABILITY AND COMPETENCE OF CONTRACTORS

Irrespective of the scale of contracting activity, there is a generally universal justification for ensuring that the potential contractor is at the least capable, financially stable, and operates to recognised standards. Where the contracted activity or project is critical to the ongoing survival and operations of employing organisation, it becomes essential that a detailed assessment of contractors is conducted.

Control Objectives for Assessing the Viability and Competence of Contractors

(a) To ensure that only stable, financially secure, and appropriately qualified contractors are engaged.

(b) To ensure that contractors have sufficient and appropriately skilled resources in order to meet the contract obligations.

(c) To ensure that contractors are selected fairly and without bias or favour.

(d) To ensure that adequate security is available in case of contract breach.

(e) To ensure that the contractor has appropriate and adequate insurance cover, and that this is maintained throughout the contract.

(f) To ensure that contractors with a propensity for contractual claims are identified and avoided.

Risk and Control Issues for Assessing the Viability and Competence of Contractors

1 Key Issues

1.1 What general measures are in place to evaluate the quality of contractors bidding for work?

1.2 What specific measures does management apply to confirm the financial stability of contractors (and what is the evidence for this)?

1.3 How does management ensure the reliability and reputation of potential contractors?

1.4 What measures are applied to ensure that contractors are appropriately qualified and hold membership of the relevant professional or trade organisations?

1.5 How is management assured that potential contractors have sufficient staff (and other) resources for the duration of the contract?

1.6 What measures ensure that contractors are selected on a fair and equitable basis (and how is staff malpractice prevented in the selection process)?

1.7 How does management confirm that adequate security or surety is available in the event of a contract breach?

1.8 How does management ensure that the contractor has in place sufficient and appropriate forms of insurance cover?

1.9 What specific measures would prevent the engagement of a contractor with a reputation or propensity for making contractual claims?

2 Detailed Issues

2.1   Are accurate and up-to-date records of contractors maintained as the basis for evaluating their suitability?

2.2   How does management specifically avoid the engagement of financially unstable contractors?

2.3   How does management ensure that engaged contractors remain financially stable for the duration of the contract?

2.4   Where applicable, does management obtain guarantees from parent companies or the contractor's bankers?

2.5   How is the technical suitability of contractors assessed (and against what benchmarks)?

2.6   How does management ensure that their records of contractors are accurate, up to date and relevant?

2.7   What measures ensure that the contractor's insurance cover remains valid and effective throughout the duration of the contract period?

2.8   Is the contractor's current and projected workload taken into account when assessing their ability to meet the contract demands?

2.9   If the contractor has been previously engaged by the organisation, how does management take account of the contractor's previous performance?

MAINTAINING AN APPROVED LIST OF CONTRACTORS

In the previous section we discussed the general issues which should be taken into account when an organisation is considering the engagement of an external contractor. However, where an organisation (such as a local authority) is regularly involved in seeking contractors for similar projects, it may prove necessary for them to maintain an approved list of reliable, trustworthy and stable contractors as the basis for selection, perhaps using tendering.

This section examines the objectives and issues surrounding the maintenance of approved lists and includes such related matters as selection criteria, maintaining the accuracy of the data, and compliance with regulations.

Control Objectives for Maintaining an Approved List of Contractors

(a)   To facilitate the selection of financially stable, competent and reliable contractors.

(b)   To ensure that contractors can achieve the required quality and technical standards.

(c)   To ensure the selection of contractors with sufficient and appropriate resources.

(d)   To ensure that the selection of contractors is based on fair and realistic criteria.

(e)   To ensure that the relevant data is accurate, complete and maintained up to date.

(f)   To ensure that the data is protected from unauthorised access, amendment, and leakage.

(g)   To ensure that all regulatory and statutory requirements are addressed.

Risk and Control Issues for Maintaining an Approved List of Contractors

1 Key Issues

1.1   How does management ensure that only financially stable, reliable and technically competent contractors are selected?

1.2   What specific measures ensure that the list of approved contractors is accurate and up-to-date?

1.3   How does management consistently assess contractors for the following attributes:

- financial status
- technical competence
- previous performance
- resources?

1.4   How does management ensure that the listing and selection criteria are fair and realistic?

1.5   Having established an approved contractor list, what specific measures prevent the engagement of an unlisted contractor?

1.6   What measures are in place to ensure that only valid contractors are entered on to the approved list?

1.7   What general measures are in place to ensure that only valid and authorised data amendments (including deletions) are applied to the approved list?

1.8   How does management ensure that all the prevailing regulatory and statutory requirements are correctly addressed?

2 Detailed Issues

2.1 Has management developed and documented formal procedures for maintaining an approved list (and have these been authorised for use)?

2.2 Who is responsible for assessing contractors and recommending their inclusion on to the list (and is adequate accountability and independence demonstrated)?

2.3 What specific measures prevent the inclusion of an unauthorised entry on to the list?

2.4 Are contractors subject to progressive evaluation in order to ensure that the listed data is relevant and accurate?

2.5 Would the engagement of an unlisted contractor be subject to specific authorisation (and how would this be evidenced)?

2.6 How is the listing data protected from unauthorised access or amendment (and how does management ensure that all amendments are authorised and accurately applied)?

2.7 What specific measures prevent staff malpractice (e.g. through collusion or bias) affecting the listing of a contractor?

2.8 What steps does management take to prove the accuracy and objectivity of the listing data?

2.9 How is confidential or commercially sensitive data protected from unauthorised leakage or access?

TENDERING PROCEDURES

Where an organisation (such as a local authority) has an obligation to demonstrate both fairness and value for money when selecting contractors, it may choose to put contract bids out to tender. The principle aim is to ensure that the optimum contractor is selected for the job, having regard for economic, quality, stability, and technical issues along the way.

Tendering is not appropriate in every case, mainly because it can be costly for employer and contractor alike.

Control Objectives for Tendering Procedures

(a) To ensure that tendering is the most appropriate and cost-effective form of contractor selection in the circumstances.

(b) To ensure that the best value for money is obtained when selecting contractors.

(c) To ensure that the most suitable and appropriate form of tendering is applied and justified.

(d) To ensure that matters of contractor reliability, stability and technical competence are adequately addressed.

(e) To ensure that authorised and documented tendering procedures are in place.

(f) To ensure that the tendering process incorporates adequate competition.

(g) To ensure that the tendering process is fair and free from the personal bias or undue influence.

(h) To ensure that the tendering instructions are accurate, complete and unambiguous.

(i) To ensure that the tendering documentation is accurate and complete.

(j) To ensure that an adequate and workable tendering timetable is applied and adhered to.

(k) To ensure that the tendering process is fairly conducted and that fraud and collusion are prevented.

(l) To ensure that the tendering process is relative to the type of contract and conforms to any legislative or regulatory requirements.

(m) To ensure that appropriate internal procedures are in place to protect the recording, handling, storage and assessment of submitted tenders.

(n) To ensure that submitted tenders are adequately protected from unauthorised access, opening, amendment or leakage.

(o) To ensure that all contractors are treated equally and fairly.

(p) To ensure that all tenders are impartially and appropriately reviewed as the basis for selection.

(q) To ensure that errors, qualifications and omissions are detected and objectively dealt with.

(r) To ensure that the optimum tender is authorised for selection.

Risk and Control Issues for Tendering Procedures

1 Key Issues

1.1 How does management ensure that tendering is justified as the most appropriate method of awarding contracts?

1.2   Has management established comprehensive, documented and authorised tendering procedures (and how is compliance with these assured)?

1.3   How does management target the tendering process and ensure that only suitable and reliable contractors are considered?

1.4   How does management ensure that the tendering procedure incorporates adequate and appropriate competition?

1.5   What selection criteria has management established as the basis for tender review and selection?

1.6   What measures are in place to ensure that the tendering procedure is fair, equitable and free from personal bias and influence?

1.7   How does management ensure that the tendering process complies with any prevailing legislation or regulations (e.g. as for EU contracts)?

1.8   How does management ensure that the tendering instructions are accurate and complete, and that a workable tendering timetable is in place?

1.9   How does management ensure that the tendering documentation accurately incorporates all the required information and correctly complies with the chosen form of contract?

1.10   How does management ensure that tenders received are impartially handled, recorded and securely stored awaiting assessment?

1.11   How are tenders protected from unauthorised opening, access, amendment or leakage?

1.12   How does management guarantee that all submitted tenders are impartially and equitably reviewed and assessed?

1.13   What measures ensure that the optimum tender solution is selected and authorised to proceed (and what is the evidence of the authorisation)?

2 Detailed Issues

2.1   Does management take appropriate account of the costs of tendering when choosing the optimum method of awarding contracts?

2.2   How does management ensure that the most suitable form of tendering (for the circumstances) is adopted?

2.3   How is the authorisation for applying a tendering approach evidenced?

2.4   How does management ensure that potential contractors are financially stable, reliable and technically competent?

2.5   What specific measures has management established to prevent staff malpractice or collusion with bidding contractors?

2.6   Has management established minimum competition criteria for the tendering process, and clearly identified the key objectives of the process beforehand?

2.7   How does management ensure that all contractors submitting bids will be treated equally and fairly (for example, in responding to specific enquiries)?

2.8   Are the costs associated with the tendering process accurately assessed, justified and monitored throughout?

2.9   How is management assured that the tendering timetable is adhered to?

2.10   How does management ensure that all submitted tenders are recorded/ acknowledged on receipt, and remain secure from tampering while awaiting review?

2.11   What specific measures are applied to the opening of tenders and the recording of key data, so that all are accurately logged and accounted for?

2.12   What action does management take with late and/or incomplete tenders?

2.13   How are tenders stored and what specifically prevents unauthorised access or amendment?

2.14   How does management ensure that any additional information (e.g. that resulting from a specific contractor enquiry) is fairly circulated to all bidding contractors?

2.15   In order that all tenders can be consistently reviewed, does management clearly establish the necessary review criteria (and if so, how can they be assured that these have been taken into account for all submitted tenders)?

2.16   How does management ensure that any errors, omissions or qualifications added by contractors will be detected and effectively dealt with?

2.17   What steps are taken to ensure that the tender review committee or team is balanced, unbiased and suitably qualified for the task?

2.18   Does the review committee document its recommendations and deliberations?

2.19   In what way is management assured that all submitted tenders are fully reviewed and assessed?

2.20   Where required, are unsuccessful contractors given access to anonymous details of the other tenderers?

CONTRACTING AND TENDERING DOCUMENTATION

Here we are concerned with the accuracy, completeness, legality and security of the documentation which supports the contracted activity.

Control Objectives for Contracting and Tendering Documentation

> (a) To ensure that all stages of contract administration are supported by accurate, complete, and legible documentation.
>
> (b) To prevent and minimise the disruption, delay, and additional costs caused by documentation errors and omissions.
>
> (c) To ensure that all contract documentation is prepared in accordance with the relevant form of contract and regulations.
>
> (d) To ensure that all documentation is securely stored and adequately protected from loss, damage, unauthorised amendment or leakage.
>
> (e) To ensure that the location of all documents can be promptly traced.
>
> (f) To ensure that only authorised and valid amendments are correctly applied to contract documents.
>
> (g) To ensure that only current versions of documents are utilised.
>
> (h) To ensure that all supporting information is correctly incorporated and to the required standard.
>
> (i) To ensure that bonds, securities, completion certificates, correspondence, etc. are accounted for and securely filed.
>
> (j) To prevent the premature or accidental disposal of contract documentation.
>
> (k) To ensure that the status of all contracts can be determined promptly and supported by the relevant documents.
>
> (l) To ensure that all relevant documents are retained and remain available for the required period.

Risk and Control Issues for Contracting and Tendering Documentation

1 Key Issues

1.1 How does management ensure that all the required contract documentation is generated at the appropriate time?

1.2 What measures are taken to ensure that documents are accurate, complete and legible?

1.3 What specific action does management take to avoid and detect errors and omissions?

1.4 What steps are in place to ensure that all relevant contract documentation is produced in the appropriate form and to the required standard?

1.5   What measures does management take to ensure that contract documents are securely stored and protected from loss, damage, and unauthorised access?

1.6   How are contract documents filed, and are they able to be traced promptly?

1.7   Where it is necessary to apply amendments to contract documents, how can management be assured that only authorised and valid changes are applied?

1.8   Where several versions of a document may exist, what steps ensure that the correct and valid version is utilised and circulated?

1.9   How does management ensure that, where necessary, documents are produced to the required technical or professional standard (i.e. as for drawings or technical specifications)?

1.10   How does management ensure that documents with a financial or specific significance (such as bonds, or securities) are adequately protected and kept secure until release?

1.11   What specific measures would prevent the premature or accidental destruction/disposal of contract documents?

1.12   What is the procedure for retaining contract documentation securely and for the appropriate period?

1.13   Does management maintain records which accurately indicate the current status of all contracting activities (and how is the accuracy and integrity of such records assured)?

2 Detailed Issues

2.1   How does management accurately identify all the documentation requirements?

2.2   Would errors and omissions be detected prior to the release of tendering and contract documents?

2.3   Where errors are noted, what steps are taken to ensure that all the affected documents are recalled and accurate replacements distributed to all affected parties?

2.4   What is the procedure for tracing and accounting for all copies of contract documentation?

2.5   What specifically prevents any unauthorised (or additional) copies being taken?

2.6   Would the loss or misplacement of contract documentation be capable of prompt detection?

2.7   How does management ensure that all copy sets are complete and legible throughout?

2.8 Are document storage conditions suitable for long-term retention?

2.9 How does management confirm that amendments are correctly applied?

2.10 What measures ensure that amended documents are correctly circulated and received?

2.11 What physically happens to outdated document copies (i.e. those that have been subject to subsequent amendment)?

2.12 How does management monitor that all bonds, securities, completion certificates, etc. are accounted for and traceable?

SELECTION AND LETTING OF CONTRACTS

Contracts represent the balancing of risks between the parties, and these are expressed in the form of documented rights and obligations. Selecting the most appropriate form of contract is often crucial in ensuring a fair balance of risks and rights, and this section examines the related issues. Additionally, it is necessary to ensure that the chosen contract is correctly enacted.

Control Objectives for Selection and Letting of Contracts

> (a) To ensure that the most appropriate form of contract is utilised and that risks are fairly balanced between parties.
>
> (b) To ensure that the optimum contract pricing method is selected for the circumstances.
>
> (c) To ensure that the organisation is adequately protected in the event of contractor breach.
>
> (d) To ensure that the contract conditions offer suitable remedies.
>
> (e) To ensure the accurate and correct completion of all contract documentation.
>
> (f) To aim to settle disputes within the contract conditions by mutual agreement.
>
> (g) To ensure that stable and reliable contractors are selected to be parties to the contract.
>
> (h) To ensure that all the key requirements, timings, and obligations are defined in the contract.

> (i)   To ensure that all contractual relationships are authorised.
>
> (j)   To ensure that contracts are correctly and legally enacted.
>
> (k)   To ensure that all applicable European and international legal implications are correctly addressed.
>
> (l)   To ensure that all contract documentation is securely stored and adequately protected from loss, theft or damage.

Risk and Control Issues for Selection and Letting of Contracts

1 Key Issues

1.1   How does management ensure that the most suitable and appropriate form of contract is selected for the circumstances?

1.2   How is management assured that the relevant contract clauses represent a fair balance of the associated risks between the parties?

1.3   What specific measures ensure that the optimum contract pricing method is applied?

1.4   What steps does management take to ensure that contracts provide adequate protection for the organisation in the event of contractor breach?

1.5   What measures ensure that contract documentation is accurately, correctly and fully completed?

1.6   In order to avoid the potentially high costs of litigation, how does management ensure that contracts facilitate alternative dispute remedies (e.g. arbitration)?

1.7   What general measures are applied to ensure that only reliable, stable and suitably qualified contractors are engaged?

1.8   How is management assured that all the relevant (and specific) requirements, timings, and obligations are appropriately and accurately incorporated into the contract?

1.9   Are all contracts subject to management authorisation (and if so, how is this evidenced)?

1.10 What steps are taken to ensure that contracts are legally enforceable and correctly enacted?

1.11 When applicable, how does management ensure that all the possible European and international legal implications are satisfactorily addressed?

1.12 What measures are in place to protect contract documentation from loss, damage, destruction, or theft?

2 Detailed Issues

2.1 How does management prevent the disruption and possible additional costs associated with utilising an inappropriate form of contract?

2.2 Are standard forms of contract ever utilised, and if so are they confirmed as offering the optimum remedy?

2.3 How does management assess the contractual requirements for a given project or scenario?

2.4 Are contracts subject to review by appropriately qualified legal experts (and what is the evidence for this)?

2.5 What steps are in place to ensure that documentation errors are effectively and promptly detected prior to the relevant contract being enacted?

2.6 What specifically prevents unauthorised or invalid contract relationships being formalised?

2.7 Where necessary, how does management ensure that contract negotiations are proficiently and adequately conducted?

PERFORMANCE MONITORING

All contracts are created for a purpose, and they will only exist where an individual or organisation has identified and justified a particular need, perhaps expressed through a number of objectives, criteria or targets. To achieve the identified objectives, the project and contract must be monitored for progress according to plan. In this section we take account of the issues for the establishment and operation of a performance monitoring environment.

Control Objectives for Performance Monitoring

(a) To ensure that all the relevant contracting and business-related objectives are fulfilled.

(b) To ensure that the contract is successfully completed on time and within budget.

(c) To ensure that quality, technical and workmanship targets are met.

(d) To ensure that key stages and milestones are identified and achieved.

(e) To enable the monitoring and assessment of contractor and consultant performances against their contractual obligations.

(f) To ensure that all contractual obligations are correctly discharged.

> (g) To ensure that all key contract events are promptly identified and reacted to.
>
> (h) To aid the effective management of the contract or project.
>
> (i) To enable the assessment of the relevance and effectiveness of the contracting management environment as the basis for identifying weaknesses to address subsequently.
>
> (j) To ensure that any apparent problems can be dealt with promptly and effectively.
>
> (k) To ensure that remedy or redress is promptly sought wherever relevant.

Risk and Control Issues for Performance Monitoring

1 Key Issues

1.1 How is management made aware of contract progress and the achievement of key stages and the underlying objectives?

1.2 What measures alert management if the contract or project is not going to be completed on time or within budget?

1.3 Would management be advised promptly of problems or delays (and how is this evidenced)?

1.4 How does management monitor that quality, technical and workmanship standards are being achieved?

1.5 How does management assess objectively the performance of a contractor or consultant during a contract (and how would management be alerted to shortcomings, delays, or other problems)?

1.6 What measures ensure that all contract obligations are being appropriately achieved?

1.7 What measures ensure that management would be made aware of the following possible contract events:

- extensions of time
- contractual claims or contractor disputes
- requirement for design changes or modifications
- problems with providing adequate resources?

1.8 How does management ensure the accuracy and reliability of performance information and reporting?

1.9 Where weaknesses, problems or shortcomings are apparent, how does management ensure that such data is complete and that appropriate corrective action has been taken in each case?

2 Detailed Issues

2.1 Has action been taken to identify accurately all the key and critical stages of the contract, so that progress can be subsequently monitored?

2.2 Have realistic budgets been established for the contract (and constituent stages) to enable subsequent comparisons with actual costs?

2.3 Would management be alerted to shortfalls in anticipated quality or workmanship standards?

2.4 What specific measures are in place to ensure that all reported problems, delays, etc. are actually followed up and effectively addressed?

2.5 Where performance shortfalls have a contractual implication, how does management ensure that the appropriate contract remedy is applied and concluded?

2.6 Are performance shortcomings and related administrative problems noted as the basis for subsequently revising and improving the quality of the contract management environment?

VALUING WORK FOR INTERIM PAYMENTS

Where a contract is set to run over a prolonged period (such as for a building or civil engineering project) the contract terms may specify the circumstances for interim or staged payments. This section considers the related objectives and issues.

Control Objectives for Valuing Work for Interim Payments

(a) To ensure that payments are made only for work actually completed and goods and services received.

(b) To ensure that payments are made only where goods and services are to the required standard and quality.

(c) To ensure that all payments are subject to suitable prior authorisation.

(d) To ensure that payments relate only to contracted activities.

(e) To ensure that work completed is accurately measured and correctly calculated using the defined methods and prices.

(f) To ensure that work completed or goods received are adequately supported by documentation in accordance with contract conditions.

> (g) To ensure that accounts are accurately settled within the timescales stipulated within the contract.
>
> (h) To ensure that all non-standard charges (e.g. for variations) are valid and supported.
>
> (i) To ensure that, where applicable, the correct value of retention is calculated and applied to interim accounts.

Risk and Control Issues for Valuing Work for Interim Payments

1 Key Issues

1.1 What measures ensure that all interim accounts are valid and relate to work actually completed and goods received?

1.2 What specific measures would prevent payments being made for work that is substandard or incomplete?

1.3 Are all payments subject to prior authorisation (and what is the evidence for this)?

1.4 How does management ensure that all contractual obligations have been met before any payments are made to contractors?

1.5 How is management assured that chargeable work has been correctly measured in accordance with the methods defined in the contract?

1.6 What measures are in place to ensure that interim accounts are accurately calculated, and that the prices used are valid and agreed?

1.7 Whenever applicable, how does management ensure that interim accounts are settled within the timescales defined in the contract?

1.8 How does management ensure that all non-standard charges and costs are valid, authorised, and correctly supported by appropriate documentation (prior to settlement)?

1.9 What measures provide assurance that retention values are accurately calculated and applied to interim accounts?

2 Detailed Issues

2.1 What specific measures would detect invalid charges for substandard or incomplete goods/services?

2.2 How does management ensure that all goods and services are provided to the defined quality and workmanship standards?

2.3   Are interim accounts correctly supported by documentary evidence, and is this examined and confirmed as correct prior to account settlement?

2.4   What measures would prevent the settlement of duplicated accounts or charges for previously costed work elements?

2.5   What specific measures would detect pricing or invoice compilation errors?

2.6   Is the calculation of retention values confirmed as being in accordance with the relevant contract conditions?

CONTRACTOR'S FINAL ACCOUNT

Upon completion of a contracted activity, the contractors will submit their final account. This may be the only account rendered or it may be preceded by previous interim accounts (as discussed in the previous section). The employer will wish to ensure the accuracy and relevance of the account, and to confirm that the effects of prior payments, outstanding claims and retained values have been accurately accounted for.

Control Objectives for Contractor's Final Account

(a)   To ensure that only valid, accurate, and authorised accounts are paid.

(b)   To ensure that accounts relate only to work actually completed or goods/services provided to the required standard.

(c)   To ensure that all accounts are costed in accordance with the measurement methods and prices contained in the contract.

(d)   To ensure that the contractor has met all contract obligations prior to account settlement.

(e)   To ensure that previous (interim) account payments have been correctly taken into account.

(f)   To ensure that retention values have been accurately calculated and applied.

(g)   To ensure that price fluctuations have been correctly calculated in accordance with the agreed formula base.

(h)   To ensure that the values of any outstanding contractual claims are valid and have been accurately incorporated.

(i)   To ensure that charges in respect of variations or modifications are valid, authorised, and correctly calculated.

(j)   To ensure that, where applicable, values of liquidated damages are correctly incorporated.

> (k) To ensure that all taxation matters are correctly addressed.
>
> (l) To ensure that any agreed damages due to the organisation have been deducted.
>
> (m) To ensure that all the key contract events reflected in the account are adequately supported by documentation.
>
> (n) To ensure that the account is settled within any agreed period stipulated in the contract.

Risk and Control Issues for Contractor's Final Account

1 Key Issues

1.1 How does the organisation confirm that all accounts are valid and accurate before settlement?

1.2 Are all contract accounts subject to formal authorisation prior to payment (and how is this evidenced)?

1.3 How does management ensure that goods and services reflected in the contractor's accounts have actually been provided?

1.4 How does management ensure that the contractor's accounts are correctly costed in accordance with the contract conditions?

1.5 How does management ensure that the contractor has satisfactorily met all contract obligations prior to settlement of accounts?

1.6 What measures are in place to ensure that retention and maintenance values are correctly calculated and withheld from the final account?

1.7 Where applicable, how does management ensure that price fluctuations during the course of the contract period have been accurately adjusted on the accounts in accordance with the agreed fluctuation formula?

1.8 What measures would ensure that the values of agreed contractual claims and damages due to the organisation have been correctly adjusted on the accounts?

1.9 How does management ensure that the charges for variations and modifications are valid, accurate, and relate only to agreed and authorised changes?

1.10 What measures are in place to confirm the accuracy and validity of VAT and other taxation calculations?

1.11 How does management ensure that all contractors' accounts are settled within the periods stipulated in the relevant contracts?

2 Detailed Issues

2.1   How are account queries, errors, and irregularities identified, brought to the attention of the contractor, and satisfactorily resolved?

2.2   What specific measures would prevent the payment of any unauthorised or invalid contractor's account?

2.3   Are all elements of contractors' accounts examined for their validity and accuracy prior to payment (and how are these checks evidenced)?

2.4   How is management assured that all the relevant goods and services meet the required quality and workmanship standards before account settlement (and what action is taken on the costs relating to any substandard elements)?

2.5   What action is taken to confirm the correct application of the agreed work measurement method?

2.6   How does management verify that the accounts are based on the agreed prices contained in the contract?

2.7   Are all the key account elements supported by accurate and reliable documentation (i.e. as a means to confirm the validity and accuracy of charges)?

2.8   Would the failure of the contractor to meet all contract obligations result in a suitable adjustment being applied to the account (where this is permitted under the terms of the contract)?

2.9   How does management confirm that previous (interim) account payments have been correctly taken into account in the final account balance?

2.10 Where retention (or maintenance) values have been deducted, what measures will ensure that these values are eventually paid over to the contractor at the appropriate time?

2.11 How would disputes arising from the final account be fairly and objectively resolved?

2.12 How does management confirm the accuracy of price fluctuation adjustments (e.g. are all such entries confirmed using a formula model)?

2.13 How does management ensure that the values of a contractor's claims added to the account are valid, authorised and correctly calculated?

2.14 What specific measures would prevent the duplicated settlement of a contractor's claims?

2.15 How does management ensure that any liquidated damage liability is identified and adjusted on the account (and how is this accurately calculated)?

2.16 What steps are taken to code accurately and enter the contractor's account on to the accounting system?

2.17 Are all key contract events (e.g. staged completions, variations, deliveries) adequately supported by accurate and complete documentary trails?

REVIEW OF PROJECT OUTTURN AND PERFORMANCE

Where a project (contracted or otherwise) has run its course, it can be beneficial to conduct a post-completion review of the project, primarily to ensure that all the objectives established at the outset have actually been achieved. Additionally, where the organisation is regularly involved in conducting such projects, it can also be useful to examine how the project progressed and the extent to which the contract/project management framework contributed to the process. There may be important administrative and control issues arising from such a post-completion review which can lead to the subsequent improvement and refinement of relevant procedures so that future projects can be more effectively managed.

Control Objectives for Review of Project Outturn and Performance

(a) To ensure that all the contract and project objectives were actually achieved.

(b) To ensure that all aspects of the contract and the contractor's performance are reviewed against expectations, requirements, and standards.

(c) To ensure that the contract management procedures and policies are reviewed so that they can be progressively improved.

(d) To ensure that all contract obligations have been satisfactorily met.

(e) To ensure that the contract was completed on time and within budget, and to note reasons for failures and shortcomings.

(f) To ensure that the accounting and management information systems are assessed for their accuracy, efficiency, and reliability.

(g) To ensure that all key contract events were effectively and efficiently handled.

(h) To ensure that all key contract events were supported by adequate and accurate documentary trails.

(i) To ensure that all non-standard events (e.g. variations and extensions of time) were suitably assessed, justified, and authorised.

(j) To ensure that all the relevant legal and regulatory issues were satisfactorily addressed and that the most appropriate form of contract was applied in the circumstances.

(k) To ensure that the performance of contractors and consultants are fully assessed.

(l) To ensure the organisation's resources and staff are reviewed in light of their performance during the contract, so that administrative improvements can be made.

(m) To ensure that all conclusions and action points are reported, agreed by senior management and subsequently authorised.

(n) To ensure that any outstanding contractual obligations are identified and resolved.

(o) To ensure that staff training and development needs are identified and addressed.

Risk and Control Issues for Review of Project Outturn and Performance

1 Key Issues

1.1 How does management confirm that all the contract objectives were fully achieved?

1.2 How does management accurately assess how a contract was conducted as a means of identifying problems and shortcomings for their attention?

1.3 How does management obtain assurance that existing contract management procedures and practices are valid, authorised, justified, effective, and are being correctly complied with?

1.4 How is management assured that contracts are completed on time and within budget (and what action do they take in the event of a shortfall)?

1.5 Does management assess the quality, accuracy, efficiency, and reliability of accounting and management information systems as the basis for their decision making?

1.6 Does management undertake an assessment of the accuracy and completeness of the contract documentation system?

1.7 How does management obtain the assurance that all non-standard contract events were authorised, justified, and fulfilled?

1.8 Does management confirm the acceptability and relevance of the chosen form of contract?

1.9 How does management confirm that all the relevant legal and regulatory issues were appropriately addressed?

1.10 Is the performance of contractors (and consultants) assessed against the defined expectations (especially where they may be considered for involvement in future contracts)?

1.11 How does management ensure that the organisation's staff and resources were efficiently utilised (and how would shortcomings and problems be addressed)?

1.12 What measures would highlight potential staff training and development needs (and how would these be addressed)?

1.13 How does management ensure that all shortcomings, problems, and potential improvements will be highlighted and appropriately addressed so that future contracts are more efficiently, securely and effectively administered?

1.14 How does management ensure that all outstanding contractual obligations would be identified and acted on?

2 Detailed Issues

2.1 What measures would ensure that any failed objectives or obligations would be identified and addressed (and is there evidence that corrective action has been agreed and taken)?

2.2 How does management ensure that all outstanding contractor obligations are identified and effectively followed up?

2.3 Are existing procedures reviewed for their relevance and contribution to efficiency and control?

2.4 How does management identify redundant, unnecessary or costly procedures (and what action is generally taken to continually improve the quality of procedures and policies)?

2.5 How does management ensure that project reviews are objectively and independently conducted (as a means of improving their potential value)?

2.6 How does management ensure that all the necessary and prescribed authorisations are in place and valid?

2.7 What specific measures would prevent unauthorised, fraudulent or invalid contracting activities or events?

2.8 Does management positively confirm that the chosen form of contract was the appropriate and optimum solution in the circumstances?

2.9 Are outstanding legal issues assessed by a suitably qualified person, so that they can be addressed and resolved in future?

2.10 Where lists of approved contractors are maintained, what measures ensure that these records are accurately updated with the results of actual contract performance reviews?

2.11 What specific measures would prevent the re-engagement of unsatisfactory contractors (i.e. based on a review of their performance during previous contracts)?

2.12 Is senior management informed of the results of the contract/project review, and how are action points confirmed as being satisfactorily addressed?

NOTE

1. For more detail on wider contract auditing see Chambers, A. D. and Rand, G. V. (1994). *Auditing Contracts*. Pitman, London.

8

Auditing Operations and Resource Management

INTRODUCTION

In this chapter we consider the operational auditing dimensions of production and manufacturing as being representative of operations in general. Although we have chosen to focus our discussion on matters relevant to production and manufacturing, there are, of course, other types of activities that could legitimately form the basis of an organisation's primary operations. For example, either the provision of a specific service to customers or retailing.

While accepting that this chapter is deliberately focused, there are many points in common between one type of operation and another. For example, they normally involve the following aspects:

- identifying an underlying requirement and endeavouring to cost-effectively exploit it
- ensuring that suitable and adequate resources (human and material) are brought together at the right time and place to fulfil the identified requirements
- ensuring that the operation is conducted safely, economically, efficiently, effectively, to the required standard, and in accordance with any prevailing regulations and laws; and so on.

Consult other chapters for discussion of related issues (refer to the Contents and the Index). For instance, just in time (JIT) management, which may be applied by management to operations and production, is looked at in Chapter 17.

First we shall consider the systems and functions that are likely to constitute this area of activity. Secondly, we shall examine each of these component functions and highlight the relative control objectives and the risk and control issues (divided into key issues and detailed issues) arising from the various constituent activities.

SYSTEM/FUNCTION COMPONENTS OF A PRODUCTION/MANUFACTURING ENVIRONMENT

We have chosen to use an essentially *functional* approach to define the production and manufacturing audit universe, which gives us the following possible breakdown of the key functions, systems or activities:

- planning and production control
- facilities, plant and equipment
- personnel
- materials and energy
- quality control
- safety
- environmental issues
- law and regulatory compliance
- maintenance.

The subject of just in time management techniques is not specifically addressed in this chapter, but see Chapter 17.

CONTROL OBJECTIVES AND RISK AND CONTROL ISSUES

We shall now examine the control objectives and the related risk and control issues for each of the production/manufacturing areas listed above. This data can be used within the format of the Standard Audit Programme Guides (SAPGs) looked at in Chapter 3. To save space we have stripped out the format and focused on the objectives to be stated and the questions to be asked and have not presented them within the SAPG format.

PLANNING AND PRODUCTION CONTROL

Here we are generally concerned with matters of planning and multi-discipline co-ordination so as to contribute to the efficient and economic use of production facilities.

Control Objectives for Planning and Production Control

(a) To ensure that production and manufacturing requirements are accurately determined, authorised, effectively communicated and suitably planned for.

(b) To ensure that adequate facilities and resources are made available at the appropriate time in order to meet the agreed production and manufacturing obligations.

(c) To ensure that the required quantity of products is manufactured to the required quality standards.

(d) To ensure that the actions of all affected departments and functions are adequately co-ordinated to achieve the defined objectives.

(e) To ensure that production resources and facilities are efficiently utilised and that waste is avoided/minimised.

(f) To ensure that the necessary production equipment is fully operational and operated efficiently.

(g) To ensure that production staff are suitably trained and experienced in order to maximise their contribution.

(h) To ensure that production downtime is minimised, suitably monitored and reacted to.

(i) To ensure that all materials, resources and finished goods are accurately accounted for.

(j) To ensure that production activities are effectively monitored, reported to management and shortfalls and problems are promptly detected and resolved.

(k) To ensure that all relevant legislation, health and safety and other regulations are complied with.

(l) To ensure that actual production plant efficiency and performance are adequately monitored for management information and action.

Risk and Control Issues for Planning and Production Control

1 Key Issues

1.1 How does management ensure that the production and manufacturing requirements are accurately defined and suitably authorised?

1.2 What mechanisms ensure that authorised production/manufacturing requirements are effectively communicated to all affected parties, and that suitable plans are agreed and implemented to meet the defined obligations?

1.3 What processes ensure that all the required resources and facilities (e.g. materials, staff, machines, knowledge) are available to meet the required production obligations?

1.4 How are actual progress and use of production facilities effectively monitored and problems, shortfalls and delays promptly detected and corrected?

1.5 What measures ensure that the required quantity of products is actually manufactured and accounted for?

1.6 How does management ensure that the items produced conform to the required quality standards, and that defect rates are effectively monitored?

1.7 What measures does management take to minimise and avoid disruption of production caused by machine breakdown, poorly experienced staff, and absence of raw materials and components?

1.8 Is the utilisation of all resources (materials and workforce) fully accounted for and would waste be identified promptly and appropriate action taken? (How is this evidenced?)

1.9 Is management kept informed of overall production performance and efficiency, and what evidence is there of corrective action being taken to address shortcomings, etc.?

1.10 What mechanisms ensure that compliance with all the prevailing legislation and regulations is confirmed?

2 Detailed Issues

2.1 Are all amendments to customer orders, production requirements, forecasts, etc. promptly and accurately identified and reported in order to modify the relevant production activities?

2.2 What measures are in place to ensure that adequate and accurate information flows are established for all affected parties?

2.3 How would uneconomic or unrealistic production runs be prevented?

2.4 How would unauthorised production activity be prevented or identified?

2.5 How does management ascertain that the practical manufacturing implications of new product lines have been identified, assessed and planned for?

2.6 Are plant utilisation records maintained and would surplus capacity be identified and reacted to?

2.7 How does management ensure that the layout of the production line maximises efficiency and avoids unnecessary movements and processes?

2.8 What processes ensure the correct flow of raw materials to the production area?

2.9 Are materials and components adequately protected from loss and damage in the production areas?

2.10 What steps are taken to avoid/minimise machine failures and downtime?

2.11 Is downtime recorded, attributed and effectively monitored by management (and how is this evidenced)?

2.12 What mechanisms ensure that the skills of the workforce are adequately maintained in line with the current requirements?

2.13 Are staff skills suitably balanced to provide adequate cover during holidays, etc.?

2.14 Would production delays be promptly detected?

2.15 Are all finished goods accounted for and trailed into the stock control system?

2.16 Are all damaged, spoilt, scrap and rejected items identified, authorised and accounted for?

2.17 How can management be assured that all production activities are accurately costed and that reliable product costings are generated?

2.18 Would uneconomic products/production runs be prevented or promptly detected?

2.19 Are machine utilisation and performance statistics accurately produced, circulated and reacted to?

2.20 Are employee productivity levels effectively monitored?

2.21 Does management periodically evaluate the adequacy of production facilities?

2.22 How does management confirm compliance with all the relevant heath and safety regulations?

2.23 How does management remain aware of the relevant regulations and keep up to date?

2.24 How would violations of regulations be detected?

2.25 Have realistic and workable contingency and disaster plans been established, and are they regularly tested for their effectiveness?

2.26 How is the accuracy of data input from other systems (e.g. sales orders, planning) confirmed?

2.27 How is the accuracy of data output to other systems (e.g. time recording to payroll, product accounting) confirmed?

FACILITIES, PLANT AND EQUIPMENT

This section addresses the requirement to provide adequate resources to facilitate the production processes, and to take proper account of them. Matters relative to the acquisition, installation and maintenance of plant and equipment are included. In addition, accounting aspects together with health and safety considerations are incorporated.

Control Objectives for Facilities, Plant and Equipment

> (a) To ensure that appropriate and sufficient facilities, plant and equipment are provided in order to support the achievement of defined business objectives.

(b)   To ensure that buildings provide adequate, efficient, and well laid out working spaces complete with all the necessary services.

(c)   To ensure that plant and equipment are properly maintained in working order, operated correctly by sufficiently trained staff and in accordance with the manufacturers' directions and recommended loadings.

(d)   To ensure that the production area is logically and safely laid out in order to maximise operational efficiency.

(e)   To ensure that machinery and equipment is correctly installed, configured, calibrated, tested and maintained in order to avoid the disruption of the production processes.

(f)   To ensure that the necessary ancillary equipment (e.g. cranes, conveyor systems, environmental systems) are provided and fully operational.

(g)   To ensure that machine loadings and performance are recorded and monitored in order to achieve the optimum safe utilisation of plant.

(h)   To ensure that all plant and equipment is adequately identified and accounted for.

(i)   To ensure that all usage, operational and overhead costs are accurately identified and reflected in the accounts.

(j)   To ensure that all plant, equipment and facilities are adequately protected from loss, damage and deterioration.

(k)   To ensure that plant and equipment requirements are monitored in accordance with current and future trends, and that acquisition of new equipment is appropriately assessed and authorised.

(l)   To ensure that all the relevant health and safety issues and regulations are satisfactorily addressed.

(m)   To ensure that disposals and transfers of plant and equipment are justified, authorised and correctly reflected in the accounts.

(n)   To ensure that staff facilities (e.g. washrooms) are adequate and of an appropriate quality.

Risk and Control Issues for Facilities, Plant and Equipment

1 Key Issues

1.1   How does management ensure that production facilities, plant and equipment are (and will remain) adequate to fulfil the defined business and operational needs?

1.2   How would facility and equipment shortcomings or surpluses be promptly identified and addressed?

1.3   What measures are in place to ensure the optimum efficiency of the production facility layout, and how are problems identified and resolved?

1.4   What steps are in place to ensure that equipment is operated correctly, appropriately maintained, and effectively utilised?

1.5   How is management made aware of production downtime caused by failure of or problems with plant and equipment, and what action is taken to avoid and minimise such disruptions?

1.6   How is all plant and equipment appropriately accounted for and correctly reflected in the accounts?

1.7   Are all acquisitions and disposals of plant and equipment subject to adequate prior assessment and authorisation, and how is this evidenced?

1.8   What measures are in place to ensure that all the relevant usage, operational and overhead costs associated with the production facilities are identified and correctly accounted for?

1.9   How does management ensure that all the relevant prevailing health and safety regulations are fully complied with?

2 Detailed Issues

2.1   How does management accurately and reliably assess the production facility, plant and equipment requirements, and ensure that future needs are both identified and planned for?

2.2   How does management avoid both shortfalls and excesses of facilities and equipment?

2.3   Has management prepared and tested contingency arrangements in the event of a major disruption to production facilities (e.g. a serious fire)?

2.4   Has appropriate, adequate, and current insurance cover been provided?

2.5   Does the production facility layout allow for the logical flow of goods and avoid unnecessary handling, etc.?

2.6   Are facilities maintained in an orderly and clean manner, and have all potential dangers and debris been removed?

2.7   How do the facilities conform to the requirements of the relevant regulations?

2.8   How does management monitor that the appropriate environmental systems (e.g. heating, lighting, air conditioning) are operating correctly, efficiently and in accordance with defined standards?

2.9   Have sufficient and appropriate staff facilities been provided and do they comply with relevant regulations and standards?

2.10   Have safe and realistic working loads been determined for production plant and equipment, and how does management ensure that actual operations conform with the required levels?

2.11   Has management implemented an ongoing programme of equipment maintenance that complies with the manufacturers recommendations, and how do they monitor that the programme is correctly conducted?

2.12   How does management ensure that all equipment is correctly installed, configured, and calibrated?

2.13   Is downtime recorded at an individual machine level, and would problems with specific equipment be actively pursued with the manufacturers (e.g. through service and warranty arrangements)?

2.14   Are standard operating procedures defined and documented for all production equipment?

2.15   How are all relevant staff made aware of the correct, standard and safe methods of operation, and how is their compliance monitored?

2.16   Are measures in place to detect and resolve instances of the inappropriate or unsafe operation of equipment?

2.17   What mechanisms ensure that production staff are appropriately and adequately trained to perform their duties efficiently and safely?

2.18   Would breaches of the defined safety codes be identified and reacted to?

2.19   Is sufficient ancillary equipment (e.g. conveyors, cranes, handling devices, specialist tools) provided and maintained?

2.20   Have accurate and appropriate performance monitoring facilities been established, and what evidence is there that the data is reviewed and actioned by management?

2.21   How does management confirm that all the production assets (e.g. plant and equipment) recorded in the accounts are valid and available for use?

2.22   What mechanisms prevent the unauthorised or premature disposal of plant and equipment?

2.23   What precautions are taken to prevent loss of, damage to, or deterioration of plant and equipment?

2.24   Would failures to comply with health and safety regulations be detected so that appropriate action could be taken?

2.25   How is the accuracy of data input from other systems (e.g. production planning) confirmed?

2.26 How is the accuracy of data output to other systems (e.g. fixed assets) confirmed?

PERSONNEL

Irrespective of the sophistication of the available facilities and equipment, the success or otherwise of a production process will inevitably be dependent on the extent and quality of the human resources. Unless staff are suitably experienced, trained, organised, supervised and equipped, there is the attendant danger that the overall process will be uneconomic or technically deficient. Our focus here is on production personnel issues, the wider implications of personnel and training are dealt with in Chapter 11.

Control Objectives for Personnel

(a) To ensure that adequate and appropriately trained staff are provided in order to fulfil the current and future production objectives.

(b) To ensure that production staff are appropriately organised, experienced and qualified to satisfactorily address the production objectives.

(c) To ensure that staff resources are efficiently and cost-effectively employed.

(d) To ensure that staff performance is effectively monitored and short-comings are detected and addressed.

(e) To ensure that production staff are adequately supervised so that the work is undertaken in the relevant timescale and to the required standard.

(f) To ensure that non-productive time is minimised.

(g) To ensure that all hours worked are correctly recorded, costed and accounted for.

(h) To ensure that employees on hourly rates are paid, at the correct rate, only for hours actually worked.

(i) To ensure that production employees are provided with relevant and sufficient equipment, tools, clothing, etc. to enable them effectively and safely to discharge their responsibilities.

(j) To ensure that all production employees (including temporary and casual staff) are stable, reliable and confirmed as suitably experienced prior to engagement.

> (k) To ensure that staff turnover and absenteeism are monitored and minimised.
>
> (l) To ensure that communication between management and staff is effectively handled and aims to foster good labour relations.

Risk and Control Issues for Personnel

1 Key Issues

1.1 What mechanisms are in place to ensure that production staffing requirements are accurately determined and procured?

1.2 How does management ensure that the required production demands will be met through the provision of sufficient staff?

1.3 How is management assured that the production workforce is appropriately and sufficiently skilled to meet the production objectives?

1.4 How does management ensure that staff resources are efficiently and cost-effectively utilised?

1.5 What mechanisms are in place to monitor production staff performance, and are shortcomings identified and suitably dealt with?

1.6 What processes ensure that goods are produced within the defined timescales and to the required quality standards?

1.7 What steps are taken to ensure that hours worked are correctly recorded and accounted for?

1.8 How does management ensure that hourly paid employees are paid only for true productive time?

1.9 How does management ensure that the workforce is adequately trained to meet the production demands and targets?

1.10 How is the engagement of unsuitable, unstable and poorly experienced staff prevented?

1.11 What steps are taken to foster and maintain good labour relations with the production employees and their representatives, and are changes in conditions and practices adequately communicated, discussed and agreed?

2 Detailed Issues

2.1 How are the current and future production staffing requirements determined, and how can management be assured of the accuracy and reliability of these data?

2.2 Are the skill requirements for production staff accurately determined and how are these data used to ensure that the workforce skills are adequately maintained?

2.3 Are staff suitably skilled to enable the effective coverage of absences, holiday periods, etc.?

2.4 What mechanisms prevent undue levels of unproductive time (e.g. during retooling)?

2.5 Are staff and supervisors appropriately organised and structured to facilitate the allocation of responsibilities and adequate lines of communication?

2.6 Are all staff aware of their explicit responsibilities, and how is this achieved?

2.7 Would surplus or underused staff resources be promptly identified and redeployed?

2.8 Would failures to meet timescale and/or quality targets be promptly identified, and how is this evidenced?

2.9 How is management assured that all the required resources are made available at the appropriate time so as to avoid/minimise non-productive time?

2.10 What measures ensure that hourly paid staff are paid only for the hours actually worked and at the appropriate rate?

2.11 What mechanisms ensure that overtime payments are valid, authorised and correctly accounted for through the payroll and accounting systems?

2.12 What measures prevent the fraudulent manipulation of time sheets?

2.13 Does management ensure that evening and night shifts are adequately supervised?

2.14 How does management ensure that all the required equipment, tools, safety devices, etc. are provided, and that staff comply with the prevailing health and safety regulations?

2.15 Are the previous employment records of staff confirmed as correct and satisfactory prior to engagement, and would shortcomings be adequately identified?

2.16 Is staff turnover a problem, and what measures are in place to monitor and minimise turnover of employees?

2.17 Is management monitoring absenteeism and taking appropriate action against persistent offenders or where production objectives are being adversely affected?

2.18 How is the accuracy of data input from other systems (e.g. production planning) confirmed?

2.19 How is the accuracy of data output to other systems (e.g. payroll, product accounting) confirmed?

MATERIALS AND ENERGY

The efficiency of the production process relies partly on the availability of the right components in the right place at the right time. If the organisation is to avoid both the unnecessary costs of holding excess stocks and the disruptions caused by inadequate levels of available material, effective stock resourcing and allocation mechanisms need to be established. Chapter 10 incorporates separate sections on related subjects such as stock control, and warehousing and storage.

This chapter also incorporates issues relative to the use of energy, especially the application of an economically viable energy strategy, so that costs are contained and waste is avoided.

Control Objectives for Materials and Energy

(a) To ensure that adequate supplies of the appropriate materials are available at the correct time to support production requirements.

(b) To avoid or minimise any disruptions caused by an inadequate flow of materials through the production facility.

(c) To ensure that all materials are protected from damage and in a suitable condition for production purposes.

(d) To ensure that all materials are fully accounted for.

(e) To ensure that the organisation has an energy strategy covering such aspects as preferred fuel types, adequate usage monitoring, economic use of energy, and an awareness of realistic conservation measures.

(f) To ensure that energy consumption is monitored and action is taken to contain energy costs and avoid waste.

(g) To ensure that energy is efficiently used.

(h) To ensure that optimum terms are obtained from the most appropriate energy suppliers.

(i) To ensure that all energy costs are monitored and authorised for payment.

(j) To provide an ongoing awareness of energy conservation methods and to promote a positive attitude to energy matters.

Risk and Control Issues for Materials and Energy

1 Key Issues

1.1 How does management ensure that adequate supplies of all the appropriate materials will be available at the correct time to support production and manufacturing requirements?

1.2   What measures ensure that shortfalls in supplies or delays in the availability of materials will be promptly detected and effectively reacted to?

1.3   How are all materials accounted for (from procurement, through delivery to eventual usage)?

1.4   Has management established a strategy or procedure to ensure that the most appropriate form of energy is utilised and that usage costs are adequately monitored (and what evidence is there that the current strategy is being complied with)?

1.5   How does management ensure that energy supplies are obtained from appropriate suppliers at the optimum cost?

1.6   What measures are in place to monitor energy usage and identify waste and inefficiencies?

1.7   What measures are in place to ensure that payments for energy costs are valid, accurate and suitably authorised?

1.8   Are alternative sources of energy and improvements in energy usage considered on an ongoing basis as a means of improving efficiency, conserving energy and reducing the associated costs?

2 Detailed Issues

2.1   How are supplies of materials co-ordinated in order to ensure that appropriate and adequate supplies are maintained?

2.2   Are changes in the production plans adequately communicated to the purchasing, stock control and other affected functions in order to ensure that the appropriate inventory levels are maintained?

2.3   What measures prevent materials from being damaged or lost in the production area(s)?

2.4   Are effective measures in place to ensure that substandard or damaged materials are promptly identified and appropriate corrective action is taken?

2.5   Would losses of materials (for example, through pilferage) be detected and effectively reacted to?

2.6   Where realistic alternative energy types/sources exist, how can management be certain that the most appropriate type/source is utilised?

2.7   What measures are in place to ensure that energy is efficiently consumed and that waste is avoided?

2.8   How are the accounts received for fuel and energy correctly quantified and priced (and how is this evidenced)?

2.9   How does management ensure that all equipment is operating efficiently and that excessive energy consumption is prevented?

2.10   Are measures in place to monitor energy usage and costs against expectations, and are unusual variations adequately followed up?

2.11   Does management monitor energy consumption and costs for each key building or facility?

2.12   What checks are in place to ensure that all the relevant control equipment is correctly and appropriately configured to safely contain energy usage within the optimum ranges?

2.13   Where alternative sources exist, how does management ensure that they obtain the best terms for energy?

2.14   Are projects designed to improve the efficiency of energy consumption fully appraised, cost justified, and suitably authorised?

2.15   Are measures in place to ensure that staff are adequately aware of and trained in the efficient use of energy?

2.16   How does management ensure that all the relevant safety factors are satisfactorily addressed?

2.17   Are measures in place to ensure appropriate compliance with all the required statutory obligations?

2.18   How is the accuracy of data input from other systems (e.g. stock control) confirmed?

2.19   How is the accuracy of data output to other systems (e.g. energy accounts payable) confirmed?

QUALITY CONTROL

At a mechanical level, adopting a quality approach to production involves the definition and subsequent monitoring of appropriate standards, thus ensuring that they are both achieved and monitored for their relevance on an ongoing basis. However, it is also crucial that the affected management and staff are suitably committed to the driving quality ethos.

Chapter 17 includes a section on total quality management, which discusses the wider implications of adopting a quality-oriented approach throughout the organisation.

Control Objectives for Quality Control

(a)   To ensure that the required quality standards are defined, monitored and complied with.

(b)   To ensure that the production methods required to achieve the prevailing quality standards are adequately defined and communicated.

(c)   To ensure that both materials received and goods produced are to the required standard.

(d)   To avoid the additional costs, wasted resources, and erosion of the organisation's reputation associated with the production of poor-quality goods.

(e)   To ensure that any relevant statutory and industry quality regulations are satisfactorily addressed.

(f)   To ensure that effective testing and inspection methods are defined and implemented.

(g)   To ensure that production output is appropriately inspected and tested to ensure the maintenance of quality standards.

(h)   To ensure that any quality problems are promptly identified, reported, evaluated, and resolved.

(i)   To ensure that management is kept informed of defect rates and the implications of quality problems.

Risk and Control Issues for Quality Control

1 Key Issues

1.1   Have quality specifications been established for materials, components and finished items, and what form do they take?

1.2   How does management ensure that the defined quality standards are being cost-effectively achieved?

1.3   What measures are in place to identify quality problems or shortcomings and how can management be certain that all such problems are promptly and effectively resolved?

1.4   What measures prevent sub-standard and poor-quality items from reaching end customers?

1.5   What mechanisms are in place to ensure compliance with any prevailing statutory or industry-level quality standards?

1.6   How does management ensure that the established quality assurance, inspection and testing arrangements are justified and effective?

2 Detailed Issues

2.1   Are quality considerations built into the product design and development processes in order to ensure that they can adequately be addressed in subsequent production runs?

2.2   Are measures in place to confirm the quality specification of materials received from outside suppliers at the time of delivery?

2.3   Is prompt action taken to reject substandard supplies and arrange replacement stocks?

2.4   What measures are in place to assess potential suppliers for their competence and commitment to quality?

2.5   Have quality specifications been defined, authorised and formally documented, and how can management be sure that the current and valid specifications are in use?

2.6   Where achievement of the defined quality standards is dependent on the correct application of a specific production process or method, have such methods been adequately recorded, tested and communicated to all affected parties?

2.7   What mechanisms are in place to achieve an up-to-date awareness of all relevant regulatory quality standards?

2.8   What measures prevent the production, circulation and marketing of substandard items?

2.9   Are the required testing and inspection programmes defined (e.g. in respect of sample sizes, the nature of tests, tolerance limits)?

2.10   What checks are in place to ensure that the defined testing and inspection programmes are being correctly applied?

2.11   Where appropriate, are the organisation's testing processes operated to all the required regulatory standards (and how is this evidenced)?

2.12   How does management ensure that the testing and inspection staff are adequately skilled and experienced to perform their duties?

2.13   Where necessary, are the organisation's quality testing facilities certified by the relevant regulatory/industry bodies?

2.14   Is management kept regularly informed of detected defect rates and the action taken to correct shortcomings, etc.?

2.15   How is the accuracy of data input from other systems (e.g. product development) confirmed?

2.16   How is the accuracy of data output to other systems (e.g. industry regulation and compliance) confirmed?

SAFETY

Management will need to ensure that employees are adequately protected from potentially hazardous processes, equipment and substances. This presupposes that management is fully aware of all the potential risks so that appropriate steps can be taken to address them. The adopted approach to safety issues will need to incorporate the provision (and maintenance) of appropriate equipment as well as suitable staff training in the use of such facilities. In the production environment many of the safety issues will be the subject of specific regulations and legislation, and management will therefore need to ensure ongoing compliance. The broader aspects of health and safety are also addressed in Chapters 11 and 14, and a sample Code of Ethical Conduct is given in Appendix 9.

Control Objectives for Safety

(a) To ensure that an comprehensive, approved and documented safety policy is established and complied with.

(b) To ensure that all the safety factors relevant to the production facility have been identified and satisfactorily addressed.

(c) To ensure that all the necessary safety equipment is provided and maintained in operational order.

(d) To ensure that all the relevant prevailing legislation and regulations are being fully complied with.

(e) To ensure that all staff are fully aware of the workplace risk, how to use correctly the safety equipment and protect themselves.

(f) To ensure that machinery and equipment are safely installed, effectively maintained and fitted with protective guards when necessary.

(g) To provide adequate and operative fire prevention and protection facilities.

(h) To ensure that building evacuation procedures and drills are established and regularly tested.

(i) To provide adequate and appropriate first aid and medical facilities.

(j) To ensure that all accidents and incidents are promptly reported and addressed.

(k) To ensure that adequate hygiene and cleaning standards are maintained.

(l) To ensure that hazardous materials are correctly and safely stored.

(m) To ensure that all the required certifications are obtained from regulatory bodies.

Risk and Control Issues for Safety

1 Key Issues

1.1 Has an authorised and documented health and safety policy been developed and implemented, and is it maintained and kept up to date?

1.2   How does management monitor, identify and adequately address all the health and safety risks and hazards within the production facility?

1.3   What measures are in place to monitor full and ongoing compliance with all the relevant legislation and regulations?

1.4   What processes ensure that all staff are fully aware of workplace risks and how to use safety equipment correctly and adequately protect themselves?

1.5   Are appropriate and safe methods used to move materials and goods around the production area, and are staff suitably instructed in the correct lifting and carrying techniques in order to avoid injury?

1.6   What measures ensure that appropriate and sufficient safety equipment has been provided, and that it remains in working order?

1.7   What checks are made to ensure that all machinery is correctly installed and maintained in safe working order?

1.8   Are all relevant machines fitted with effective and operational guards, safety cut-outs, etc.?

1.9   Have sufficient and effective fire prevention and protection systems been provided, and is there evidence that they are regularly tested?

1.10   Have adequate first aid and medical facilities (equipment and personnel) been provided, and are supplies replenished when used?

1.11   What steps are taken to ensure that all incidents and accidents are promptly reported and appropriately dealt with?

1.12   Are adequate hygiene and cleanliness standards established, and what measures ensure that the required standards are maintained?

1.13   How does management ensure that adequate and appropriate insurance cover is provided and maintained?

1.14   Have adequate and appropriate procedures been defined for the storage, movement and handling of hazardous materials (and how is compliance confirmed)?

1.15   Where it is essential for continued operations, what mechanisms ensure that all the required regulatory inspections are conducted at the relevant time and that the appropriate certification is obtained?

2 Detailed Issues

2.1   Has management undertaken a risk assessment of health and safety implications throughout the organisation in order to identify the risks and ensure that they are addressed?

2.2   How does management maintain an up-to-date awareness of all the relevant health and safety regulations?

2.3   Are all staff adequately trained in safety matters, including the use of relevant equipment and clothing (and how can management be certain that all the relevant staff actually receive the appropriate training)?

2.4   Are staff progressively tested on their level of understanding of safety measures in order to identify further training needs?

2.5   How does management ensure that appropriate and adequate lifting and materials handling equipment is provided?

2.6   Are building evacuation, fire and security drills regularly conducted and assessed for effectiveness?

2.7   What measures ensure that all access points and traffic areas are kept clear of obstructions?

2.8   Are adequate fire alarms installed, tested and maintained (and would faults be detected promptly)?

2.9   What processes ensure that the records of incidents and accidents are fully and correctly maintained in accordance with any regulatory requirements?

2.10   Are sufficient and suitably trained first aid and medical personnel available, and how are they promptly summoned to an incident?

2.11   Are medical staff suitably trained and equipped to cope with industry or process-specific incidents (e.g. chemical spillage, high voltage shocks)?

2.12   In the event of an emergency, how can management be sure that all staff and visitors will be accounted for?

2.13   Are transitory safety risks (such as trailing power leads, or wet floors due to cleaning) adequately avoided and addressed?

2.14   What measures prevent the accumulation of waste materials, combustible materials, etc. in working areas?

2.15   What processes ensure that all the required certificates and licences are obtained to enable the lawful operation of the production facilities?

2.16   What measures ensure that any failures to fully comply with the regulatory requirements are promptly identified and effectively dealt with?

2.17   What mechanisms prevent unauthorised access to hazardous materials?

2.18   How is accuracy of data input from other systems (e.g. risk management) confirmed?

2.19   How is the accuracy of data output to other systems (e.g. the staff training records) confirmed?

ENVIRONMENTAL ISSUES

Our focus here is on the environmental implications of production processes, but we also aim to encompass the issues relative to product design as well as those relating to the production processes themselves. The selection of environmentally friendly or renewable materials may be an issue, particularly when viewed against the background of increased customer concern for the general environment. Sector-specific or national regulations may apply, especially in the area of materials disposal, and management will need to be assured about compliance. All these areas underpin the relevance of establishing an overall environmental policy for the organisation, so that management and staff are fully aware of their responsibilities.

Chapter 15 examines the broader implications of environmental interactions against a background of increasing concern with and awareness of environmental issues.

Control Objectives for Environmental Issues

(a) To provide an authorised and documented policy on environment issues as a framework for conducting production activities.

(b) To minimise the impact of production activities on the environment.

(c) To ensure that the organisation's products are environmentally friendly.

(d) To ensure that waste is minimised and properly disposed of.

(e) To avoid pollution and environmental contamination.

(f) To assess, on an ongoing basis, the environmental impacts of production and define the requirements to be adhered to.

(g) To ensure that alternative and potentially environmentally friendly processes and technologies are considered and implemented where justified.

(h) To minimise/avoid the use of scarce materials and non-renewable energy sources.

(i) To ensure that harmful or hazardous materials and waste products are safely and responsibly transported and disposed of.

(j) To ensure that all environmental legislation and regulations are fully complied with.

(k) To avoid adverse impacts upon the organisation's reputation and image.

(l) To ensure that environmental issues are subject to monitoring and management.

Risk and Control Issues for Environmental Issues

1 Key Issues

1.1 Has an approved and documented environment policy been established for the production facility?

1.2 What measures ensure that the principles of the environmental policy are complied with, and how would non-compliance be promptly detected?

1.3 Have the production processes and activities been assessed for their environmental impacts (and how is the necessary corrective action evidenced)?

1.4 How does management ensure that all the relevant environmental legislation and regulations are fully complied with, thus avoiding penalties and adverse effects on the organisation's public image?

1.5 How does management monitor that all waste products are correctly and safely treated, discharged or disposed of?

1.6 What measures prevent the pollution and contamination of the environment?

1.7 Are the organisation's products assessed for "environmental friendliness" (e.g. impact during production/use, potential to be recycled, safe disposal at end of product life, restricted use of scarce resources)?

1.8 Has management actively considered alternative and less environmentally harmful production processes?

1.9 Are measures in place to ensure that all environmental impacts are identified, monitored and effectively managed (and what is the evidence for this)?

2 Detailed Issues

2.1 Is the environmental policy supported by the commitment of senior management and a suitable staff training/awareness programme?

2.2 Are all projects to reduce the impact of production activities on the environment subject to a full feasibility and cost appraisal, before being authorised?

2.3 Is the assessment of environmental impacts kept up to date in order that management action is relevant and targeted?

2.4 Has a responsibility for environmental management been defined and allocated?

2.5 What measures ensure that all waste products are identified, assessed for their environmental impact, and appropriately treated/processed?

2.6   Are all discharges of waste products subject to monitoring and permitted within the prevailing regulations (and how would non-compliance be detected)?

2.7   How does management ensure that all waste product treatment processes are operating correctly and efficiently?

2.8   What measures ensure that management would be made aware of all accidental and unintentional spillages of potentially harmful materials?

2.9   Are contingency plans and resources in place to deal effectively with the likely range of environmental accidents?

2.10   How does management confirm that waste disposal sites and operators are appropriately licensed to handle the specific by-products generated by the organisation?

2.11   Is management considering utilising alternatives to hazardous or scarce materials as a means of reducing the environmental impacts?

2.12   Are the potential long-term environmental liabilities adequately assessed for both newly acquired sites and those being disposed of?

2.13   Are environmental impact audits regularly conducted by appropriately experienced personnel and are their findings and recommendations effectively followed up?

2.14   Does the design and development of new products take into account the potential environmental impact of production, and what measures ensure that such impacts are minimised and contained?

2.15   How is the accuracy of data input from other systems (e.g. new product development or design) confirmed?

2.16   How is the accuracy of data output to other systems (e.g. industry regulation and compliance) confirmed?

LAW AND REGULATORY COMPLIANCE

The scope in this section takes into account local, national and sector-specific regulatory issues, encompassing such matters as awareness, ensuring ongoing compliance, and thus avoiding the adverse impacts of non-compliance.

Control Objectives for Law and Regulatory Compliance

> (a)   To ensure that management and staff maintain an accurate awareness of all relevant legislation and regulations.
>
> (b)   To ensure full compliance with the prevailing legislation and regulations.

(c)   To ensure that business operations are reviewed and assessed for legal and regulatory implications.

(d)   To ensure that specific responsibility for addressing the relevant requirements is defined and allocated.

(e)   To take the legislative and regulatory requirements into account when planning change.

(f)   To prevent and minimise penalties and litigation arising from non-compliance.

(g)   To seek reliable professional advice on legal matters in order to select the optimum solutions.

Risk and Control Issues for Law and Regulatory Compliance

1 Key Issues

1.1   How does management ensure full awareness of all the relevant legal and regulatory implications for the production facility?

1.2   What measures are in place to ensure that all the relevant legislation and regulations are correctly complied with?

1.3   Would management be promptly made aware of any failure to comply or breaches of regulations, and how is this evidenced?

1.4   What mechanisms ensure that all staff are suitably aware of their responsibilities for legal and regulatory matters?

1.5   Does management take the legal and regulatory implications into account when considering or planning changes within the production environment?

1.6   Does management have access to reliable sources of professional legal advice when necessary?

1.7   What steps would be taken to minimise the extent of penalties, litigation cost, and adverse impacts on the organisation's image and reputation in the event of a serious breach of regulations?

2 Detailed Issues

2.1   Has the production facility/environment been fully assessed for all the relevant legal and regulatory implications as the basis for defining the compliance requirements?

2.2   How does management maintain awareness of new and changed legal and regulatory requirements, and how is this evidenced?

2.3   Are any forms of independent inspection undertaken as a means of further ensuring the necessary compliance?

2.4   Are the relevant regulatory and legal requirements correctly incorporated into operating procedures and policies (and are they maintained and kept up to date)?

2.5   Are measures in place to address the specific regulations for the following areas:

- employment
- hours of work
- working conditions
- safety
- facilities
- equipment?

2.6   How is the accuracy of data input from other systems (e.g. the legal department) confirmed?

2.7   How is the accuracy of data output to other systems (e.g. staff training records) confirmed?

MAINTENANCE

Continuity is the keyword here; ensuring that production processes are not unduly disrupted by equipment failure due to any inadequacies in the maintenance of same. Beyond the cost implications of production disruption, management would also seek to ensure that the organisation's investment in plant and machinery is protected through adequate and regular maintenance, and that serious and potentially costly faults are minimised.

Control Objectives for Maintenance

(a)   To ensure that all production equipment and machinery is cost-effectively maintained in working order.

(b)   To prevent/minimise any disruption to production caused by the failure of equipment, plant and machinery.

(c)   To define and implement a structured and planned approach to preventive maintenance in order to ensure that all relevant devices are regularly inspected and serviced.

(d)   To ensure that adequate and appropriately skilled maintenance staff are employed to fulfil the defined maintenance obligations.

(e) To provide a prompt and effective response to emergency maintenance problems during working hours.

(f) To ensure that preventive maintenance work is conducted at a time to avoid undue disruption of production processes.

(g) To ensure that the maintenance programme does not contravene any current supplier/manufacturer warranties and service conditions.

(h) To ensure that all maintenance work is conducted to the required standard and complies with any prevailing safety regulations.

(i) To ensure that the performance of external maintenance contractors is monitored and confirmed as being effective and acceptable.

(j) To ensure that all maintenance costs are accurately identified, justified, recorded, authorised and accounted for.

(k) To ensure that all spares and materials used during maintenance are correctly accounted for.

(l) To ensure that maintenance costs are adequately monitored and that the appropriate action is taken with regard to troublesome or costly pieces of production machinery.

Risk and Control Issues for Maintenance

1 Key Issues

1.1 What measures are in place to ensure that all production equipment and machinery is maintained in working order?

1.2 Has management defined, documented and implemented a suitable maintenance plan which identifies the servicing needs for all key equipment?

1.3 How is management assured that all the intended maintenance work is correctly conducted?

1.4 How does management ensure that adequate and appropriately skilled maintenance staff are provided?

1.5 What mechanisms minimise the disruptions caused by the failure of machinery during production runs?

1.6 When appropriate, are external suppliers and maintenance contractors used to conduct regular servicing and emergency repairs (and is their performance monitored for effectiveness and value for money)?

1.7 Are all machines and equipment maintained to the required standard (and how is this evidenced)?

1.8   How are all maintenance costs (labour and materials) accurately identified, justified, authorised and correctly accounted for?

1.9   Is regular and accurate information on maintenance costs and machine performance provided, and what action is taken by management in respect of persistently faulty equipment?

1.10   Is management made aware of the need to replace or upgrade production equipment, and what is the evidence that such replacements are fully examined, justified and authorised to proceed?

2 Detailed Issues

2.1   Are machine failures and operational problems promptly reported to the appropriate staff to enable effective action to be taken?

2.2   What measures prevent equipment being overlooked for maintenance purposes?

2.3   Are maintenance requirements documented and differentiated between items to be serviced by internal staff and external contractors/suppliers?

2.4   Is a preventive maintenance plan documented and in place, and how can management be sure that it is adhered to?

2.5   Is equipment under the supplier's warranty adequately identified so that all maintenance is handled by the supplier or the manufacturer?

2.6   What measures prevent unauthorised or unqualified staff from tampering with or servicing production equipment?

2.7   Is preventive maintenance conducted out of normal working hours (or during re-tooling or production set-up periods) in order to avoid any undue disruption of production processes?

2.8   Is the performance of key pieces of equipment subject to effective monitoring so that potentially disruptive faults can be anticipated and countered?

2.9   Are accurate and up-to-date servicing records maintained for each piece of key production equipment?

2.10   Are effective and workable contingency arrangements in place (and tested) in the event of the failure of a key piece of machinery?

2.11   How does management ensure that any devices used in continuous manufacturing processes are operating correctly and receive the necessary maintenance attention?

2.12   Are all claims against suppliers for persistently faulty equipment effectively pursued and compensation sought?

2.13 Are maintenance staff suitably trained to deal with the range of production equipment in place, and how is this confirmed?

2.14 Are maintenance staff resources adequate to ensure appropriately skilled coverage during holiday periods, etc.?

2.15 Are out-of-hours maintenance activities suitably justified and authorised?

2.16 Are maintenance activities (both internally and externally resourced) subject to monitoring for justification and performance purposes?

2.17 How would management be made aware of any unnecessary or unjustified activities?

2.18 Does management conduct appraisals of the performance of external service contractors and take remedial action when necessary?

2.19 What measures ensure that claims are pursued against external maintenance contractors in the event of unsatisfactory or delayed service provision?

2.20 Where safety and other regulatory implications apply, how can management be certain that the required maintenance standards are achieved?

2.21 What mechanisms ensure that relevant production equipment is correctly calibrated, configured, and operating at the optimum level recommended by the manufacturer?

2.22 Are purchase orders for spare parts and maintenance consumables suitably justified, authorised and accounted for?

2.23 Are stocks of maintenance parts accounted for and regularly verified (and what prevents pilferage and other losses occurring)?

2.24 How is the accuracy of data input from other systems (e.g. external contractors charges from the accounts payable system) confirmed?

2.25 How is the accuracy of data output to other systems (e.g. overtime hours worked by the maintenance team for payroll calculation purposes) confirmed?

9

Auditing
Marketing and Sales

INTRODUCTION

In this chapter we consider the operational auditing dimensions of the marketing and sales functions.

SYSTEM/FUNCTION COMPONENTS OF THE MARKETING AND SALES FUNCTIONS

We have chosen to use an essentially *functional* approach to define the marketing and sales audit universe, which gives us the following possible breakdown of the key functions, systems or activities, further subdivided between marketing and sales and after sales support:

Marketing and sales:

- product development
- market research
- promotion and advertising
- pricing and discount policies
- sales management
- sales performance and monitoring
- distributors[1]
- relationship with parent company
- agents
- order processing

After sales support:

- warranty arrangements
- maintenance and servicing
- spare parts and supply

In common with other chapters in this book, the component activities/functions noted for the given subject area are closely interconnected, and should not be viewed in isolation, as there inevitably will be synergy and information flow between the separate elements. The points of interconnection should be of particular concern (to auditors and management alike) as they can represent changes of managerial responsibility and jurisdiction, which often results in reduced control effectiveness at the interface.

GENERAL COMMENTS

The specific marketing stance taken by an organisation will be relative to its particular industry, and also strongly determined by wider economic and general market influences, such as:

- increasing price competition;
- the increasing role and importance of customer service quality
- the level of general competition
- the implications of consolidation of the competition (i.e. into fewer and larger market players)
- the globalisation of competitors and markets
- the need to improve products and service quality.

Customer focus is seen as increasingly important and many organisations have oriented their marketing approach accordingly, perhaps to the extent of viewing their customers as assets, through the use of such techniques as MCSA (managing customers as strategic assets).

Although we have opted to adopt a functional approach to marketing, there is a trend to move away from a centralised marketing approach (typified by a specialist department serving the whole organisation) to a *line marketing* orientation, which devolves marketing responsibilities to line management for a given product, range or segment. The reasoning behind this move is to achieve improved synergy and integration between the marketing activities and the day-to-day decisions taken in a wider business management context. In other words, marketing is being moved closer to the front line. In tandem with this change, marketing can become a more generalised and widespread thread running through the organisation so that it becomes "everyone's business".

The functional components we have identified can be used in any marketing situation, but the devolution of marketing responsibility may result in audit coverage being spread across a number of areas of influence where an organisation has many discrete products or segments.

CONTROL OBJECTIVES AND RISK AND CONTROL ISSUES

We shall now examine the control objectives and the related risk and control issues (divided into key issues and detailed issues) for each of the marketing, sales and after sales support areas listed above. This data can be used within the format of the Standard Audit Programme Guides (SAPGs) introduced in Chapter 3. To save space we have here stripped out the format and focussed on the objectives to be stated and the questions to be asked.

PRODUCT DEVELOPMENT

This subject area is predominantly about the future cost-effective positioning of product lines in association with the driving strategic direction of the organisation and taking into account the implications of external market and economic forces. Where product developments are justified, appropriate, realistic, and suitable, co-ordinated plans will be required to support the development process and bring the product to the market on time and at the right price.

Chapter 12 contains a section on product development from a research and development viewpoint. Chapter 6 includes a related section on product/project accounting.

Control Objectives for Product Development

(a) To ensure that new and existing products are developed in accordance with market factors and the strategic objectives of the organisation.

(b) To ensure that product lines do not become prematurely obsolete.

(c) To ensure that all product developments are fully assessed in relation to the potential market, estimated production costs and selling price.

(d) To ensure that all product development projects are suitably authorised to proceed.

(e) To ensure that the design assessment and product specification processes are adequate and address matters of quality and performance.

(f) To ensure that the product development is timed so that market and competitive advantages are optimised.

(g) To ensure that the resources required to undertake the development are accurately identified, costed, justified and authorised.

(h) To ensure that the activities of all the affected functions (e.g. production, advertising, quality control and sales team) are co-ordinated in order to achieve the defined objectives.

(i) To ensure that the eventual product is adequately and appropriately protected from exploitation by others (e.g. through the use of patents).

(j) To ensure that all information about the organisation's product developments remains confidential.

(k) To ensure that the progress of the development project is adequately monitored by management and appropriate changes are applied when necessary and authorised.

(l) To ensure that all the actual development costs are correctly identified and monitored against the established budgets.

(m) To ensure that all significant project variations or problems are promptly reported to management for corrective action.

(n) To ensure that the product is thoroughly tested throughout the development and subject to appropriate consumer testing prior to launch.

(o) To ensure that the market launch of new or modified products is adequately planned and monitored.

(p) To ensure that the initial sales performance of new products is closely monitored.

(q) To ensure that shortfalls in sales performance are promptly detected and reacted to.

(r) To ensure that the objectives and performance criteria established at the outset of the development are actually achieved.

Risk and Control Issues for Product Development

1 Key Issues

1.1 Has management defined and authorised strategic business objectives, and what measures are in place to ensure that all product developments comply with these targets?

1.2 Has management established, authorised and implemented documented procedures for the development and evolution of all product ranges?

1.3 What checks are in place to monitor that product plans remain adequate, appropriate, viable, etc.?

1.4 How does management ensure that all product development projects are valid and authorised?

1.5 What mechanisms ensure that the product design and specification stages are effectively conducted so as to avoid problems and repercussions during later development stages (e.g. production or cost implications)?

1.6 Are all the appropriate and relevant recognised quality and performance standards adequately addressed in the product development process?

1.7 What forms of market research are undertaken, and how can management be sure that the target product has a viable market?

1.8   How are all the relevant issues addressed to ensure the most appropriate launch of the eventual product?

1.9   What processes ensure that all the resources required to undertake the development are accurately identified, costed, justified and authorised?

1.10   Are all product developments subject to adequate project management in order to cater for the following aspects:

   - adequate co-ordination of all affected functions to ensure achievement of development objectives
   - definition of key stages of the project and the ongoing monitoring of actual progress against target
   - authorisation and control of all project resources and costs?

1.11   What measures ensure that new or modified products are subject to extensive, adequate and appropriate testing (including any sector specific or specialist product testing requirements)?

1.12   What processes ensure that the launch of new products is adequately planned for and co-ordinated (e.g. in terms of supporting promotion, adequacy of stocks)?

1.13   Are actual sales of new products adequately monitored in order to ensure that the overall business objectives are achieved?

2 Detailed Issues

2.1   What mechanisms prevent the investigation or development of a product outside the defined and authorised strategic parameters of the business?

2.2   Has management defined and authorised product development plans with the intention of extending and prolonging the life of existing products and introducing viable new lines?

2.3   How does management ensure that its product plans remain relevant, up to date and in step with customer needs and market developments?

2.4   Are product developments geared to a price-driven market, and what measures does management take to ensure that the costing criteria are accurate?

2.5   Is appropriate account taken of competitor analysis and are critical marketing timing considerations identified and planned for?

2.6   How does management ensure that all the affected functions are adequately consulted during the product development?

2.7   How would all the implications of a new product reliably be identified and planned for?

2.8   How does management ensure that product details and development plans and business development strategies remain confidential?

2.9   What steps are taken to protect product designs, related production techniques and technologies from exploitation by others?

2.10   Are key staff involved in product development subject to fidelity bonding or commercial confidentiality clauses in their employment contracts?

2.11   How is management confident that problems, shortcomings, cost overruns, etc. would be promptly detected and reported?

2.12   Have adequate arrangements been made to provide management with regular, accurate and relevant project information?

2.13   Where appropriate, are products subject to testing under recognised trade, national or international quality/standards schemes?

2.14   Upon product launch, how does management ensure that all the necessary promotional activities are co-ordinated?

2.15   What measures are in place to provide adequate stocks of new products upon launch?

2.16   What mechanisms ensure that all affected staff (e.g. sales, servicing, customer enquiries clerks, etc.) are suitably trained to respond effectively to customers' requirements?

2.17   What procedures ensure that management is promptly made aware of sales and performance shortfalls?

2.18   How is the accuracy of data input from other systems (e.g. market research or planning) confirmed?

2.19   How is the accuracy of data output to other systems (e.g. production control, sales management) confirmed?

MARKET RESEARCH

To keep the marketing direction of the organisation pertinently focused, it is critical that an accurate and up-to-date awareness of customer and market expectations is maintained. Where it is justified, the use of market research techniques can provide the necessary marketing intelligence to reinforce or influence the marketing strategy. In this section, we consider the implications of market research for the business and seek to ensure that such techniques are cost-effectively and efficiently applied.

Control Objectives for Market Research

(a)   To ensure that the organisation remains aware of the needs of their target customers.

(b)   To ensure that all product development, marketing and sales activities are based on accurate determinations of the prevailing economic, market and customer trends.

(c)   To ensure that market research activities are accurately costed, justified and authorised.

(d)   To ensure that the organisation is kept informed about competitor products and activities.

(e)   To ensure that promotional and advertising activities are appropriately targeted as a means to ensure value for money and effectiveness.

(f)   To identify potential new markets or opportunities to differentiate products and services.

(g)   To ensure that the organisation's products and services match the market expectation in respect of quality, price and performance.

(h)   To ensure that customer complaints and product returns are appropriately analysed as the basis for taking corrective action.

(i)   To maintain a database of market intelligence relevant to the operating sector to support effective decision making.

Risk and Control Issues for Market Research

1 Key Issues

1.1   How does management maintain an accurate and up-to-date awareness of market trends, customer needs and competitor activities as the basis for their own planning and decision making?

1.2   What steps are taken to ensure that customer requirements are identified and effectively addressed?

1.3   How does management correlate market research findings with product development, promotional and sales activities?

1.4   Are all market research activities accurately costed, and justified as being worthwhile and authorised?

1.5   How does management assess that promotional activities and advertising are appropriately targeted and offer value for money?

1.6   How does management identify potential new markets or opportunities to differentiate their products?

1.7   What measures ensure that products continue to match the required performance, quality and price criteria?

1.8   Are new and prototype products/services realistically market tested prior to full launch, and how are the results utilised?

1.9 How is management assured that market research data is accurate and reliable?

2 Detailed Issues

2.1 Are suitably skilled and experienced marketing staff employed to conduct or direct market research activities?

2.2 How does management ensure that external market research agencies and consultants are reliable, qualified and cost-effective?

2.3 Is the performance of market research activities reviewed and assessed for effectiveness (over a suitable period)?

2.4 Are macroeconomic events, general sector trends and other market influences taken into account by management, what assurances are there that interpretations of such factors are accurate?

2.5 Does management conduct a comprehensive competitor analysis as the basis for determining the appropriate tactical responses?

2.6 Are customer complaints and comments recorded, assessed and used to define the necessary corrective action?

2.7 How is the accuracy of data input from other systems (e.g. sales performance, financial reporting) confirmed?

2.8 How is the accuracy of data output to other systems (e.g. planning function, promotion and advertising) confirmed?

PROMOTION AND ADVERTISING

Setting the appropriate tone and approach for advertising and promotion can be seen as a crucial requirement given the high costs normally associated with these processes. It is debatable whether they are, in truth, arts or sciences—much depends on the study and interpretation of human expectation, susceptibility and desire. In this section, we consider the key business-related issues, incorporating those relating to the engagement and use of external specialists in the field.

Control Objectives for Promotion and Advertising

> (a) To ensure that a planned approach (perhaps by product type) to promotion and advertising is agreed, authorised and implemented.
>
> (b) To ensure that promotional and advertising budgets are agreed, authorised and adhered to.

(c) To ensure that advertising activity is of an appropriate type, sufficient in quantity, adequately targeted at the relevant market, represents value for money, and is monitored for effectiveness.

(d) To ensure that the engagement and utilisation of external advertising agencies and consultants is accurately costed, justified and authorised.

(e) To ensure that the organisation pays for only confirmed advertising activities.

(f) To ensure that advertising and promotional budgets allocated to external agencies are authorised and confirmed as used for the defined purpose.

(g) To ensure that the expenditure of promotional budgets is accurately accounted for and reflected in the accounts.

(h) To ensure that budgets for individual promotions are agreed, authorised and monitored.

(i) To ensure that the advertising and promotional plans and strategy are kept confidential and are protected from unauthorised access.

(j) To ensure that promotional literature (e.g. point of sale materials, leaflets, price lists) is accurate, lawful and that sufficient supplies have been obtained.

(k) To ensure that promotions are lawful, fairly conducted, active for a defined but limited period, and that adequate resources are allocated.

(l) To ensure that promotional staff are adequately trained so as to project a positive and informed image.

(m) To ensure that promotional items (e.g. gifts exchanged for coupons, redeemable vouchers) and merchandising stocks are accounted for.

(n) To ensure that staff and agents are prevented from taking part in, and benefiting from, promotional activities.

(o) To ensure that advertising and promotional budgets passed over to agents, etc. are accounted for and used only for the prescribed purpose.

(p) To ensure that sponsorship deals are justified, authorised, and subject to a written agreement which defines the fees payable and the type and level of service(s) to be provided in exchange.

(q) To ensure that all promotional and advertising activities are reviewed and appropriately amended on an ongoing basis.

Risk and Control Issues for Promotion and Advertising

1 Key Issues

1.1 Has a planned approach to advertising and promotion been agreed, authorised and implemented?

1.2 How does management ensure that advertising and promotional expenditure is adequately targeted, budgeted, effectively used and fully accounted for?

1.3 What mechanisms prevent expenditure on unauthorised advertising and promotional schemes?

1.4 Is the engagement of external advertising agencies, creative consultants, and marketing companies subject to adequate assessment, justification and authorisation?

1.5 How does management verify that the organisation is paying only for actual advertising and promotional activities?

1.6 What measures ensure that all advertising and promotional activities are lawful, accurate and project a positive corporate image?

1.7 Are budgets established and is actual expenditure monitored against budget?

1.8 What precautions prevent unauthorised access to or leakage of advertising and promotional plans?

1.9 How does management ensure that promotional activities are adequately defined, authorised, proficiently conducted and adequately resourced?

1.10 What measures ensure that sales, marketing and promotional staff are well informed about the products and present a positive corporate image?

1.11 Are all sponsorship deals subject to a written agreement, and are they monitored to confirm that all the prescribed obligations have been satisfactorily discharged?

2 Detailed Issues

2.1 What processes prevent the operation of unauthorised advertising and promotional activities?

2.2 Does management measure and monitor the effectiveness of advertising and promotional activities?

2.3 Are the merits of alternative advertising media, coverage frequency, etc. explored in order to implement the optimum approach?

2.4 How does management know that the adopted approach is adequate and effective?

2.5   If a specific advertising agency or consultant is hired, is management sure that alternatives would not offer improved service and value for money?

2.6   What measures are in place to prevent payments being made for invalid advertising and promotional services?

2.7   Are external agencies held accountable for all expenditure on the organisation's behalf?

2.8   What monitoring processes ensure that allocated budgets are being correctly and appropriately utilised?

2.9   What measures ensure that all promotional and advertising literature is accurate, up to date, lawful and correctly utilised?

2.10   Are all promotional and merchandising stocks securely held, used only for the defined purpose, regularly verified, and fully accounted for?

2.11   How does management verify that all advertising and promotional expenditure is correctly reflected in the accounts?

2.12   How are staff and agents prevented from taking part in or benefiting from promotional schemes?

2.13   How are potential sponsorship arrangements assessed and judged to be worthwhile?

2.14   Are all sponsorship arrangements authorised and subject to a written agreement?

2.15   Are all the obligations of sponsorship clearly defined (for all parties) and monitored for full compliance?

2.16   How does management determine the "value" and benefits of sponsorship and related promotional activities?

2.17   How are agents assessed for their stability, reliability, suitability, etc.?

2.18   How is accuracy of data input from other systems (e.g. sales performance and monitoring) confirmed?

2.19   How is the accuracy of data output to other systems (e.g. planning, product development) confirmed?

PRICING AND DISCOUNT POLICIES

When an organisation establishes its pricing policy it needs to ensure that all the internal and external economic and market-related factors have been duly considered and incorporated; otherwise there is the danger that the product or service will fail in the real world. This section explores the related accounting, marketplace and business strategy issues.

Chapter 6 includes an examination of the issues surrounding the related subject of product/project accounting.

Control Objectives for Pricing and Discount Policies

> (a) To ensure that pricing and discount structures are authorised and documented.
>
> (b) To ensure that pricing levels are competitive, profitable, and adequately cover the underlying costs.
>
> (c) To ensure that an awareness of market trends, competitor pricing, etc. is maintained to enable the appropriate commercial response.
>
> (d) To ensure that authorised prices and discounts are correctly applied to invoices.
>
> (e) To ensure that changes to prices and discounts are authorised and correctly implemented.
>
> (f) To ensure that accurate and reliable records of costs are maintained in support of determining the pricing policy.
>
> (g) To provide adequate costing information as a means of identifying the potential for cost savings, etc.
>
> (h) To ensure that the effects of taxation and duty are taken into account when setting prices.
>
> (i) To ensure that, when applicable, geographic differentials and the effects of cyclical sales patterns are taken into account when determining variations to the pricing policy.
>
> (j) To ensure that pricing structures accord with the relevant distributor, agent, retailer chain and are competitive at each stage.
>
> (k) To ensure that government, national and international pricing restrictions are taken into account when applicable.

Risk and Control Issues for Pricing and Discount Policies

1 Key Issues

1.1 Have documented pricing and discount policies been authorised and implemented (and are they based on established profit margins, etc.)?

1.2 What steps are taken to ensure that prices remain competitive, profitable and sustainable?

1.3 How is management assured that the correct prices and discounts are always applied to invoices (and what mechanisms are in place to detect and report any unauthorised variations)?

1.4   How does management confirm that product costing information is accurate, complete, and reliable as the basis for determining prices?

1.5   What measures ensure that changes to prices and discount structures are justified, authorised and correctly applied?

1.6   Does management take into account the effects of taxation (e.g. VAT or sales tax), duty and any prevailing price constraints when determining pricing levels?

2 Detailed Issues

2.1   How does management ensure that the most appropriate form of product costing is applied?

2.2   How does management maintain an accurate awareness of market trends, competitor prices, etc. as determinants of pricing policy?

2.3   Are the required profit levels and returns realistically established?

2.4   What processes link individual customers to the correct pricing and discount structure, so as to ensure the accurate calculation of invoices?

2.5   What parameters govern the eligibility for discounts, and what mechanisms ensure that they are correctly applied?

2.6   What steps are taken to protect commercially sensitive pricing information from unauthorised access and leakage?

2.7   Does management take into account the potential for geographic differentiation in pricing policy, and if so what assurances are there that the variations are correctly applied to invoices?

2.8   Where the sales of a product are affected by cyclical patterns, does the pricing structure vary in relation to demand (and is this process duly authorised)?

2.9   Where prices vary according to cyclical sales patterns, how does management ensure that the correct price is applied?

2.10   What measures prevent the set-up and application of invalid or unauthorised prices and discounts?

2.11   How does management verify that the prevailing pricing structure complies with any national or international pricing regulations?

2.12   How is the accuracy of data input from other systems (e.g. product costing) confirmed?

2.13   How is the accuracy of data output to other systems (e.g. accounts receivable or advertising and promotion) confirmed?

SALES MANAGEMENT

How best to organise, target and utilise the sales force resources are the key points here. On the one hand we are concerned with the development of a clear overall strategy for achieving the desired sales levels, but on the other hand there is a need to contain the costs of seeking out suitable and stable customers and maintaining their ongoing interest in the organisation's products and services.

Control Objectives for Sales Management

(a) To ensure that realistic sales strategies and quotas are developed, authorised, implemented and monitored.

(b) To ensure that customers and potential customers are identified and pursued.

(c) To ensure that accurate and up-to-date customer and sales activity data is obtained and maintained in support of sales activities and reporting.

(d) To ensure that adequate and appropriately trained sales staff are provided.

(e) To ensure that sales staff are adequately managed to maximise their performance and attain the defined sales quotas.

(f) To ensure that workable sales territories are established and suitably staffed.

(g) To ensure that sales staff operate within the defined and authorised company policies (e.g. for prices, discounts, credit rating, etc.).

(h) To ensure that new customers are confirmed as being bona fide, financially stable, etc. prior to a trading relationship being established.

(i) To ensure that order data is accurately captured and subsequently processed.

(j) To ensure that sales staff expenses, commissions, bonuses, etc. are valid, correctly calculated and authorised.

(k) To ensure that the costs associated with maintaining the sales force are accurately identified, authorised, accounted for, and monitored against performance.

(l) To ensure that delinquent sales accounts and customers are pursued.

(m) To ensure that customer enquiries and complaints are recorded and adequately followed up.

> (n) To ensure that all the requirements of export sales are correctly addressed.
>
> (o) To ensure that sales staff account for all trade samples, etc.

Risk and Control Issues for Sales Management

1 Key Issues

1.1 Are sales activities conducted in accordance with defined and authorised strategies and quotas?

1.2 What measures are in place to ensure that current and potential customers are identified and that customer data is accurately maintained and kept up to date?

1.3 How does management ensure that adequate (and justifiable) sales staff are provided and that they are suitably trained and knowledgeable about the company products?

1.4 How are sales staff workloads allocated (e.g. through defined territories or specific customer allocations) and how does management measure and monitor performance (e.g. for leads and confirmed sales)?

1.5 What mechanisms ensure that all orders fully comply with company policies on:

- prices
- discounts
- credit ratings and limits, etc.

1.6 What measures are applied to ensure that customers are financially stable and reliable (and what prevents the acceptance of unsuitable customers)?

1.7 How are individual customer credit limits determined and are they subject to a higher level of authority prior to orders being accepted?

1.8 How does management confirm that all order data is accurately captured, conforms to company policies, and is accurately reflected through delivery and invoice accounting?

1.9 What mechanisms are in place to confirm the accuracy and validity of sales staff expenses, commissions, bonuses, etc.?

1.10 Is management made aware of the actual costs associated with maintaining the sales force, and is this data related to budgets and required levels of sales activities as a means of determining the effectiveness of sales activities?

1.11 Are sales staff engaged in following up delinquent accounts and resolving customer complaints (and how is management assured that such actions are effectively conducted)?

1.12 How does management verify that all the administrative and regulatory requirements of export sales are correctly fulfilled?

2 Detailed Issues

2.1 Upon what basis have sales quotas and targets been produced (and are they realistic and reliable)?

2.2 How are sales quotas rolled down to the sales team?

2.3 What levels of authority would be applied to amendments of the sales strategy and quotas (and how is this authority evidenced)?

2.4 Are product development, marketing, promotional and advertising activities co-ordinated to support actively sales staff activities?

2.5 How is the success (or otherwise) of the defined strategy measured, and how are changes agreed and implemented?

2.6 Have mechanisms been established to reliably identify potential customers and marketing opportunities?

2.7 How is customer and sales lead data protected from unauthorised access and amendments (and how is management assured that it remains up to date and relevant)?

2.8 What checks are in place to ensure that data on sales activities (e.g. leads, confirmed orders) is accurate?

2.9 Would management promptly be made aware of unproductive or under-achieving sales staff?

2.10 What mechanisms prevent the establishment of unauthorised, unlawful or uneconomic trading terms with a customer?

2.11 How does management ensure that adequate time is allowed for sales staff to implement major changes in sales policy?

2.12 How does management ensure that all sales staff are suitably experienced and demonstrate an accurate knowledge of company products and trading terms?

2.13 What measures are in place to ensure that all sales leads are captured, trailed and accounted for?

2.14 Are sales leads and transactions reported through the agents' network accurately captured, in compliance with the prevailing terms, and taken into account when allocating commission payments?

2.15 Have authorised procedures been established and applied for determining and operating credit and trading limits?

2.16 What mechanisms prevent established credit and trading limits being exceeded?

2.17 Is the acceptance of new customers (or increased limits for existing customers) subject to suitable authorisation (and how is this evidenced)?

2.18 What measures prevent the acceptance of orders where prices and/or discounts are outside the authorised range?

2.19 What measures does management take to avoid losses associated with trading with financially unsuitable customers?

2.20 Are all orders accounted for?

2.21 Have standard rates for sales staff expenses (mileage charges, hotel accommodation, subsistence, entertaining, etc.) been agreed, authorised and implemented?

2.22 What mechanisms prevent the payment of sales staff expenses claims that fall outside of the authorised rates?

2.23 Are sales staff expense claims subject to scrutiny for validity and accuracy (and are they authorised for settlement)?

2.24 Are sales territories and staff journeys optimised in relation to their operational base, so as to contain travel and overnight accommodation costs?

2.25 What steps are taken to verify that payments of sales commission and bonus are accurate, based on actual sales achievements, correctly calculated, and authorised?

2.26 What mechanisms prevent the payment of invalid or unauthorised expenses, commissions and bonuses?

2.27 Are established expense rates, commission and bonuses subject to regular review, justification and authorised amendment?

2.28 How does management maintain an awareness of all customer complaints/comments, and what checks are in place to ensure that such queries are effectively dealt with?

2.29 What mechanisms are in place to detect failures to comply with all the prevailing export sales regulations?

2.30 Are sales staff held to account for all product samples, demonstration products and merchandising stocks in their possession (and would shortfalls be promptly detected and followed up)?

2.31 How is the accuracy of data input from other systems (e.g. planning or pricing policy) confirmed?

2.32 How is the accuracy of data output to other systems (e.g. order processing or petty cash reimbursement) confirmed?

SALES PERFORMANCE AND MONITORING

The overall development, production, pricing, promotion and marketing strategies associated with a given product or service will interface with the real world through a comparison between forecast and actual sales performance levels. The initial determination of sales forecasts needs to be both realistic and accurate. The actual performance of the sales force (in terms of both sales achievement and operating costs) will require accurate ongoing monitoring against the predicted targets, in order that management are provided with up-to-date and reliable data to support their decision making. It will also be necessary to evaluate whether an adequate and suitably trained sales force is provided and maintained in relation to the performance requirements.

Control Objectives for Sales Performance and Monitoring

(a) To ensure that realistic and accurate sales forecasts, targets and quotas are calculated, authorised and implemented.

(b) To ensure that accurate sales performance data is obtained and monitored against the authorised targets.

(c) To ensure that the performance of the sales function is subject to ongoing monitoring and that any shortcomings are satisfactorily addressed.

(d) To ensure that the organisation's marketing and performance objectives are met.

(e) To ensure that adequate sales staff are engaged and effectively managed to maximise their performance and achieve the defined quotas.

(f) To ensure that sales staff are suitably trained to adequately represent the company and its products.

(g) To ensure that significant fluctuations in margins, sales volumes, and revenue generation are accurately reported to management.

(h) To ensure that the sales function operating costs are justified in relation to performance achievements.

Risk and Control Issues for Sales Performance and Monitoring

1 Key Issues

1.1 How does management ensure that projected sales targets are accurately and realistically determined?

1.2 Is the establishment of sales targets/quotas and any subsequent amendment subject to suitable authorisation (and how is this evidenced)?

1.3 Does management maintain adequate records of historical sales trends, volumes, etc. as the basis for sales planning (and how can they be sure of the accuracy and validity of such data)?

1.4 How does management ensure that all actual sales data is accurately and completely captured?

1.5 Is management provided with accurate and up-to-date sales performance statistics?

1.6 What action is taken to detect and react promptly to sales performance shortcomings, etc.?

1.7 How does management determine and justify the staffing establishment of the sales function so as to avoid under or over-staffing?

1.8 How does management ensure that sales staff are adequately trained and knowledgeable about company products and terms of business?

2 Detailed Issues

2.1 Are up-to-date sales forecasts (by product where applicable) available that reflect the following elements:

- unit volumes
- revenue levels?

2.2 What factors are taken into account when determining the sales forecasts and targets?

2.3 How does management confirm that the data and methods used to generate sales forecasts are accurate and reliable?

2.4 How does management ensure that sales quotas are accurately rolled down to members of the sales team?

2.5 Are actual sales figures differentiated between in-house sales force, agents, distributors, etc. (and is each group separately monitored for performance and achievement of objectives)?

2.6 Is account taken of market trends and the potential for securing increases in market share?

2.7 Is the underlying sales strategy and generated forecast subject to ongoing review and modification (and how are amendments authorised)?

2.8 Are all actual sales activities accurately captured and incorporated into the appropriate information system?

2.9 What mechanisms protect the sales data from unauthorised access and amendment?

2.10 How does management ensure that sales returns, cancelled orders, rejected orders, discounts and allowances are all correctly and accurately reflected in the sales performance statistics?

2.11 Where sales performance is related to staff rewards (e.g. commissions), what mechanisms ensure that the calculation and payment of such rewards is correct and not based on inaccurate or manipulated data?

2.12 Would management be made aware of deviations from established margins?

2.13 Would management be made aware of unproductive or under-achieving sales staff?

2.14 Is "sales performance" assessed in any of the following ways, and if so how are variations reported and reacted to:

- selling costs as a percentage of total sales
- sales personnel remuneration and other costs as a percentage of total sales
- agent sales and commissions as a percentage of total sales
- discounts given as a proportion of total sales
- call success rates and average cost?

2.15 How is accuracy of data input from other systems (e.g. order processing or accounts receivable) confirmed?

2.16 How is the accuracy of data output to other systems (e.g. payroll or management information system) confirmed?

DISTRIBUTORS

The use of external distributors may offer an organisation competitive, strategic or economic advantages. For example, using an established external distribution infrastructure, avoids the substantial costs associated with the development of an internal distribution system. In this section we take into consideration the relevant internal and customer-related issues, with the underlying objective of seeking the most advantageous, efficient and cost-effective distribution solution.

The following material on distributors is duplicated in Chapter 10, which takes a broader view of the overall subject of distribution.

Control Objectives for Distributors

(a) To ensure that the use of distributors offers the organisation competitive or strategic advantage.

(b) To ensure that customers' needs are best served by a distribution arrangement.

(c) To ensure that external distributers are appropriately qualified, suitably resourced, financially stable and provide a cost-effective and efficient service.

(d) To ensure that engagement of external distributors is subject to adequate assessment, justification and authorisation.

(e) To ensure that all arrangements with external distributors are the subject of a suitable and enforceable legal agreement.

(f) To ensure that responsibility for advertising and promotion of company products is clearly defined and that appropriate budgets are authorised and established.

(g) To ensure that territories and geographic operational areas are clearly defined so that there is no conflict with other distributors or with company direct selling operations.

(h) To ensure that customer enquiries and orders are routed accordingly and that the distributor is responsible for accurately fulfilling the order.

(i) To ensure that all aspects of distributor performance are monitored and reacted to when necessary.

(j) To ensure that all payments to external distributors (e.g. fees or commissions) are valid and authorised.

(k) To ensure that external distributors have sufficient, suitable and secure storage facilities, and are adequately insured.

(l) To ensure that external distributors are capable of installing and appropriately configuring company products when applicable.

(m) To ensure that stocks of company products held by distributors are fully accounted for, verified and correctly invoiced.

(n) To ensure that distributors are not subject to conflicts of interest with either their own or a competitor's product.

(o) To ensure that any settlements due from the distributor are correctly accounted for.

> (p) To ensure, where necessary, that distributors are proficient in the maintenance and after sales servicing of company products.
>
> (q) To ensure that all the relevant legislation and regulations are fully complied with.
>
> (r) To ensure that distributors project a positive image of the company.

Risk and Control Issues for Distributors

1 Key Issues

1.1   In the determination of the agreed sales policy, have the benefits of indirect versus direct sales organisations been fully assessed?

1.2   Has management determined the competitive or strategic advantages of entering into a distributed sales arrangement, e.g.:

- access to new or overseas markets
- greater market penetration
- benefiting from an established infrastructure?

1.3   How does management assess the proficiency of potential and current distributors, and what checks are in place to ensure that the end customer is receiving a suitable and high-quality service?

1.4   What measures are in place to assess the financial stability and suitability of distributors?

1.5   Are all distribution arrangements adequately assessed, authorised and subject to a suitable legal agreement?

1.6   Are geographic distribution areas clearly established, and how does management ensure that there are no conflicts with existing distributors and direct sales activities?

1.7   What mechanisms prevent an association with a distributor involved in marketing similar products (e.g. either the distributor's own or from a competitor)?

1.8   How does management ensure that responsibilities for related costs (e.g. advertising, promotion, staff training, etc.) are clearly defined, and authorised where necessary?

1.9   How does management monitor the performance of distributors, and what action is taken with those performing below expectations?

1.10   Have the prices for the organisation's products been agreed, authorised and defined in writing, and what measures ensure that accounts are accurately produced?

1.11   What steps are taken to ensure that invoices for goods supplied to distributors are promptly and fully paid on time?

1.12   When appropriate, are fees or commissions due to distributors accurately calculated and authorised?

1.13   How does management determine that the distributor (and the distributor's staff) are sufficiently skilled to promote, install and maintain the organisation's products (and how are shortcomings identified and addressed)?

1.14   Does management confirm that the distributor's storage facilities are adequate and secure, and that all company goods held are adequately protected and covered by the distributor's insurance?

1.15   How does management ensure that all the relevant prevailing legislation and regulations are fully complied with (and has specific responsibility or liability been clearly allocated)?

2 Detailed Issues

2.1   Are all alternative sales approaches (including the use of distributors) subject to full assessment?

2.2   How does management justify the use of distributor arrangements?

2.3   Are distributors used solely for selling-on company products, or are they also involved in any of the following variations:

- adding value through modification or incorporation
- providing full training and support to end customers
- installing and maintaining products, etc.?

2.4   Are the costs of establishing new or overseas markets using direct selling techniques compared to the use of distributors?

2.5   How does management accurately assess the technical ability, resources, staff proficiency and facilities of distributors?

2.6   What mechanisms prevent an arrangement being made with an unsuitable, financially unstable, poorly resourced or technically deficient distributor?

2.7   Are all distributor arrangements subject to suitable authority, and how is this evidenced?

2.8   Are all initial distributor arrangements subject to a satisfactory probationary period?

2.9   Does management have the right of access to the distributor's records?

2.10   How does management decide the nature of distribution arrangements to establish (e.g. "exclusive" or "sole"), and how is conflict with any direct sales activity avoided?

2.11   Who is responsible for funding local advertising and product promotion (if this is the organisation, how is management assured that budget limits are adhered to and the expenditure is valid and represents value for money)?

2.12   Is the organisation responsible for training the distributor's staff in respect of company products (and is there a financial limit applied and enforced on such expenditure)?

2.13   How are agreed performance criteria established and monitored (and would management promptly be made aware of shortcomings, etc.)?

2.14   What measures are in place to prevent incorrect prices and terms being invoiced to the distributors?

2.15   Are all supplies forwarded to distributors fully accounted for, regularly verified and securely held?

2.16   Are claims lodged for company products stolen or damaged while in the distributor's care?

2.17   What measures ensure that all relevant customer enquiries and orders are routed to the correct distributor?

2.18   How does management verify that any fees or commissions due to distributors are valid and accurately calculated and paid?

2.19   Does management periodically review all the costs associated with maintaining the distribution network as a means of justifying the approach in comparison to other techniques?

2.20   How does management ensure that all the regulatory requirements of export sales and movements of stocks to overseas distributors are fully complied with?

2.21   Is the distributor authorised to use company trade marks in the promotion and advertising of products, and how does management confirm that such marks are properly used for the agreed purposes?

2.22   How is the accuracy of data input from other systems (e.g. pricing policy or product development) confirmed?

2.23   How is the accuracy of data output to other systems (e.g. order processing, after sales support) confirmed?

RELATIONSHIP WITH THE PARENT COMPANY

Taking a marketing and sales standpoint, we are concerned here with the efficacy (or otherwise) of the relationship established between the parent company and any overseas (or satellite) operations. For example, there may be the need to take account of local taxation implications so that the relationship is specifically established to optimise the taxation conditions. Other significant aspects, such as foreign exchange issues or local regulations may also require management attention.

Control Objectives for Relationship with the Parent Company

(a) To ensure that the establishment and operation of overseas and satellite activities are adequately assessed in order to optimise the fiscal, legal and operational factors.

(b) To ensure that the financial and funding arrangements made for overseas/satellite operations legally optimise the taxation advantages for the parent company.

(c) To ensure that the set-up conditions of subsidiary operations are suitably authorised.

(d) To ensure that local economic and currency factors are accurately monitored and reacted to.

(e) To ensure that management maintains an accurate awareness of all the relevant, fiscal, legal and political factors which could affect overseas and satellite operations as the basis for effective decision making.

(f) To ensure that the parent organisation adequately monitors all subsidiary, overseas and satellite operations for their effectiveness, performance, contribution, stability, etc.

(g) To ensure that suitably experienced and trustworthy local management are engaged in order to sustain operations and achieve strategic business objectives.

(h) To ensure that the parent organisation provides sufficient and appropriate support and resources.

(i) To ensure that adequate and effective lines of communication are established between the subsidiary and parent organisations.

(j) To ensure that accurate, reliable and appropriate management information is generated and circulated to parent company management.

(k) To ensure that local legislation and regulations are fully complied with.

(l) To generally protect and safeguard company assets and investments in subsidiary, overseas and satellite operations.

Risk and Control Issues for Relationship with the Parent Company

1 Key Issues

1.1 How does management confirm that all the relevant fiscal, legal and operational factors have been satisfactorily assessed and addressed?

1.2   How does management maintain an accurate awareness of all the relevant factors (legal, fiscal, etc.) which could affect the subsidiary operation?

1.3   How does management ensure that the establishment and operation of subsidiary activities is optimised for the benefit of the parent company and supports the achievement of business objectives?

1.4   Are all subsidiary operations based on agreed and authorised criteria, and what measures prevent the establishment of unsuitable or unauthorised conditions?

1.5   What steps does management take to ensure that local managers and staff are of the appropriate calibre and are capable of effectively handling the relevant operations?

1.6   How does management satisfy itself that it has taken all the possible (and legal) precautions to protect the parent company from penalty or other adverse consequence?

1.7   What steps are taken to ensure that adequate and accurate management information is provided to support effective decision making, etc. (and would management promptly be made aware of significant events or problems)?

1.8   What mechanisms ensure that all the relevant and prevailing legislation and regulations are fully complied with?

2 Detailed Issues

2.1   Are the relevant overseas, subsidiary and satellite operations subject to formal (perhaps legally binding) and authorised agreements (and if so, how does management ensure ongoing compliance)?

2.2   What steps does management take to optimise the taxation implications of overseas and subsidiary operations?

2.3   How does management remain adequately aware of the key taxation and other fiscal factors that could affect specific operations?

2.4   Are investments in subsidiary operations subject to adequate prior assessment by suitably experienced individuals, and how are such investments protected?

2.5   What mechanisms would prevent parent company investment and involvement in potentially unprofitable or commercially unstable subsidiary ventures?

2.6   In areas where there are known potential risks, are the investment and activity levels restricted (perhaps initially) so as to contain any adverse impact?

2.7   How does management check that all arrangements are within the prevailing law and regulations in the target country?

2.8   Are currency exchange rates (and any possible currency restrictions) adequately monitored, and how are the necessary actions authorised and legally implemented?

2.9   Has management access to appropriate legal and fiscal expertise to support their decisions and actions, and how is the accuracy and reliability of such advice ensured?

2.10   Have contingency plans been defined in the event of an emergency befalling the subsidiary operation (e.g. political instability)?

2.11   How does management ensure that the organisation's quality and performance standards are maintained by subsidiary operations, and how would they be made aware of related failures?

2.12   How is the accuracy of data input from other systems (e.g. from legal department or risk assessment) confirmed?

2.13   How is the accuracy of data output to other systems (e.g. management information) confirmed?

AGENTS

If there are notable commercial advantages in the engagement of external agents to promote the company's products and services, the organisation will need to ensure that such relationships are established only with financially stable, reliable, suitably experienced and adequately resourced entities.

Control Objectives for Agents

(a)   To ensure that the use of agents offers the organisation either competitive or strategic advantage.

(b)   To ensure that customers' needs are best served by an agency arrangement.

(c)   To ensure that external agents are appropriately qualified, suitably resourced, financially stable and provide a cost-effective and efficient service.

(d)   To ensure that engagement of external agents is subject to adequate assessment, justification and authorisation.

(e)   To ensure that all arrangements with external agents are the subject of a suitable and enforceable legal agreement.

(f)   To ensure that responsibility for advertising and promotion of company products is clearly defined and that appropriate budgets are authorised and established.

(g) To ensure that territories and geographic operational areas are clearly defined so that there is no conflict with other agents or company direct selling operations.

(h) To ensure that all aspects of agency performance are monitored and reacted to when necessary.

(i) To ensure that all payments to external agents (e.g. fees or commissions) are valid and authorised.

(j) To ensure that stocks of company products held by agents are fully accounted for, verified and correctly invoiced.

(k) To ensure that agents are not subject to conflicts of interest with either their own or a competitor's product.

(l) To ensure that all the relevant legislation and regulations are fully complied with.

(m) To ensure that agents project a positive image of the company and its products.

Risk and Control Issues for Agents

1 Key Issues

1.1 In the determination of the agreed sales policy, have the benefits of agencies versus direct sales operations been fully assessed?

1.2 Has management determined the competitive and strategic advantages of entering into an agency arrangement, i.e.:

- access to new or overseas markets
- greater market penetration
- benefiting from an established infrastructure?

1.3 How does management assess the proficiency of potential and current agents?

1.4 What measures are in place to assess the financial stability and suitability of agents?

1.5 Are all agency arrangements adequately assessed, authorised and subject to a suitable legal agreement?

1.6 Are geographic areas of operation clearly established, and how does management ensure that there are no conflicts with existing agents, distributors or direct sales activities?

1.7 What mechanisms prevent an association with an agent involved in marketing similar products (e.g. the distributor's own or from a competitor)?

1.8   How does management ensure that responsibilities for related costs (advertising, promotion, staff training, etc.) are clearly defined, and authorised where necessary?

1.9   How does management monitor the performance of agents, and what action is taken with those performing below expectations?

1.10   Are fees or commissions due to agents accurately calculated and authorised?

1.11   How does management assess that the agent (and the agent's staff) are sufficiently skilled to promote the organisation's products (and how are shortcomings identified and addressed)?

1.12   How does management ensure that all the relevant prevailing legislation and regulations are fully complied with (and has specific responsibility or liability been clearly allocated)?

2 Detailed Issues

2.1   Are all alternative sales approaches (including the use of agents or distributors) subject to full assessment?

2.2   How does management justify the use of agents?

2.3   Are agents used solely for selling-on company products, or are they also involved in any of the following variations:

- adding value through modification or incorporation
- providing full training and support to end-customers
- installing and maintaining products?

2.4   Are the costs of establishing new or overseas markets using direct selling techniques or distributors compared to the use of agents?

2.5   How does management accurately assess the technical ability, resources, staff proficiency and facilities of its agents?

2.6   What mechanisms prevent an arrangement being made with an unsuitable, financially unstable, poorly resourced or technically deficient agent?

2.7   Are all agency arrangements subject to suitable authority, and how is this evidenced?

2.8   Are all initial agency arrangements subject to a satisfactory probationary period?

2.9   Does management have the right of access to the agent's records?

2.10   Who is responsible for funding local advertising and product promotion (if this is the organisation, how does management ensure that budget limits are adhered to and the expenditure is valid and represents value for money)?

2.11   Is the organisation responsible for training the agent's staff in respect of company products (and is there a financial limit applied and enforced on such expenditure)?

2.12   How are agreed performance criteria established and monitored (and would management promptly be made aware of shortcomings, etc.)?

2.13   How does management check that all that all relevant customer enquiries and orders are routed to the correct agent?

2.14   How does management ensure that all fees or commissions due to agents are valid and accurately calculated and paid?

2.15   Does management periodically review all the costs associated with maintaining the agency network as a means of justifying the approach in comparison to other techniques?

2.16   Are agents authorised to use company trade marks in the promotion and advertising of products, and how does management confirm that such marks are properly used for the agreed purposes?

2.17   How is the accuracy of data input from other systems (e.g. pricing policy) confirmed?

2.18   How is the accuracy of data output to other systems (order processing or sales performance) confirmed?

ORDER PROCESSING

Sales orders may be generated in a number of ways (e.g. through a dedicated internal sales force, external agents, telephone sales enquiries). Irrespective of how they are generated, the organisation's management will need to be assured that all orders are accounted for and efficiently processed. However, there will be the attendant requirement to ensure that customers are (and remain) suitable, financially stable and that they operate within the confines of realistic credit limits so as to contain any financial exposures. This section is concerned with all these issues; however, the related aspects for the effective operation of an accounts receivable system are addressed in detail within a separate section of Chapter 6.

Control Objectives for Order Processing

(a)   To ensure that all valid orders are correctly identified, accounted for and processed in accordance with the organisation's policies and procedures.

(b) To ensure that official orders are accepted only from bona fide, authorised and suitable customers.

(c) To ensure that orders are accepted only for creditworthy customers with sufficient available credit limits.

(d) To ensure that new customers are properly assessed and authorised for set-up with an appropriate credit limit.

(e) To ensure that the determination and amendment of credit limits is appropriately authorised.

(f) To ensure that effective credit control is exercised to ensure that customers' accounts are promptly followed up and payments obtained.

(g) To ensure that all order details are accurately captured for subsequent processing purposes.

(h) To ensure that all affected functions are co-ordinated so that the order is promptly and efficiently fulfilled.

(i) To ensure that orders are promptly and accurately acknowledged.

(j) To ensure that delivery and any other special customer requirements are identified and appropriately addressed.

(k) To ensure that all orders are promptly fulfilled, delivered and confirmed as received.

(l) To ensure that invoices are raised against all fulfilled orders and accounted for within the accounts receivable system and accounts.

(m) To ensure that the correct terms, prices, and discounts are reflected on subsequent invoices.

(n) To ensure that key data (product prices, order records, etc.) are adequately protected from unauthorised access and amendment.

(o) To ensure that export orders are handled in accordance with all the prevailing regulations.

(p) To ensure that all the current laws and regulations are correctly and fully observed.

Risk and Control Issues for Order Processing

1 Key Issues

1.1 What measures ensure that all orders (from all possible sources) are correctly identified, logged, reviewed, authorised to proceed, and accounted for?

1.2   What measures prevent the acceptance of orders based on invalid or unauthorised terms and conditions (e.g. those outside the defined company policies)?

1.3   What measures are applied to ensure that only orders from established, authorised, bona fide customers are accepted?

1.4   What mechanisms prevent the acceptance and processing of orders from customers who have an outstanding/overdue balance on their account or insufficient authorised credit remaining?

1.5   How does management assess new customers for their financial stability and suitability, etc. (and what measures prevent the acceptance of inappropriate customers)?

1.6   Are all new customers and the setting of their initial credit limits subject to suitable authorities?

1.7   How is management assured that credit limits are strictly observed and amended only when suitably authorised?

1.8   What measures ensure the accurate capture of order data?

1.9   What mechanisms ensure the appropriate co-ordination of the following functions in the correct and prompt processing of customer orders:

- sales
- production
- stock control
- export department
- accounts receivable
- credit control
- despatch/distribution
- after sales support?

1.10   What measures ensure that all orders are acknowledged and efficiently fulfilled?

1.11   How is management assured that accurate invoices are raised and accounted for within the accounts receivable system?

1.12   How does management ensure that all export orders are correctly processed and handled in accordance with all the prevailing regulations?

1.13   What measures are in place to ensure that all the relevant legislation and regulations are correctly observed?

2 Detailed Issues

2.1   Have authorised and documented policies been established for the following:

- new customer acceptance
- setting credit limits
- credit control
- pricing and discounting
- standard terms/conditions
- export sales procedures?

2.2 How is compliance with all the authorised policies assured?

2.3 Are accurate and reliable records of authorised existing customers maintained, and how are they protected from unauthorised access and invalid amendments?

2.4 What form of assessment and verification is applied to new or potential customers to confirm their acceptability?

2.5 What measures prevent the set-up of a customer record when the required assessment and credit checks have *not* been applied?

2.6 Are procedures in place governing the determination and amendment of credit and trading limits, and how is management sure that they are always correctly complied with?

2.7 What mechanisms prevent the acceptance of an order where the customer has previous accounts overdue for payment?

2.8 Are measures in place to identify and cater for any special customer requirements (e.g. specific delivery dates, modified specification)?

2.9 What measures are in place to identify accurately the status of all orders and highlight those outstanding for delivery?

2.10 What processes identify and accordingly progress outstanding orders?

2.11 Are all deliveries accurately recorded and documented as either received or rejected (in whole or in part)?

2.12 What procedures link orders delivered to the accurate generation of the relevant invoices?

2.13 What mechanisms ensure that the correct, appropriate and authorised details (prices, discounts, quantities, terms, etc.) are reflected on invoices?

2.14 What processes prevent the delivery of an order without the generation of the relevant invoice?

2.15 What measures protect key data (prices, discounts, order records, invoice records, etc.) from unauthorised access and amendment?

2.16 Are all invoices correctly and accurately accounted for on the customer's debtors accounting record?

2.17 What measures ensure that all invoices are promptly despatched to customers?

2.18   In order to prevent staff malpractice and fraud, are key duties adequately segregated?

2.19   Is management provided with adequate, accurate and timely management information about orders received and in progress, etc.?

2.20   How is the accuracy of data input from other systems (e.g. agencies or stock control) confirmed?

2.21   How is the accuracy of data output to other systems (e.g. distribution or account receivable) confirmed?

WARRANTY ARRANGEMENTS

Control Objectives for Warranty Arrangements

(a)   To ensure that after sales support and warranty arrangements are defined, documented and authorised for all products.

(b)   To ensure that customers are accurately advised of the conditions of the organisation's warranty arrangements.

(c)   To ensure that liabilities for warranties are accurately recorded and maintained as the basis for validating requests and claims.

(d)   To ensure that customers are provided with an adequate timely, and cost-effective after sales warranty service.

(e)   To ensure that all warranty requests are valid and eligible.

(f)   To ensure that authorised charges are applied for after sales service and support outside the warranty period.

(g)   To ensure that all the costs associated with the provision of warranty services are identified, accounted for, and monitored.

(h)   To ensure that all warranty requests, claims and action taken are accurately recorded.

(i)   To ensure that the underlying causes of warranty problems are identified, monitored, and reported to the affected function (design, quality control, production, etc.).

(j)   To ensure that adequate and appropriate resources are provided to support the required service levels.

(k)   To ensure that problems caused by external factors (e.g. the supply of substandard components) are identified and appropriately followed up with suppliers and contractors.

(l)   To ensure that all consumer and warranty legislation and regulations are fully complied with.

(m) To ensure that the establishment of extended warranty schemes is adequately assessed, justified, authorised and appropriately implemented.

(n)   To ensure that the charges made for out-of-warranty and extended warranty work are adequate to cover the costs.

(o)   To ensure that ongoing product development and research contributes to increasingly reliable and quality products in order to further reduce or to contain after sales and warranty liabilities.

Risk and Control Issues for Warranty Arrangements

1 Key Issues

1.1   Are all after sales support and warranty arrangements authorised, documented and adequately communicated to eligible customers?

1.2   How does management check that the existing warranty arrangements fully comply with all the prevailing consumer and general legislation and regulations?

1.3   How does the organisation's warranty and after sales conditions compare with both those applicable within the sector/industry and those offered by competitors?

1.4   How does management verify that all warranty requests, claims and enquiries relate to valid customers with products still within the applicable warranty period?

1.5   What mechanisms prevent the servicing and follow-up of products that fall outside the warranty arrangements or period of eligibility?

1.6   Are all warranty requests/claims accurately recorded, accounted for, and confirmed as satisfactorily addressed?

1.7   What measures are in place to ensure that the appropriate charges for work outside the warranty arrangements are applied and fully paid by the relevant customers?

1.8   What mechanisms ensure that the charges made for out-of-warranty work are sufficient to cover the actual costs?

1.9 Are steps taken to accurately identify, account for and monitor all the costs associated with the provision of warranty and after sales support?

1.10 Has management taken effective action to identify the underlying causes of service problems as the means of taking remedial action (e.g. with suppliers, contractors or internal departments)?

1.11 Where applicable, is the establishment of extended warranty schemes subject to adequate assessment, justification, and authorisation (and are such schemes adequately monitored for effectiveness and profit contribution)?

2 Detailed Issues

2.1 What mechanisms prevent or detect the operation of an unauthorised or illegal warranty scheme?

2.2 How does management confirm that the established warranty policy is complied with?

2.3 Have adequate steps been taken to record all the relevant sales as a basis for validating warranty claims?

2.4 What steps ensure that all warranty and service requests are promptly and effectively dealt with?

2.5 Are warranty and servicing performance statistics circulated to management for monitoring purposes, and would shortfalls, delays, and problems be detected and resolved?

2.6 What prevents servicing work being conducted outside the warranty period where no charge is made to the customer?

2.7 How does management ensure that service personnel are engaged only on official workloads?

2.8 Would management be alerted to unpaid charges for servicing work?

2.9 Does management regularly monitor the costs associated with warranty activities and take action either to reduce costs or to improve efficiencies?

2.10 Are warranty and after sales support resources subject to ongoing monitoring by management, and what is the evidence that corrective action is being taken when necessary?

2.11 How is the accuracy of data input from other systems (e.g. sales order and customer data) confirmed?

2.12 How is the accuracy of data output to other systems (e.g. accounts receivable for recovering servicing costs from customers) confirmed?

MAINTENANCE AND SERVICING

Control Objectives for Maintenance and Servicing

(a) To ensure that an authorised product maintenance and servicing system is documented and established to support customers and discharge the organisation's liabilities.

(b) To ensure that all service requests are validated and classified as either chargeable or non-chargeable (e.g. within warranty).

(c) To ensure that all service requests are accurately logged, recorded, allocated and subsequently confirmed as completed.

(d) To ensure that adequate staff, stock and other resources are made available to support an efficient and cost-effective service.

(e) To ensure that servicing staff are adequately trained and appropriately equipped to conduct their duties effectively.

(f) To ensure that all the costs associated with the provision of maintenance and servicing facilities are identified, accounted for, authorised and monitored.

(g) To ensure that the performance and cost-effectiveness of the maintenance and servicing facilities are subject to ongoing monitoring and management.

(h) To ensure that alternative methods of providing maintenance and servicing (e.g. contracting out to an external service organisation) are considered and kept under review.

(i) To ensure that the customers are charged for servicing work at the recognised rate.

(j) To ensure that debtors accounts for servicing activities are accurately established and maintained.

(k) To ensure that outstanding debtor accounts are actively pursued and paid.

(l) To ensure that the hours worked by all service engineers and maintenance staff (including travelling) are accurately recorded, accounted for, and charged out when necessary.

(m) To ensure that the usage of all spares and parts is valid, authorised, accurately accounted for, and costed.

(n) To ensure that faulty or substandard components are referred to the suppliers for replacement or credit.

> (o) To ensure that accurate data is obtained on fault histories and recurrent problems as the basis for continually improving the product.

Risk and Control Issues for Maintenance and Servicing

1 Key Issues

1.1   Has management established an authorised maintenance and servicing policy which defines the conditions, charges and performance criteria?

1.2   How does management check that servicing activities fully comply with the documented policy?

1.3   How does management ascertain that all maintenance and service requests relate to valid customers?

1.4   What mechanisms prevent the servicing of products for non-registered or invalid customers?

1.5   Are measures in place to record accurately all service requests and differentiate between those within and outside warranty as the basis for determining the charging arrangements?

1.6   What measures ensure that all service calls are promptly allocated to an engineer and regularly progressed until completion is confirmed?

1.7   Are outstanding or particularly problematic service calls adequately identified and progressed to the customer's satisfaction?

1.8   Has management established service level criteria which are subject to performance monitoring and follow up?

1.9   How does management ensure that adequate and appropriately trained staff, materials, servicing equipment and all other resources are made available to fulfil the obligations and workload?

1.10   Are all the costs associated with the provision of maintenance and servicing accurately identified, accounted for, authorised, and monitored?

1.11   What mechanisms ensure that all valid customer charges (labour and materials) are accurately applied and pursued for settlement?

1.12   Are all service debtor accounts accurately reflected and accounted for in the accounts receivable system?

1.13   What mechanisms ensure that the charges made for out-of-warranty work are sufficient to cover the actual costs of provision?

1.14   Is management provided with accurate data on the actual labour and material costs incurred?

1.15 How does management monitor that spare parts are utilised for only bona fide purposes and are fully accounted for (including periodic verification)?

2 Detailed Issues

2.1 Have adequate steps been taken to record all the relevant sales as a basis for validating service requests?

2.2 How is management assured that all service requests are promptly and effectively dealt with?

2.3 Are servicing performance statistics produced and circulated to management for monitoring purposes, and would shortfalls, delays and problems be detected and resolved?

2.4 What mechanisms prevent servicing work being conducted outside the warranty period where no charge is made to the customer?

2.5 How would management be alerted to potential staff training needs?

2.6 Has adequate and operational servicing equipment been provided?

2.7 How does management confirm that the present servicing arrangements are the best option (and are alternatives assessed)?

2.8 How does management verify that servicing personnel are engaged only on official workloads?

2.9 What measures ensure that the correct labour rates and component costs are reflected on customer invoices?

2.10 Where faults or recurring problems appear to be related to externally sourced components, is management taking action to seek redress from the supplier?

2.11 How does management monitor that all the relevant legislation and regulations are being complied with?

2.12 How is the accuracy of data input from other systems (e.g. sales records and component costings) confirmed?

2.13 How is the accuracy of data output to other systems (e.g. accounts receivable) confirmed?

SPARE PARTS AND SUPPLY

Control Objectives for Spare Parts and Supply

(a) To ensure that adequate stocks of spare parts are maintained to support customer requirements and future servicing requirements.

(b)   To ensure that all stock issues/movements are valid, authorised, and accounted for.

(c)   To ensure that under-stocking, over-stocking and obsolete holdings are avoided.

(d)   To ensure that spares can be cost-effectively produced or purchased in good time to support requirements.

(e)   To ensure that stocks are accurately valued and periodically verified.

(f)   To ensure that re-order levels are accurately determined and effectively used to avoid out-of-stock situations.

(g)   To ensure that spares used for warranty and other non-chargeable work are identified and costed.

(h)   To ensure that chargeable spares are invoiced to customers at authorised prices.

(i)   To ensure that persistent faults relating to components are accurately identified and followed up with the production function or the relevant external supplier.

Risk and Control Issues for Spare Parts and Supply

1 Key Issues

1.1   What measures ensure that stocking levels of spare parts are accurately and cost-effectively determined in order to support anticipated demands?

1.2   What mechanisms prevent under or over-stocking of spare parts?

1.3   What processes ensure that all stock movements are valid, authorised and correctly accounted for?

1.4   Are re-order levels realistically set and effectively used to trigger the required (and authorised) production or purchase?

1.5   Are all production runs and purchase orders suitably authorised and optimised for quantity and price (e.g. how are uneconomic requests avoided)?

1.6   How does management ensure that stocks of spares are accurately and appropriately valued in the accounts (and how can they be sure that the stocks actually exist)?

1.7   Are all the costs associated with the usage of spare parts accurately identified, accounted for, and effectively monitored against expectations?

1.8   Are spare part costs for chargeable (e.g. non-warranty) work validated, accounted for, and recovered from customers (and what measures prevent the unauthorised or invalid usage of components)?

1.9   What steps are in place to ensure that persistent component faults or problems are promptly identified, verified and appropriately followed up?

2 Detailed Issues

2.1   Has management defined, documented and authorised a policy governing the permitted use of spares, and how do they ensure that it is fully complied with?

2.2   What is the applied policy on supplying components for discontinued products, and how is the accumulation of obsolete spares avoided?

2.3   What measures prevent the unauthorised usage or pilferage of spares (and would such events be capable of detection)?

2.4   Are accurate sales records maintained to support decision making about potential spares stock requirements (and if so, how does management ensure the accuracy of such data over time)?

2.5   Are the relevant stock records subject to periodic and effective verification, and how are variances and anomalies reported and resolved?

2.6   Are production and supplier lead times accurately identified and taken into account when determining re-order levels for spares?

2.7   How does management ensure that the cost of components recovered from customers continues to reflect accurately their true cost and the required margins?

2.8   What measures prevent unauthorised access to and unauthorised amendment of stock and costing records?

2.9   Would potential design or performance weaknesses promptly be detected and resolved?

2.10   How is the accuracy of data input from other systems (e.g. the warranty customer records) confirmed?

2.11   How is the accuracy of data output to other systems (e.g. accounts receivable for chargeable spares or the stock control system) confirmed?

NOTE

1. The use of distributors may represent an important component in the adopted marketing strategy. In Chapter 10 we examine the broader operational implications of distribution, including the use of external distributors. For convenience, we have duplicated the detailed material addressing *distributors* in both this chapter and Chapter 10

10

Auditing Distribution

INTRODUCTION

In this chapter we consider the subject of distribution, and the related subjects of stock control, and warehousing and storage. Our discussion of distribution incorporates two logical areas: general distribution principles and utilisation of external distributors.

Consult other chapters for discussion of related issues—see the Contents and the Index. For instance, just in time (JIT) management, which may be applied by management to distribution, is discussed in Chapter 17.

SYSTEM/FUNCTION COMPONENTS OF DISTRIBUTION

We have used an essentially *functional* approach to define the distribution audit universe, which gives us the following possible breakdown of the key functions, systems or activities:

- distribution, transport and logistics
- distributors
- stock control
- warehousing and storage.

The distribution methods employed will vary between organisations, for example they may include:

- indirect shipment through a network of strategically located warehouses
- direct shipment from the production unit using in-house transport
- via third-party distributors and/or haulage contractors.

The objectives and risk issue questions provided in this chapter are deliberately wide-ranging and take into consideration the variations noted above; as a result they will require editing prior to use so that the points covered more closely follow the actual scenario encountered by the auditor.

CONTROL OBJECTIVES AND RISK AND CONTROL ISSUES

We shall now examine the control objectives and risk and control issues (divided into key issues and detailed issues) for each of the distribution areas listed above. This data can be used within the Standard Audit Programme Guides (SAPGs) looked at in Chapter 3. To save space we have concentrated on the objectives to be stated and the questions to be asked and have not presented them within the SAPG format.

DISTRIBUTION, TRANSPORT AND LOGISTICS

In an attempt to apply the optimum distribution and transport solution, the use of both in-house resources and external contractors may need to be considered. The following objectives and risk and control issues cover points relevant to both these potential situations. Where there is an established in-house transport function, additional factors are noted covering areas such as the maintenance of the vehicle fleet, ensuring compliance with all the prevailing laws and regulations, and economic planning of delivery runs.

Control Objectives for Distribution, Transport and Logistics

(a) To ensure that an adequate, appropriate, efficient and cost-effective distribution and transport infrastructure is provided to meet the needs of customers.

(b) To ensure that goods are distributed and delivered in the most efficient manner.

(c) To ensure that stock is located in the optimum position to fulfil the anticipated demands and to avoid localised shortages.

(d) To ensure that only correctly constituted and valid consignments are actioned and accurately reflected in the accounts.

(e) To ensure that the appropriate goods in the relevant quantities are delivered on time.

(f) To ensure that goods are adequately protected from loss and damage during intermediate storage and transit.

(g) To ensure that contracts with external distributors and haulage contractors are suitable and authorised.

(h) To ensure that external distribution and transport contractors are paid at the agreed rate for work actually done.

(i) To ensure that the performance and cost-effectiveness of external contractors is monitored as a means of ensuring that they offer the appropriate quality and value for money.

(j) To ensure that exports and all overseas consignments are correctly handled, documented and comply with the relevant regulations.

(k) To ensure that an adequate number of appropriate delivery vehicles are provided and operated cost-effectively.

(l) To ensure that the most efficient and cost-effective means of delivery is used.

(m) To ensure that the delivery demands are adequately and accurately determined and planned for.

(n) To ensure that delivery journeys/runs are sufficiently and economically planned so as to avoid delays and excess mileages, etc.

(o) To ensure that transport facilities are operated legally and in accordance with the prevailing regulations for drivers and vehicles.

(p) To ensure that correct type and quantity of goods are safely loaded and that the relevant materials handling devices are provided.

(q) To ensure that deliveries are agreed and signed for, and that any discrepancies are identified, documented, investigated and resolved.

(r) To ensure that adequate and appropriate insurance cover is provided for goods while in store and transit.

Risk and Control Issues for Distribution, Transport and Logistics

1 Key Issues

1.1 How does management assess that the distribution facilities in place are adequate, efficient and able to cater for current and future demands?

1.2 Is there adequate and timely liaison and information flow between the sales, production, stock control, distribution and transport functions in order to ensure that customer demands are fulfilled?

1.3 How does management ensure that the most appropriate, efficient and cost-effective distribution and transport options are used?

1.4 How is management certain that only correctly constituted and valid consignments are actioned, and that they are accurately reflected in the relevant accounting systems?

1.5 Are all external distribution and transport contract arrangements appropriate, authorised and regularly monitored for quality, performance and value for money?

1.6   How does management ensure that external contractors' charges are valid and authorised, and what mechanisms prevent the payment of invalid or erroneous charges?

1.7   Are adequate precautions taken to protect goods in intermediate storage and transit from damage and loss?

1.8   How does management verify that all deliveries are undertaken in the required timescale and agreed and signed for?

1.9   Are all delivery discrepancies identified, documented, investigated and resolved (and how is this evidenced)?

1.10   How does management ensure that the delivery vehicle fleet is appropriate, adequate and is operated efficiently and legally?

2 Detailed Issues

2.1   Are accurate and appropriate delivery schedules prepared as the basis for loading, distribution and delivery (and how would errors be prevented)?

2.2   Are distribution and transport facilities provided on a stable and planned basis in line with the anticipated demands?

2.3   How does management maintain an awareness of the alternative distribution and transport options as a means to ensure that the optimum solution is applied?

2.4   Are distribution depots and intermediate storage facilities located in accordance with the organisation's trading patterns and customer base?

2.5   Would management be able to detect any underused, surplus or redundant storage facilities?

2.6   How does management check that the flow of goods from production through sales to the customer is accurately anticipated and planned for, so that the customer's requirements are efficiently fulfilled?

2.7   Are all stocks and movements of goods adequately tracked and trailed in order to determine their whereabouts?

2.8   Are distribution stocks accurately organised and identified so that orders can be efficiently prepared for despatch and all items accounted for?

2.9   Are all stock movements supported by authorised documentation and what processes ensure that all movements are correctly reflected in the accounting system for the appropriate accounting period?

2.10   What processes ensure that the correct type and quantity of goods are prepared for despatch?

2.11   What mechanisms prevent shortages of goods or unreasonable order backlogs at the distribution centres?

2.12   What processes prevent the despatch of incorrect or false consignments?

2.13   What processes ensure that goods are stored and delivered in saleable and good condition?

2.14   How is the financial stability, suitability and reliability of external distribution and transport contractors evaluated and confirmed?

2.15   How is management made aware of poor external contractor performance?

2.16   What prevents the acceptance of false, invalid or unauthorised distribution and transport charges from external contractors?

2.17   Are individual consignments assessed for the optimum delivery method, and how can management be sure that delivery costs are contained?

2.18   Would late, delayed or missing deliveries be detected and appropriate action taken?

2.19   Are all goods damaged in transit accurately identified, investigated and action taken to promptly despatch suitable replacements?

2.20   Are all export and overseas consignments correctly documented in accordance with customs and export regulations?

2.21   Are export and overseas consignments despatched by the most efficient and economic means?

2.22   Are the additional costs of overseas deliveries recovered?

2.23   How does management verify that the delivery vehicle fleet is suitable and efficiently utilised?

2.24   Are transport fleet operating costs monitored and reacted to?

2.25   What mechanisms prevent uneconomic and poorly planned delivery journeys?

2.26   How does management ensure that the vehicle fleet is operated in accordance with the prevailing laws and regulations (including conforming with required driving periods, distances and rest periods)?

2.27   Are all transport drivers suitably qualified, experienced and licensed?

2.28   Are vehicles loaded logically and efficiently in accordance with the scheduled delivery run?

2.29   Are goods loaded safely on delivery vehicles and have the appropriate loading devices been supplied to unload safely at the destination without damaging the goods?

2.30   Are drivers held to account for all the goods loaded on their vehicles and delivered to customers?

2.31   Are vehicles and goods in transit covered by adequate, suitable and current insurance provision?

2.32 Are goods held in distribution and intermediate stores covered by appropriate and current insurance?

2.33 How is the accuracy of data input from other systems (e.g. sales orders) confirmed?

2.34 How is the accuracy of data output to other systems (e.g. stock control) confirmed?

DISTRIBUTORS

It may be more viable for the organisation to outsource the distribution of its products through an established and stable contractor, and thereby take advantage of an existing infrastructure. This option will also avoid funds being tied up in the in-house development and running of such activities, and therefore enable their more effective application elsewhere. However, this requires the careful selection of a suitable and financially stable contractor with the necessary resources to fulfil both the organisation's requirements and any existing workloads to the required standards.

The points noted below are also listed in Chapter 9 as part of the consideration of the use of distributors in the development of a strategic approach to marketing.

Control Objectives for Distributors

(a) To ensure that the use of distributors offers the organisation either competitive or strategic advantage.

(b) To ensure that customers' needs are best served by a distribution arrangement.

(c) To ensure that external distributors are appropriately qualified, suitably resourced, financially stable and provide a cost-effective and efficient service

(d) To ensure that engagement of external distributors is subject to adequate assessment, justification and authorisation.

(e) To ensure that all arrangements with external distributors are the subject of a suitable and enforceable legal agreement.

(f) To ensure that responsibility for advertising and promotion of company products is clearly defined and that appropriate budgets are authorised and established.

(g) To ensure that territories and geographic operational areas are clearly defined so that there is no conflict with other distributors or with company direct selling operations.

(h) To ensure that customer enquiries and orders are routed accordingly and that the distributor is responsible for accurately fulfilling the order.

(i) To ensure that all aspects of distributor performance are monitored and reacted to when necessary.

(j) To ensure that all payments to external distributors (e.g. fees or commissions) are valid and authorised.

(k) To ensure that external distributors have sufficient, suitable and secure storage facilities, and are adequately insured.

(l) To ensure that external distributors are capable of installing and appropriately configuring company products when applicable.

(m) To ensure that stocks of company products held by distributors are fully accounted for, verified and correctly invoiced.

(n) To ensure that distributors are not subject to conflicts of interest with either their own or a competitor's product.

(o) To ensure that any settlements due from the distributor are correctly accounted for.

(p) To ensure, where necessary, that distributors are proficient in the maintenance and after-sales servicing of company products.

(q) To ensure that all the relevant legislation and regulations are fully complied with.

(r) To ensure that distributors project a positive image of the company.

Risk and Control Issues for Distributors

1 Key Issues

1.1 In the determination of the agreed sales policy, have the benefits of indirect versus direct sales organisations been fully assessed?

1.2 Has management determined the competitive or strategic advantages of entering into a distributed sales arrangement, e.g.:

- access to new or overseas markets
- greater market penetration
- benefiting from an established infrastructure?

1.3 How does management assess the proficiency of potential and current distributors, and what checks are in place to ensure that the end customer is receiving a suitable and high-quality service?

1.4   What measures are in place to assess the financial stability and suitability of distributors?

1.5   Are all distribution arrangements adequately assessed, authorised and subject to a suitable legal agreement?

1.6   Are geographic distribution areas clearly established, and how does management ensure that there are no conflicts with existing distributors and direct sales activities?

1.7   What mechanisms prevent an association with a distributor involved in marketing similar products (e.g. either the distributor's own or from a competitor)?

1.8   How does management ensure that responsibilities for related costs (advertising, promotion, staff training, etc.) are clearly defined, and authorised where necessary?

1.9   How does management monitor the performance of distributors, and what action is taken with those performing below expectations?

1.10   Have the prices for the organisation's products been agreed, authorised and defined in writing, and what measures ensure that accounts are accurately produced?

1.11   What steps are taken to ensure that invoices for goods supplied to distributors are promptly and fully paid on time?

1.12   When appropriate, are fees or commissions due to distributors accurately calculated and authorised?

1.13   How does management determine that the distributor (and the distributor's staff) are sufficiently skilled to promote, install and maintain the organisation's products (and how are shortcomings identified and addressed)?

1.14   Does management confirm that the distributor's storage facilities are adequate and secure, and that all company goods held are adequately protected and covered by the distributor's insurance?

1.15   How does management ensure that all the relevant prevailing legislation and regulations are fully complied with (and has specific responsibility or liability been clearly allocated)?

2 Detailed Issues

2.1   Are all alternative sales approaches (including the use of distributors) subject to full assessment?

2.2   How does management justify the use of distributor arrangements?

2.3   Are distributors used solely for selling-on company products, or are they also involved in any of the following variations:

- adding value through modification or incorporation
- providing full training and support to end customers
- installing and maintaining products, etc.?

2.4   Are the costs of establishing new or overseas markets using direct selling techniques compared to the use of distributors?

2.5   How does management accurately assess the technical ability, resources, staff proficiency and facilities of distributors?

2.6   What mechanisms prevent an arrangement being made with an unsuitable, financially unstable, poorly resourced or technically deficient distributor?

2.7   Are all distributor arrangements subject to suitable authority, and how is this evidenced?

2.8   Are all initial distributor arrangements subject to a satisfactory probationary period?

2.9   Does management have the right of access to the distributor's records?

2.10   How does management decide the nature of distribution arrangements to establish (e.g. "exclusive"), "sole", and how is conflict with any direct sales activity avoided?

2.11   Who is responsible for funding local advertising and product promotion (if this is the organisation, how is management assured that budget limits are adhered to and the expenditure is valid and represents value for money)?

2.12   Is the organisation responsible for training the distributor's staff in respect of company products (and is there a financial limit applied and enforced on such expenditure)?

2.13   How are agreed performance criteria established and monitored (and would management be promptly made aware of shortcomings, etc.)?

2.14   What measures are in place to prevent incorrect prices and terms being invoiced to the distributors?

2.15   Are all supplies forwarded to distributors fully accounted for, regularly verified and securely held?

2.16   Are claims lodged for company products stolen or damaged while in the distributor's care?

2.17   What measures ensure that all relevant customer enquiries and orders are routed to the correct distributor?

2.18   How does management ensure that any fees or commissions due to distributors are valid and accurately calculated and paid?

2.19   Does management periodically review all the costs associated with maintaining the distribution network as a means of justifying the approach in comparison to other techniques?

2.20   How does management ensure that all the regulatory requirements of export sales and movements of stocks to overseas distributors are fully complied with?

2.21   Is the distributor authorised to use company trade marks in the promotion and advertising of products, and how does management confirm that such marks are properly used for the agreed purposes?

2.22   How is the accuracy of data input from other systems (e.g. pricing policy, product development) confirmed?

2.23   How is the accuracy of data output to other systems (e.g. order processing, after sales support) confirmed?

STOCK CONTROL

Effective and accurate stock control is important in maintaining the adequacy of supplies to sales and/or production activities. See also the following related sections of other chapters:

- Chapter 6 contains a section on the subject of inventories
- Chapter 7 features the implications for the interface between the receipt of goods and the accurate updating of stock control records
- Chapter 8 includes a discrete section on the subject of materials and energy, which has connotations for accurate stock control.

Control Objectives for Stock Control

(a)   To ensure that adequate and appropriate stocks are held to meet the demands of sales and production.

(b)   To avoid overstocking.

(c)   To ensure that all stock movements are valid, authorised, correctly processed, accounted for, and accurately reflected in the accounts.

(d)   To ensure stocks are securely and appropriately stored in order to prevent loss, theft, deterioration or misappropriation of stock items.

(e)   To ensure that stock records are accurately maintained, adequately protected from unauthorised access, and regularly verified.

(f)   To ensure that stock discrepancies are promptly highlighted, investigated and resolved.

> (g) To ensure that stock write-offs, scrap and other disposals are justified, authorised and correctly handled.
>
> (h) To ensure that stock levels are monitored in order to detect and react to replenishment requirements, obsolete and slow-moving items.
>
> (i) To ensure that all stockholdings are traceable to a known storage location.
>
> (j) To ensure that management is provided with accurate and timely information on stock levels and usage.
>
> (k) To ensure that liaison between the stock control function and other relevant activities (e.g. sales and production) is sufficient to achieve the organisation's objectives.

Risk and Control Issues for Stock Control

1 Key Issues

1.1 Have authorised and documented stock control policies and procedures been implemented, and how is management sure that they are fully complied with?

1.2 How does management determine the current and future stock requirements, and what checks are in place to monitor that actual stock levels can accurately meet sales and production demands?

1.3 Is management made aware of overstocking and stock shortages, and how are remedial actions evidenced?

1.4 What measures ensure that all stock movements are valid, authorised, correctly processed, and accounted for?

1.5 What mechanisms prevent the acceptance and processing of invalid or unauthorised stock movements?

1.6 What measures are in place for storing stock securely?

1.7 What processes ensure that stock valuations are accurate and correctly reflected in the inventory and accounting records?

1.8 What mechanisms prevent the manipulation, distortion or falsifying of stock records?

1.9 How does management verify that all stock adjustments, write-offs, and scrap disposals are justified, authorised and correctly processed?

1.10 How would management promptly be made aware of slow-moving and potentially obsolete stock items?

2 Detailed Issues

2.1   Are processes in place which ensure that adequate information is provided to facilitate adequate stock planning to achieve business objectives?

2.2   Have suitably trained and experienced stock control staff and management been provided?

2.3   What prevents the overstocking of items?

2.4   How are stocks maintained at the optimum level, taking into account such factors as supplier or production lead time, etc.?

2.5   Are raw materials, items in production and finished goods discretely identified, physically tracked, and correctly reflected in the accounts?

2.6   Is management promptly alerted to low stock levels, and how are responses evidenced and monitored?

2.7   Are all stock movements and adjustments supported by documentation and trailed?

2.8   Are all damaged items and those returned from customers, etc. accurately identified and appropriately returned for credit?

2.9   Is it possible to verify the validity of stock sales through to the accounts receivable system?

2.10 Is it possible to verify all stock movements to the production facility and agree stock inputs to the output of finished goods?

2.11 Are stock issues of raw materials promptly actioned and the associated items moved into the production area to minimise workflow disruptions?

2.12 What are the procedures for authorising and accounting for all stock issues?

2.13 What processes ensure that stock items are used in rotation so that items do not deteriorate?

2.14 How does management ensure that all stock deliveries (including those made directly to production or sales locations) are identified, confirmed as correct, and duly accounted for?

2.15 How is management certain that the appropriate accounting treatment is applied to stock items (i.e. fixed or current assets, write-off to revenue, appropriate timing, etc.)?

2.16 What measures prevent the theft or misappropriation of stock items?

2.17 Is stolen or damaged stock reported to the police (where appropriate), and claimed against the insurers?

2.18 What checks are in place to ensure that all stock movements are accurately reflected on the stock control/inventory records?

2.19   Are stock records adequately protected from unauthorised or false entries?

2.20   Are the stock records subject to regular verification; if so, how often and how is this evidenced?

2.21   How does management ensure that all stock items are subject to reliable verification and that the valuations contained in the published accounts are complete and accurate?

2.22   How does management ensure that the prices used to evaluate stock-holdings are valid, accurate and up to date?

2.23   What mechanisms ensure that all stocktaking variances are accurately recorded, reported to management, investigated and resolved?

2.24   Is adequate authorisation applied and evidenced in support of all stocktaking adjustments?

2.25   Are adequate and secure stock storage facilities provided in order to prevent deterioration of items and losses due to theft?

2.26   Can the precise storage locations of all stock items promptly be determined?

2.27   Are stock write-offs, disposals, etc. authorised at the appropriate level and how is this evidenced?

2.28   What measures ensure that the best price is obtained for stock disposals (i.e. for scrap) and are such transactions authorised and the relevant proceeds confirmed?

2.29   How is accuracy of all data input from other systems (e.g. purchasing) confirmed?

2.30   How is the accuracy of data output to other systems (e.g. product costing, accounts receivable) confirmed?

2.31   How is the accuracy and integrity of the stock system records assured, and what measures prevent unauthorised access to the stock data?

2.32   How does management confirm that management information extracted from the stock system is accurate, timely and complete?

WAREHOUSING AND STORAGE

This section examines a number of interrelated issues which should aim to support the provision of goods at the right place, at the right time and in good condition. The requirements also have linkages with choosing the optimum location(s) for warehousing and ensuring that goods are safely and securely stored. There may also be health and safety implications wherever hazardous materials are stored.

Control Objectives for Warehousing and Storage

(a) To ensure that materials, goods and products are adequately and securely stored in order to facilitate their prompt identification and despatch.

(b) To ensure that sufficient storage space is available and the layout of storage facilities is suitable to meet the operational requirements of the organisation.

(c) To ensure that goods are effectively stored in order to provide an efficient service to customers and internal users.

(d) To ensure that the optimum warehouse locations are utilised to maximise the efficiency of distribution to customers, etc..

(e) To ensure that all goods are adequately protected from damage, deterioration and loss, in order that they remain in optimum condition for use.

(f) To ensure that all stock movements are valid, authorised and properly executed.

(g) To ensure that goods are stored safely.

(h) To ensure that staff are appropriately trained in the handling of goods in order to avoid damage to the goods and injury to staff.

(i) To provide adequate and serviceable materials handling devices as an aid to efficiency and cost-effectiveness.

(j) To ensure that hazardous items are safely stored.

(k) To ensure that all relevant regulations and legislation are complied with.

(l) To ensure that stocks are used in rotation.

(m) To ensure that adequate and relevant insurance cover is provided for both the stocks and storage facilities.

Risk and Control Issues for Warehousing and Storage

1 Key Issues

1.1 How is management made aware of the current and future storage capacity requirements, and what is the evidence of effective planning to meet the identified demands?

1.2 How does management decide where to locate warehouses, and is adequate account taken of the relevant logistical, transport and customer service considerations?

1.3 Are the storage locations (i.e. bins or bays) adequately identified to enable the prompt location of stock units?

1.4 Are storage facilities adequate to protect goods from damage or deterioration?

1.5 What mechanisms are in place to ensure that all stocks are adequately protected from theft and pilferage?

1.6 What measures are in place to prevent unauthorised access to the storage areas?

1.7 How does management verify that all movements of stock are valid, authorised and correctly executed?

1.8 Are goods (especially hazardous materials) stored safely and in accordance with established regulations and good practice, and how is management assured that this is the case?

1.9 Are staff adequately trained in the various materials handling techniques, and how does management confirm this?

1.10 Is the efficiency of the storage facility enhanced with the use of appropriate handling devices (trolleys, pallets, forklift trucks, cranes, etc.) and how is management assured that all such devices are serviceable and contributing to the overall cost-effectiveness of the operation?

1.11 How does management ensure that all the relevant regulations and legislation are being complied with?

1.12 What mechanisms ensure that adequate, up-to-date and relevant insurance cover is in place for both the stocks and the storage facilities?

2 Detailed Issues

2.1 Is space allocated in order to cope with peak loads rather than normal or minimum requirements?

2.2 Has management provided spare storage capacity as a contingency to cater for expansion, etc. (and how was this accurately determined)?

2.3 Is space usage monitored and action taken to avoid wasted or excess space?

2.4 Are raw materials, goods and finished goods appropriately segregated?

2.5 How does management avoid excess storage space and aim to contain the costs of providing storage facilities?

2.6 Are fast-moving items accurately identified and conveniently located for efficient handling?

2.7 Are items adequately trailed to all the relevant storage locations?

2.8 Are stocks used in rotation (as appropriate) in order to avoid the build-up of older or outdated items?

2.9 Is there sufficient space between storage locations to enable effective and safe access, the use of handling equipment, and the safe evacuation of the building in case of emergency?

2.10 How does management ensure that production and sales requirements are promptly and accurately advised to the warehouse?

2.11 Have specific responsibilities for the warehouse operation been allocated (and does this include maintaining an awareness of current materials handling trends and relevant regulations)?

2.12 Are packaging, storage and handling techniques adequate to protect the goods from damage and deterioration?

2.13 Are damaged items promptly identified and appropriate action taken (and how is this evidenced)?

2.14 Are the appropriate environmental conditions (i.e. air conditioning, humidity, and temperature) provided and maintained at the required level?

2.15 Are storage areas well lit for safety and security purposes?

2.16 What physical and other security measures are in place to protect goods and personnel, and are they regularly tested for effectiveness?

2.17 Are adequate and operational intruder alarm systems installed and regularly tested?

2.18 Are adequate and operational fire prevention, protection, and containment facilities provided, and are they regularly tested and maintained?

2.19 Would the fire containment systems (e.g. sprinklers, foam inlets) cause significant damage to stocks?

2.20 What measures prevent staff pilferage of stock items?

2.21 Are adequate staff provided to meet the operational demands of the organisation, and how does management determine and maintain the staffing requirements?

2.22 Are staff aware of the required and safe handling techniques, and how is this confirmed?

2.23 Has management provided adequate and suitable protective equipment and clothing for staff, and how is its use confirmed?

2.24 What checks are in place to ensure that goods are stacked and stored safely?

2.25 Are sufficient and adequate facilities provided for moving heavy items, and are staff aware of the correct use of such facilities?

2.26   Are delicate items adequately protected during storage and when being moved?

2.27   How is the accuracy of data input from other systems (e.g. stock control or sales order processing) confirmed?

2.28   How is data output to other systems (e.g. distribution) confirmed?

11

Auditing Personnel and Management Development

INTRODUCTION

In this chapter we consider the operational auditing dimensions of the personnel function.

SYSTEM/FUNCTION COMPONENTS OF THE PERSONNEL FUNCTION

Adopting an essentially *functional* approach to define the Personnel audit universe results in the following possible breakdown of the key functions, systems or activities. The first item listed is intended to be a general and top-level review of the overall personnel (or human resources) function and touches on each of the other noted components in summary terms, whereas the other components tackle the given subjects in considerably more depth.

- human resources department
- recruitment
- manpower and succession planning
- staff training and development
- welfare
- pension scheme (and other benefits)
- health insurance
- staff appraisal and disciplinary matters
- health and safety
- labour relations
- company vehicles.

CONTROL OBJECTIVES AND RISK AND CONTROL ISSUES

We shall now examine the control objectives and risk and control issues (divided into key issues and detailed issues) for each of the personnel functions listed above. This data can be used within the Standard Audit Programme Guides (SAPGs) looked at in Chapter 3. To save space we have concentrated on the objectives to be stated and the questions to be asked and have not presented them within the SAPG format.

HUMAN RESOURCES DEPARTMENT

Personnel are likely to represent the largest proportion of operating costs for an organisation. Furthermore, the performance of (and the contribution made by) employees is normally crucial to the success or otherwise of the entity. Management is responsible for ensuring that adequate numbers of suitably experienced, trained and motivated employees are provided in support of the organisation's objectives. In organisations of any size, the application of agreed employment policies and practices are normally administered by the human resources (or personnel) department.

The objectives and risk/control issues that follow in this particular section are concerned with the set-up and ongoing operation of a human resources (HR) function with defined responsibilities for such elements as recruitment, training and management development, staff appraisal schemes and labour relations.

The programme of risk and control issues noted below could be used for a high-level review of the HR function so that the top-level findings can be used, by the internal auditor, as pointers to those specific constituent areas which may require subsequent in-depth examination.

Control Objectives for the Human Resources Department

(a) To ensure that adequate and suitably experienced staff are recruited and provided in order that the organisation's business objectives are achieved.

(b) To ensure that policies which support the recruitment, retention, training and development, performance appraisal, remuneration, welfare, disciplining and employment termination of the personnel are developed, implemented and monitored.

(c) To ensure that all the prevailing employment and employee legislation and regulations are fully complied with.

(d) To ensure that the organisation's remuneration and benefits remain competitive and relative to the industry standards.

(e) To ensure that staff are adequately trained to perform their duties and that their skills and abilities are developed and maintained in accordance with the current and future business operational requirements.

(f) To foster positive labour relations at all levels and to avoid disruptive disputes.

> (g) To ensure that personnel turnover and absenteeism are monitored, maintained at acceptable levels, and problems are promptly reacted to.
>
> (h) To ensure that staff recruitment is suitably authorised in accordance with the operational demands of the business and cost-effectively conducted.
>
> (i) To ensure that staff performance is monitored and the necessary remedial action is taken.
>
> (j) To ensure that adequate personnel records are maintained and protected from unauthorised access.
>
> (k) To provide information and a cost-effective and professional service to management on all human resource matters.

Risk and Control Issues for the Human Resources Department

1 Key Issues

1.1 How does management ensure that there will be adequate and suitably skilled staff available now and in the future, to ensure the achievement of their business objectives?

1.2 Have documented policies been established for staff recruitment, training, remuneration, performance appraisal, and disciplinary matters?

1.3 What measures are in place to prevent the engagement of staff on terms outside the prevailing policies, terms and conditions?

1.4 What measures ensure that all staff recruitment is authorised and that only suitably skilled persons are employed?

1.5 How is ongoing compliance with all the prevailing employment regulations and laws confirmed, and would failure to comply be promptly detected?

1.6 What measures ensure that salaries, benefits and all other terms and conditions remain competitive and realistic in relation to the sector and national norms?

1.7 How does management ensure that skill requirements are identified and staff are adequately trained and developed to meet the demands of the business?

1.8 What measures ensure that good labour relations are maintained and costly disputes are avoided?

1.9 Is management made aware of absenteeism and staff turnover levels, and what action is taken in the event of increased or unacceptable levels?

1.10 How does management monitor staff performance to check it is at the appropriate level and proficiency, and what action is taken to identify and correct any shortfalls?

1.11 Is there a documented disciplinary and grievance procedure in place, and does it conform to the necessary regulations?

1.12 What measures are in place to ensure that human resource staff maintain an accurate and up-to-date awareness of all the relevant regulations and professional practices (and is line management also kept informed)?

1.13 How does management ensure that all staff are made aware of their responsibilities and entitlements under the prevailing personnel policies?

1.14 How does management verify that the personnel records are up to date, accurate and adequately protected from unauthorised use and access?

2 Detailed Issues

2.1 How are the current and future staffing levels and skills geared to the needs of the strategic plans for the organisation?

2.2 How is over-staffing avoided?

2.3 What actions ensure that there are always adequate numbers of suitably experienced and trained staff available to meet the organisation's needs?

2.4 What measures prevent the build-up of inappropriately skilled or inadequately qualified staff?

2.5 How does the organisation avoid the high costs associated with staff redundancies?

2.6 How are the various documented personnel policies and standards maintained and kept up to date and relevant?

2.7 Have standard pay/salary scales been established, and what prevents the engagement and set-up of an employee on non-standard rates and conditions?

2.8 Are the official salary scales accurately maintained and amended only when authorised?

2.9 Who is responsible for determining remuneration and benefits packages and how is management authorisation for these evidenced?

2.10 What measures ensure that salary reviews are suitably authorised, accurately calculated and correctly applied to the payroll?

2.11 Are all new positions independently evaluated in respect of grade, applicable salary, special conditions, etc., and how is this process evidenced?

2.12   What measures prevent the establishment of an unauthorised or non-graded position?

2.13   Has management agreed and defined the required staffing establishment levels, and are these used to verify all recruitment activity?

2.14   Are all positions supported by an authorised and up-to-date job description or specification?

2.15   Is recruitment driven, in every case, by the requirements of an authorised job description?

2.16   How are high recruitment costs avoided (for example, unreasonable recruitment consultancy commissions)?

2.17   Are recruitment activities suitably targeted?

2.18   Are temporary or short-term staffing requirements accurately identified and authorised?

2.19   Are candidates for temporary positions suitably assessed?

2.20   How does management avoid the engagement of unsuitable staff, those with a previous poor employment/attendance record, or those with unconfirmed qualifications?

2.21   How does management make sure that training resources are appropriately targeted in accordance with need?

2.22   How does management monitor that the available training resources are appropriate, up to date and effective?

2.23   How does management ensure that individuals' training needs are being accurately identified and effectively addressed?

2.24   How are staff and management kept aware of current employment regulations and their relevant responsibilities?

2.25   Have adequate sources of employment and human resource information been established for the use of staff and management?

2.26   If management failed to comply with relevant employment legislation, would the transgression be capable of prompt detection?

2.27   Have adequate channels of communication been established to enable the prompt identification and reporting of potential staffing problems?

2.28   Is management provided with accurate, reliable and regular information on such matters as staffing levels, days lost due to sickness, absenteeism, etc., and is it obliged to take corrective action when necessary?

2.29   Are staff kept sufficiently aware of changes and developments which affect them?

2.30   What measures ensure that staff who perform below the required standard are accurately identified?

2.31 Have suitable and lawful mechanisms been provided to enable staff to bring their concerns and grievances to the attention of management as the basis for a fair and full review?

2.32 Has management provided the necessary facilities to deal sympathetically and effectively with employee problems and personal matters, taking into account any relevant local regulations?

2.33 What processes ensure that all staff leavers are correctly dealt with (i.e. paid all their entitlements, removed from the payroll, company property recovered, other benefits discontinued, etc.)?

2.34 What mechanisms ensure that staff dismissed for disciplinary reasons are correctly and lawfully treated?

2.35 What prevents the unauthorised access to or use of personnel data, and would violations be detected and reacted to?

2.36 Does the personnel data maintained by the organisation conform to the requirements of any relevant legislation?

2.37 How can management be assured that the current practices conform to the relevant equal opportunities and anti-discrimination regulations?

2.38 How is the accuracy of data input from other systems confirmed?

2.39 How is the accuracy of personnel data output to other systems confirmed?

RECRUITMENT

Identifying and engaging the right person for the job can be an expensive process, especially where the vacancy is a specialist one and external recruitment agencies are involved. Recruitment is initially about the accurate identification of a justified need and then selecting the most effective and cost-effective methods to fulfil the requirement.

Control Objectives for Recruitment

(a) To ensure that appropriately experienced and stable staff are recruited to meet the organisation's business and operational objectives.

(b) To ensure that a structured, targeted, and cost-effective approach to recruitment is adopted.

(c) To ensure that all recruitment and appointments are suitably authorised.

(d) To ensure that recruitment activities comply with current legislation and regulations.

(e) To ensure that new employees are engaged in compliance with the prevailing remuneration and conditions policies.

(f) To ensure that all positions are suitably evaluated and that the key recruitment criteria are identified.

(g) To ensure that candidates are evaluated against the job specification and adequately screened to confirm their previous employment and educational record.

(h) To ensure that personnel and employment records are correctly established and accurately maintained in accordance with any applicable legislation.

(i) To ensure that valid and correct employment contracts are agreed, signed and retained.

Risk and Control Issues for Recruitment

1 Key Issues

1.1 Have documented recruitment policies and procedures been established, and how is management assured that they are up to date and complied with?

1.2 Have standard remuneration scales and employment conditions been implemented, and would management be made aware of staff engagements which fall outside these standards?

1.3 How is management certain that all staff recruitment and appointments are warranted and authorised?

1.4 What processes ensure that the requirements of a particular position are clearly established as the basis for evaluating subsequent applicants?

1.5 How does management ensure that the most appropriate and cost-effective method of recruitment is used, and that excessive recruitment costs are avoided?

1.6 What steps are taken to confirm the previous employment record and educational qualifications of candidates, and what prevents the engagement of someone with an invalid or unsuitable record?

1.7 How does management monitor that all the prevailing employment and engagement legislation and regulations are being correctly observed?

1.8 Are all staff engagements supported by a valid, accurate, agreed, and signed contract of employment, and what prevents staff being engaged without a contract being in force?

1.9   What measures ensure that new employees are correctly set up on the payroll and that their salary rate is valid for the position?

1.10   How does management check that accurate, complete and up-to-date personnel records are maintained which conform to any relevant laws and regulations?

1.11   Are personnel and employment records adequately protected from unauthorised access and use?

2 Detailed Issues

2.1   How are recruitment requirements identified and are they all subject to suitable authorisation (and how is this evidenced)?

2.2   What prevents an unauthorised position being filled?

2.3   Are all new positions and replacements subject to assessment and management authority?

2.4   Are all positions supported by an up-to-date job description and specification?

2.5   How can management be certain that recruitment is directed by the requirements of the job description or specification?

2.6   Is a planned approach adopted for recruitment which defines the optimum method(s) to be used?

2.7   Is the recruitment method agreed with the relevant manager and an overall budget established (for advertising, use of agencies, etc.)?

2.8   Is recruitment advertising appropriately directed (i.e. to relevant journals and locations)?

2.9   How does management verify that recruitment costs (including advertising and external agency fees) are valid, authorised and within budget?

2.10   Are recruitment efforts suitably targeted and are internal candidates sought and considered?

2.11   Are the established job criteria (salary range, preferred age range, etc.) realistic and current in relation to the local employment conditions?

2.12   Where recruitment activities are either protracted or unsuccessful, is management consulted and a revised approach agreed?

2.13   Is recruitment performance monitored by management and is there evidence of the corrective action taken?

2.14   Are all those concerned with recruitment suitably aware of the implications of all the prevailing recruitment and employment legislation and regulations (and how is this evidenced)?

2.15 What processes would detect actual or potential infringements of the prevailing employment legislation?

2.16 How is management assured that prevailing equal opportunity and anti-discrimination laws are being complied with?

2.17 Are applicant/staff complaints about the recruitment process promptly and effectively dealt with in accordance with the current law?

2.18 Are references obtained and checked for validity, etc.?

2.19 Are claimed educational and vocational qualifications verified, and how are anomalies followed up?

2.20 Are interviews professionally conducted by suitably experienced personnel and are interview objectives established as the basis for the conduct of the interview?

2.21 Are standard rates established for interview expenses and are claims checked for validity and suitably authorised for payment?

2.22 How are interview expense payments outside the standard rates prevented?

2.23 Where specific skills are required, are candidates adequately tested and evaluated prior to engagement?

2.24 Are candidates required to undergo a medical examination as a condition of employment (e.g. for acceptance into the company health insurance scheme), and how is management assured that unsuitable candidates are identified?

2.25 Are applications efficiently dealt with and are rejected candidates informed?

2.26 Are accurate records maintained of all applicants (including current employees)?

2.27 How does management ensure that all offers of employment are valid, accurate and lawful?

2.28 Are all offers of employment accounted for and are acceptances correctly acknowledged and processed?

2.29 Are the contents of employment contracts verified for accuracy before release, and how would errors be prevented?

2.30 Are all employment contracts accounted for, and how can management be certain that all contracts are signed and in force?

2.31 Are new staff made aware of all relevant conditions of employment, operational practices, safety regulations, etc., and how is this evidenced?

2.32 Are suitable arrangements made for new employees (e.g. issue of security cards, induction or safety training)?

2.33 Would inaccurate or incomplete personnel/employment records be detected and what action is taken to correct such records?

2.34 Is management information generated from the personnel and employment records accurate, reliable, timely and appropriate?

2.35 How is the accuracy of data input from other systems (e.g. manpower planning) confirmed?

2.36 How is the accuracy of data output to other systems (e.g. payroll) confirmed?

MANPOWER AND SUCCESSION PLANNING

Nothing is ever static in business, and the general ability of the organisation to pre-empt anticipated change and adequately plan for its consequences can be a fundamental matter of survival. This can be particularly true where staff are concerned. Even setting aside the effects of natural levels of staff turnover, any company will need to ensure that the workforce is capable of meeting both the current and foreseeable demands. Changes in staffing skills may, for example, be required as a consequence of introducing new technology or the effects of external market influences.

This section aims to explore the issues arising from the need to ensure that future staff skill demands are planned for and accordingly met. In a dynamic employment situation, staff will be promoted and move into other areas of the organisation, and there should be mechanisms in place to ensure that other employees are suitably groomed and waiting in the wings to move into the vacated positions. Where the vacant roles are especially critical, the need to plan for the succession is even more vital.

Control Objectives for Manpower and Succession Planning

(a) To ensure that sufficient and suitable staff are provided now and in the future so that corporate objectives are achieved.

(b) To determine a staffing policy which takes into account the need to adapt to both internal and external changes.

(c) To ensure that recruitment and staff allocation activities are co-ordinated to ensure the optimum staffing level and to avoid over-staffing.

(d) To ensure that the workforce is adequately and appropriately skilled to meet the ongoing business and operational demands.

(e) To ensure that staff training and development are co-ordinated to provide an adequate reserve of experienced staff.

> (f)   To ensure that staffing levels and costs are contained within defined limits.
>
> (g)   To ensure that any need to reduce staffing levels is determined in good time so that the appropriate implications can be evaluated and suitable consultations/arrangements made.

Risk and Control Issues for Manpower and Succession Planning

1 Key Issues

1.1   Has management implemented a structured approach to manpower and succession planning?

1.2   Have the implications of the mid to long-term strategic business objectives of the organisation been appropriately taken into account when considering the manpower and succession requirements?

1.3   In determining the ongoing staffing requirements, has management taken appropriate account of technical, social and economic influences?

1.4   Has a suitable staffing policy been established, and are line management fully aware of the requirements?

1.5   Are all recruitment and/or staff reduction activities undertaken in accordance with the manpower plan, and how is this evidenced?

1.6   Have current and future skill requirements been accurately identified, and what action is being taken to ensure that staff are appropriately developed and trained to meet the requirements?

1.7   What measures prevent the recruitment of staff outside the established levels?

1.8   Are unavoidable staff reductions adequately planned for (including appropriate staff communication, assessment, counselling and redundancy arrangements, etc.)?

2 Detailed Issues

2.1   What measures are in place to ensure that manpower and succession plans are up to date, relevant and attainable?

2.2   How does management monitor that all the necessary implications of their business plans have been taken into account when undertaking staff planning?

2.3   Are all new or revised business activities reviewed in the context of their implications for manpower requirements?

2.4   What measures prevent the necessity for urgent or emergency recruitment of temporary staff?

2.5   Does the manpower plan contain accurate and up-to-date financial implications, and are these correctly reflected in the budgeting system?

2.6   How does management remain fully aware of all the potential influences on staffing, recruitment, training, etc.?

2.7   Have effective measures been established to ensure that there is an adequate reserve of trained staff for both key executive replacement and to cover natural wastage?

2.8   Have the objectives of the manpower and succession processes been adequately communicated to affected management personnel, and are they aware of their relevant responsibilities?

2.9   Are training and staff development strategies/plans positively linked to the projected manpower requirements, so that unnecessary or wasteful training is avoided?

2.10   Is management undertaking ongoing monitoring of the actual staffing situation in relation to the planned requirements, and is appropriate action being taken to correct deviations, etc.?

2.11   Are staff subject to regular performance and skill appraisals as a means of determining the current status of staff proficiency?

2.12   Where the manpower and succession plans contain confidential or sensitive data, are adequate precautions taken to prevent unauthorised access or leakage?

2.13   When significant staff reductions are foreseen, are adequate procedures and plans established to ensure that staff transfers, redundancies, etc. are appropriately, legally and sympathetically handled?

2.14   How is the accuracy of data input from other systems confirmed?

2.15   How is the accuracy of data output to other systems confirmed?

STAFF TRAINING AND DEVELOPMENT

Staff need to be suitably trained to discharge their responsibilities effectively and efficiently. The cost of providing adequate training can be high and management will need to ensure that precious training resources are targeted to the areas of the greatest need. Where an organisation is going through far-reaching changes, staff training may be an essential ingredient in the achievement of the related objectives. In the points that follow, the need for an agreed and justified policy on training is regarded as a key requirement as a point of reference for all the related activities. The importance of monitoring the effects of training is also emphasised.

Control Objectives for Staff Training and Development

(a)   To ensure that training and staff development resources are accurately targeted in order to maximise their effects and avoid wasteful activity.

(b)   To ensure that employees are adequately trained to enable them to discharge their responsibilities effectively.

(c)   To ensure that the skills of the workforce are maintained at the appropriate level and in line with the business objectives of the organisation.

(d)   To motivate staff and increase their commitment by providing suitable personal and skill development facilities.

(e)   To anticipate the future skill needs of the business and ensure that relevant training is planned for.

(f)   To provide adequate and appropriate training facilities and resources on a cost-effective basis.

(g)   To maximise the benefits available from government or trade training schemes and subsidies.

(h)   To consider the use of training and staff development as means to gain a competitive advantage.

Risk and Control Issues for Staff Training and Development

1 Key Issues

1.1   Has management defined, documented and implemented a training policy which incorporates training programmes and timetables, required standards of skill proficiency, training methods to be used, authority limits for training expenditure, and so on?

1.2   How is management assured that all training and staff development activities are justified, authorised and appropriately targeted?

1.3   Is expenditure on training and development subject to budgetary control, and what prevents unauthorised or unnecessary training activities from taking place?

1.4   Has management determined the required skill and knowledge base for the workforce and implemented a planned training approach to ensuring that the employees remain competent and able to discharge their duties?

1.5   How is management certain of identifying and suitably addressing individual training and development needs?

1.6   Are training activities actively monitored for their effectiveness, so that deficiencies can be recognised and remedied?

1.7   How does management ensure that the most suitable and cost-effective training methods and resources are used?

1.8   Are the costs of training and staff development offset, whenever possible, by obtaining government or trade-related training subsidies?

1.9   Is training conducted to a suitable trade or nationally recognised standard?

1.10   Whenever possible, does management consider the use of training in order to gain a competitive or strategic advantage?

2 Detailed Issues

2.1   Are all new employees promptly provided with adequate induction training to inform them about the organisation and its aims?

2.2   Are all relevant employees provided with a personal training and development plan, and how does management ensure that the established objectives are met?

2.3   Are future skill requirements anticipated and adequately planned for, and how is this evidenced?

2.4   How are the development and training needs of individual employees identified, justified and fulfilled?

2.5   How is a training requirement justified and authorised?

2.6   How does management ensure that all training requirements are addressed?

2.7   What mechanisms prevent unauthorised or unjustified training activities?

2.8   What procedures are established for the review and authorisation of training and support for relevant professional qualifications, and how is the authorisation evidenced?

2.9   Are clear procedures available which define the extent to which the organisation will contribute to the fees for relevant professional qualification training?

2.10   Are staff who pursue relevant professional qualifications entitled to study leave and how is this controlled?

2.11   Are all specialist training requirements identified and addressed in order that key business processes and activities are protected?

2.12   Does management allow sufficient time to address the recognised training needs?

2.13   How does management monitor that training activity is (and remains) effective?

2.14   Are training staff kept abreast of the available and relevant training techniques and methods, and are they in a position to recommend the optimum form?

2.15   Are training methods, tools and facilities regularly reviewed for their relevance and effectiveness?

2.16   Is the use of external training facilities subject to adequate prior assessment and authorisation, and how is this evidenced?

2.17   How does management ensure that the organisation receives value for money in respect of training?

2.18   Whenever possible, is training conducted to a recognised standard?

2.19   Are there mechanisms in place to identify employees with a high development potential?

2.20   Are senior and key employees further motivated by the establishment and implementation of personal development programmes, and are such regimes monitored for their effectiveness and contribution to retaining key staff?

2.21   Does management take full advantage of any available government or trade-related training subsidies or grants?

2.22   Has management considered the role of training to improve the appeal of the organisation's products or services (for example, through improved customer advice and support)?

2.23   How is the accuracy of data input from other systems (e.g. staff appraisal scores) confirmed?

2.24   How is the accuracy of data output to other systems (e.g. personnel records) confirmed?

WELFARE

Individual organisations will take different views of staff welfare, and not all will provide all the facilities hinted at in the section that follows, as they can be seen as costly options.

Control Objectives for Welfare

(a)   To ensure that adequate provision is made for the protection of staff from injury or death in the course of their duties.

(b)   To ensure that appropriate and relevant employer's liability insurance cover is provided in accordance with the prevailing legal requirements.

(c) To motivate staff, to maintain staff morale, and improve their working conditions by providing, as appropriate, refreshment facilities, medical services, sporting and recreational facilities, transport facilities to/from sites, crèche facilities, staff shops/discounts, etc.

(d) To ensure that all staff welfare facilities are provided on an authorised and cost-effective basis.

(e) To ensure that only eligible employees benefit from welfare and other general facilities.

(f) To ensure that all goods and stock associated with welfare activities is adequately accounted for.

(g) To ensure that both unauthorised access to and abuse of staff welfare facilities is prevented.

(h) To ensure that the costs associated with the provision of welfare and fringe benefits are contained within budget.

Risk and Control Issues for Welfare

1 Key Issues

1.1 Has management defined, agreed, documented and implemented a policy and procedures on the provision of and eligibility for staff welfare facilities?

1.2 What does management do to provide adequate facilities to protect staff from injury or death in the course of their duties?

1.3 Are all relevant staff made aware of the specific health and safety regulations?

1.4 How does management confirm that the organisation is correctly complying with all the relevant health, safety and insurance requirements and regulations?

1.5 Are all accidents and incidents recorded and reported (in accordance with the prevailing regulations)?

1.6 Are all staff welfare facilities subject to suitable authorisation and management monitoring?

1.7 What measures prevent the use of staff facilities by outsiders and unauthorised employees?

1.8 How does management verify that all assets, goods and stock associated with staff welfare facilities are secure and accounted for?

1.9 Are staff welfare facilities operated within the agreed budgets, and are variances reported to management and acted upon?

2 Detailed Issues

2.1   What does management do to ensure that all the required staff protection and safety facilities are provided to the relevant standards?

2.2   Are staff fully aware of their responsibilities with respect to their well-being?

2.3   Are security facilities at company buildings and sites adequate?

2.4   Are staff who are involved in hazardous or potentially dangerous activities (such as transporting large amounts of cash) suitably trained and protected?

2.5   How does management confirm that insurance cover is appropriate, sufficient and currently in force?

2.6   Are all claims processed against the company insurance policies suitably documented, verified and pursued?

2.7   Are staff made aware of the available facilities and their eligibility to use them?

2.8   How does management justify and authorise staff welfare facilities?

2.9   Are staff welfare facilities monitored for usage and their contribution to staff motivation and morale (and are under-used or ineffective facilities withdrawn)?

2.10   How does management verify that the organisation is providing all the facilities required by local or national regulations and laws?

2.11   Are all the costs associated with the provision of welfare facilities accounted for and compared to the relevant budgets for management action?

2.12   How does management prevent unofficial, illegal or unauthorised activities?

2.13   Are club membership fees correctly accounted for?

2.14   Are company subsidies (e.g. for staff canteen or site transport) accounted for, within the agreed budget and suitably authorised?

2.15   Are suitably experienced or qualified staff provided (e.g. for medical services) and appropriate regulations (e.g. licensing arrangements) fully observed?

2.16   Are independent staff counsellors available to confidentially assist staff with their personal problems and concerns?

2.17   Are welfare facilities withdrawn from individual employees in proven cases of abuse or malpractice?

2.18   Are employees asked to prove their identity when using company facilities, and how is this achieved?

2.19   How are ex-employees or outsiders prevented from benefiting from welfare facilities?

2.20 How is accuracy of data input from other systems (e.g. from personnel records or payroll) confirmed?

2.21 How is the accuracy of data output to other systems (e.g. to payroll) confirmed?

PENSION SCHEME (AND OTHER BENEFITS)

The ethical administration of pension schemes has become a high-profile issue in the UK following the well-publicised Maxwell situation, where pension funds were supposedly used to prop up an ailing business empire. The improper use of the Maxwell pension scheme funds led to pension payments to thousands of pensioners being put in jeopardy. This case has raised issues about the prudent management and trusteeship of pension funds, which often represent very large sums.

In addition to the issues surrounding pension schemes, this section also considers other systems provided for the benefit of employees and directors, such as employee share schemes, share option schemes, and profit related pay (PRP) schemes. The noted control objectives and key issues cover all the above mentioned types of schemes; the detailed issues are subdivided into the various schemes.

Control Objectives for Pension Scheme (and Other Benefits)

(a) To ensure that pensions schemes are correctly established and operated in accordance with the prevailing legislation and good practice, so as to protect members' interests and safeguard the funds.

(b) To ensure that the scheme is suitably authorised and subject to a suitable trust deed if required.

(c) To ensure that pension funds are kept completely separate from company funds and fully accounted for.

(d) To ensure that membership eligibility rules are established and that only bona fide employees are accepted as members in accord with the membership rules.

(e) To ensure that the prescribed investment and funding policy is followed in all transactions, and periodically reviewed in order to remain pertinent.

(f) To ensure that all contributions (employee and employer) are accurately calculated, recorded, deducted, paid over and fully accounted for.

(g) To ensure that trustees (and management) are kept regularly informed of the performance and status of the fund.

(h) To ensure that the accumulated funds are adequate in order to meet the projected pension and benefits demands.

(i) To ensure that the fund is subject to external audit scrutiny and that any recommendations are appropriately followed up.

(j) To ensure that members are kept informed of their accrued pensions rights and other benefits.

(k) To ensure that all death in service and lump sum claims are validated and handled in accordance with the prevailing legislation and tax regulations.

(l) To ensure that pension payments are correctly calculated, accounted for and only paid over to bona fide pensioners.

(m) To ensure that refunds of contributions are valid, permissible under the law and fully accounted for.

(n) To ensure that transfers to/from other pension schemes are correctly valued and accounted for.

(o) To provide suitably experienced and qualified staff to administer the scheme and respond efficiently to members' enquiries, etc.

(p) To ensure that any employee share, share option or profit related pay schemes are correctly established, comply with the relevant legislation, are fully accountable, and are only operated for the benefit of bona fide and eligible members.

Risk and Control Issues for Pension Scheme (and other benefits)

1 Key Issues

1.1 How does management ensure that the pension scheme is correctly established and operated, and complies with the current legislation and good practice?

1.2 Is the scheme in its current form authorised by management and supported by documented procedures, rules and a suitable trust deed (if applicable)?

1.3 Would any failure to comply with either the established rules or prevailing legislation be promptly detected?

1.4 How do management and trustees confirm that all pension funds are kept strictly separate from company activities and remain fully accounted for?

1.5 What mechanisms prevent unauthorised or ineligible employees becoming members of the pension scheme?

1.6   Has the preferred investment policy and strategy been defined, agreed and documented, and how are management and trustees assured that it is always followed in investment transactions?

1.7   How are members, management and trustees assured that all pension contributions are valid, correctly calculated, deducted, paid over, and accounted for?

1.8   What processes would detect anomalies or irregularities in respect of contribution accountability, and how is any corrective action evidenced?

1.9   Are management and trustees regularly supplied with accurate, timely and relevant information on the scheme in order to discharge their responsibilities?

1.10   Is the fund subject to regular scrutiny by suitably qualified external auditors (or any other regulatory bodies), and are their recommendations and observations adequately followed up?

1.11   Are there processes in place to ensure that all payments from the fund are valid, authorised, correctly calculated, paid over to bona fide persons, and fully accounted for?

1.12   How does management ensure that the operations of any other schemes (e.g. employee shares, share options, profit related pay) fully comply with the current legislation and tax regulations, and are fully accounted for?

2 Detailed Issues

Pensions

2.1   Are the pension administrators and trustees kept fully aware of the current legislation and good practice affecting the operation of pension schemes, and how is this evidenced?

2.2   Has the establishment and ongoing operation of the pension scheme been subject to appropriate authorisation?

2.3   Has senior management sanctioned the extent of the company contributions to the scheme, the costs of operation, the methods of funding and the membership rules?

2.4   Are adequate and up-to-date pension scheme rules and procedures in place, and made available to scheme members and potential members?

2.5   Has a suitable trust deed been established for the scheme, and does it define:

- the nature and purpose of the scheme
- the names of the trustees
- the rules for appointing trustees
- the trustees' terms of reference

- the method of funding
- the investment policy
- benefits and conditions of membership
- the reporting and auditing requirements?

2.6   How are management and members assured that the requirements of the trust deed are complied with?

2.7   Do the nomination and election processes for trustees comply with the regulations and good practice, and are the appointed trustees suitably experienced and adequately represent the interest of scheme members?

2.8   Are trustees and/or the scheme administrators held accountable for their actions, and have their responsibilities and duties been clearly defined?

2.9   Are separate bank accounts and fund accounts maintained for the operation of the fund, and is there adequate segregation from company funds and activities?

2.10 Are all investment transactions authorised and confirmed as being in accordance with the documented investment policy and aims of the scheme, and what prevents the processing of invalid or unauthorised transactions?

2.11 How are members and potential scheme members confirmed as being eligible for membership, and how are all eligible members identified at the appropriate time?

2.12 Are all contributions (employee and employer) calculated in accordance with the rules of the scheme?

2.13 What prevents the level of individual members' contributions exceeding any statutory or regulatory limits?

2.14 Are all additional voluntary contributions (AVCs) in accordance with the prevailing regulations and scheme rules, and correctly accounted for?

2.15 Are all scheme contributions accounted for within the fund, and what prevents the incorrect calculation and deduction of contributions?

2.16 Are all staff leavers identified and correctly notified of their options under the pension scheme, and what processes prevent incorrect or invalid advice/ data being provided?

2.17 How are all contribution refunds confirmed as being valid, accurate, within the scheme rules, and in compliance with current legislation?

2.18 Are all contribution refunds correctly calculated, accounted for, trailed and confirmed as paid only to bona fide members?

2.19 How do trustees, members and management ensure that the accumulated fund is sufficient to meet the projected pension demand, and how can they be confident that the current fund valuation is accurate and realistic?

2.20   Are trustees kept informed of the fund performance in order that they can appropriately discharge their responsibilities to members?

2.21   What evidence is there that appropriate action is taken by trustees to respond to investment or fund concerns?

2.22   Are trustees obliged to meet regularly and are minutes of their meetings and details of the authorised actions appropriately maintained?

2.23   Are audited accounts provided to members on a regular basis?

2.24   Are all members' queries and concerns about the fund and its administration recorded and confirmed as being adequately (and independently) dealt with?

2.25   Are the conditions under which the organisation can declare a contribution holiday clearly defined and subject to adequate review and authorisation?

2.26   Are regular statements of their entitlements provided to members, and how is the accuracy and validity of this data confirmed?

2.27   How are death-in-service payments confirmed as being valid, authorised, correctly calculated and paid over to bona fide beneficiaries?

2.28   What mechanisms prevent pension department staff, trustees and management from misappropriating members funds?

2.29   How are tax-free lump sum payments confirmed as being valid, correctly calculated in accordance with the relevant regulations, and accounted for?

2.30   Are all members approaching retirement identified and correctly advised of their pension valuations?

2.31   What measures are in place to prevent pension payments being made to invalid persons?

2.32   How are trustees and pension administrators made aware of all pensioner deaths so that the payments of pension benefit are accordingly ceased or correctly routed to eligible and valid dependents, and how is this documented?

2.33   Are all transfers from other schemes accurately assessed for their eligibility, confirmed value, and the relative value in the target scheme?

2.34   Are the best interests of the members taken into account when transfers to and from the scheme are being considered, and how are members assured that they are receiving accurate and appropriate information and guidance?

2.35   How are all transfers into and from the pension fund accounted for, authorised and trailed?

2.36   Are pension administration staff suitably experienced and qualified?

2.37   How are surplus scheme funds identified and dealt with, and is the action taken authorised and confirmed to be within the law and in the best interests of scheme members?

2.38   How is accuracy of data input from other systems (e.g. payroll and bank accounts) confirmed?

2.39   How is the accuracy of data output to other systems (e.g. accounting systems) confirmed?

2.40   What mechanisms prevent the unauthorised access to and misuse of pension scheme and membership data?

2.41   Are pension administration and any external fund costs authorised and monitored by management?

Employee Share Schemes
2.42   Has management authorised the scheme and ensured that it conforms to the prevailing legislation and regulations?

2.43   Have the scheme rules been defined, agreed and documented?

2.44   How is membership eligibility confirmed and what prevents the acceptance of invalid members?

2.45   Are staff leavers accurately identified, correctly notified of their options under the scheme, correctly processed, and removed?

2.46   Are staff share holdings held in trust for the prescribed period and are all holdings accurately identified and accounted for?

2.47   How are the periodic allocation of shares calculated and the individual allocations recorded and accounted for?

2.48   Are appropriate individual share holdings transferred from the trust to personal ownership at the correct time (as determined by the current regulations)?

2.49   Are all scheme and individual share holdings correctly registered (and are accurate holding certificates issued in good time)?

2.50   How does management ensure that all dividends due on scheme and individual holdings are accurately calculated and paid over to bona fide share holders?

2.51   Are all ownership transfers of scheme/individual holdings (i.e. upon the death of the employee) confirmed as valid, authorised and accounted for?

2.52   How is accuracy of data input from other systems confirmed?

2.53   How is the accuracy of data output to other systems confirmed?

2.54   What mechanisms prevent the unauthorised access to and misuse of scheme and membership data?

Share Option Scheme

2.55 Has management authorised the scheme and ensured that it conforms to the prevailing legislation and regulations?

2.56 Have the scheme rules been defined, agreed and documented, and how is compliance with them confirmed?

2.57 How is membership eligibility confirmed and what prevents the acceptance of invalid members?

2.58 How is the accuracy and validity of the option allocations confirmed?

2.59 Is the accuracy of scheme data confirmed?

2.60 When members wish to exercise their rights to purchase shares from the scheme, are their requests validated to the rules and confirmed as complying with the current taxation regulations?

2.61 Are members' payments for shares confirmed as being correct, recorded and fully accounted for?

2.62 Are all shares purchased by members from the scheme subsequently correctly registered and the appropriate ownership documentation issued?

2.63 Are members leaving the scheme or the organisation correctly advised as to their rights and liabilities?

2.64 How is accuracy of data input from other systems confirmed?

2.65 How is the accuracy of data output to other systems confirmed?

2.66 What mechanisms prevent the unauthorised access to and misuse of scheme and membership data?

Profit Related Pay

2.67 Has management authorised the scheme and ensured that it conforms to the prevailing legislation and regulations?

2.68 Have the scheme rules been defined, agreed and documented, and how is compliance with them confirmed?

2.69 How is membership eligibility confirmed and what prevents the acceptance of invalid members?

2.70 What checks are in place to confirm that all entitlements are correctly calculated, disbursed and accounted for?

2.71 What processes ensure that only eligible staff partake in the scheme and what prevents unauthorised and ineligible participation?

2.72 Are payments under the scheme authorised by management, and how is this evidenced?

2.73 Is the scheme subject to management review as to its effectiveness?

2.74   How is accuracy of data input from other systems confirmed?

2.75   How is the accuracy of data output to other systems confirmed?

2.76   What mechanisms prevent the unauthorised access to and misuse of scheme and membership data?

HEALTH INSURANCE

Many employers will provide health insurance cover for their employees (with eligibility perhaps linked to a qualifying job grade, or following a probationary employment period). This section examines the issues emerging from such schemes, and includes points relevant to both externally sourced and in-house funded schemes.

Control Objectives for Health Insurance

(a)   To provide an authorised and cost-effective health insurance scheme for eligible staff.

(b)   To ensure that only eligible staff become members of the scheme.

(c)   To ensure that premiums paid by the company are correctly calculated, authorised, relative to actual membership, accounted for, and are competitive.

(d)   To ensure that any additional contributions made by employees are correctly calculated, received and paid over to the scheme.

(e)   To ensure that the provision of the scheme fully complies with all the relevant legislation and taxation regulations.

(f)   To ensure that claims against the scheme are correctly routed and dealt with.

(g)   To prevent the processing of invalid or excessive claims so as to contain the operating costs to the organisation.

(h)   To ensure that management periodically reviews the performance and costs of the scheme so as to ensure that it continues to represent good value for money.

Risk and Control Issues for Health Insurance

1 Key Issues

1.1   Has the scheme been suitably authorised and the costs justified and negotiated on the best terms?

1.2 Have appropriate membership eligibility rules been established, and are only eligible employees accepted for membership at the appropriate time?

1.3 How does management make sure that the operation of the scheme complies with all the relevant legislation and current taxation regulations?

1.4 How are the organisation's premiums calculated, and does this process represent the actual level/type of membership?

1.5 How does management ensure that the premiums represent good value for money and that they are competitive (e.g. are they subject to review by management upon renewal)?

1.6 Are all premium payments authorised, recorded and adequately accounted for?

1.7 Are all scheme claims assessed for validity and recorded as passed over to the scheme providers?

1.8 Are excessive or invalid claims identified and prevented from being processed?

2 Detailed Issues

2.1 What processes prevent the acceptance of unauthorised, ineligible, invalid or high risk scheme members?

2.2 Has the responsibility for administering the scheme been allocated?

2.3 Have realistic and economic benefit limits been established (as a means to contain the premium costs), and are members fully aware of any such limits to scheme coverage?

2.4 Is the scheme arranged with a recognised, stable and reliable provider?

2.5 Is the performance of the scheme provider monitored and regularly assessed for value for money, etc.?

2.6 How does management ensure that any available company taxation advantages of the scheme are appropriately and legally exploited?

2.7 When applicable, are the individual members' personal benefit taxation liabilities accurately recorded and reported to the relevant authorities (e.g. as for P11D returns in the UK)?

2.8 How does management verify that the premiums paid by the organisation are accurately based on the actual scheme membership (excluding staff leavers)?

2.9 Are additional premiums to be paid directly by members correctly calculated, deducted, paid over and accounted for?

2.10 How is accuracy of data input from other systems (e.g. human resources or payroll) confirmed?

2.11   How is the accuracy of data output to other systems (e.g. general ledger) confirmed?

STAFF APPRAISAL AND DISCIPLINARY MATTERS

Staff motivation can be aided by the setting (either globally or individually) of performance and personal development targets, against which actual achievement is subsequently measured. In some formal schemes, the achievement success of employees may be linked to rewards (for example, the extent of the annual pay review). Alongside these elements is the need to identify the training and development requirements of individuals so that costly training resources can effectively be targeted and staff skill levels suitably maintained in step with the current environmental factors.

This section also addresses staff disciplinary matters and the need to establish formal complaints and disciplinary procedures.

Control Objectives for Staff Appraisal and Disciplinary Matters

(a)   To ensure that staff performance is monitored and regularly appraised so that employee contributions are maximised.

(b)   To ensure that the staff appraisal system is authorised by management and that the scheme is supported by realistic and workable procedures.

(c)   To ensure that management and staff are fully aware of the aims of the system and their role in the process.

(d)   To ensure that staff are aware of their responsibilities and have determined measurable goals and objectives to achieve.

(e)   To ensure that the achievement of personal goals and objectives is monitored and reasons for non-achievement identified and reviewed.

(f)   To link performance and personal achievement to the reward structure.

(g)   To ensure that personal training and development needs are assessed and addressed.

(h)   To ensure that the appraisal process is fair, unbiased, and gives employees the opportunity to comment on and agree their obligations and performance standards.

(i)   To ensure that staff with consistently poor performance records are detected and dealt with accordingly.

(j)   To ensure that all appraisal and disciplinary schemes operate within the confines of the prevailing employment legislation.

(k)   To ensure that matters of absenteeism and misconduct are formally dealt with.

> (l)   To provide facilities to enable staff to bring their problems and concerns to the attention of management without fear of retribution.
>
> (m)   To provide a formal complaints and disciplinary procedure, incorporating escalation procedures, rights of appeal and representation, and defined disciplinary stages (letters of warning, withdrawal of privileges, dismissal, etc.).

Risk and Control Issues for Staff Appraisal and Disciplinary Matters

1 Key Issues

1.1   How does management confirm that staff are performing at the appropriate level and standard?

1.2   Has management authorised and established a staff appraisal system supported by documented procedures?

1.3   Does the staff appraisal scheme have the commitment of senior management, and are staff and management aware of their roles in the process?

1.4   Are staff performances assessed against realistic and measurable factors and objectives, and how are these recorded?

1.5   Is line management adequately trained and briefed for their role and responsibilities in the appraisal scheme?

1.6   Are individuals' performances regularly assessed against their defined goals and objectives, and are failures to achieve the desired standard examined to determine the underlying reasons?

1.7   Are performance shortcomings used as the basis for determining and agreeing the personal training and development needs of staff?

1.8   How does management ensure that staff training and development needs are satisfactorily and cost-effectively addressed?

1.9   Have formal, authorised and documented disciplinary procedures been established, and how is compliance assured?

1.10   Do all staff appraisal and disciplinary procedures comply with the current and relevant employment legislation, and how is compliance confirmed?

1.11   Is management assured that cases of persistent absenteeism or serious misconduct would be detected and appropriately dealt with?

1.12   In dealing with disciplinary matters, are the rights of employees adequately catered for?

2 Detailed Issues

2.1   Are all staff made aware of their responsibilities and the scope of their position?

2.2   Is line management adequately trained to consistently and fairly conduct appraisal interviews and assessments?

2.3   Is adequate account taken of employees' views and comments?

2.4   Does the system cater for the comments of management above the level of appraiser as a means of quality control?

2.5   How does management monitor that the appraisal scoring method is consistent and reliable?

2.6   Is the appraisal scheme used in a positive context as the basis for improving and developing staff, rather than in a punitive context?

2.7   Does the appraisal system enable the detection of exceptional or high performing employees who could be groomed for promotion?

2.8   Where appraisal results/scores are used as a basis for pay reviews, how can management be certain that the scores are valid and not manipulated?

2.9   Are employees required to signify their agreement to the recorded goals and objectives?

2.10 What mechanisms are in place to detect poor performance on the job?

2.11 Are regular staff, department, team or quality circle meetings encouraged in order to promote a positive attitude towards performance and contribution?

2.12 Do staff have access to alternative independent channels of communication for their problems and concerns, and the right formally to escalate their grievances (and is the relevant procedure formalised)?

2.13 Are employees' rights to have trade union, staff association or legal representation at disciplinary hearings complied with?

2.14 What steps does the organisation take to avoid the escalation of disciplinary disputes to public industrial tribunals?

2.15 What processes ensure that all the stages of the disciplinary procedure are conducted in compliance with the relevant legislation?

2.16 How is the accuracy of data input from other systems (e.g. attendance records or performance statistics) confirmed?

2.17 How is the accuracy of data output to other systems (e.g. personnel records) confirmed?

HEALTH AND SAFETY

Health and safety matters will range from general (perhaps even common sense) measures that will normally apply to every employer through to those which are specifically relative to the sector or operations of the organisation. In either case, there is an obligation on employers to ensure that all the required health and safety issues are satisfactorily addressed. Management will need to be assured that all the relevant and prevailing regulations are being complied with. Additionally, it is crucial that staff are fully aware of their responsibilities and are suitably trained in the use of any required safety equipment.

This section also touches on general security matters. Chapter 14 also features the following points about health and safety in the context of providing a suitably safe environment for staff and visitors as a part of ensuring their overall security.

Control Objectives for Health and Safety

(a) To ensure that risk assessment identifies all potential health and safety implications as the basis for rectifying exposures.

(b) To ensure that all health and safety matters are addressed for the protection of staff, visitors and customers.

(c) To ensure the relevant legislation and regulations are fully complied with.

(d) To ensure that all staff are fully aware of workplace risks, how to use safety equipment and protect themselves.

(e) To ensure that adequate safety equipment and training are provided.

(f) To ensure that machinery and equipment is effectively maintained, safely installed and protected where necessary.

(g) To provide adequate and operative fire prevention and protection facilities.

(h) To ensure that building evacuation drills are effective and regularly tested.

(i) To provide adequate security measures for the protection of staff and visitors.

(j) To ensure that all accidents and incidents are promptly reported.

(k) To ensure that appropriate, sufficient and current insurance cover is in place.

(l) To provide adequate first aid and medical facilities.

(m) To ensure that adequate hygiene and cleaning standards are maintained.

> (n) To ensure that hazardous materials are correctly and safely stored.
>
> (o) To ensure that all required certifications are obtained from regulatory bodies.

Risk and Control Issues for Health and Safety

1 Key Issues

1.1   How does management verify that they have identified and adequately addressed all health and safety risks and hazards within the organisation?

1.2   Has an authorised and documented health and safety policy been developed and implemented, and is it maintained up to date?

1.3   How does management confirm compliance with all the relevant legislation and regulations?

1.4   What processes ensure that staff are fully aware of workplace risks and how properly to use safety equipment and protect themselves?

1.5   Has sufficient and appropriate safety equipment (e.g. fire extinguishers, protective clothing) been provided, and what measures ensure that it all remains in working order and effective?

1.6   Have sufficient and effective fire prevention and protection systems been provided, and are they regularly tested?

1.7   Are adequate security measures in place to restrict access to facilities and protect staff and equipment from attack?

1.8   What steps are in place to ensure that all incidents and accidents are reported and appropriately dealt with?

1.9   Have adequate first aid and medical facilities (equipment and personnel) been provided, and are supplies replenished when used?

1.10 Are adequate hygiene and cleanliness standards established, and what mechanisms ensure that the required standards are maintained?

1.11 How does management provide and maintain adequate and appropriate insurance cover?

1.12 What mechanisms ensure that all the required regulatory inspections are conducted and that the appropriate regulatory certification is obtained?

1.13 How does management ensure that all hazardous materials are safely, correctly and securely stored?

2 Detailed Issues

2.1   Has management undertaken a risk assessment of health and safety implications throughout the organisation in order to identify the risks and ensure that they are addressed?

2.2   Has a health and safety policy been introduced, and have specific responsibilities for safety issues been allocated?

2.3   What mechanisms prevent non-compliance with the prevailing health and safety regulations?

2.4   How does management maintain an up-to-date awareness of all the relevant health and safety regulations?

2.5   Are all staff adequately trained in safety matters, including use of equipment and clothing (and how can management be certain that all the relevant staff actually receive the appropriate training)?

2.6   Are staff progressively tested on their level of understanding of safety measures in order to identify further training needs?

2.7   How does management monitor that all the relevant safety equipment is maintained in working order?

2.8   Are all relevant machines fitted with guards, safety cut-outs, etc. to the required standard?

2.9   How does management monitor that all computer equipment conforms to the required standards (e.g. screen radiation levels)?

2.10 Are building evacuation, fire and security drills regularly conducted and assessed for effectiveness?

2.11 Are adequate fire alarms and security systems installed, tested and maintained (and would faults be detected promptly)?

2.12 How does management monitor that all building environmental systems (heating, lighting, air conditioning, etc.) are working correctly and to the required legal standards?

2.13 What mechanisms prevent unauthorised access to buildings and facilities?

2.14 Are the relevant staff (receptionists, door guards, post room staff, etc.) aware of the action required in the event of a bomb alert, an attack on the building, a suspicious package, and so on?

2.15 What processes ensure that the records of incidents and accidents are fully and correctly maintained in accordance with any regulatory requirements?

2.16 Are sufficient and suitably trained first aid and medical personnel available, and how can they promptly be summoned to an incident?

2.17 In the event of an emergency, how does management account for all visitors?

2.18   Are transitory safety risks (such as trailing power leads, wet floors due to cleaning) adequately addressed?

2.19   What does management do to maintain sufficient insurance cover in the event of the organisation being sued for negligence with regard to health and safety conditions?

2.20   What processes ensure that insurance cover is renewed, on time and at the appropriate level?

2.21   What processes ensure that all the required certificates and licences are obtained to enable the lawful operation of facilities?

2.22   What mechanisms prevent unauthorised access to hazardous materials?

2.23   How is accuracy of data input from other systems (e.g.human resources) confirmed?

2.24   How is the accuracy of data output to other systems (e.g. estates management) confirmed?

LABOUR RELATIONS

In larger organisations, this can be a vital area. Wherever there is a sizable (perhaps specially skilled) workforce, it is obviously important that disruptions to such aspects as production, customer service, etc. are minimised through prompt and effective action. Dealing effectively and fairly with workforce concerns (perhaps involving trades union representation) calls for great skill and diplomacy. In the following section we incorporate pre-emptive points such as establishing effective channels of communication with staff and ensuring that all staff are kept informed of significant change and developments.

Control Objectives for Labour Relations

(a)   To ensure that good labour relations are developed and maintained in order that operations and processes are not interrupted.

(b)   To avoid the disruption of services to customers.

(c)   To avoid costly disputes and adverse impact on the organisation's public image and reputation.

(d)   To ensure that the company policy on labour relations is suitably authorised and complied with.

> (e) To ensure that labour relations and negotiations are handled in accordance with the requirements of the prevailing legislation.
>
> (f) To secure the trust and involvement of employees as a means of effectively managing change and business development.
>
> (g) To ensure, where applicable, that relationships and negotiations with trade unions, staff associations, etc. are appropriately handled.
>
> (h) To enable the prompt identification and rectification of potential labour problems.

Risk and Control Issues for Labour Relations

1 Key Issues

1.1 Has the organisation developed, agreed, authorised and documented a labour relations policy?

1.2 Has the basis for communicating with the workforce and their representatives been clearly established, endorsed and communicated?

1.3 How does management ensure that the organisation's labour relations policy and associated procedures fully comply with the prevailing legislation and regulations?

1.4 How does management make sure that all the requirements of the labour relations policy are complied with?

1.5 What measures are in place to avoid or cater for the disruptions and impacts of labour relation problems?

1.6 How is management sure that it would detect potential labour relations problems and be able to react promptly?

1.7 Have suitably experienced and qualified staff, familiar with negotiation and other relevant techniques, been employed and allocated the responsibility for dealing with labour relations?

1.8 Are staff (and their officially recognised representatives) actively involved in the development of the business and instances of major change?

1.9 How does management ensure that the balance of power between the organisation and staff representation is maintained?

2 Detailed Issues

2.1 Has management established effective channels of communication between themselves and the workforce (including trade unions and staff associations when applicable)?

2.2 Has management allocated a defined responsibility for handling public and media relations in the event of a labour dispute?

2.3 How does/would management protect the organisation's public image and corporate reputation during any labour dispute?

2.4 Have procedures been established which define the framework for negotiating change, pay reviews, etc., and how is management assured that all such procedures are being complied with?

2.5 Has management recognised the role of arbitration in the settlement of disputes and agreed a formal arbitration procedure with other affected parties?

2.6 Has adequate provision been made to enable staff to communicate their views to management (i.e. through staff meetings, works committees or board representation)?

2.7 Is there a formal agreement in place addressing the recognition of nominated trade unions and other representative bodies?

2.8 How is the accuracy of data input from other systems (e.g. manpower and succession planning) confirmed?

2.9 How is data output to other systems (e.g. personnel system) confirmed?

COMPANY VEHICLES

The determination of corporate company vehicle policy often resides with the human resources function, and they may even control the allocation of vehicles to staff based on the agreed policy. Although the day-to-day administration of the fleet may rest with an appropriately skilled transport function, we have intentionally included all the issues relating to company vehicles in this section.

Control Objectives for Company Vehicles

(a) To ensure that an authorised vehicle policy is established and adhered to.

(b) To ensure that vehicles are allocated to and used only by authorised and eligible staff for defined purposes.

(c) To ensure that vehicles of the appropriate type are acquired at the optimum cost.

(d) To ensure that all vehicle acquisitions are authorised.

(e) To ensure that vehicles are operated legally and comply with all the relevant regulations.

(f) To ensure that vehicles are adequately and economically maintained and operated.

(g) To ensure that all vehicle expenditure is justified and authorised.

(h) To ensure that vehicles are disposed of at the optimum time and price.

(i) To ensure that vehicles are maintained in accordance with the warranty conditions.

(j) To ensure that all accidents and damage are reported, claimed via the insurers, and satisfactorily settled.

(k) To ensure that all fuel costs are valid, authorised and accounted for.

(l) To ensure that all vehicle costs are correctly identified, authorised, and accounted for.

(m) To ensure that vehicles used to deliver and distribute goods are suitably licensed and conform to the relevant regulations.

(n) To ensure that suitably qualified and experienced staff are employed to administer the vehicle fleet.

Risk and Control Issues for Company Vehicles

1 Key Issues

1.1 Has a suitable company vehicle policy been developed, authorised and implemented?

1.2 What mechanisms are in place to ensure that all company vehicle purchases and allocations are authorised, in accordance with the policy, and correctly treated in the accounts?

1.3 What processes ensure that all vehicles are operated legally and in accordance with all the relevant regulations?

1.4   How does management verify that all vehicle operating costs are justified, correct, authorised, and accounted for in the accounts?

1.5   What mechanisms ensure that all vehicles are regularly and adequately maintained in accordance with the warranty conditions?

1.6   What are the procedures to ensure that vehicles are disposed of at the optimum time and price, and that all disposal proceeds are correctly accounted for?

1.7   Are all accidents involving company vehicles correctly reported, processed and settled through the insurers?

1.8   How does management exercise control over fuel costs, so that only justified, appropriate and authorised fuel costs are accounted for?

2 Detailed Issues

2.1   Does the prevailing vehicle policy adequately define the authorised vehicle types and applicable staff categories?

2.2   What mechanisms prevent the acquisition of an unauthorised vehicle type?

2.3   If vehicle price limits are established, how are purchases exceeding the limit prevented?

2.4   How does management ensure that vehicles are purchased at the best negotiated prices?

2.5   Are vehicles purchased only from reputable dealers/agents, and what mechanisms prevent dealings with unauthorised suppliers?

2.6   Are appropriate discounted terms arranged with manufacturers in the event of quantity purchases?

2.7   How are all vehicle purchases authorised, and what prevents an invalid transaction being processed?

2.8   Are all new vehicles subject to inspection and would faulty or damaged vehicles be detected and rejected?

2.9   How can management be certain that all vehicle purchase costs are accurately identified and correctly accounted for (i.e. in the fixed assets records)?

2.10   Has an authorised company vehicle depreciation policy been implemented, and does it follow normal accounting practice or fiscal legislation?

2.11   Has an adequate vehicle fleet administration department been established, with suitably qualified and experienced staff?

2.12 How are all legal and regulatory matters dealt with (road fund licences, adequate insurance cover, vehicle roadworthiness, legal emission levels, etc.)?

2.13 Would failures to comply with legal and regulatory requirements be promptly detected and rectified?

2.14 How does management monitor that all company vehicle drivers are (and remain) correctly licensed and eligible (including heavy goods vehicle and specialist vehicle drivers)?

2.15 What mechanisms ensure that goods vehicle drivers are operating in accordance with the prevailing legislation (including permitted driving hours, correct utilisation of tachographs, etc.)?

2.16 Are drivers made fully aware of their responsibilities for vehicles allocated to them and made to sign for the vehicle in good condition upon allocation?

2.17 Are all company vehicles correctly and adequately insured, and are drivers aware of their responsibilities in the event of an accident ?

2.18 Are company vehicles adequately protected against theft?

2.19 What checks are in plae to monitor that vehicles are serviced and maintained in accordance with the manufacturers' recommendations and relevant warranty conditions?

2.20 What mechanisms ensure that all valid warranty claims are identified, processed and settled?

2.21 How does management verify that all vehicle maintenance and repair costs are justified and authorised?

2.22 What controls prevent non-company vehicle costs being accepted and processed?

2.23 Are all company vehicles traceable to a named driver and location?

2.24 Does the vehicle administration system alert management to forthcoming events and actions (e.g. renewal of taxation)?

2.25 Would management be able promptly to identify unusually high vehicle servicing costs for an individual vehicle?

2.26 Is regular and accurate vehicle fleet management information provided, and how is follow-up action to reported anomalies evidenced?

2.27 Is the system capable of highlighting vehicles that are either approaching their disposal date or have excessive associated costs?

2.28 Are all maintenance and repairs conducted only by suitably qualified and authorised suppliers to the necessary standard (and how is the standard confirmed)?

2.29   Have emergency and out-of-hours breakdown facilities been cost-effectively provided, and are the relative costs monitored?

2.30   Has management established an authorised policy for vehicle fuel costs, and what prevents unauthorised or invalid fuel costs being met by the company (e.g.for private journeys)?

2.31 · Are company fuel cards issued only to authorised employees, and what mechanisms prevent their misuse?

2.32   Are fuel costs reported, adequately monitored and followed up by management?

2.33   What is the procedure for reporting accidents?

2.34   What steps are in place to ensure that all accident damage is suitably inspected and assessed for repair cost in order that actual costs are reasonable and authorised?

2.35   How does management confirm that all accident repair costs are justified, authorised and reclaimed from insurers whenever possible?

2.36   Are accident claims adequately monitored to ensure prompt and appropriate settlement?

2.37   How does management verify that vehicle insurance arrangements are appropriate, legal, and offer good value for money?

2.38   How are vehicles for disposal identified, and is the basis for disposal at the optimum time for the company and the resale market?

2.39   How does management ensure that the company receives a fair market price for vehicle disposals?

2.40   Are all vehicles assessed for their likely disposal value and monitored to ensure that the actual proceeds are reasonable?

2.41   Has management established authorised disposal methods for company vehicles (e.g. via car auctions, dealers, staff sales) and how can they be sure that only authorised disposal outlets are used?

2.42   How is management certain that all vehicle disposal proceeds are correctly identified and fully accounted for?

2.43   Are management made aware of the value of disposal proceeds against the written-down value of the vehicle in the company books, and would unfavourable variances be promptly highlighted?

2.44   Are disposal proceeds subject to management authority and monitoring, and how is this evidenced?

2.45   How are all vehicle write-offs justified and suitably authorised, and what prevents the unauthorised write-off of a vehicle?

2.46 How is the accuracy of data input from other systems (e.g. authorised drivers from the personnel records) confirmed?

2.47 How is accuracy of data output to other systems (e.g. vehicle disposals to the fixed asset system, or servicing costs to the accounts payable system) confirmed?

Auditing Research and Development

INTRODUCTION

In this chapter we consider research and development (R&D).

Ethics

Before looking at the individual functions of R&D, we'll look briefly at a subject of growing importance within research and development—ethics.

Ethics is a theme never far away from the contents of this book. For instance, Chapter 15 considers environmental ethics issues. Appendix 9 is an example Code of Ethical Conduct, which covers both scientific and environmental matters. Much of the contents of this suggested *Code* is directly applicable to R&D. The Code of Ethical Conduct can be used as a model basis for designing specific organisational policy statements on these matters. Appendix 9 should be used in conjunction with the Statement of Corporate Principles (Appendix 7) and the Code of Business Conduct (Appendix 8). The Statement of Corporate Principles is the overarching group board level policy statement of general corporate principles, and the underlying Codes (Code of Business Conduct and Code of Ethical Conduct) are conversions of the general principles into what on the whole are more detailed guidelines applying to commercial issues on the one hand and to scientific and environmental issues on the other hand. All three documents are intended to have been endorsed by formal board resolution so as to become company policy. There is some common ground and thus some common wording between these two Codes. These three appendices have grown out of a set of documents originally designed for a multinational pharmaceutical company, though their wording has been modified to make them more generally applicable.

SYSTEM/FUNCTION COMPONENTS OF RESEARCH AND DEVELOPMENT

We have chosen to use an essentially *functional* approach to define the research and development audit universe, which gives us the following possible breakdown of the key functions, systems or activities:

- product development
- project appraisal and monitoring
- plant and equipment
- development project management
- legal and regulatory issues.

CONTROL OBJECTIVES AND RISK AND CONTROL ISSUES

We shall now examine the control objectives and risk and control issues (divided into key issues and detailed issues) for each of the research and development functions listed above. This data can be used within the Standard Audit Programme Guides (SAPGs) looked at in Chapter 3. To save space we have concentrated on the objectives to be stated and the questions to be asked and have not presented these within the SAPG format.

The data supplied in the following sections are deliberately general and broad in nature, so that they can be related to a range of possible organisational scenarios. However, in practice, all manner of specific industry or sector factors may apply and these should then be suitably incorporated into the data. Conversely, some of the issues raised may not apply (either in organisational or national terms) and these can accordingly be disregarded. The overall aim of the supplied data is to provide a general awareness of the likely elements for each activity.

PRODUCT DEVELOPMENT

Organisations will need to define the future strategy for their products and allocate appropriate resources to support their objectives in this area. This section examines such objectives from the research and development viewpoint, where such R&D activities are handled in-house. This stance presupposes that the relevant organisation has the requisite facilities, resources and expertise to conduct an R&D exercise, and therefore we exclude the considerations applicable to the set-up of an R&D facility.

See also the points discussed in Chapter 9 under the heading "Product Development", which refer to the ongoing development of new and improved products as a vital part of an overall marketing policy and plan.

Control Objectives for Product Development

(a) To ensure that new and existing products are researched and developed in accordance with market factors and the defined strategic objectives of the organisation.

(b) To ensure that all product developments are fully assessed in relation to the potential market, estimated production costs and selling price.

(c) To ensure that R&D resources are adequate and targeted on those areas with the greatest potential for the organisation.

(d) To ensure that R&D facilities, resources and costs are commensurate with the planned activities.

(e) To ensure that management maintains an accurate and up-to-date awareness of current technological trends and their potential application for the organisation.

(f) To ensure that an adequate level of general/speculative research is undertaken to enable the organisation to achieve a technological advantage over its competitors.

(g) To ensure that the resources required to undertake research and development are accurately identified, costed, justified and authorised.

(h) To ensure that all product development and research projects are suitably assessed and authorised to proceed.

(i) To ensure that the design assessment, feasibility, and product specification processes are adequate and address matters of quality and performance.

(j) To ensure that the research activity, theories, specifications, drawings, technology, and the eventual products are adequately protected from exploitation by others.

(k) To ensure that research and development activities do not, in themselves, violate existing patents and copyrights.

(l) To ensure that the use of external research and specialist facilities is subject to assessment, authorisation, monitoring, and effective levels of security.

(m) To ensure that specialist staff are recruited, appropriately trained, and retained for the benefit of the organisation.

(n) To ensure that all information about the organisation's product developments and research programme remains confidential.

(o) To ensure that all the actual development costs are correctly identified and monitored against the established budgets.

(p) To ensure that the progress of all research and development projects is adequately monitored by management and appropriate changes are applied when necessary and authorised.

(q) To ensure that adequate, appropriate and legally required levels of testing are conducted and evidenced.

> (r) To ensure that all significant project variations or problems are promptly reported to management for corrective action.
>
> (s) To ensure that the objectives and performance criteria established at the outset of the development are actually achieved.
>
> (t) To ensure that all the relevant legal and regulatory requirements are met.
>
> (u) To ensure that the market launch of new or modified products is adequately planned, appropriately timed to maximise the market impact, co-ordinated between the affected functions, and monitored.

Risk and Control Issues for Product Development

1 Key Issues

1.1   Has management defined and authorised strategic business objectives, and what checks are in place to ensure that all product developments and research activities comply with these targets?

1.2   Has management established, authorised and implemented documented procedures for the development and evolution of all product ranges?

1.3   How does management keep product plans adequate, appropriate, viable, etc.?

1.4   How is management sure that all product development projects are valid, justified and authorised?

1.5   What processes govern the direction of research activities in order to ensure that attention is focused on those projects with the greatest potential benefit and implications for the organisation?

1.6   Have an R&D strategy and plan been developed, documented and authorised, and what steps are taken to monitor progress and achievements?

1.7   How does management ensure that R&D resources are justified, adequate, and relative to the planned activities?

1.8   How does management maintain an accurate and up-to-date awareness of all current technologies, innovations, etc. with a potential impact for the organisation?

1.9   Beyond the specific product development projects, is the organisation sufficiently active in general and sector-related speculative research in order that a technological advantage is maintained over competitors and industry entrants?

1.10 What processes ensure that all the resources required to undertake the development are accurately identified, costed, justified and authorised?

1.11   What measures ensure that clear (and authorised) objectives and targets are established for each project (and is their achievement monitored and confirmed)?

1.12   How is management assured that the design assessment, feasibility, and specification processes are adequate and satisfactorily address quality, performance, and regulatory standards?

1.13   What measures are taken for adequate protection of research activities, intellectual property, specifications, and all research plans and data from exploitation by others or unauthorised exposure?

1.14   How does management ensure that research activities do not violate existing patents and copyrights?

1.15   Are all product developments subject to adequate project management in order to cater for the following aspects:

- adequate co-ordination of all affected functions to ensure achievement of development objectives
- definition of key stages of the project and the ongoing monitoring of actual progress against target
- authorisation and control of all project resources and costs?

1.16   What steps does management take to retain the skills and knowledge of key specialist staff, and prevent others benefiting from the individual's expertise?

1.17   What measures ensure that new or modified products are subject to extensive, adequate and appropriate testing (including any sector-specific, legally required, or specialist product testing requirements)?

2 Detailed Issues

2.1   What mechanisms prevent the investigation or development of a product outside the defined and authorised strategic parameters of the business?

2.2   Has management defined and authorised product development plans with the intention of extending and prolonging the life of existing products and introducing viable new lines?

2.3   How does management ensure that its product plans remain relevant, up to date and in step with customer needs and market developments?

2.4   Is appropriate account taken of competitor analysis and are critical marketing timing considerations identified and planned for in the research programme?

2.5   What measures are in place to ensure that crucial costs and selling price targets are identified and monitored for achievement throughout the project?

2.6   How does management ensure that research projects, product details, development plans and business development strategies remain confidential?

2.7   What measures would prevent unauthorised research and development costs?

2.8   When applicable, does the organisation take appropriate advantage of available government and research grants (and what measures ensure that eligibility for such schemes is maintained)?

2.9   Are all appropriate technologies, processes and techniques developed by the organisation adequately protected (at the most appropriate time) from exploitation by others (and how can this be assured)?

2.10   Are key staff involved in product development subject to fidelity bonding or commercial confidentiality clauses in their employment contracts?

2.11   What steps does management take to ensure that adequate numbers of specialist staff are recruited and that their skill levels are maintained through authorised training, etc.?

2.12   If relevant expertise or specialist knowledge exists outside the organisation, how does management ensure that the engagement of such external specialists is justified, authorised, accurately costed, and that progress is monitored?

2.13   What measures ensure that external consultants will not exploit and/or pass on details of the research they are conducting on the organisation's behalf?

2.14   How does management ensure that problems, shortcomings, cost overruns, etc. would promptly be detected and reported?

2.15   What processes ensure that all R&D costs are identified, accounted for, and reflected in the corporate accounts?

2.16   What mechanisms ensure the correct accounting treatment of R&D costs and the recovery of related taxation benefits whenever applicable?

2.17   Have adequate arrangements been made to provide management with regular, accurate and relevant project information (progress, costs versus budgets, failures to achieve deadlines, technical problems, etc.)?

2.18   Where appropriate, are products subject to testing under recognised trade, national or international quality/standards schemes?

2.19   Prior to commercial launch, how does management know that products are subject to the appropriate licensing by government or trade regulators?

2.20   Upon launch of the product, how does management ensure that adequate plans are in place to address such matters as:

- adequacy of stocks
- provision of staff training
- launch timing to maximise the market impact
- co-ordination of all affected functions, etc.?

2.21   How is the accuracy of data input from other systems (e.g. market research or planning) confirmed?

2.22   How is the accuracy of data output to other systems (e.g. production control, sales management, etc.) confirmed?

PROJECT APPRAISAL AND MONITORING

Here we examine the issues surrounding the identification of potential projects, the appraisal of R&D projects leading to their justification and authorisation to proceed, and the general monitoring of costs and progress against those planned for and approved.

Control Objectives for Project Appraisal and Monitoring

(a)   To ensure that all research and development activities are in accordance with the defined and authorised strategic objectives of the organisation.

(b)   To ensure that all R&D projects are fully assessed in respect of technical implications, product potential, equipment and tooling costs, timescale, research costs, production costs, selling price, and so on.

(c)   To ensure that project appraisals are effectively conducted in order to assure management as to the value and justification of the project under review.

(d)   To provide (where justified) a formal, documented, and authorised project appraisal procedure and ensure compliance.

(e)   To recommend to management those projects that should be implemented and to obtain management authorisation to proceed.

(f)   To ensure that the appraisal process identifies and accurately costs the R&D resources required to fulfil the project.

(g)   To ensure that the key project stages and deliverables are identified and monitored for achievement.

(h)   To ensure that key responsibilities are defined and allocated.

> (i) To ensure that an appropriate project management framework is defined and established.
>
> (j) To ensure that budgets are established and monitored against actual expenditure and efforts;
>
> (k) To ensure that the progress of the research and development project is adequately monitored and that shortcomings, variations, etc. are promptly identified and dealt with.
>
> (l) To ensure that all the key stages and project objectives are met on time and within budget.
>
> (m) To ensure that management is provided with adequate, timely and accurate information on project progress, costs, etc.
>
> (n) To ensure that all the relevant legal and regulatory requirements are identified, monitored, and fulfilled.

Risk and Control Issues for Project Appraisal and Monitoring

1 Key Issues

1.1 Has management defined and authorised strategic business objectives, and how can they be sure that all R&D activities comply with these targets?

1.2 Have formal, documented and authorised project appraisal procedures been defined and implemented (and if so, how is compliance with them ensured)?

1.3 How does management verify that all R&D activities are valid, justified and authorised (and what mechanisms prevent unauthorised activities)?

1.4 Are all R&D projects subject to adequate appraisals incorporating the following factors:

- technical implications
- product and market potential
- research costs
- equipment and tooling costs
- estimated production costs
- project timescale
- specialist requirements, etc.?

1.5 How does management make sure that the appraisal staff will conduct the assessment in an objective, considered and professional manner?

1.6 How does management signify their authorisation to proceed with an R&D project, and what prevents the initiation of an unauthorised project?

1.7 Does the appraisal process identify and cost all the R&D resources required to fulfil the project?

1.8 What measures ensure that clear (and authorised) objectives, key stages, targets, and deliverables are identified and established for each R&D project?

1.9 What mechanisms ensure that the project budgets, and all the factors noted in point 1.4 above are adequately monitored and achieved?

1.10 What measures ensure that all key responsibilities are defined, allocated, and monitored?

1.11 Would management promptly be made aware of project progress short-comings, problems and delays, and what measures ensure that objectives are met on time and within budget?

2 Detailed Issues

2.1 Are all R&D project costs subject to effective accounting and budgetary control (and would significant variations promptly be brought to management's attention)?

2.2 Are all the management information requirements identified and addressed (and how can the accuracy and reliability of such data be assured)?

2.3 Is overall responsibility for managing and co-ordinating the project allocated, and is the nominated individual charged with the appropriate authority to achieve the defined objectives?

2.4 Has a formal, documented and appropriate project management framework been established to progress and monitor the project?

2.5 Have steps been taken to consult with and co-ordinate the action of all the affected functions so that the project objectives and timescales are satisfactorily achieved?

2.6 Are all costs outside the authorised budgets subject to prior justification and special authority?

2.7 What measures ensure that all the relevant legal and regulatory requirements are identified and appropriately addressed?

2.8 How is accuracy of data input from other systems (e.g. corporate planning or industry regulation) confirmed?

2.9   How is accuracy of data output to other systems (e.g. budgetary control) confirmed?

PLANT AND EQUIPMENT

R&D projects often require the acquisition or manufacture of specialised pieces of equipment (such as test or calibration devices). In this section we consider the procurement, accounting treatment, installation, usage, maintenance, and eventual disposal of such R&D equipment.

Control Objectives for Plant and Equipment

(a)   To ensure that all R&D plant and equipment requirements are accurately identified, justified, and authorised.

(b)   To ensure that appropriate resources are made available in order to support project activities and meet the defined R&D objectives.

(c)   To ensure that R&D equipment and associated costs are commensurate with planned activities.

(d)   To ensure that R&D assets are accurately identified, recorded, correctly accounted for, suitably valued, and periodically verified.

(e)   To ensure that all R&D equipment costs are accurately identified, authorised, and allocated to related projects, etc.

(f)   To ensure that R&D and specialist equipment is adequately maintained in full working order and accurately calibrated.

(g)   To ensure that redundant, underused, surplus or obsolete equipment is promptly identified and authorised for appropriate disposal.

(h)   To ensure that staff have the relevant skills to correctly use R&D and specialist equipment.

Risk and Control Issues for Plant and Equipment

1 Key Issues

1.1   How are R&D plant and equipment requirements defined, and is the acquisition of such equipment subject to formal prior justification and authorisation (and if so, how is this evidenced)?

1.2   What mechanisms prevent the unauthorised procurement of R&D equipment outwith the project budget?

1.3   How does management ensure that equipment is obtained using the most advantageous funding method (i.e. purchase, leasing, etc.)?

1.4   What measures ensure that all R&D assets are accurately identified, recorded in the accounts, and correctly valued?

1.5   What mechanisms ensure that the correct and appropriate accounting treatment is applied to R&D assets?

1.6   Does management take adequate steps periodically to confirm the existence and valuation of all R&D assets (and would untraced or incorrectly valued items be identified and investigated)?

1.7   Are all R&D equipment costs (i.e. acquisition, supply of consumables, and ongoing maintenance) identified, accounted for, and accurately allocated to specific R&D projects?

1.8   How does management monitor that all R&D equipment is appropriately and regularly maintained in working order (and are the associated costs authorised and accounted for)?

1.9   What steps does management take to avoid the accumulation of under-used, redundant or obsolete items of R&D equipment?

1.10   What measures ensure that surplus items of R&D equipment are authorised for disposal and that the relevant proceeds are maximised and accounted for?

1.11   How does management monitor that specialist equipment is being correctly used by research staff in order to support the validity of research and development activities?

2 Detailed Issues

2.1   How does management verify that decisions to obtain R&D equipment are appropriately related to the significance, length and perceived value of projects (e.g. are those high-value items required for short-term projects leased or hired, rather than being purchased outright)?

2.2   Can all R&D assets be promptly traced and located at any time?

2.3   Are orders and invoices for all R&D equipment authorised at the appropriate level?

2.4   How does management verify that the values of R&D equipment reflected in the company accounts are accurate, up to date and verified?

2.5   Are write-offs of R&D assets subject to specific authorisation, and how is this evidenced?

2.6   What measures ensure that items of long-term R&D plant are correctly treated as fixed assets and appropriately depreciated over an acceptable period?

2.7   Are R&D equipment requirements for specific projects justified and authorised as part of the overall project appraisal process?

2.8   Are project equipment budgets authorised, established, effectively monitored, and followed up when necessary (and how are investigations of variances evidenced)?

2.9   What steps are taken to ensure that specialist equipment is correctly installed and calibrated?

2.10 What measures prevent the unauthorised disposal of R&D equipment?

2.11 How are all disposal proceeds identified and accounted for?

2.12 How does management ensure that the best prices are obtained against equipment disposals (and are such arrangements authorised)?

2.13 How is the accuracy of data input from other systems (e.g. project appraisal) confirmed?

2.14 How is the accuracy of data output to other systems (e.g. fixed assets or project accounting) confirmed?

DEVELOPMENT PROJECT MANAGEMENT

Here we consider the management and progress of an R&D project from the point of authorisation to its ultimate completion. On the way, aspects such as cost and progress monitoring, the provision of adequate and accurate project information, and the achievement of defined objectives are considered. See also Chapter 6, which has a section on "'Product/Project Accounting".

Control Objectives for Development Project Management

(a) To ensure that all R&D projects are effectively managed so that the objectives and key criteria established at the outset of the project are cost-effectively and efficiently achieved.

(b) To ensure that all the resources required to undertake research and development projects are accurately identified, costed, justified, authorised, and provided.

(c) To ensure that project management responsibilities and accountabilities are defined and allocated.

(d) To ensure that all the actual project costs are correctly identified, accounted for, and monitored against the established budgets.

(e) To ensure that the progress of all projects is adequately monitored by management and that appropriate changes are authorised and applied when necessary.

(f) To ensure that adequate, accurate, and timely management information is provided.

(g) To ensure that adequate, appropriate, and legally required levels of testing are conducted and evidenced.

(h) To ensure that all the relevant legal and regulatory requirements are correctly addressed.

Risk and Control Issues for Development Project Management

1 Key Issues

1.1 Have formal project management procedures been defined, authorised and implemented (and if so, how is management assured that the procedures are adhered to)?

1.2 Has management defined and authorised the project objectives, and how can they be sure that these will be achieved?

1.3 Have key project targets and deliverables been identified, and are they subject to ongoing monitoring throughout the project?

1.4 What processes ensure that all the required project resources are accurately identified, costed, justified, authorised and provided?

1.5 What measures are in place to ensure that adequate and suitable staff resources are made available for the duration of the project (and have any training requirements been satisfactorily addressed)?

1.6 Have management responsibilities been formally allocated to named individuals, and how do they report on their progress, etc.?

1.7 How is management assured that all project costs are correctly accounted for and monitored against the defined budgets?

1.8 Are all R&D projects subject to adequate ongoing management in order to cater for the following aspects:

- adequate co-ordination of all the affected functions to ensure achievement of the project objectives
- definition of key stages of the project and the ongoing monitoring of actual progress against targets and budgets
- authorisation and control of all project resources and costs?

1.9   What steps are taken to ensure that adequate, timely, accurate, and relevant project information is generated and circulated to management?

1.10   What measures are in place to ensure that any project problems, shortcomings, or budget problems would promptly be identified and reported for action?

1.11   How does management keep abreast of all the relevant legal and regulatory requirements, and ensure appropriate compliance is attained?

2 Detailed Issues

2.1   Have accurate and realistic timing and cost targets been set for projects?

2.2   What measures prevent unauthorised project expenditure or activities, and how would management be made aware of them?

2.3   Have sufficiently detailed budgets been established, and are they subject to ongoing monitoring against actual costs?

2.4   What processes ensure that all R&D costs are identified and correctly reflected in the project and company accounts?

2.5   Have adequate arrangements been made to provide management with regular, accurate and relevant project information (such as progress, actual costs versus budgets, failures to achieve deadlines, technical problems)?

2.6   Have quality and performance targets been established, and what measures ensure that they are cost-effectively achieved?

2.7   If project objectives prove to be impossible or unreasonably expensive to achieve, are they reviewed by senior management so that either expenditure limits are authorised for amendment or the objectives are amended?

2.8   Who has the authority to abandon an unsuccessful project, and what measures are in place to fully assess the impact of such a decision?

2.9   How does management monitor that products and technologies under development are adequately and appropriately tested?

2.10   Where necessary, are product testing programmes related to the achievement of recognised national, regulatory or legally required standards?

2.11   How are the conclusions and outcomes of R&D projects presented and converted into the related production processes, and are they subject to formal commercial and financial assessment before proceeding?

2.12   How is the accuracy of data input from other systems (e.g. budgetary control and project control system) confirmed?

2.13   How is the accuracy of data output to other systems (e.g. project accounting) confirmed?

LEGAL AND REGULATORY ISSUES

Many industries (e.g. pharmaceuticals and chemicals) are governed by an array of legal and regulatory conditions. This segment takes account of the need to ensure that any legal and/or regulatory requirements are accurately identified and effectively addressed as part of the overall R&D environment. Also included are aspects such as protecting research activities (e.g. through patents), ensuring that new R&D projects do not violate existing patents and copyrights, and identifying possible sources of external funding for R&D.

Control Objectives for Legal and Regulatory Issues

(a) To ensure that all the relevant and prevailing legal and regulatory issues are identified, addressed, and complied with.

(b) To ensure that defined quality, performance, and testing standards are achieved.

(c) To ensure that all research activity, theories, specification, drawings, technologies, and products are adequately protected from exploitation by others.

(d) To ensure that research and development activities do not, in themselves, violate existing patents and copyrights.

(e) To ensure that projects comply with the conditions of any grant funding schemes.

(f) To ensure that all processes utilised during the R&D project fully comply with the relevant health and safety standards.

(g) To ensure that, when appropriate, project facilities and products obtain the necessary certifications.

Risk and Control Issues for Legal and Regulatory Issues

1 Key Issues

1.1 How does management verify that all the relevant and prevailing legal and regulatory issues have been accurately identified and planned for?

1.2 What mechanisms are in place to prevent liabilities for legal penalties and related commercial and reputation implications?

1.3 Has management identified and addressed all the industry quality, safety, testing, and performance standards, and have the relevant certifications and accreditations been obtained?

1.4   Have the resource and cost implications of compliance been accurately determined and authorised?

1.5   What measures are taken to protect adequately research activities, intellectual property, specifications, technologies, innovations, and data from exploitation by others and unauthorised exposure?

1.6   How does management ensure that research activities do not violate existing patents and copyrights?

1.7   Does management fully investigate the possibility of offsetting R&D costs by identifying and applying for available government and trade research funding grants?

1.8   What steps are taken to ensure that the project remains eligible to receive grant funding and that amounts due are received, correctly applied, and accounted for?

1.9   Does management ensure that all projects are assessed for health and safety implications as the basis for providing all the required precautions, equipment and staff training?

1.10   How is management confident that any failure to comply with relevant laws and regulations would be promptly identified for action?

2 Detailed Issues

2.1   Are the costs associated with regulatory and legal compliance accurately identified, authorised, accounted for and monitored against budget?

2.2   Does management take appropriate and prompt action to protect the various aspects of in-house research by filing patent applications?

2.3   How does management ensure that the level of legal protection obtained for R&D activities is sufficient (e.g. are overseas patents required and justified)?

2.4   What precautions are in place to prevent unauthorised access, copying or manipulation of R&D project materials?

2.5   How does management ensure that adequate investigations are conducted into existing third-party research activities, patents, and published materials which may present legal implications for the proposed R&D project?

2.6   How does management maintain an accurate awareness of all the potential sources of grant funding?

2.7   What steps are taken to ensure that grant income is fully accounted for and only used for the defined purposes?

2.8   How does management ensure that the maximum benefit is derived from grant income?

2.9   When considering applications for grants, are all the implications assessed (e.g. stipulations that the resultant research must be published for general use)?

2.10   Where products have to be officially registered before being marketed, what steps are taken to minimise the possibility of failure?

2.11   When applicable and commercially acceptable, are the benefits of jointly funded research projects fully assessed and authorised?

2.12   How is the accuracy of data input from other systems confirmed?

2.13   How is the accuracy of data output to other systems (e.g. industry regulation) confirmed?

13

Auditing Information Technology

INTRODUCTION

In this chapter we consider the audit review of information technology (IT) activities. This chapter is not intended to be a technical manual for computer or IT auditors; rather, it approaches IT activities from business and operational viewpoints.

Before examining, in some detail, the various IT activities, we open the chapter with a discussion of fundamental IT security issues as embodied in the *Code of Practice for Information Security Management* published as BS7799 in 1995 by the British Standards Institute.

INTRODUCTION TO INTERNATIONAL STANDARDS FOR INFORMATION SECURITY MANAGEMENT

Four out of five UK organisations suffered a breakdown in their information technology systems in 1993 and 1994, according to a UK government sponsored survey, co-sponsored by the IT company ICL. The survey of 850 organisations estimated that the annual cost of such incidents exceeds £1.2 billion—a 12% increase on a similar survey two years previously. Only one in seven companies had a specialist IT security function and only 43% used formal risk analysis techniques.

A recent important advance in the development of standards for information security is the development in the UK in 1993 of a *Code of Practice for Information Security Management*. This was written by the Department of Trade and Industry, together with major blue-chip user organisations. The participating bodies set out to agree and define a set of standards drawn from industry leading companies' best practices, for any organisation to work to, to ensure compliance with baseline security measures (so-called because they collectively define an industry baseline of good security practice).

This *Code* has since been published by the British Standards Institute (BSI) as BS7799 [1995]. It is intended to form a basis for the development, implementation and measurement of information security management. A second objective is to provide confidence that data is secure in the course of inter-company electronic trading. BSI has plans to introduce an accreditation and certification scheme for BS7799 similar to that relevant to quality standards BS5750 and the International Standards Organisation's ISO9000.

We focus on this *Code* as it seems likely that it will be the basis for the development of codes (a) in other nation states, (b) at European Union level, and (c) internationally. In the past British Standards have become the basis for international standards—for instance the British Standards on quality systems became the basis for the ISO9000 series of standards.

Overview of BS7799

The BS7799 *Code* provides guidance and recommendations for information security management via three basic components:

- *Confidentiality*—protecting sensitive information from unauthorised disclosure.
- *Integrity*—safeguarding the accuracy and completeness of information.
- *Availability*—ensuring that information and vital services are available to users.

Meaning of "Integrity"

The following important insight into the meaning of *integrity* is given by Melville and List[1] who define integrity as the condition when:

Information is sufficiently right at the time of use for the purpose to which the user wishes to put the output.

Their definition has the merit of encompassing the whole system—clerical procedures, IT procedures, and all the computer processing.
    And they go on to say:

"Sufficiently right" can be specified exactly in specific circumstances—even when the "user" may be another part of the information system. Equally "sufficiently right" encompasses the probability that a person may judge rightness in the light of experience and external factors of which the information system is totally unaware.

"At the time of use" is important in the definition because all processing is time dependent and the time of use specifies the time requirement for the information.

"For the purpose" is included because accuracy requirements for information derived from the same data vary widely from minimal discrepancies required in, for example, air plane navigation or payroll to the much larger tolerances allowed in reported financial statements, government returns and future business projections.

"Output" can be in any form. In commercial systems today it is usually a printout or screen display; in other systems it may be LED display or a virtual reality projection. As technology develops, output will include voice and multimedia presentations. Where the output from a system is automatically input to another system, external or internal, then the criteria which constitute "sufficiently right" at the transfer point will require to be specified in detail.

Sections and Controls in BS7799

BS7799 has ten sections and in each section a number of controls are recommended. Taking all ten sections together, there are 108 specific controls of which BS7799 specifies that ten are key or mandatory controls. Most of them may seem to be common sense, but they are often dangerously neglected in practice by many businesses. The 108 specific controls are grouped under 33 higher level, more generalised controls—which in turn are grouped into the ten sections. The mandatory controls are drawn from six of the ten sections of BS7799.

The Sections in BS7799 are:

Section 1   Security Policy
Section 2   Security Organisation
Section 3   Assets Classification and Control
Section 4   Personnel Security
Section 5   Physical and Environmental Security
Section 6   Computer and Network Management
Section 7   System Access Control
Section 8   System Development and Maintenance
Section 9   Business Continuity Planning
Section 10   Compliance

Mandatory Controls

The Mandatory Controls in BS7799 relate to the following. There must be:

1. an information security policy document
2. allocation of information security responsibilities
3. information security education and training
4. reporting of security incidents
5. virus controls
6. business continuity planning process
7. control of proprietary software copying
8. safeguarding of organisational records
9. compliance with data protection legislation
10. security policy compliance.

We will look at each of these key control areas in turn, giving the BS7799 wording of each and referring to the section to which they belong.

1. An Information Security Policy Document

Section: 1 (Security Policy)
BS7799 ref.: 1.1.1
Wording: "A written policy document available to all employees responsible for information security."

This will usually comprise a written document to confirm management direction and support for information security. The policy will cover the definition, intention, explanation, responsibilities and a process to report suspected security incidents.

2. Allocation of Information Security Responsibilities

Section: 2 (Security Organisation)
BS7799 ref.: 2.1.3
Wording: "Responsibilities for the protection of individual assets and for carrying out specific security processes should be explicitly defined."

3. Information Security Education and Training

Section: 4 (Personnel Security)
BS7799 ref.: 4.2.1
Wording: "Users should be given adequate security education and technical training."

This means they should receive appropriate training in organisational policies and procedures, including security requirements and other business controls as well as training in the correct use of IT facilities.

4. Reporting of Security Incidents

Section: 4 (Personnel Security)
BS7799 ref.: 4.3.1
Wording: "Security incidents should be reported through management channels as quickly as possible."

A formal reporting procedure should be established and followed for the reporting of security incidents, together with an incidence response procedure, setting out the action to be taken on receipt of an incident report. This should cover all employees and contractors.

5. Virus Controls

Section: 6 (Computer and Network Management)
BS7799 ref.: 6.3.1
Wording: "Virus detection and prevention measures and appropriate user awareness procedures should be implemented."

The areas of compliance with software licences, unauthorised use of software and virus detection software is also covered together with the checking of diskettes (and CD ROMS) for viruses before use.

6. Business Continuity Planning Process

Section: 9 (Business Continuity Planning)
BS7799 ref.: 9.1.1
Wording: "There should be a managed process in place for developing and maintaining business continuity plan across the organization."

This covers the identification of critical business processes, the impact of various disasters on business activities, emergency arrangements, documentation of agreed procedures and processes, education of staff and testing and updating of plans.

7. Control of Proprietary Software Copying

Section: 10 (Compliance)
BS7799 ref.: 10.1.1
Wording: "Attention is drawn to the legal restrictions on the use of copyright material."

To do with ensuring that the organisation has in place a policy to ensure that no copyright material is copied without the owner's consent. Users should not copy software or use software on other systems. Regular audits of software should be made.

8. Safeguarding of Organisational Records

Section: 10 (Compliance)
BS7799 ref.: 10.1.2
Wording: "Important records of an organisation should be protected from loss, destruction and falsification."

Some records will need to be securely retained to meet statutory requirements as well as to support essential business functions. Records should be destroyed that have been retained beyond their statutory retention time. Guidelines should be issued on the retention, storage, handling and disposal of records and information. An inventory of key information should be kept.

9. Data Protection

Section: 10 (Compliance)
BS7799 ref.:   10.1.3
Wording: "Applications handling personal data on individuals should comply with data protection legislation and principles."

Personal information on individuals that is stored or processed on computers should be obtained and processed in accordance with the country's data protection legislation. (Later in this chapter we consider the internationally, generally accepted data protection principles).

10. Compliance with Security Policy

Section: 10 (Compliance)
BS7799 ref.:   10.2.1
Wording: "All areas within the organization should be considered for regular review to ensure compliance with security policies and standards."

This should include IT systems and system providers, information and data owners, users, and management.

Data Protection Principles

Most European countries now have data protection legislation which circumscribes the collection, maintenance and uses of personal data so as to protect individuals' rights to privacy in a computer environment. It is now a European Union requirement. Any country in the world without such legislation risks becoming a "data dustbin"—a location for disreputable databases holding personal information where the owner of the database wishes to avoid controlling legislation. A corollary of this is that multinational companies are unlikely to establish transnational personnel databases in countries not subject to data protection legislation as, to do so, would be likely to place them in breach of data protection requirements in other countries within which they have operations and therefore staff.

In some countries data protection legislation is limited to computer-held personal data, but in other countries it extends to personal data held in any form.

Leading companies now regard the principles which underpin data protection legislation to be broadly applicable to *all* their databases, and wherever located. In general these principles represent good IT practice for any system. In addition there is always a possibility that an IT system not originally designed to hold personal data might in due course do so—so it is advisable to develop it from the outset with the data protection principles in mind.

The data protection laws of different nation states usually enshrine the following data protection principles:

1. Data on individuals should be obtained and processed fairly.
2. It should be held for specified and lawful purposes only.
3. It should not be used or disclosed in any other ways.
4. Data held on an individual should be adequate, relevant, but not excessive.
5. It should be accurate and kept up to date
6. An individual upon whom data is held should have access to it at reasonable intervals and without undue delay or cost.
7. There should be an entitlement for an individual to require the correction or deletion of data relating to the individual that is in breach of any of these data protection principles.
8. There should be security against unauthorised access, use of or accidental loss of personal information held on individuals.

Security on the Internet

By the beginning of 1996 the Internet (or the "Net") had an estimated 50 million users connected worldwide. It is a genuinely global network which allows individuals to exchange electronic mail, files and other messages, to participate in common interest groups and to access thousands of computer databases worldwide. Many organisations feel an urgent need to get connected to the Internet. But it has security risks and few understand the complexities of the problems or their solutions.

The Internet is inherently dangerous since it allows users into a system. There is at present little security for information transferred across the Net. This means that, unless the user takes precautions, messages travel "in the clear" and are vulnerable to interception, misrouting or tampering. Viruses can also be attached to files sent via electronic mail (e-mail).

The generic information security principles and controls discussed earlier in this chapter need to be applied to Internet use as well.

The advice, in general, is:

- If the Internet server is connected to a corporate system or network, there is a need to secure the system/network from the Internet server—perhaps through use of a "Firewall" or secure authentication service—so as to reduce the risk of an attacker accessing corporate information.
- If a company sends sensitive information or financial transactions over the Internet, the information must be protected while in transit, probably through the use of cryptography.
- A formal risk analysis of the company's use of the Internet should be performed periodically and appropriate security measures developed, implemented and monitored.

- The company should develop and circulate an Internet Connection Policy so as to make users aware of the potential risks and their safeguards.

SYSTEM/FUNCTION COMPONENTS OF INFORMATION TECHNOLOGY

We have elected to use an essentially *functional* approach to define the information technology auditing universe, which gives us the following possible breakdown of the key functions, systems or activities:

- IT strategic planning
- IT organisation
- IT sites
- processing operations
- back-up and media
- system and operating software
- system access control
- personal computers
- software maintenance
- local area networks (LANs)
- databases
- Data Protection Act
- facilities management
- system development
- software selection
- contingency planning
- electronic data interchange (EDI)
- viruses
- electronic office
- user support
- BACS (i.e. automated cash/funds transfer)
- spreadsheet design
- expert systems
- IT accounting.

This listing of activities and functions is deliberately pitched to take account of a potentially wide range of possible IT scenarios. For example, some of the items are more akin to traditional mainframe installations, whereas others are geared to the contemporary business use of networks and personal computers. This broadbrush approach is intended to enable auditors to identify and extract those elements that match their own organisation's use of IT. We should not become too transfixed by the definition of this list of activities, as they will rarely operate in complete isolation from each other—for example, IT strategic planning outputs may have direct relevance to system developments or the expansion of local area networks.

CONTROL OBJECTIVES AND RISK AND CONTROL ISSUES

We shall now examine the control objectives and the related risk and control issues (divided into key issues and detailed issues) for each of the information technology activity areas listed above. This data can be used within the format of the Standard Audit Programme Guides (SAPGs) looked at in Chapter 3. To save space we have concentrated on the objectives to be stated and the questions to be asked and have not presented them within the SAPG format.

For greater detail on the application of the control matrix technique (introduced in Chapter 3) to a universe of IT activities, see *Auditing the IT Environment*.[2]

Appendix 11 highlights the essential issues for a range of IT-related activities based upon the format of a Standard Audit Programme Guide, together with some illustrative controls and measures.

IT STRATEGIC PLANNING

Here we are primarily concerned with planning for the use of IT in the business so as to ensure that the business objectives and operational requirements are effectively met. There are many possible choices for IT-based business solutions, and selecting the most appropriate can be both difficult and crucial for the business. There is the medium-term danger that the organisation will become locked into a quickly outdated and inflexible IT environment which fails to deliver any commercial or competitive advantages.

Applying formal strategic planning techniques to the business use of IT will normally concentrate on the key business requirements and the objectives set by management as part of their wider long-term planning. Against these targets, goals and objectives it is then usual to map the existing use of IT to support the business, highlighting any high value and data related activities that could be improved by the use of IT-based methods. The key output of any IT strategy exercise is an action plan designed to take the business forward from the current IT scenario to the future environment. If the output represents extensive change, the action plan is likely to be a staged programme which may include such elements as:

- acquiring and moving over to new hardware platforms (e.g. the migration from traditional mainframes to client/server-based systems)
- improving or extending the data communications infrastructure (e.g. installing local and wide area networks, dedicated communication lines, etc.)
- improving or upgrading existing application systems (e.g. extending the types of data held or extending the processing functionality)
- commissioning new application software to support business activities (e.g. the internal or external development of software)
- introducing new or improved IT development and management techniques to contribute to efficiency and cost-effectiveness (e.g. the use of formal system development methodologies or the introduction of a revised user support system).

Not all the changes generated through the IT strategy process will necessarily be hardware or software related; there may be a case for introducing new or revised techniques which aid the efficiency of the IT function.

The approach adopted for conducting an IT strategy plan will, of course, depend on the scale and type of the underlying business and the current level of IT involvement. For example, larger organisations may be able to justify an in-house software development team to create and support their business-specific application systems, whereas the norm may be to engage external software developers to tailor an existing standard system or to build a new one.

Whatever form the recommended action plans take, the key point is that they must be justified in business terms. There is no place for IT for IT's sake, otherwise the IT tail starts to wag the business dog!

Control Objectives for IT Strategic Planning

(a) To ensure that the IT facilities and services support both the strategic objectives of the business and the maintenance of competitive advantage.

(b) To ensure that the use of IT throughout the organisation is adequately planned and geared to the underlying business needs.

(c) To ensure that investments in IT facilities are justified and represent value for money.

(d) To ensure that a stable, reliable and secure IT environment is provided to support the business.

(e) To ensure that both the current and anticipated requirements of the business are appropriately served by the IT facilities.

(f) To ensure that adequate and appropriately skilled personnel are provided to support the achievement of established objectives.

(g) To ensure that the IT environment incorporates appropriate and justifiable hardware, software, methods, facilities and tools to support the business.

(h) To ensure that the information needs of the business are best served by current and planned systems.

(i) To ensure that a suitable planning methodology is utilised in order to accurately identify underlying requirements and convert them into action plans.

(j) To ensure that only justified and authorised systems are developed and maintained.

(k) To ensure that all IT projects and acquisitions are authorised and in accord with the established planning objectives.

(l) To ensure that cost-effective and optimum solutions are applied.

(m) To ensure that IT-related costs are accurately identified and contained within budgeted limits.

Risk and Control Issues for IT Strategic Planning

1 Key Issues

1.1 How does management ensure that the provision of all IT hardware, software, methods and resources remains in step with the strategic direction of the business and the achievement of competitive advantages, etc.?

1.2 What action does management take to identify and review possible ways of achieving competitive advantage through the application of IT?

1.3 How is management certain that the use of IT facilities best serves the organisation and that unnecessary, inadequate or outdated systems and methods are identified and avoided?

1.4 Has management established a mechanism to ensure that both current and future business needs will be appropriately supported by the use of IT (and how is this evidenced)?

1.5 How does management ensure that the information needs of the business are adequately served?

1.6 What processes ensure that the IT facilities remain relevant and in step with business changes and developments?

1.7 What measures are in place to ensure that all IT costs and investments are in step with the agreed plans and appropriately authorised?

1.8 What mechanisms prevent the acquisition and development of un-authorised systems and facilities (i.e. those outside the agreed direction)?

2 Detailed Issues

2.1 How is management certain that the key business objectives are identified as the basis for accurate IT planning (and what checks are in place to ensure that the objectives remain up to date)?

2.2 How does management ensure that IT planning takes account of current and emerging technical trends as the basis for assessing potential benefits?

2.3 How does management monitor that potential IT projects and facilities are adequately assessed, justified and authorised?

2.4 Has management established a range of agreed and documented policies to support the application of IT throughout the organisation, and to ensure that the objectives of the business are adequately addressed?

2.5 How does management ensure that all IT facilities support a stable, reliable and secure environment, (and what checks are in place to establish that key suppliers are stable)?

2.6   What mechanisms ensure that agreed changes to the business operations and objectives are promptly identified and assessed for their impact upon the IT facilities?

2.7   How does management ensure that adequate and appropriately skilled IT staff are available to support the current and anticipated needs?

2.8   How does management ensure that the impacts of adopting specific IT hardware, software, methods and facilities are identified, assessed and adequately planned for?

2.9   Have the data needs of the business been identified as the basis for both current and future systems (and how is redundant or duplicate data avoided)?

2.10   What mechanisms ensure that all new systems and amendments to existing ones are justified and authorised?

2.11   How is the commitment of senior management to the defined IT strategy evidenced?

2.12   How does management ensure that all affected staff are aware of the requirements of the IT strategy and their responsibilities?

2.13   Are all potential systems and IT environmental changes subject to a formal feasibility assessment, justification and approval processes?

2.14   What procedures ensure that all the IT-related costs are accurately identified, monitored and contained?

2.15   Are all amendments to the IT strategy formally reviewed and authorised (and how is this evidenced)?

2.16   How does management ensure that all affected parties (users, system owners, etc.) are adequately consulted and involved in the IT planning process?

2.17   What measures ensure that only accurate and reliable data is used in the IT planning process?

2.18   How is commercially sensitive or confidential information used in the planning process protected from leakage or misuse?

IT ORGANISATION

This section looks at the organisational structure of an in-house IT function. In practice, such functions vary considerably in size and operational scope, so there are no universal models. The organisation will need to consider the primary purposes of the IT function and how they are to be delivered. Once completed, the key factors can be defined in agreed and authorised policies, such as:

- optimum organisational structure
- terms of reference for the IT function

- service level agreements
- definition of roles and responsibilities (i.e. job descriptions)
- required operational and technical standards, etc.

Control Objectives for IT Organisation

(a) To ensure that an appropriate and efficient organisational structure is established for the IT function.

(b) To ensure that responsibilities and accountabilities are defined, agreed and allocated.

(c) To ensure that adequate and appropriate IT resources and skills are provided to support the business.

(d) To ensure that an appropriate framework of operating standards, procedures and policies is established, adhered to, maintained and kept up to date.

(e) To ensure that the required levels and standards of IT service provision are established, agreed and can be observed.

(f) To ensure that key duties are appropriately segregated in order to protect the integrity of operations, systems and data.

(g) To ensure that skill requirements are identified and met through ongoing training and staff development.

(h) To ensure the accuracy and security of user application systems and data.

(i) To ensure that the continuity of operations can be maintained in the event of a disaster or failure.

(j) To ensure that effective channels of communication are provided and that staff remain aware of the required performance, quality and service objectives.

Risk and Control Issues for IT Organisation

1 Key Issues

1.1 Has management adequately defined the organisational structure and responsibilities of the IT function (and how is this kept up to date and relevant)?

1.2 How is management assured that the IT function organisational structure is best placed to support the operation and objectives of the business?

1.3   Have the organisational structure and specific responsibilities been formally agreed and authorised (and how is this evidenced)?

1.4   What mechanisms ensure that agreed responsibilities and accountabilities are accurately and effectively communicated to the IT staff?

1.5   How does management ensure that sufficient levels of IT resource (including suitably skilled staff) are provided to support the current and future needs of the business?

1.6   What steps does management take to ensure that the skills of the IT staff remain relevant and up to date?

1.7   Has a framework of authorised and documented operating standards, procedures and policies been established and implemented?

1.8   How does management ensure that the established standards, procedures and policies are effectively complied with?

1.9   How does management monitor that the required and necessary levels of IT service provision are being appropriately delivered?

1.10   How does management prevent the potential for staff fraud or malpractice in order to protect the integrity of systems and data?

1.11   What steps have been taken to ensure that IT operational facilities are capable of prompt and effective recovery in the event of a disaster or major failure?

1.12   What measures are in place to ensure that operational systems are secure and that operations are correctly conducted?

2 Detailed Issues

2.1   Have formal terms of reference for the IT function been agreed, documented and authorised?

2.2   Have the organisational structure and staffing establishment level been ratified and authorised by senior management (and how is this evidenced)?

2.3   Are changes to the organisational structure and establishment levels formally reviewed, documented and authorised?

2.4   How does management ensure that business objectives and plans are appropriately converted into action plans?

2.5   Has management established monitoring processes to ensure that defined responsibilities, standards and performance objectives are being appropriately met?

2.6   Have agreed budgets been established for the IT function and are they subject to regular and effective monitoring by management?

2.7   What measures ensure that all the required procedures, standards and policies are kept up to date?

2.8   Are changes to procedures and policies subject to management authorisation (and how is this evidenced)?

2.9   How is IT management sure that the level of service provision is adequate and appropriate, and what mechanisms are in place to ensure that users' requirements are identified and addressed?

2.10   How does management ensure that agreed levels of staff training and development resource are effectively targeted in order to avoid waste?

2.11   Has management taken action to prevent important skills being restricted to a limited number of individual employees?

2.12   How does management confirm that the measures in place to aid recovery from disaster or failure remain effective, up to date, and relevant?

2.13   What specific policies or procedures have been established to ensure that processing operations are correctly conducted and that data is adequately protected from corruption, loss or destruction?

2.14   Has management taken steps to ensure that cost-effective and appropriate industry standards and practices are applied in the IT function (i.e. the use of a recognised system development methodology or appropriate programming standards)?

2.15   What mechanisms ensure that adequate lines of communication are established (and used) with system users and owners?

2.16   How does IT management maintain an up-to-date awareness of the current business objectives and requirements?

IT SITES

Here we are principally concerned with the provision of an adequate and secure IT facility, where equipment and operations are protected from damage, disruption or loss.

Control Objectives for IT sites

(a) To provide a secure and reliable environment for all IT activities.

(b) To ensure that all IT facilities are adequately protected from damage, loss or disruption.

(c) To ensure that adequate plans are in place to deal effectively with emergencies.

(d) To ensure that appropriate and reliable environmental and physical conditions are provided and maintained.

(e) To prevent unauthorised access to the IT facility.

(f) To ensure that risks are assessed and IT facilities are adequately and appropriately insured.

(g) To ensure that staff maintain an up-to-date awareness of their responsibilities for security and safety.

(h) To ensure that buildings, persons and property are effectively protected from fire.

Risk and Control Issues for IT sites

1 Key Issues

1.1 What general steps does management take to identify and address the potential risks in respect of the IT facility?

1.2 How does management ensure that all IT sites are secure and adequately protected from unauthorised access?

1.3 How does management take due regard of the location of the IT facility and the potential hazards?

1.4 What specific measures are in place to further restrict access to the main computer room or processing facility (and how does management ensure that the measures are effective)?

1.5 What measures are in place both to prevent and to detect the unauthorised removal of IT equipment?

1.6 Have steps been taken during the design and construction of the IT facility to ensure that water, power and fuel are stored and routed so as to avoid any adverse impact due to leakage, short circuit, etc.?

1.7 Have adequate physical security and fire prevention systems been installed (and how does management ensure that they remain operational, appropriate, and effective)?

1.8 How does management ensure that adequate and effective plans and procedures are in place to deal with emergencies, disasters, bomb threats, attacks on the building, etc.?

1.9 Are regular emergency, fire, and contingency drills conducted as a means of evaluating the effectiveness of the prevailing measures?

1.10 How does management ensure that staff are sufficiently aware of their responsibilities in respect of fire detection/prevention, and emergency evacuation drills, etc.?

1.11 How does management verify that all the environmental requirements (such as air conditioning, temperature, and humidity) have been identified, provided, and maintained?

1.12 How is management assured that adequate and appropriate levels of insurance cover are in place for the IT facilities?

2 Detailed Issues

2.1 What measures are in place to protect the IT installation from staff malpractice?

2.2 How are existing access control measures tested for effectiveness?

2.3 How does management ensure that staff access control measures are kept up to date?

2.4 What specific measures are in place to control access by visitors, delivery staff, etc.?

2.5 What measures are in place to deal with out-of-hours access?

2.6 Are "high risk" or sensitive areas provided with additional access measures?

2.7 Have specific security and storage needs been effectively addressed (i.e. media library)?

2.8 Are computer room staff aware of the actions to be taken in the event of an emergency (i.e. the correct power-down procedure)?

2.9 Have adequate fire detection systems been installed (and how does management ensure that they remain operational and effective)?

2.10 Does the design of the building adequately support the containment of fire (i.e. provision of fire doors, sealed conduits, and fire-proof barriers, etc.)?

2.11 Have suitable fire containment systems (e.g. sprinklers or gas-smothering facilities) been installed?

2.12 Does the air-conditioning system shut-off automatically in the event of a fire being detected?

2.13 Has management consulted with the local fire fighting service when determining the necessary precautions and facilities?

2.14 How does management monitor that appropriate steps are taken to protect the well-being and safety of staff and visitors?

2.15 What measures ensure that the relevant and correct temperature and humidity are maintained for the IT facilities?

2.16 Where necessary or justified, have back-up or secondary environmental systems been provided?

2.17 Have facilities been provided to address the loss or disruption of the power supply?

2.18 Does the prevailing insurance cover address the potential for the following categories of risk.

- material damage (e.g. to buildings, hardware, etc.)
- consequences of the damage (e.g. disruption of business operations, loss of data, etc.)
- risks to and from personnel or third parties (e.g. injury liability or staff negligence/fraud).

PROCESSING OPERATIONS

The contents of this section are designed so that they can be applied to a variety of different processing situations. For example, the traditional batch-oriented methods normally associated with mainframe systems or the more direct (and usually informal) entry of data in to freestanding or networked personal computers.

Irrespective of the hardware platform in use, the auditor will mainly be concerned with matters of data accuracy, validity, authorisation, and completeness. These factors are linked not only to matters of access control, but are also dependent on the use of the authorised and valid versions of computer programs. Beyond these points, it is probable that there will be performance considerations to take account of; for example, is the output data available on time for its use in other interfaced systems and for circulation to staff in order to support their activities?

Control Objectives for Processing Operations

(a) To ensure that all processing is valid, authorised and accurate.

(b) To ensure that data is protected from unauthorised access and use.

(c) To ensure that the required service levels are achieved in support of the business objectives.

(d) To ensure that only authorised and tested programs are used.

(e) To ensure that only accurate, complete and timely data is provided.

(f) To ensure that IT processing facilities are operated at optimum performance/efficiency without jeopardising system integrity and reliability.

Risk and Control Issues for Processing Operations

1 Key Issues

1.1 What general measures are in place to ensure that processing activity is valid, accurate and authorised?

1.2 What specific measures prevent unauthorised transactions and/or system amendments being applied?

1.3 How can management be assured that data is accurate, complete, authorised and reliable?

1.4 How is commercially sensitive or confidential data protected from unauthorised access or leakage?

1.5 What measures ensure that only authorised and tested versions of programs are utilised?

1.6 How would management promptly be made aware of any abnormal processing activity?

1.7 What steps are in place to prevent development staff directly accessing the live production environment?

1.8 How does management monitor that the skills of the operating and technical support staff are kept up to date and relevant?

1.9 How does management ensure that the mainframe and distributed systems are operated at optimum efficiency (and that facility overloads are prevented)?

1.10 What measures prevent unauthorised usage of mainframe (or equivalent) facilities?

1.11 How does management check that the operating system is efficiently configured and that adequately skilled staff are available to maintain and/ or rebuild the system in the event of major failure?

1.12 Have adequate steps been taken to ensure that all key hardware is regularly and appropriately maintained in order to avoid unnecessary disruption of services, etc.?

1.13 What measures ensure that the use of job control language (JCL) or system control language (SCL) is optimised and that inefficient or inappropriate tasks are not loaded?

1.14 Is access to the JCL and SCL facilities adequately restricted in order to avoid unauthorised amendments?

1.15 What steps are in place to ensure that all the necessary processing stages are correctly applied in the appropriate sequence?

1.16   What measures ensure that processing is conducted in accordance with the business requirements and within the required timescales?

1.17   What steps ensure that only authorised, accurate and appropriate data is loaded for access by users?

1.18   Have management defined the required service provision levels, and what measures ensure that the agreed performance criteria are achieved?

2 Detailed Issues

2.1   How would management promptly be made aware of any corrupt or inaccurate data?

2.2   What specific steps would prevent the loading and use of unauthorised and untested programs or system amendments?

2.3   What measures are in place to assess and promptly deal with processing problems and delays?

2.4   What measures are in place to confirm positively the accuracy and completeness of processing operations?

2.5   What measures prevent the delivery or provision of inaccurate output to users?

2.6   Are contingency measures in place to restore promptly disrupted services?

2.7   How does management ensure that access to and use of utility programs is valid, appropriate and trailed?

2.8   Are the actions of operations staff capable of being identified and trailed (and are they made accountable for their actions)?

2.9   Are the activity logs routinely reviewed in order to ensure that unauthorised activities would be detected?

2.10   What specific measures prevent the application of inefficient or invalid JCL or SCL?

2.11   What steps are in place to ensure that all general processing operations are conducted in the correct sequence and at the relevant time?

2.12   What measures ensure that only the correct data files are loaded, and that invalid files are detected?

2.13   What measures prevent the premature overwriting or erasure of data files?

2.14   What measures would enable the continuation of processing activities if a key data or program was lost or destroyed?

2.15   Has management provided adequate operational procedures and policies in order to ensure that operating staff are fully aware of their responsibilities?

2.16   What steps are taken with urgent or non-standard processing jobs in order to prevent the disruption of mainstream processing?

2.17   What measures prevent unauthorised access to confidential data output, and how is such data securely distributed to authorised users?

BACK-UP AND MEDIA

Paying attention to the back-up and secure storage of data is often (falsely!) seen as a chore which can be left to another day. It is all too easy to overlook the real value of business data and not take adequate precautions to protect it should a problem occur with the computer or the application system. The situation is exacerbated by the widespread use of personal computers (PCs) in business, where the option to take the necessary precautions with data are usually left to the discretion of the user. The formal data handling and security techniques that emerged from mainframe installations over the years do not readily translate into the more informal and open world of the PC. In addition, unless the responsibility for data and system back-up is clearly defined and complied with, it is all too easy for end-users to assume that someone else is securing *their* systems.

In this section we examine the issues relating to protection of data through adequate back-up, and also include details of the related practices of secure storage and media handling.

Control Objectives for Back-up and Media

(a)   To ensure that critical systems and data are adequately and frequently backed up to protect the business operations and integrity of the organisation.

(b)   To provide the means to recover promptly and accurately from system failure or invalid processing situations.

(c)   To ensure that the organisation's data is adequately protected from loss, damage and leakage.

(d)   To ensure that all corporate data is safeguarded and retained.

(e)   To ensure that retained data remains in a usable and accessible form.

(f)   To ensure that the organisation is capable of complying with the prevailing data retention legislation and regulations.

(g)   To ensure that data storage facilities provide the appropriate environmental conditions to prevent deterioration or damage to media.

(h)   To ensure that media staff are appropriately skilled in media handling techniques.

(i) To ensure that all media and data are accurately identified, trailed, and accounted for.

(j) To ensure that media and data are not prematurely disposed of or destroyed.

(k) To prevent the infection of media and systems with viruses.

(l) To ensure that users are made aware of their responsibilities with regard to the back-up and protection of PC data.

(m) To ensure that only the correct data are used for processing operations.

(n) To ensure that faulty or defective media are identified, replaced and disposed of.

(o) To prevent the unauthorised use of media and data.

Risk and Control Issues for Back-up and Media

1 Key Issues

1.1 How does management ensure that all the key systems and data are effectively protected in the event of a failure or breakdown in order to avoid disruption to business operations and requirements?

1.2 How is management assured that systems and data files are appropriately backed up at the right time?

1.3 What checks are in place to monitor that the prescribed data (and system) back-up routines are being correctly applied in practice?

1.4 How does management ensure that the current data back-up and recovery procedures are adequate so that systems could be restored promptly and accurately?

1.5 What measures ensure that all data and system back-ups are securely stored and adequately protected from damage, loss or deterioration?

1.6 What steps are in place to protect key elements of corporate data in the event of a major systems failure or disaster befalling the IT facility?

1.7 What measures ensure that all key data and system back-ups can be accurately and promptly identified and traced?

1.8 How does management ascertain that the organisation is correctly complying with all the prevailing and relevant data retention legislation and regulations (i.e. for accounting and financial data)?

1.9 What measures ensure that long-term back-up media remains readable and usable?

1.10   What measures ensure that only the correct and valid data and systems files are used in processing activities?

1.11   What specific measures prevent the premature erasure, disposal, or reuse of back-up media?

1.12   What measures are in place to prevent and/or detect the virus infection of media and the spreading of that infection throughout the corporate systems?

2 Detailed Issues

2.1   Has management established an agreed back-up procedure which defines, among other things, the following elements:

- back-up frequency
- number of copies
- retention period?

2.2   How does management ensure that the back-up procedures remain appropriate in relation to changing business requirements, etc.?

2.3   What measures are in place to detect any failure to undertake a prescribed back-up at the appropriate time?

2.4   How is management sure that systems and data could be promptly recovered from back-up copies (i.e. has the recovery process been tested to prove its effectiveness)?

2.5   How does management check that end-users are applying adequate data back-up routines in order to protect their PC-based activities?

2.6   Does management ensure that all key back-ups are regularly accounted for?

2.7   Where are the back-up storage facilities located (and does this location afford appropriate protection in the event of a disaster, such as a fire, affecting the main IT facility)?

2.8   How is the disposal of outdated or unwanted media controlled so that valid items are not destroyed or overwritten?

2.9   Are the staff involved in media handling suitably trained in handling and transporting techniques in order to protect corporate data and systems?

2.10   Have adequate copies of key data been provided in case one copy becomes damaged or unreadable?

2.11   What measures ensure that virus infections are promptly detected, contained and effectively dealt with?

2.12   What specific measures prevent the transfer of virus-infected media to third parties (such as suppliers or customers)?

2.13   How would unauthorised access to or use of back-up media be prevented (or detected)?

SYSTEM AND OPERATING SOFTWARE

Here we are concerned with the category of software which is fundamental to the operation of computers. System and operating software will determine how the computer basically handles data, stores files, etc. In the more familiar personal computer environment, operating system software examples would be MS-DOS, Windows and Windows 95.

PC users who use the Windows environment, will probably be aware that there are many configuration options provided and that it can take some time to settle upon the particular set-up which most suits their needs. Windows has the benefit of being fairly user-friendly, once you have understood the jargon and the range of possibilities. The available options have the potential to effect the speed and efficiency of operations, the appearance of the screens, and the range of options offered to users. However, operating systems for networking and mainframe environments are normally much more complex and usually require considerable expertise in their configuration and use.

This section is not intended to be technically oriented, but concentrates on the business and operational implications of systems and operating software. The commercially available operating systems are normally the subject of dedicated technical books which explore the depths of their complexity for the benefit of system managers and other IT specialists. Indeed there are such texts specifically designed for internal auditors.[3]

Control Objectives for System and Operating Software

(a)   To ensure that only authorised and reliable systems and operating software are used in order to provide a stable basis for data processing operations.

(b)   To ensure that the configuration of the systems/operating software supports the efficient running of systems.

(c)   To ensure that the operating system prevents unauthorised access to systems, data and facilities.

(d)   To ensure that adequate and appropriately skilled staff are available to maintain the systems/operating software.

(e) To ensure that all configuration changes or software amendments applied to the operating software are valid, authorised and fully tested prior to implementation.

(f) To ensure that the use of privilege user or high level facilities is valid, authorised, and suitably trailed.

(g) To ensure that the operating systems for personal computers are appropriately configured for maximum performance and integrity.

(h) To ensure that personal computer operating systems are adequately protected from unauthorised tampering.

(i) To ensure that the capability to recover from a major systems failure is maintained and periodically tested.

(j) To ensure that error conditions, etc. are appropriately logged and followed up.

(k) To ensure that the use of powerful utility and diagnostic software is controlled and monitored in order to prevent disruption of services or corruption of data and systems.

Risk and Control Issues for System and Operating Software

1 Key Issues

1.1 What measures ensure that only recognised, reliable, industry standard, and correctly configured operating systems are used throughout the organisation?

1.2 How does management ensure that the various operating systems are appropriately configured to support the efficient and secure running of systems?

1.3 What measures prevent unauthorised access to and amendment of operating systems and systems software?

1.4 Are all systems software upgrades and fixes adequately assessed, tested and authorised prior to application to the live environment?

1.5 How does management monitor that the efficiency and performance of the operating system is optimised?

1.6 Are systems and operating software facilities effectively configured and established so that unauthorised access to data and systems is prevented (or at least detected)?

1.7 What is the procedure to ensure that full recovery from a major systems failure can be achieved promptly (i.e. the ability to quickly and correctly rebuild the operating environment)?

1.8   How does management ensure that adequate and appropriately skilled staff are available to maintain operating and systems software?

1.9   Are abnormal or unauthorised events promptly and independently brought to the attention of management for action?

1.10   Is access to "privilege user" facilities adequately restricted and trailed?

1.11   Has management established adequate and appropriate levels of operating system journals in order to maintain an accurate awareness of system usage and operating efficiency?

1.12   How does management ensure that all personal computers throughout the organisation are appropriately and consistently configured?

1.13   What measures prevent users from applying unauthorised or inappropriate amendments to PC configurations?

2 Detailed Issues

2.1   How does management ensure that the organisation is using the most appropriate operating systems to support their requirements?

2.2   Would management promptly be made aware of the use of unauthorised or unsuitable operating systems?

2.3   What measures prevent the inappropriate or disruptive configuration of operating/systems software?

2.4   Do access facilities reflect both the operational requirements of the organisation and protect users' data?

2.5   Are up-to-date records maintained which reflect the current and authorised condition and configuration of operating systems?

2.6   What measures prevent the application of invalid, unsuitable or unauthorised amendments to the operating system?

2.7   How does management verify that all operating system amendments are fully and effectively tested prior to update in the live environment?

2.8   How is the performance of the operating system monitored (and would this process enable the prompt detection of potential problems)?

2.9   Who has the responsibility and authority to amend the "workmix"?

2.10   How is management made aware of error conditions, abnormal events or the use of "privilege user" facilities?

2.11   Is access to utility and diagnostic facilities suitably restricted and trailed?

2.12   How does management check that all job control language (JCL) or systems control language (SCL) instructions are valid, authorised and tested prior to introduction to the live environment?

2.13 What specific measures prevent the introduction and use of unauthorised or unreliable PC operating systems?

2.14 What measures prevent PC users from introducing unauthorised operating systems by rebooting from a system disk placed in the floppy disk drive?

2.15 Would the measures in place enable the detection of unauthorised amendments to PC operating systems?

SYSTEM ACCESS CONTROL

Under this topic we consider the protection of data and systems from unauthorised use as a means of ensuring that data remains accurate, reliable and confidential.

Control Objectives for System Access Control

(a) To ensure that systems and data are secure from unauthorised access and usage.

(b) To prevent disruption of the business caused by unauthorised access to computing facilities.

(c) To ensure that data are adequately protected from unauthorised amendment, loss or leakage.

(d) To ensure that all system usage is recorded and accounted for.

(e) To ensure that potential breaches of access security are promptly detected and reacted to.

(f) To ensure that staff are aware of their responsibilities for protecting company systems and data.

(g) To ensure that access passwords are of an acceptable standard and kept confidential.

(h) To ensure that access rights and associated records are kept up to date.

Risk and Control Issues for System Access Control

1 Key Issues

1.1 Has management established a policy of system and data ownership whereby users take responsibility for their systems and data?

1.2 What measures are in place to ensure that data and systems are effectively protected from unauthorised access and/or amendments?

1.3 How is system usage identified (and charged for, where necessary)?

1.4 What measures ensure that the access control arrangements are kept up to date and relevant to the underlying business needs?

1.5 Who controls the granting of access rights, and how does management check that this operation is correctly conducted?

1.6 How does management monitor that staff are fully aware of their responsibilities with regard to data and system security?

1.7 How does management ensure that user access passwords are effective and are protected from leakage and misuse?

1.8 What specific measures prevent the casual use of terminals (and personal computers) left switched on and unattended?

1.9 How does management ensure that users access systems on a strictly "need to know" basis?

2 Detailed Issues

2.1 How are valid access rights to systems and data determined?

2.2 What mechanisms ensure that leavers and those changing position are appropriately amended on the access system(s)?

2.3 Are the established access rights periodically checked for accuracy and relevance (with outdated entries being removed or edited)?

2.4 Will attempted security breaches or violations be promptly detected and reported to management for action?

2.5 What additional measures are in place to ensure that high-level or privilege access rights are effectively controlled and that relevant actions are trailed (and authorised)?

2.6 Has management established that attempted security breaches are staff disciplinary offences?

2.7 Are access arrangements subject to periodic review and assessment (and how is this evidenced)?

2.8 Have standards been established for passwords (minimum length, regular changing, avoidance of obvious or previous used words, etc.)?

2.9 If password standards have been established, how is management certain that they are complied with?

2.10 How are initial passwords communicated to the relevant user, and what measures ensure that the password remains secure in transit?

PERSONAL COMPUTERS

The business (and leisure) use of personal computers has mushroomed in popularity. PCs are approachable, easy to use, increasingly reliable and ever more powerful. When linked together through networks they become even more flexible and enable the sharing and exchange of data. They have also been responsible for changing working methods. They do however, have a down side.

The very ease of approach afforded by the PC presents problems of security, access control, and so on. The growth in an organisation's reliance upon PCs can be insidious, and unless sensible security and usage methods are concurrently introduced, exposure to real risks will follow.

This section addresses the primary concerns of PC usage in a business environment.

Control Objectives for Personal Computers

(a) To ensure that personal computers are consistently and securely used throughout the organisation as a means of contributing to efficiency and the achievement of business objectives.

(b) To ensure that the use of all personal computers is justified and authorised.

(c) To ensure that only suitable industry standard personal computers are acquired from stable and reliable suppliers capable of providing the required support.

(d) To ensure that all personal computers and ancillary equipment is effectively protected from loss, theft or damage.

(e) To ensure that staff are suitably trained in the effective and efficient use of personal computing facilities.

(f) To ensure that only authorised and licensed versions of software are used throughout the organisation.

(g) To ensure that all PC equipment is correctly installed and appropriately configured.

(h) To prevent unauthorised configuration and software amendments being applied.

(i) To ensure that only authorised users are granted access to PC facilities.

(j) To ensure that the organisation conforms to the prevailing software licensing conditions.

(k) To prevent the unauthorised copying and theft of PC software and data.

(l)   To prevent the loading of unauthorised software.

(m)   To ensure compliance with the requirements of the Data Protection legislation.

(n)   To ensure that business disruption caused by hardware failure is minimised.

(o)   To prevent the infection of PC equipment and other IT facilities with viruses, and to deal promptly and effectively with any suspected or actual infection.

Risk and Control Issues for Personal Computers

1 Key Issues

1.1   How does management ensure that personal computing supports the objectives of the IT strategic plan?

1.2   How does management ensure that PC facilities are justified and contribute to business efficiency and/or the achievement of corporate objectives?

1.3   What measures are in place to ensure that personal computers are consistently and securely used throughout the organisation?

1.4   How does management ensure that suitable personal computers are obtained from reliable suppliers and that they meet the relevant performance and facility requirements?

1.5   Does management take effective steps to ensure that PC hardware is of an appropriate (and recognised) type and quality, and is capable of future expansion?

1.6   What steps are taken to protect PC hardware from theft, damage or misuse?

1.7   How does management ensure that only authorised and appropriate software is loaded on to personal computers (and what specifically prevents users from loading their own software files)?

1.8   What measures prevent users from applying unauthorised or inappropriate configuration amendments which could adversely affect performance and reliability?

1.9   How is the unauthorised use of personal computers and the relevant data prevented?

1.10   How are staff adequately trained in the correct and efficient use of PC facilities and specific software applications?

1.11   What steps does management take to ensure that the requirements of the prevailing data protection legislation are fully complied with?

1.12   What measures are in place to prevent undue disruption in the event of hardware failure?

1.13   What measures protect personal computers from virus infections?

1.14   What measures prevent users from making unauthorised copies of licensed software and sensitive data files?

1.15   What measures prevent users from circumventing access and operating system controls?

2 Detailed Issues

2.1   What measures ensure that only justified and authorised PC equipment is acquired (and how is the authorisation evidenced)?

2.2   How are staff made aware of their responsibility for accurate and appropriate usage of PC facilities?

2.3   Are all personal computers of an acceptable industry standard (and is the acquisition of non-standard items subject to suitable authorisation)?

2.4   How does management ensure that PC suppliers are capable of providing an effective support and maintenance service?

2.5   What mechanisms ensure that the most appropriate method of financing PC acquisition is used in the circumstances?

2.6   How is the unauthorised movement or removal of PC equipment prevented?

2.7   How does management monitor that the number of software packages used throughout the organisation conforms to the licences held?

2.8   How is management made aware of the use of unlicensed or pirated software systems?

2.9   What measures prevent users from applying unauthorised or inappropriate software updates (and how can management be assured that the use of software is consistent throughout the organisation)?

2.10   How does management ensure that only authorised and valid users can gain access to corporate systems and data?

2.11   Would attempted access violations or system security breaches be promptly and effectively detected and reported?

2.12   What measures are in place to ensure that system/data access rights are kept up to date and are relevant to operational needs?

2.13   Are staff made aware of the need to regularly back up and securely store their data (and how does management ensure that such precautions are actually taken)?

2.14   How is management assured that back-up and other precautionary measures are effective (for example are system recovery processes periodically tested for their effectiveness)?

2.15   Are all hardware and software upgrades applied only by suitably trained and authorised staff (and how is this confirmed)?

2.16   Would virus infections be promptly identified, and what arrangements are in place to deal effectively with such infections?

2.17   What measures would prevent the uncontrolled spread of virus infections (e.g. through local area networks)?

SOFTWARE MAINTENANCE

Our focus here is on applications system software and its maintenance and amendment. Where a system has a critical role in the business operations, management will need to be assured that it can continue to operate in a secure and reliable manner. From time to time, it may be necessary to apply amendments to the functionality and operational aspects of the programs, and in order for the overall integrity of the system to be maintained, such modifications will need to be applied proficiently and tested thoroughly prior to live use.

The application of software amendments and updates can be undertaken either by in-house system development staff, or by external software companies where the standard "off-the-shelf" application system is involved.

Control Objectives for Software Maintenance

(a)   To ensure that systems are capable of being maintained in order to prolong their useful life and continue to serve the business.

(b)   To ensure that all system amendments are justified and authorised.

(c)   To ensure that system amendments are comprehensively and independently tested prior to being correctly applied in the live environment.

(d)   To ensure that only authorised and tested amendments are applied.

(e)   To ensure that systems are adequately documented so that they can be effectively maintained.

(f)   To ensure that the various versions of programs are accurately identified so that only the authorised versions can be used.

(g)   To ensure that the systems documentation is appropriately updated following software amendments.

(h)   To ensure that live programs are strictly separated from those under development, and that movements between the live and development environments are adequately controlled.

(i)   To ensure that the live program library only contains valid and authorised versions of current programs.

(j)   To ensure that personal computer application software is correctly updated with officially recognised upgrades and fixes.

(k)   To ensure that facilities are in place to deal effectively with emergency program fixes.

Risk and Control Issues for Software Maintenance

1 Key Issues

1.1   Are all key systems adequately documented to a defined standard so as to ensure that they can be maintained effectively?

1.2   What steps ensure that software amendments are accurately defined, justified, and authorised?

1.3   What steps ensure that all software amendments and corrections are fully and satisfactorily tested before being introduced into live use?

1.4   Are all software amendments appropriately coded and valid for the purpose?

1.5   What procedures ensure that only authorised and current versions of programs are used in the live production environment?

1.6   What measures ensure that all amendments are suitably specified and documented to the required standard?

1.7   What mechanisms ensure that live programs and those under development are kept strictly separate?

1.8   What checks are in place to monitor the validity of the contents of the live and production program libraries?

1.9   What procedures ensure that personal computers are correctly updated with only official and appropriate software upgrades and fixes?

1.10 Has management established effective routines to deal with emergency (i.e. out of hours) program fixes without jeopardising system integrity or business operations?

2 Detailed Issues

2.1   What mechanisms ensure that all systems are suitably documented and that the records are updated whenever an amendment is applied?

2.2   What measures ensure that all proposed software amendments are appropriately specified to the satisfaction of users?

2.3   What specific measures prevent the application of unauthorised or invalid system amendments to the live environment?

2.4   What is the documentary evidence for the comprehensive testing of software amendments (and does this have to be reviewed and authorised by management prior to acceptance of the amendment)?

2.5   What measures ensure that additional functionality (perhaps with a fraudulent or malicious intent) is not incorporated into software fixes?

2.6   How does management ensure that all programming is conducted in accordance with best practice and to the required standard?

2.7   Are the contents of the various program libraries periodically checked to ensure that only valid items are held?

2.8   What measures prevent the unauthorised transfer of programs between the development and live program libraries?

2.9   How is the testing of programs and amendments defined (and what prevents the application of ineffective or inadequate levels of testing)?

2.10   How does management ensure that the versions of personal computer applications used throughout the organisation are consistent (i.e. would invalid or outdated versions be promptly identified)?

LOCAL AREA NETWORKS

Data communication technology has undergone a period of rapid and explosive development in recent years, with notable gains in transmission speeds and the interconnectivity of systems. Businesses will use variations of the networking theme to achieve the effective (and secure) sharing and communication of business data.

Local area networks (LANs) are now commonplace, and larger geographic areas of data communication coverage can be achieved by using wide area networks (WANs) or metropolitan area networks (MANs). The growing use of fibre optic systems and the development of dedicated communication networks are pushing us inexorably towards a global networking future.

Although we use the term LAN throughout, the business-oriented issues noted within this section can be generally applied in any network communications environment. The underlying control and risk principles can equally be applied to WANs, MANs, etc. We have deliberately avoided a technically driven approach.

Control Objectives for Local Area Networks

(a) To ensure that appropriate, justified and authorised network facilities are provided to support the business.

(b) To ensure that local area network facilities are secure and adequately protected from unauthorised access and tampering.

(c) To ensure that the optimum networking solution is applied in the circumstances.

(d) To ensure that adequate account is taken of future expansion needs.

(e) To ensure that systems and data are adequately protected from unauthorised use.

(f) To ensure that network installations are suitably planned and implemented.

(g) To ensure that only recognised and industry standard network hardware and software are used.

(h) To ensure the integrity and reliability of the network system software.

(i) To ensure that the required performance and response criteria are achieved.

(j) To ensure that file and system servers, gateway PCs and other network equipment are protected from unauthorised access and tampering.

(k) To ensure that supervisor and other high-level user facilities are protected from unauthorised usage.

(l) To ensure that network support staff are adequately and appropriately skilled to support the network operations.

(m) To ensure that external (i.e. dial-up) access to the network facilities is valid and authorised.

(n) To ensure that adequate and effective contingency and recovery plans are in place to enable the controlled and prompt recovery of service in the event of a major failure, etc.

Risk and Control Issues for Local Area Networks

1 Key Issues

1.1 How does management ensure that LAN requirements are fully assessed, justified, and accord with the needs of the business and the IT strategic plan?

1.2 Are performance and service availability requirements accurately identified as the basis for determining the optimum networking solution(s)?

1.3 How does management take due account of predicted future needs when planning and providing LAN facilities?

1.4   What specific measures prevent unauthorised access to the networking facilities, and protect user systems and data from invalid access and usage?

1.5   How is management assured of the integrity of the network system software and its contribution to general data and system security?

1.6   How are file and system servers, gateway PCs and other LAN hardware protected from unauthorised access, tampering, etc.?

1.7   How are supervisor and other high-level user facilities protected from unauthorised usage?

1.8   Has management made adequate arrangements to ensure that network support staff are suitably skilled?

1.9   How does management ensure that effective plans have been established to support the prompt recovery of critical LAN systems following a major failure or disaster?

2 Detailed Issues

2.1   What specific measures prevent the unauthorised introduction or updating of LAN facilities?

2.2   How does management ensure that the defined performance and response requirements are being consistently achieved in practice?

2.3   How does management monitor that planned LAN development keeps pace with the needs of the business?

2.4   Has management established a planned approach to the expansion of the LAN in step with anticipated business growth?

2.5   Who is responsible for defining access rights and how does management ensure that such rights do not jeopardise the integrity of systems and data?

2.6   How are access rights accurately kept up to date?

2.7   Are measures in place to ensure that only industry standard LAN hardware is acquired from stable and proven suppliers (who are capable of providing ongoing support and maintenance)?

2.8   What steps are taken to ensure that all LAN software is reliable and proven?

2.9   What checks are in place to ensure that the LAN software is correctly, appropriately and efficiently configured?

2.10 What specific measures are in place to prevent unauthorised external access to the LAN (i.e. through dial-up services)?

2.11 How is management made aware of invalid amendments to the configuration of LAN hardware and software?

2.12 Are unusual (or potentially damaging) events prevented, logged or reported?

2.13 What measures prevent users from applying unnecessary and invalid amendments to LAN hardware and software configurations?

2.14 Are LAN recovery plans periodically tested for their effectiveness (and how is this evidenced)?

DATABASES

This section relates to use of database techniques to support a business. Many of the formal system analysis and development techniques are built around a data-driven approach, where the information needs of the relevant organisation are accurately established as the foundations for the development and operation of all the related business systems. Normally, the data approach is typified by data modelling and database techniques, which aim to reduce (or eliminate) instances of data duplication and redundancy through the creation of a relational database.

From the management standpoint, it is important that the chosen data structure and the database management system used to contain and manipulate information, are secure, reliable and provide accurate information to support the business needs.

Control Objectives for Databases

(a) To ensure that the information needs of the organisation are appropriately reflected and addressed in the data structure.

(b) To ensure that the most suitable, reliable, secure and flexible database system is established.

(c) To ensure that users embrace the concept of system and data ownership.

(d) To ensure that data are adequately protected from unauthorised access, amendments, usage, and leakage.

(e) To ensure that the database system and the data it contains are accurately set up and maintained.

(f) To ensure that the ongoing integrity of the database is maintained.

(g) To ensure that all subsequent amendments to the database form and structure are valid and authorised.

(h) To ensure that suitably skilled staff are available to support the operation and maintenance of the database.

(i) To ensure that the database is resilient and can be promptly and fully recovered in the event of a major failure or disaster.

> (j)   To ensure that the data are regularly and appropriately backed up to protect the business operations.
>
> (k)   To ensure that users are appropriately trained in the use of ancillary database facilities (such as query languages) so that they are efficiently and effectively used.
>
> (l)   To ensure that all systems developments and amendments fully take into account the implications for the database structure and system.
>
> (m) To avoid the holding and processing of duplicated or redundant data.

Risk and Control Issues for Databases

1 Key Issues

1.1   How does management ensure that the data needs of the organisation are accurately identified and reflected in current systems and databases?

1.2   How has management ensured that appropriate, secure, reliable and flexible database management systems are in place and maintained?

1.3   How can management be assured that appropriate control is exercised over systems and data ownership and the determination of access rights?

1.4   How are data protected from unauthorised access and amendments?

1.5   What measures ensure that the initial set-up of the database structure is relevant, accurate and reflects the agreed corporate data requirements?

1.6   How is the ongoing integrity of the database structure and contents assured?

1.7   Are all subsequent amendments to the database structure and contents subject to authorisation, and what measures prevent unauthorised structural amendments?

1.8   What steps does management take to ensure that sufficiently skilled staff are available to support the operation and maintenance of the database?

1.9   What specific measures ensure that the database can promptly and accurately be rebuilt in the event of a major failure?

1.10 Are adequate and effective database back-up precautions taken?

1.11 How does management ensure that query languages are efficiently and appropriately used (and that enquiries are neither excessive nor over-demanding on systems resources)?

1.12 What measures ensure that all system developments and amendments conform to the agreed structure and contents of the database system?

2 Detailed Issues

2.1   Has the required data structure been documented and formally authorised (and how is this evidenced)?

2.2   What measures are in place to prevent the holding (and processing) of redundant or duplicated data items?

2.3   How does management verify that the chosen database supplier is stable, reliable and capable of providing ongoing support?

2.4   Does the selected database management system conform to recognised industry standards?

2.5   Has the capacity and flexibility of the database system been assessed in light of anticipated growth (and has the ability to meet future demands been confirmed)?

2.6   Are users/system owners held responsible for defining and authorising access rights?

2.7   How does management monitor that the access rights to data and systems are accurately kept up to date?

2.8   Are the database rebuilding procedures subject to periodic testing as a means of assessing their effectiveness?

2.9   Is the database backed up at the appropriate frequency (and are the back-up media tested for readability)?

2.10 How is management made aware of attempts to violate access arrangements or other unusual database activities?

DATA PROTECTION ACT

It could be said that all data protection legislation principles are formalised common sense. However, a business registered under the UK Data Protection Act 1984, will need to ensure that the principles are effectively applied throughout the organisation. This is partly a matter of clear communication of staff responsibilities, underpinned by defined procedures which are capable of being monitored for compliance.

Since the passing of the Data Protection Act 1984, there has been an underlying problem with the unscrupulous trade in personal information as operated by some (albeit a minority of) organisations and individuals who use devious means to obtain data. In specific circumstances, these activities were not regulated by the Data Protection Act 1984, and therefore prosecution under that act was ruled out. In order to address this problem, three new criminal offences were incorporated into the Criminal Justice and Public Order Act 1994, which came into effect on 3 February 1995.

It is now an offence "for a person to procure the disclosure of personal information to him, where he knows or has reason to believe that he is not a person to whom the data user is registered to disclose the data". Guidance issued by the Data Protection Registrar[4] goes on to say: "In cases where either bribery or deception is used, it may be fairly clear that the person obtaining the data in that way has good reason to believe that the organisation approached would not, in normal circumstances, authorise the disclosure in question. If this is the case, then the person seeking the data is likely to have committed a criminal offence."

The other two new offences created by the amendments "relate to the sale, or offering for sale (including advertising for sale) of personal data (or information extracted from such data) procured in the manner described above". Internal auditors should be aware of these amendments to the UK legislation when considering reviews of data protection measures.

Control Objectives for Data Protection Act

(a) To ensure compliance with the prevailing data protection legislation.

(b) To ensure that staff are aware of their responsibilities in respect of the data protection regulations.

(c) To ensure that the organisation's data protection registration is accurate and maintained up-to-date.

(d) To ensure that data protection implications are appropriately addressed for all system developments and amendments.

(e) To ensure that enquiries from data subjects are promptly, efficiently and accurately dealt with.

(f) To ensure that data errors are promptly corrected.

Risk and Control Issues for Data Protection Act

1 Key Issues

1.1 How does management ensure that all the prevailing data protection requirements are cost-effectively complied with (and how is such compliance evidenced)?

1.2 What steps has management taken to ensure that all affected staff are made aware of their responsibilities under the prevailing data protection legislation?

1.3 What measures ensure that the organisation's registration details remain accurate and up to date (e.g. for new systems and business activities)?

1.4 How does management ensure that data protection implications are appropriately considered for all systems under development (or where significant amendments are being applied)?

1.5   What systems are in place to ensure that all enquiries from data subjects are promptly identified and actioned?

1.6   What processes ensure that data errors are promptly and appropriately corrected?

2 Detailed Issues

2.1   How does management maintain staff awareness of data protection issues and their correct treatment?

2.2   Has the responsibility for periodically confirming the accuracy of the organisation's data protection registration been allocated?

2.3   How is management assured that personal data is obtained fairly and lawfully?

2.4   How is management assured that personal data is only held for the required purpose?

2.5   How is management assured that personal data is disseminated in accord with the registration?

2.6   How is management assured that personal data is accurate and up to date?

2.7   What measures are in place to ensure that unwanted, surplus or obsolete personal data is erased?

2.8   How is personal data restricted to authorised users only?

2.9   What procedures avoid unauthorised amendment of data?

2.10   How does management ensure that data is protected from accidental loss, leakage or destruction?

2.11   How does management confirm that printed or filmed personal data is securely disposed of?

2.12   How is management assured that all data subject enquiries are accounted for?

FACILITIES MANAGEMENT

The current vogue for outsourcing extends to IT activities, especially where an organisation wishes to concentrate its internal resources upon the business activities it is best placed to handle. The outsourcing of IT activities is normally referred to as facilities management (FM), where an external organisation takes over the day-to-day running of such functions as mainframe computer operations, system development or system maintenance. In some instances, this transfer of responsibility includes the transfer of the employing organisation's former staff in the relative area.

The application of facilities management solutions can remove the onerous and often costly need for the organisation to maintain specialist staff skills and equipment. This off-loading can free resources and funding which can be concentrated on more worthwhile activities; for example, the development of new products and services designed to enhance the continued survival of the business.

The engagement of an FM contractor should be preceded by an accurate determination of the relevant IT service requirements including consideration of service levels, required quality standards, etc.

Control Objectives for Facilities Management

(a) To ensure that the IT requirements are accurately determined and the optimum solution is adopted.

(b) To ensure that the use of facilities management solutions is fully assessed, justified, and authorised as part of the strategic direction for IT.

(c) To ensure that the required service levels and performance criteria are accurately determined and addressed by the FM contractor.

(d) To ensure that the selected FM contractor is stable, reliable and capable of delivering the required services.

(e) To ensure that the contractual arrangements accurately and appropriately define the respective responsibilities, rights, and liabilities.

(f) To ensure that adequate and effective security will be exercised over the organisation's systems and data in order to protect its business operations.

(g) To ensure that the ownership of hardware, software, systems and data are clearly defined.

(h) To ensure that cost and performance measures are monitored against targets and that prompt action is taken in the event of shortfalls, etc.

(i) To ensure that adequate and proven contingency and disaster recovery arrangements are in place to protect the ongoing business operations.

(j) To ensure that all transactions and processing are accurately trailed and accounted for.

(k) To ensure that any proposed operational changes or developments are subject to prior mutual agreement and authorisation.

(l) To ensure that adequate operational and quality standards are in place.

(m) To ensure that any migration to third-party FM arrangements is adequately planned for and implemented.

Risk and Control Issues for Facilities Management

1 Key Issues

1.1   How has management determined that the use of FM services is appropriate and justified?

1.2   How is management sure that the optimum FM solution has been selected?

1.3   Is the use of FM services subject to formal authorisation (and how is this evidenced)?

1.4   How does management ensure that the required levels of service and cost saving are accurately identified, addressed and achieved?

1.5   How is management assured that the selected FM contractor is stable, reliable, and fully capable of providing the required service(s)?

1.6   Have all the relevant responsibilities, rights and liabilities been fairly allocated between the parties and accurately reflected in the contractual documents?

1.7   How can management be assured that adequate and effective security will be exercised over company systems and data?

1.8   Has management clearly established the ownership of hardware, general software and specific company systems?

1.9   How does management ensure that cost and performance targets are actually achieved?

1.10   Has management confirmed that adequate (and regularly tested) contingency plans are in place to protect ongoing processing and service provision?

1.11   Are measures in place to ensure that all new systems or process amendments are subject to prior agreement, authorisation and effective testing?

1.12   Is the FM contractor responsible for ensuring that all processing is subject to accurate and adequate trailing?

1.13   How does management ensure that the migration to FM services is adequately planned and implemented in order to minimise disruption, etc.?

2 Detailed Issues

2.1   Have all the viable alternatives to FM been fully assessed?

2.2   What measures prevent the unauthorised establishment or amendment of FM arrangements?

2.3   How does management monitor that the selected FM contractor operates to recognised and appropriate quality and performance standards (and are such standards defined in the contractual documents)?

2.4   What specific measures prevent unauthorised amendment of (or access to) the organisation's systems and data?

2.5   What measures ensure that any cost or performance shortcomings are promptly identified and effectively reacted to?

2.6   How does management ensure that the required service levels are actually achieved?

SYSTEM DEVELOPMENT

Beyond the common types of business systems (e.g. payroll, general ledger, word processing) businesses often have the need for very specific types of computer application system to support their particular business and operational needs. For example, a hotel will require a room booking, allocation and billing system.

A requirement to develop a new application can be addressed in a number of ways, for example using an in-house system development team or by going out to tender to a number of external software development companies. The maintenance of a dedicated in-house development team can be expensive, partly because it is necessary to maintain the staff skill levels in a constantly evolving technical environment. In either case, the costs of such system developments may represent a considerable investment. Development projects should be fully appraised, justified and subject to proficient project management techniques with defined testing stages, so that the output system is seen to be reliable, secure and robust.

The following points are designed so that they can be applied in a variety of different development scenarios.

Control Objectives for System Development

> (a)   To ensure that all systems developments are authorised and in accord with the IT strategic objectives.
>
> (b)   To ensure that all developments are assessed and justified on business, cost and benefit grounds.
>
> (c)   To ensure that an adequate, structured and secure systems development environment is provided and maintained.
>
> (d)   To ensure that adequate and appropriately skilled development staff are provided to support the creation and maintenance of reliable systems.
>
> (e)   To ensure that systems are developed to a stable and recognised standard.

(f)   To ensure that users are adequately represented in the realistic and accurate definition of functional requirements.

(g)   To ensure that systems are secure and offer suitable protection of data and business interests.

(h)   To ensure that development projects are effectively managed and are delivered on time and within budget.

(i)   To ensure that all systems are fully and satisfactorily tested prior to live use.

(j)   To ensure that systems are accurately and appropriately documented in order to support their ongoing maintenance.

(k)   To ensure that systems are effectively implemented and all considerations and impacts are appropriately taken into account.

(l)   To ensure that the required benefits and performance requirements are actually achieved.

Risk and Control Issues for System Development

1 Key Issues

1.1   Has management established the authorised strategic direction for information technology within the organisation, and are all systems developments authorised in relation to this agreed strategy?

1.2   How does management ensure that all systems developments are justified and authorised (i.e. on cost, business or benefit grounds)?

1.3   What steps has management taken to provide a secure and stable environment for the development of systems (i.e. the provision of recognised development methodologies and standards)?

1.4   How can management ensure that only stable, reliable and secure systems are developed?

1.5   What measures ensure that the relevant staff skills are acquired and maintained to support the creation of appropriate systems?

1.6   What measures ensure that accurate and appropriate system requirements and functional specifications are used as the basis for developments?

1.7   How does management ensure that delivered systems provide adequate protection of data from misuse and unauthorised access?

1.8   What action is taken to ensure that development projects are efficiently managed and delivered on time and within budget?

1.9   How does management verify that delivered systems conform to the agreed requirements and are free from errors?

1.10   What measures are in place to document systems accurately and comprehensively so that they can be maintained efficiently?

1.11   How does management identify all the implications and impacts of systems under development and plan for their successful and smooth introduction?

1.12   Are all developments monitored and reviewed after completion to ensure that all the anticipated benefits (i.e. cost savings or performance improvements) are actually achieved?

2 Detailed Issues

2.1   What specific measures would prevent the development of unauthorised, or inappropriate IT systems?

2.2   Are developments that involve the acquisition of new hardware platforms, development tools or skills subject to appropriate prior assessment and authorisation (and how is this evidenced)?

2.3   Are all major system developments subject to formal feasibility study, financial assessment and/or authorisation?

2.4   What measures ensure that systems are developed to an acceptable quality?

2.5   How does management ensure that system specifications take sufficient account of the users?

2.6   Are documented system specifications provided as the basis for all development projects (and are they subject to formal prior authorisation)?

2.7   Has management established a data security and access policy, and if so how is this enforced during systems development projects?

2.8   How does management ensure that program coding is of an acceptable quality and satisfactorily addresses the authorised requirements?

2.9   Are all development projects related to authorised budget and targets, and how does management ensure that projects are delivered within the agreed limits?

2.10   How is management made aware of project delays and shortfalls, and is this done promptly?

2.11   Does management ensure that all new systems are fully tested to the satisfaction of users prior to live usage (and if so, how is this evidenced)?

2.12   Have system documentation standards been adopted, and if so how is compliance assured?

2.13   Where external resources are used in a development project, how does management ensure that all the required quality, specification and performance issues are satisfactorily addressed?

SOFTWARE SELECTION

This section contrasts with the previous section in that it is concerned with the selection of software solutions from outside contractors and this normally relates to fairly general types of computer system (e.g. a stock control system) rather than the specialised system requirements normally addressed by bespoke developments.

In opting to source software externally, management will be looking to ensure that the suppliers are stable, reliable and capable of satisfying their needs.

Control Objectives for Software Selection

> (a) To ensure that the acquisition of software is justified, authorised and accords with the agreed IT strategic direction.
>
> (b) To ensure that all software is reliable, secure, flexible, and adequately supported.
>
> (c) To ensure that software suppliers are stable and able to provide ongoing product support.
>
> (d) To ensure that all impacts and costs associated with the acquisition of software are accurately identified and addressed.
>
> (e) To ensure that the optimum software solution is selected.
>
> (f) To ensure that staff are adequately trained and supported in the efficient use of software.

Risk and Control Issues for Software Selection

1 Key Issues

1.1 Are all software acquisitions subject to formal assessment, justification and authorisation (and how is this evidenced)?

1.2 How does management ensure that acquired software conforms to the agreed IT strategy and established platforms, etc.?

1.3 How does management ensure that only reliable, proven and secure software products are acquired?

1.4 How does management confirm that the optimum software solution is selected (and are all possible solutions examined)?

1.5 What steps does management take to confirm the stability and reliability of potential software suppliers?

1.6   How does management confirm that software suppliers are capable of providing suitable product support (including implementation and staff training where necessary)?

1.7   Upon what basis are market solutions sought (i.e. are requirement specifications used to assess software suitability)?

1.8   How does management ensure that all the costs and implications of software acquisition are assessed and authorised?

1.9   Are software products subject to formalised testing and the achievement of satisfactory results prior to purchase being authorised?

1.10 Does management ensure that adequate user support facilities (including documentation and training) are provided in order to maximise the benefits of the system?

1.11 What measures ensure that the implementation of the new software is adequately planned for and that appropriate resources are made available?

2 Detailed Issues

2.1   What specific measures prevent the acquisition of unauthorised and poor quality software packages?

2.2   Is due account taken of the market position and reputation of the software supplier?

2.3   Are existing users contacted for their comments about the software prior to acquisition?

2.4   How does management ensure that software products have a demonstrable upgrade path relevant to the platforms used within the organisation?

2.5   Are the costs of future product upgrades and staff training accurately assessed prior to purchase?

2.6   If changes or enhancements to the standard product are deemed necessary, are they and the associated costs subject to prior justification and authorisation (and how is this evidenced)?

2.7   Are performance shortcomings (in actual use) detected and resolved?

CONTINGENCY PLANNING

As an organisation's dependence on IT grows, the development of suitable contingency arrangements in the event of disaster can become vital to ensure the ongoing survival of the business. The contingency solution chosen will, in part, depend on the extent and degree of risks associated with major failures.

Control Objectives for Contingency Planning

(a) To ensure that adequate and effective contingency plans have been established to support the prompt recovery of crucial IT facilities in the event of major failure or disaster.

(b) To ensure the survival of the business and to minimise the implications of a major IT failure.

(c) To ensure that all the potential risks to the IT facility are identified and assessed in preparation of the contingency plans.

(d) To ensure the optimum contingency arrangements are selected and cost-effectively provided.

(e) To ensure that an authorised and documented disaster recovery plan is created, kept up to date, and securely stored.

(f) To ensure that the recovery plan is periodically tested for its relevance and effectiveness.

(g) To ensure that all internal and external parties to the recovery process are fully aware of their responsibilities and commitments.

(h) To ensure that appropriate liaison is maintained with external parties (i.e. insurers, emergency services, suppliers, etc.).

(i) To ensure that both the damaged and recovery sites are secure and that IT systems are securely operated in support of the business.

(j) To ensure that systems and procedures are adequately and accurately documented to aid the recovery process.

(k) To ensure that public and media relations would be addressed effectively during an emergency in order to minimise adverse publicity and business implications.

Risk and Control Issues for Contingency Planning

1 Key Issues

1.1 What measures are in place to prevent, avoid or minimise the potential for a disaster befalling the IT facility?

1.2 Has management given formal consideration to the potential for an IT related disaster, the relevant risks, and the implications for the business operations?

1.3 What action has management taken to plan for dealing with the effects of a major failure or disaster affecting the IT installation?

1.4   How is management assured that the prescribed contingency arrangements would lead to the prompt and effective recovery of IT services?

1.5   How can management be certain that the current contingency arrangements are the most appropriate and cost-effective in the circumstances?

1.6   How does management ensure that the recovery arrangements remain up to date?

1.7   How is management certain that all affected parties (internal and external) are fully aware of their responsibilities and commitments in the event of a disaster?

1.8   Has the recovery plan been formally documented (and if so, how are the copies protected from loss or damage so that they would remain accessible in the event of a disaster)?

1.9   What measures would ensure that systems and data could promptly be rebuilt (and is this capability regularly tested)?

1.10   Has provision been made to deal effectively with media and public relations in the event of a disaster, so that the image and reputation of the business is appropriately maintained?

2 Detailed Issues

2.1   Have matters of physical security, fire prevention, detection and control within the IT installation been effectively addressed in order to reduce the possibility of a disaster?

2.2   Has management taken steps to identify the most vulnerable and crucial aspects of the IT and business operations?

2.3   What measures have been taken to ensure that IT facilities would promptly be re-established?

2.4   Has management identified the minimum level of IT service required in order to maintain business operations (and the means to ensure that this level can be reinstated and/or maintained)?

2.5   Has management accurately determined the critical timescale following a disaster, during which IT services must be recovered in order for the business to survive?

2.6   Has management authorised a recovery plan and fully documented the related actions and responsibilities?

2.7   How does management ensure that this documented plan is accurately kept up to date?

2.8   Were all the possible recovery and contingency options assessed and costed as the basis for selecting the optimum solution?

2.9   Has management sought and obtained commitments in writing from key suppliers and contractors as to their level of response in the event of an IT-related disaster (and are these kept up to date)?

2.10   Has the recovery plan been subject to regular and realistic testing in order to confirm that it remains appropriate?

2.11   How is management assured that adequate and appropriate insurance cover is in place to address both the direct losses and the business impacts of an IT related disaster?

2.12   Are up-to-date copies of the recovery plan and all other system and procedural documentation securely stored and accessible?

ELECTRONIC DATA INTERCHANGE

Electronic data interchange (EDI) has become a key technology for companies engaged in businesses where there are high levels of transactions regularly flowing between parties (e.g. invoices moving between suppliers and customers). Industry standards have been established and the electronic transfer of data between entities is now commonplace with notable advantages, such as:

- accuracy and completeness of transaction data moved between parties
- reduction of errors caused by the previous need to rekey transactions
- removal of processing and postal delays.

Control Objectives for Electronic Data Interchange

(a)   To ensure that the use of EDI is fully assessed, justified and authorised as part of the adopted IT and business strategies.

(b)   To ensure that all the business and legal implications of using EDI are fully assessed and addressed.

(c)   To ensure that the optimum EDI solution is identified and implemented.

(d)   To ensure that relationships with suppliers and customers are not adversely affected by the introduction of EDI.

(e)   To ensure that the chosen method and technology are secure and that traffic is suitably authenticated.

(f)   To ensure that all transactions are confirmed as valid and reconciled.

(g)   To ensure that data from feeder systems is accurate, complete and valid.

(h)   To ensure that commercially sensitive data remains confidential.

(i)   To ensure that the approval of the required regulatory body (i.e. HM Customs & Excise) is obtained as necessary for the chosen system.

(j)   To ensure that all EDI systems are fully and satisfactorily tested before live use.

(k)   To ensure that contingency plans are in place to provide emergency cover in the event of a failure or breakdown.

(l)   To ensure that only recognised and reliable EDI systems and protocols are used.

(m) To ensure that the anticipated benefits and strategic advantages are actually achieved.

Risk and Control Issues for Electronic Data Interchange

1 Key Issues

1.1   Have the business and strategic advantages of using EDI been formally assessed, justified, and authorised (and how is this evidenced)?

1.2   How has management assessed the business and operational implications of introducing EDI (and has its introduction been adequately planned for)?

1.3   Has management taken professional legal advice on the legal status of EDI transactions, and resolved any potential areas of concern?

1.4   What steps were taken to ensure that the optimum EDI solution was adopted?

1.5   How is management assured that suppliers and customers affected by the introduction of EDI are committed to the concept and prepared to accept this type of relationship?

1.6   How does management verify that the adopted EDI system is reliable and secure (and that transaction data is adequately protected)?

1.7   What measures ensure that all EDI transactions are accurate, valid and authorised?

1.8   What specific measures ensure that commercially sensitive data remains confidential and secure?

1.9   Where necessary, has management obtained the required approval of the appropriate regulatory body for the operation of the EDI system?

1.10 Was the EDI system fully tested to the satisfaction of users, prior to live use (and how can management be assured that the testing was suitably comprehensive)?

1.11 What measures are in place to enable the continuation of EDI services following a major systems failure or disaster (and how can management be assured that any disruption will be minimised)?

1.12 Has management reviewed the performance and benefits of the EDI system and confirmed the achievement of their initial objectives?

2 Detailed Issues

2.1 How is management assured that the chosen EDI system is stable, reliable, and uses recognised protocols and standards?

2.2 How was the EDI system selected and was the ability of the suppliers to provide adequate support and maintenance taken into account?

2.3 Have the costs of introducing and using EDI systems been accurately identified, justified and authorised?

2.4 What specific measures prevent unauthorised access to (or usage of) EDI facilities?

2.5 What measures prevent both the transmission and receipt of unauthorised, duplicated or erroneous transactions?

2.6 How does management ensure that data extracted from feeder systems is accurate, complete and valid prior to EDI transmission?

2.7 Is all EDI data traffic satisfactorily reconciled between source and target systems?

2.8 Are the EDI contingency arrangements/plans regularly tested to ensure that they remain effective (and what is the evidence for this)?

VIRUSES

Although media hype can be said to have unduly raised the level of fear about the likelihood and effects of computer viruses within the business community, the actual effects of virus infection upon IT operations can still be very disruptive and costly to eradicate. The attendant dangers normally rise in proportion to the level of IT dependency and the associated devolvement of IT operational responsibility to end-users, who may be inexperienced in the methods of avoiding infection.

Control Objectives for Viruses

(a) To ensure that all systems are adequately protected from virus infections.

(b) To ensure that the impact and disruption caused by virus infections is prevented and/or minimised.

(c) To ensure that virus infections cannot be spread outside of the organisation (i.e. to customers or suppliers).

(d) To ensure that staff are fully aware of their responsibilities in the avoidance of virus infections.

(e) To ensure that only valid and authorised software is loaded on to company computers.

(f) To ensure that adequate arrangements are in place to enable the prompt identification of virus infections.

(g) To ensure that the company is able to achieve a complete recovery from virus infection.

(h) To ensure that the measures in place keep pace with virus developments and remain effective.

Risk and Control Issues for Viruses

1 Key Issues

1.1 What measures are in place to prevent systems from becoming infected by viruses?

1.2 How are personal computers protected from virus infection?

1.3 What procedures are in place to ensure that management is promptly made aware of any virus infections?

1.4 What specific measures prevent the export of virus infections to suppliers or customers (e.g. via magnetic media or on-line services)?

1.5 How does management ensure that staff are adequately aware of their responsibilities for preventing viral infection (and what is the evidence for this)?

1.6 Have procedures been established that promptly isolate any suspected infection as a means of reducing the opportunity of it spreading?

1.7 Has management established a planned approach for dealing with infections, and how are they assured that this remains potentially effective?

2 Detailed Issues

2.1   What measures would detect infected media and/or prevent the loading of same?

2.2   What measures prevent the loading of unauthorised or pirated software?

2.3   How does management ensure that all magnetic media is free from infections?

2.4   In the event of an infection being detected, how does management ensure that it will not spread in an uncontrolled way?

2.5   What steps are in place to prevent the spreading of virus infections via the local area network or wide area network systems?

2.6   Do technical support staff have the necessary skills to identify, isolate and effectively deal with viral infections?

2.7   Are the procedures for dealing with infections subject to regular testing in order to confirm their effectiveness?

2.8   How does management ensure that measures for dealing with infections keep pace with both the virus developments and the evolution of corporate systems?

ELECTRONIC OFFICE

Here we are targeting integrated electronic office systems which aim to support the easy flow of data from one system (or process) to another. Whereas this type of system approach can lead to more efficient working methods and the easy sharing of corporate data, it also affords greater opportunities for data and systems to be subject to unauthorised use.

The selection of a stable and proven systems environment is essential if all the anticipated efficiency benefits are to be achieved. Software suppliers should be vetted to ensure that they are stable and capable of providing the required ongoing support for the system.

Control Objectives for Electronic Office

(a)   To ensure that electronic office systems contribute to the efficiency and consistency of administration tasks.

(b)   Ensure that only appropriate, reliable and secure electronic office software is obtained.

(c)   To ensure that the selected software is compatible with the chosen hardware platforms.

(d) To ensure that the acquisition of software is justified and authorised.

(e) To ensure that adequate user support is available for the selected systems.

(f) To ensure that only official and recognised upgrades and fixes are applied.

(g) To ensure that all systems are consistently configured throughout the organisation.

(h) To ensure compliance with the software licence conditions.

Risk and Control Issues for Electronic Office

1 Key Issues

1.1 Have all electronic office systems been justified and authorised?

1.2 How does management ensure that all electronic office software is appropriate, secure and reliable?

1.3 What precautions does management take to confirm the stability of software suppliers and their ability to provide ongoing support and maintenance?

1.4 Are software products assessed for the suitability of their features, performance criteria, and compatibility with the preferred hardware platforms?

1.5 How does management ensure that users are given appropriate support in their use of the software products (e.g. user documentation, help facilities, training)?

1.6 How does management ensure that only officially recognised and valid software upgrades are correctly applied?

1.7 What specific measures ensure that software is consistently and efficiently configured throughout the organisation?

1.8 How does management confirm that all the software licence conditions are being complied with (number of copies and avoidance of unauthorised copying, etc.)?

2 Detailed Issues

2.1 What specific measures prevent the loading and use of unauthorised software and systems?

2.2 How does the organisation review the suitability and functionality of software products, and justify the acquisition of same?

2.3   How can management be sure that all the hardware implications are identified, assessed and justified where necessary (i.e. additional memory and hard disk storage requirements)?

2.4   Would management be made aware of the inefficient or inappropriate use of software (e.g. electronic mail systems)?

2.5   What measures ensure that all registered users of the software are using the same versions and configurations (and would it be possible to detect anomalies)?

2.6   What mechanisms prevent users from applying unauthorised system upgrades and amendments?

2.7   How does management confirm that the anticipated benefits of using a particular application are in fact being achieved?

USER SUPPORT

With increasing levels of IT responsibility being allocated to end users, it is vital that adequate provision is made to support users and the systems they use. Where they have a problem with their computer or software, users need prompt and effective action to resolve the problem so that they can concentrate on their business responsibilities.

In this section we address the issues related to the provision of a centralised end-user support service.

Control Objectives for User Support

(a)   To provide adequate and effective user support services so as to ensure that IT facilities are consistently, correctly, and securely used.

(b)   To ensure that hardware and software faults are promptly remedied and that business disruption is minimised.

(c)   To ensure that system availability complies with the prevailing service level agreements.

(d)   To ensure that end-users do not apply their own software and hardware solutions, which could result in damage and/or business disruption.

Risk and Control Issues for User Support

1 Key Issues

1.1   Has management taken steps to ensure that adequate and appropriate user support facilities are provided, as a means to ensure the consistent and secure use of IT facilities?

1.2   How does management ensure that adequate and sufficiently skilled support staff are available to provide an effective service (and how do they monitor the effectiveness of the service)?

1.3   Have clear reporting lines been established for hardware and software faults, and how does management ensure that all such problems are promptly and effectively dealt with?

1.4   Have service-level agreements been established, and how is management assured that such performance levels are being achieved?

1.5   What specific measures ensure that all user support enquiries/calls are logged, trailed and subsequently satisfactorily cleared?

1.6   What measures prevent end-users taking unauthorised action to investigate and rectify faults and problems?

2 Detailed Issues

2.1   Are all hardware and software faults logged and analysed?

2.2   What procedures ensure that faults referred out to external suppliers or engineers are promptly and cost-effectively dealt with?

2.3   How does management ensure that all charges from external suppliers and engineers for user support are correct and valid?

2.4   What mechanisms prevent reported faults from being disregarded or left unresolved?

2.5   Is the performance of the user support and fault service monitored (i.e. against defined service levels)?

2.6   How can management be assured that the skills of the user support staff remain compatible with the systems and hardware in use throughout the organisation?

2.7   Are sufficient copies of hardware and systems documentation available as reference sources (and what measures ensure that such documents are kept up to date)?

2.8   What measures ensure that user support staff do not breach either systems or data security facilities in the course of their duties?

BACS

Although we have chosen to label this section as being applicable to BACS (Bankers Automated Clearing Service), the following points can generally be applied to any system involving the electronic transfer of funds.

Control Objectives for BACS

> (a) To ensure that BACS facilities are only used for valid and authorised purposes.
>
> (b) To ensure that all BACS transactions are valid, accurate, trailed, reconciled, and correctly accounted for.
>
> (c) To prevent staff fraud or malpractice.
>
> (d) To ensure that data rejections are promptly identified and corrected.
>
> (e) To ensure the integrity of the BACS data conversion programs.
>
> (f) To ensure that data is submitted in accordance with the prevailing BACS processing timetables.
>
> (g) To ensure that all interfacing systems comply with the required transmission and format protocols.
>
> (h) To ensure that all BACS tapes and media are identified, securely stored, and accounted for.
>
> (i) To ensure that transactions are protected from tampering prior to transmission.

Risk and Control Issues for BACS

1 Key Issues

1.1 What general measures has management established in order to ensure that only valid and authorised use is made of BACS facilities?

1.2 How does management ensure that all transactions destined for BACS transmission, are accurate, complete, valid, and authorised?

1.3 How does management ensure that all BACS activity is accounted for?

1.4 How does management verify that the programs used to prepare data for BACS processing are accurate and authorised for use?

1.5 What specific measures ensure that all BACS processing is conducted at the correct time and in accordance with the prevailing processing timetables and deadlines?

1.6 What mechanisms ensure that the relevant programs conform to the required BACS format and protocol standards?

1.7 Are all BACS tapes securely held, appropriately handled, and accounted for?

1.8 What general measures would prevent the unauthorised tampering with BACS data?

2 Detailed Issues

2.1   Has management documented the procedural requirements for BACS processing, and clearly allocated relevant responsibilities and accountabilities?

2.2   What measures actively prevent the introduction of invalid, fraudulent or unauthorised BACS transactions?

2.3   Would management be made aware of unusual or over-frequent transactions (prior to transmission)?

2.4   Is someone held responsible for ensuring the accuracy and completeness of BACS data prior to authorising the release of the relevant media?

2.5   What steps has management taken to prevent internal fraud through staff collusion?

2.6   Are all records of BACS activity reconciled to source (or target) systems?

2.7   How are data rejections handled so as to ensure their subsequent correct processing?

2.8   What measures prevent the submission of duplicated transactions through the BACS systems?

2.9   What mechanisms prevent the use of unauthorised programs in the preparation of BACS data?

2.10   Are all BACS service charges verified for accuracy and validity prior to payment?

SPREADSHEET DESIGN

Current spreadsheet software is easy to use, feature-rich and a familiar part of the PC environment. Spreadsheets are often—officially or unofficially—woven into the corporate information system. Because they are so approachable and easy to use, spreadsheets often evade any scrutiny during their development or live use. They may be rarely evaluated for their logic, resilience and reliability.

This section aims to raise the important profile of spreadsheets and address the potential adverse business impacts they can represent.

Control Objectives for Spreadsheet Design

(a)   To ensure that when spreadsheets are used, they are consistent and reliable.

(b)   To ensure that spreadsheet data is accurate, complete and authorised to facilitate secure decision making.

(c)   To ensure that best practice and secure techniques are used in the development of spreadsheet solutions.

(d)   To ensure that staff involved in generating spreadsheets are appropriately skilled.

(e)   To ensure that spreadsheets are given ongoing maintenance and support.

(f)   To ensure that adequate and appropriate security is exercised over the access to key management spreadsheets.

(g)   To ensure that spreadsheets are accurately specified and documented.

(h)   To ensure that all key spreadsheets are comprehensively and satisfactorily tested prior to live use.

(i)   To ensure that spreadsheets are protected from unauthorised amendment.

(j)   To ensure that sensitive or confidential data is adequately protected.

Risk and Control Issues for Spreadsheet Design

1 Key Issues

1.1   How does management decide whether a spreadsheet is the most suitable form of data presentation and analysis in order to protect the integrity of decision making within the organisation?

1.2   What measures ensure that spreadsheet solutions are fit for the purpose, accurate, reliable and secure from unauthorised tampering?

1.3   What measures are in place to provide accurate guidance to spreadsheet developers as to best practice and methods?

1.4   Are spreadsheets subject to formal processes governing the following stages:

- specification
- determining the required logic
- testing
- documentation for maintenance purposes?

1.5   How does management ensure that critical spreadsheet models are adequately protected from unauthorised access?

1.6   How does management verify that the initial logic and construction of a spreadsheet remains constant?

1.7   What mechanisms ensure that all subsequent amendments and updates made to spreadsheets are valid, authorised and correctly applied?

2 Detailed Issues

2.1 How does management avoid the proliferation of inaccurate or unreliable spreadsheets which may undermine the quality of management data and decision making?

2.2 Has management established formal guidelines for the development of critical spreadsheet systems?

2.3 What steps has management taken to ensure that relevant staff are suitably trained in the use and development of spreadsheets?

2.4 Are spreadsheet developments documented so that they can be subsequently maintained and updated?

EXPERT SYSTEMS

Expert systems are often developed to augment (or perhaps even replace) expensive specialist skills that may be vital to an organisation.

Control Objectives for Expert Systems

(a) To ensure that the use of expert systems is fully assessed, justified, and authorised.

(b) To ensure that the appropriate and optimum type of expert system is used.

(c) To ensure that the "rules" and "knowledge" components are accurate and valid.

(d) To ensure that the system is fully and satisfactorily tested prior to live use.

(e) To ensure that subsequent amendments to the system are authorised, accurate and fully tested.

(f) To ensure that the components of the system are adequately protected from unauthorised amendment or tampering.

(g) To ensure that the operational use of the expert system is supported by appropriate procedures in order that its use is valid, reliable and supports the business objectives.

(h) To ensure that commercially sensitive or confidential data used by the expert system is adequately protected from unauthorised leakage or access.

Risk and Control Issues for Expert Systems

1 Key Issues

1.1 What measures are in place to ensure that expert systems are developed only where there is a justified requirement and such systems represent the optimum solution?

1.2 How does management know that the most appropriate form of expert system and model is used in the relevant circumstances?

1.3 What specific measures ensure that the "knowledge" and "rules" are accurately and completely determined, and correctly correlated?

1.4 What steps has management taken to ensure that the system is reliable, secure and delivers accurate conclusions?

1.5 What specific measures ensure that unauthorised amendments are not applied to the system?

1.6 What steps has management taken to ensure that the operational use of the expert system will positively contribute to the business and achieve the anticipated benefits?

1.7 What specific measures are in place to protect sensitive or confidential data from unauthorised access or leakage?

2 Detailed Issues

2.1 Has the expert system been subject to a comprehensive testing program in order to guarantee the quality and reliability of the output?

2.2 Does management monitor the actual benefits derived from the use of the expert systems and compare these with the anticipated ones?

2.3 Have up-to-date and appropriate procedures been provided to guide users of the system in its correct use and interpretation?

2.4 Has management taken appropriate steps to protect details and the knowledge inherent in the expert system from leakage (e.g. to competitors)?

IT ACCOUNTING

Here we examine the issues arising from the need to account accurately for the various aspects of the IT environment. Of course, in practice the extent and range of such IT activities will vary enormously, and the level of specific accounting treatment will also differ in proportion. However, IT resources often represent considerable levels of investment.

Control Objectives for IT Accounting

> (a) To ensure that a documented and agreed accounting policy is created for the IT operations.
>
> (b) To ensure that the cost and accounting structure accurately reflects the organisation and supports a meaningful accounts reporting system.
>
> (c) To ensure that the accounts are accurate, complete and timely.
>
> (d) To ensure that management information generated from the accounting system is accurate.
>
> (e) To ensure that the accounting systems and practices fully comply with all the prevailing legislation and regulations.
>
> (f) To ensure that all assets are correctly identified and accounted for.
>
> (g) To ensure that reliable budget procedures are established, enabling the setting and monitoring of agreed budgets.
>
> (h) To ensure that all accounting entries are authorised, valid, and accurately processed within the correct accounting period.
>
> (i) To ensure that all projects are accurately costed.
>
> (j) To ensure that an accurate and fair basis is established for charging out IT facility usage to users.

Risk and Control Issues for IT Accounting

1 Key Issues

1.1 Has management agreed, documented and circulated an accounting policy for the IT function?

1.2 How does management verify that the adopted accounting structure accurately and appropriately reflects the IT operations and the information needs of management?

1.3 What measures ensure that the accounting data is accurate, complete, up to date and reliable?

1.4 How does management confirm that the accounting systems and surrounding practices fully comply with all the relevant accounting legislation and regulations?

1.5 What measures ensure that all assets are identified and correctly treated within the accounting system (additionally, are they regularly confirmed)?

1.6   Have agreed and authorised budgets been set for the IT function/ operations?

1.7   How does management ensure that budgeted targets are achieved, and that variances are effectively reacted to?

1.8   How does management ensure that all accounting entries are valid, authorised, and accurately processed within the relevant accounting period?

1.9   Have project accounting systems been established to enable actual costs to be accurately determined?

1.10   Have end-users been allocated responsibility for their IT related costs?

1.11   What measures have management taken to ensure that IT facility usage costs are fairly, accurately and completely accounted for and charged out to users where necessary?

2 Detailed Issues

2.1   What measures ensure that the agreed accounting policy is adhered to?

2.2   Would potential breaches of the prevailing accounting regulations be promptly identified and followed up?

2.3   What measures ensure that all the management information generated from the accounting system is accurate and reliable?

2.4   What prevents the unauthorised amendment of previously agreed budgets?

2.5   What prevents major actual versus budget variances from being disregarded?

2.6   What specific measures prevent the processing of unauthorised or invalid accounting entries?

2.7   What specific measures would detect incorrect account postings and duplicated transactions?

HIGH-LEVEL CONSIDERATION OF RISK AND CONTROL ISSUES FOR A RANGE OF IT-RELATED ACTIVITIES WITH ILLUSTRATIVE CONTROLS

We provide as Appendix 11 an example of a Standard Audit Programme Guide (SAPG) in truncated format, which addresses the subject of information technology within an organisation at a summary level. This type of review, which examines a broad range of related activities at a top level, may be applicable where either: (a) it is necessary to gather an overall impression of the information technology environment in a restricted timescale, or (b) where the audit function is undertaking an initial review in order to gather data so that subsequent full-scale reviews can be targeted appropriately.

A typical information processing facility is explored through a selection of the previously identified discrete IT activity areas. The data implies a mixed platform IT environment with mainframe equipment, networks and personal computers all in evidence.

Each IT topic is addressed by the inclusion of a number of essential (or key) control and risk issues. Additionally, each issue is complemented by illustrative controls and measures.

The scenario depicted by the issue and control data is intended to be neither definitive nor comprehensive, but rather to provide some general guidance as to the nature of controls that could be found in practice.

NOTES

1. List, W. and Melville, R. (October 1994) 'Integrity in Information Systems'. City University Business School, Working Paper, October 1994; International Federation for Information Processing (IFIP) Working Group 11.5.
2. Chambers, A. D. and Rand, G. V. (1994) *Auditing the IT Environment*. Pitman, London.
3. The following examples are all published by the Institute of Internal Auditors, UK: *An Introduction to Auditing MVS*, Research Report 36, 1991; *Audit and Control of ICL's VME Operating System*, Research Report 20, 1987; and *Unix Control and Security Manual*, Research Report 41, 1993.
4. *Data Protection Guidance on the Criminal Justice Act Amendment*, December 1995, available from The Data Protection Registrar, Wycliffe House, Water Lane, Wilmslow, Cheshire SK9 5AF.

14

Auditing Security

INTRODUCTION

In this chapter we shall examine security matters within a typical organisation. This subject is, as you would expect, primarily concerned with the protection of property, premises and persons so that the business can continue to be conducted without disruption or material loss. However, when considering the broader implications of security, account should also be taken of matters beyond the physical—for example, of less tangible elements such as corporate data or intellectual property.

Protection processes aim to avoid theft of and/or damage to property and premises owned or used by the organisation. Where an organisation is involved in trading, the loss of or damage to stock not only represents an unwanted disruption, but may actually result in an inability to continue operating.

So that management can take appropriate, adequate and cost-effective steps to prevent or contain such disruptions, it will be necessary for them to take a realistic view of their situation from a risk assessment standpoint. Without obtaining an accurate assessment of the inherent risks, management cannot expect to react accordingly and cost-effectively. Indeed, one of the essential elements of any effective control environment is the practice of risk assessment (see Chapter 4). Most areas of operational risk can be offset by the provision of suitable and cost-effective insurance and we shall also be looking at the arrangements for insurance cover.

Although this subject area is normally focused on those physical and preventive measures that guard against unauthorised access and unrestricted movement within company premises, there are related safety aspects that also need to be taken into consideration. These range from the obvious fire prevention and detection systems to more explicit situations where the very operations themselves have significant safety implications. For example, the storage and use of hazardous chemicals or the dangers associated with a large-scale industrial process. Beyond the practical dimensions associated with these subjects and the physical dangers they can present, there are likely to be stringent regulatory and legislative requirements that will need to be addressed. Accordingly, management will have to actively demonstrate that the appropriate action has been taken and that the prevailing laws have been complied with.

In the context of protecting employees we also set out control objectives and risks and control issues for the subject of health and safety; this is also covered in the chapter on personnel, Chapter 11.

As with most fundamental elements of business operations, the topics of security and health and safety should ideally be the subject of a formal and documented corporate policy, so that all affected parties are aware of their responsibilities and the required actions.

CONTROL OBJECTIVES AND RISK AND CONTROL ISSUES

We shall now examine the control objectives and the related risk and control issues (divided into key issues and detailed issues) for each of the following activity areas:

- security
- health and safety
- insurance.

This data can be used within the Standard Audit Programme Guides (SAPGs) looked at in Chapter 3. To save space we have concentrated on the objectives to be stated and the questions to be asked and have not presented them within the SAPG format.

SECURITY

Control Objectives for Security

(a) To ensure that adequate and appropriate security measures are in place in order to protect assets, persons and business activities.

(b) To ensure that company property is adequately protected from theft, loss and damage.

(c) To ensure that risks are appropriately assessed as the basis for providing effective counter-measures.

(d) To ensure that the costs associated with security measures are accurately determined, justified and authorised.

(e) To ensure that adequate, trustworthy and appropriately trained security staff are provided.

(f) To ensure that adequate and operational security and fire alarms systems are provided, tested and maintained.

(g) To ensure that staff are aware of their responsibilities in respect of security (i.e. personal and company property).

> (h) To ensure that adequate emergency and evacuation drills are defined and regularly tested for their effectiveness.
>
> (i) To prevent unauthorised access to company premises and to account for the movement and access of all visitors.

Risk and Control Issues for Security

1 Key Issues

1.1 What measures are in place to prevent the following:

- unauthorised access to company premises.
- theft of company property from premises.
- damage and disruption caused by vandalism, burglary and other security threat?

1.2 Have potential risks and security threats been adequately defined and assessed?

1.3 Are authorised and documented security policies in place (e.g. for controlling access to premises by visitors), and how is management assured that the procedures are adhered to?

1.4 How does management monitor that security measures are effective and in line with changing situations?

1.5 What measures are applied to ensure that security staff are suitably trained, appropriately experienced, and trustworthy?

1.6 What processes ensure that security, intruder and fire alarm systems are adequate, operative, suitably maintained and tested?

1.7 How are staff made aware of their security and personal safety responsibilities (and how does management ensure that staff awareness of such matters is adequately maintained)?

1.8 Have documented procedures and instructions been implemented for emergency drills, building evacuations, and contingency arrangements (and how is their effectiveness assessed)?

1.9 How does management accurately identify the costs associated with all security measures, and are these subject to effective authorisation and monitoring?

2 Detailed Issues

2.1 How does management ascertain that current security measures relate to and address the potential risks?

2.2 Are all operational and physical changes adequately assessed for their impact on the security arrangements (and how is this review process evidenced)?

2.3 How does management ensure that only staff and suitably authorised visitors gain access to company premises?

2.4 What security precautions are taken to prevent unauthorised access to especially sensitive or critical facilities (e.g. main computer installation or cash handling areas)?

2.5 Are the staff employed in sensitive areas subject to appropriate pre-employment checks and/or fidelity bonding (where this is justified)?

2.6 How can bona fide employees be reliably identified by security personnel and other employees?

2.7 What measures are in place to identify and trail all keys to company premises?

2.8 How are building and office keys allocated to employees; and what measures prevent unauthorised staff, past employees, and other persons gaining access to company keys?

2.9 What steps are in place to ensure that all keys and other access devices are recovered from employees leaving the company?

2.10 How are staff made aware of their responsibilities for security?

2.11 What measures are in place to prevent the unauthorised removal of company property and goods from the premises?

2.12 What measures are in place to identify and effectively deal with suspicious or unattended packages on company premises?

2.13 Are reception and security staff aware of the required action to take in the event of a bomb threat, physical assault on the building, etc.?

2.14 Are fire and security alarms systems regularly tested and any faults reported and dealt with?

2.15 What security measures are taken out of normal office/operational hours (and are they justified)?

2.16 Are documented procedures in place in the event of a fire, and are all staff and visitors accounted for?

2.17 Are procedures in place to summon the relevant emergency services (fire, police or ambulance)?

2.18 How does management ensure that existing security and related safety matters fully comply with the prevailing laws, bye-laws and regulations?

2.19   Have all company premises been assessed by the appropriate external agency and confirmed or certified as being of an appropriate standard (and if not, are all shortcomings adequately dealt with)?

2.20   Would management be made aware of uneconomic or unjustified security measures?

2.21   Are costs associated with security incidents accurately determined and claimed via the insurers whenever appropriate?

2.22   What specific access arrangements are made for visiting consultants, tradesmen, representatives and contractors (and how is their access restricted to the relevant areas)?

2.23   How is the accuracy of data input from other systems (e.g. staff recruitment) confirmed?

2.24   How is the accuracy of data output to other systems confirmed?

HEALTH AND SAFETY

Health and safety matters will range from general (perhaps even common sense) measures that will normally apply to every employer through to those which are specifically relative to the sector or operations of the organisation. In either case, there is an obligation on employers to ensure that all the required health and safety issues are satisfactorily addressed. Management will need to be assured that all the relevant and prevailing regulations are being complied with. Additionally, it is crucial that staff are fully aware of their responsibilities and are suitably trained in the use of any required safety equipment.

Control Objectives for Health and Safety

(a)   To ensure that risk assessment identifies all potential health and safety implications as the basis for rectifying exposures.

(b)   To ensure that all health and safety matters are addressed for the protection of staff, visitors and customers.

(c)   To ensure the relevant legislation and regulations are fully complied with.

(d)   To ensure that all staff are fully aware of workplace risks, how to use safety equipment and protect themselves.

(e)   To ensure that adequate safety equipment and training are provided.

(f)   To ensure that machinery and equipment is effectively maintained, safely installed and protected where necessary.

(g)   To provide adequate and operative fire prevention and protection facilities.

(h)   To ensure that building evacuation drills are effective and regularly tested.

(i)   To provide adequate security measures for the protection of staff and visitors.

(j)   To ensure that all accidents and incidents are promptly reported.

(k)   To ensure that appropriate, sufficient and current insurance cover is in place.

(l)   To provide adequate first aid and medical facilities.

(m)   To ensure that adequate hygiene and cleaning standards are maintained.

(n)   To ensure that hazardous materials are correctly and safely stored.

(o)   To ensure that all required certifications are obtained from regulatory bodies.

Risk and Control Issues for Health and Safety

1 Key Issues

1.1   How does management verify that it has identified and adequately addressed all health and safety risks and hazards within the organisation?

1.2   Has an authorised and documented health and safety policy been developed and implemented, and is it kept up to date?

1.3   How does management confirm compliance with all the relevant legislation and regulations?

1.4   What processes ensure that staff are fully aware of workplace risks and how properly to use safety equipment and protect themselves?

1.5   Has sufficient and appropriate safety equipment (e.g. fire extinguishers, protective clothing) been provided, and what measures ensure that it all remains in working order and effective?

1.6   Have sufficient and effective fire prevention and protection systems been provided, and are they regularly tested?

1.7   Are adequate security measures in place to restrict access to facilities and protect staff and equipment from attack?

1.8   What steps are in place to ensure that all incidents and accidents are reported and appropriately dealt with?

1.9   Have adequate first aid and medical facilities (equipment and personnel) been provided, and are supplies replenished when used?

1.10 Are adequate hygiene and cleanliness standards established, and what mechanisms ensure that the required standards are maintained?

1.11 How does management provide and maintain adequate and appropriate insurance cover?

1.12 What mechanisms ensure that all the required regulatory inspections are conducted and that the appropriate regulatory certification is obtained?

1.13 How does management ensure that all hazardous materials are safely, correctly and securely stored?

2 Detailed Issues

2.1 Has management undertaken a risk assessment of health and safety implications throughout the organisation in order to identify the risks and ensure that they are addressed?

2.2 Has a health and safety policy been introduced, and have specific responsibilities for safety issues been allocated?

2.3 What mechanisms prevent non-compliance with the prevailing health and safety regulations?

2.4 How does management maintain an up-to-date awareness of all the relevant health and safety regulations?

2.5 Are all staff adequately trained in safety matters, including use of equipment and clothing (and how can management be certain that all the relevant staff actually receive the appropriate training)?

2.6 Are staff progressively tested on their level of understanding of safety measures in order to identify further training needs?

2.7 How does management monitor that all the relevant safety equipment is maintained in working order?

2.8 Are all relevant machines fitted with guards, safety cut-outs, etc. to the required standard?

2.9 How does management monitor that all computer equipment conforms to the required standards (e.g. screen radiation levels)?

2.10 Are building evacuation, fire and security drills regularly conducted and assessed for effectiveness?

2.11 Are adequate fire alarms and security systems installed, tested and maintained (and would faults be detected promptly)?

2.12 How does management monitor that all building environmental systems (heating, lighting, air conditioning, etc.) are working correctly and to the required legal standards?

2.13 What mechanisms prevent unauthorised access to buildings and facilities?

2.14   Are the relevant staff (receptionists, door guards, post room staff, etc.) aware of the action required in the event of a bomb alert, an attack on the building, a suspicious package, and so on?

2.15   What processes ensure that the records of incidents and accidents are fully and correctly maintained in accordance with any regulatory requirements?

2.16   Are sufficient and suitably trained first aid and medical personnel available, and how can they promptly be summoned to an incident?

2.17   In the event of an emergency, how does management account for all visitors?

2.18   Are transitory safety risks (such as trailing power leads, wet floors due to cleaning) adequately addressed?

2.19   What does management do to maintain sufficient insurance cover in the event of the organisation being sued for negligence with regard to health and safety conditions?

2.20   What processes ensure that insurance cover is renewed, on time and at the appropriate level?

2.21   What processes ensure that all the required certificates and licences are obtained to enable the lawful operation of facilities?

2.22   What mechanisms prevent unauthorised access to hazardous materials?

2.23   How is accuracy of data input from other systems (e.g. human resources) confirmed?

2.24   How is the accuracy of data output to other systems (e.g. estates management) confirmed?

INSURANCE

Control Objectives for Insurance

(a)   To ensure that all relevant business and operational risks are accurately assessed as the basis for providing adequate and appropriate insurance cover.

(b)   To ensure that prevailing insurance cover would remove, reduce or minimise risk exposures as appropriate.

(c)   To ensure that insurance cover arrangements are justified and authorised.

(d)   To ensure that insurance costs represent value for money and are competitive, effectively monitored and contained.

(e)   To ensure that insurance arrangements are made through competent, reliable and stable brokers/companies.

(f) To ensure that insurance cover is renewed when appropriate and remains current.

(g) To ensure that claims are reviewed, agreed and authorised prior to release.

(h) To ensure that insurance claims are valid, correctly costed and pursued with the insurers until settled.

(i) To ensure that insurance claims are controlled to prevent excessive levels and the potential for increased premiums.

(j) To ensure that insurance arrangements comply with all the applicable legal and regulatory requirements.

(k) To ensure that measures designed to reduce risks and related insurance costs are assessed, justified and authorised.

Risk and Control Issues for Insurance

1 Key Issues

1.1 How does management ensure that all insurable risks are identified, assessed and adequately covered?

1.2 What processes ensure that the levels and types of insurance cover are appropriate and adequate?

1.3 Are insurance arrangements subject to prior authority, and what mechanisms prevent the establishment of invalid, unauthorised or unnecessary insurance arrangements?

1.4 How does management ensure that insurance costs are competitive and represent value for money?

1.5 What processes ensure that all insurance arrangements are arranged with suitable and reliable insurance institutions?

1.6 How does management verify that the required insurance cover is current and in force?

1.7 Are insurance claims subject to appropriate assessment and authority prior to submission?

1.8 How does management ensure that all insurance claims are appropriately costed and eventually settled?

1.9 How does management ensure that suitable insurance cover is obtained for all areas where it is required by law (e.g. for employer's liability and motor vehicles)?

1.10 What measures are in place to monitor and assess methods of reducing risks and their impact on insurance costs?

2 Detailed Issues

2.1 Are new or modified business operations adequately assessed for their inherent risks, and how can management be certain that the prevailing insurance arrangements remain suitable and adequate?

2.2 What mechanisms prevent the continuation of unwanted, uneconomic or unwarranted insurance arrangements?

2.3 Is current insurance cover available for the following areas (as applicable):

- employer's liability
- third party
- buildings/premises
- equipment/plant
- key assets
- IT equipment
- vehicles
- interruption/loss of business;
- stocks?

2.4 Are payments of all insurance premiums (including renewals) suitably authorised?

2.5 Are insurance renewal premiums subject to review and authorisation?

2.6 What mechanisms prevent the automatic renewal of insurance premiums where the cover is no longer valid or required?

2.7 Are brokers' fees subject to authorisation prior to payment?

2.8 What mechanisms prevent the arrangement of insurance cover with unreliable or financially unstable insurance companies?

2.9 Are small or uneconomic claims prevented in order to avoid the potential for increased renewal premiums?

2.10 Are all claims based on realistic, accurate and legitimate cost data?

2.11 Are policy documents scrutinised for inappropriate conditions or unreasonable exclusion clauses (and what action would be taken in such instances)?

2.12 What measures ensure that the proceeds from all insurance claims are identified and correctly accounted for?

2.13 Are certificates of insurance obtained, securely stored and/or displayed when required by the prevailing regulations?

2.14 Are adequate, accurate and up-to-date records of all current insurance policies maintained?

2.15 How does management ensure that the status of all insurance cover can be promptly and accurately determined?

2.16 What processes ensure that all the prevailing laws and regulations are fully complied with?

2.17 How is the accuracy of data input from other systems (e.g. risk assessment or fixed assets) confirmed?

2.18 How is the accuracy of data output to other systems (e.g. to the general ledger) confirmed?

15

Auditing Environmental Responsibility

INTRODUCTION

All businesses interact with the wider environment, whether through the procurement of materials, the impact of manufacturing processes or the disposal of waste products.

In recent years there has been a growing global recognition that the physical environment needs to be protected from damage. The planet is being viewed as a total mechanism with finite resources and a limited capability to regenerate. This raising of environmental awareness has taken place not only at a general public level, but has been increasingly supported by emerging scientific evidence. Past industrialisation has had an enormous impact on the land, water and air. Environmental protection legislation from the UK government and the EU is now in force, but there is still a great deal that individual businesses can do to ease the impact of their operations on the environment and perhaps make financial savings as well. In the public consciousness it is no longer acceptable for businesses to be reactive in relation to environmental impacts; instead, they are encouraged to adopt a proactive stance in their attitudes and deeds. Indeed, it could be said that is in the best interests of the wider business community to ensure that its impact on the environment does not jeopardise future opportunities for sustained growth.

Public awareness about environmental matters has also undergone a drastic change and personal initiatives (such as recycling) have hesitantly emerged. Some organisations have exploited the currency of environmental matters and now deliberately project a more caring and concerned image to their potential customers. Environmental responsibility can be good for business.

Later in this chapter we examine the European Commission's Eco-Management and Audit Scheme and we will note that one of its requirements is for a company-wide environmental policy to be established. In Appendix 9 we provide an example Code of Ethical Conduct which covers both scientific and environmental matters. Of course, these two intermesh intensely. Auditors may wish to use the Code of Ethical Conduct as a model basis for designing their own policy statement on environmental and other ethical issues. Appendix 9 should be used in conjunction with the Statement of Corporate Principles (Appendix 7) and the Code of Business Conduct (Appendix 8). The Statement of Corporate Principles is the overarching group board-level policy statement of general corporate principles, and the underlying Codes (Code of Business Conduct and Code of Ethical Conduct) are conversions of the general principles into what on the whole are more detailed guidelines applying to commercial issues on the one hand and to scientific and environmental issues on the other. All three documents should be endorsed by formal board resolution and become company policy. There is some common ground and thus some common wording between these two Codes. These three documents were designed for a multinational pharmaceutical company, and their wording has since been modified to make them more generally applicable.

The principle of "the polluter pays" is now widely recognised as the foundation for both formal regulation and individual environmental action programmes. This premise has motivated companies to find alternative business strategies which take due account of environmental concerns. In some high-profile industries (such as mineral extraction and chemicals) the potential costs associated with the aftermath of an environmental disaster are considerable. This, together with the public relations and other longer-term implications for the survival of the business, has encouraged such organisations to take their environmental responsibilities very seriously. In other sectors, some companies have instigated product recycling programmes as recognition of their ongoing responsibility for the environmental impact of their products. In the motor industry, both BMW and Mercedes Benz have decreed that a notable percentage of the materials used in their new vehicles should be recyclable. In the office equipment market, Hewlett Packard have established a programme that lets users return their used laser printer toner cartridges for recycling.

When considering the environmental impact of the business, a wide range of factors should be examined for their environmental implications, for example the following questions may be applicable:

- Are more environmentally friendly materials available? (i.e. naturally sustainable)?
- Can we use renewable energy sources?
- Can we use less material?
- Can the choice of materials influence the useful life of the product or improve the opportunities for eventual recycling?
- Can we make savings by recovering and reusing materials?
- Can we adequately protect the product with less packaging material?
- How can waste be minimised?
- How can we protect and conserve surrounding land?

In this chapter, we will look at the emergence of environmental management standards and how they can be applied. The environmental management and audit framework will be examined and the possible role of internal auditors discussed. The chapter concludes with an example audit programme for conducting a high-level review of environmental issues within an organisation.

This programme includes control objectives and risk/control issues in the form of key questions.

ENVIRONMENTAL AUDITING—A DEFINITION

The following definition of environmental auditing was taken from *Environmental Auditing*, published by the International Chamber of Commerce in 1989:

A management tool comprising a systematic, documented, periodic and objective evaluation of how well environmental organisation, management and equipment are performing with the aim of helping to safeguard the environment by:

(i) facilitating management control of environmental practices;
(ii) assessing compliance with company policies, which would include meeting regulatory requirements.

From this definition it can be discerned that the responsibility for environmental management spans the organisation and is not necessarily the sole preserve of one specialist function. In many respects the broader issues of environmental responsibility (and accountability) are matters of organisational culture. In some industries (such as petrochemicals), operations that are likely to have an environmental impact are already governed by combinations of industry best practice and specific laws and regulations.

THE EMERGENCE OF ENVIRONMENTAL CONCERNS

The emergence of environmental regulations and increased general awareness has been most apparent in the developed industrial nations. Economic reality in the developing world has limited the necessary investment in alternative environmentally friendly technologies and methods. New techniques of material extraction and production may have higher associated costs which must be justified and sustainable within the target marketplace.

Initial warnings of the consequences of environmental damage were particularly noticeable in the 1960s, especially in relation to the widespread use of chemical pesticides. Although environmental concerns were initially seen as marginal matters that were the province of a few dedicated activists and scientists, the spread of general interest in the environment, underpinned by a number of well-publicised disasters and expanding scientific findings, soon reached a point when positive action was being demanded of governments.

In the United States, the US Environmental Protection Agency published (in 1969) an outline approach to environmental auditing which coincided with the passing of the National Environmental Policy Act, which required that the environmental impacts of major projects be properly assessed and addressed.

There have been parallel and equally significant developments in environmental awareness elsewhere in the world, for example in Japan where very demanding and rigorously policed pollution control criteria have been established.

Within the European Union (EU; known as the European Community [EC] before 1 November 1993) selected member states have developed regulations and legislation relating to environmental issues. The Single European Act (1987) incorporated responsibilities for environmental aspects which led to the subsequent issue of legally binding regulations and directives. We discuss relevant EU regulations and the related national and international standards in the following section.

RELEVANT STANDARDS

European Union Regulations

During the 1980s and 1990s a large number of EU Directives on environmental issues were introduced.[1]

In order to set the scene for all future EU legislative efforts, a draft Directive for Civil Liability for Damage caused by Waste was published in 1991 which contained the following key elements:

- the legal principle of strict liability in environmental regulations
- the principle of "the polluter pays"
- extension of liability to *carriers* in addition to the *producers* of waste
- the need for compulsory insurance programmes
- the power given to public interest groups to more easily initiate legal actions against polluters.

An EC Council Regulation[2] was enacted in 1993 which "allows voluntary participation by companies in the industrial sector in a Community eco-management and audit scheme". An EU regulation is directly applicable to all member states. The contents of this document are supported by other separately developed standards, such as BS7750 and ISO14000, which we discuss later. In addition, this Regulation aims to support other related EU objectives in such areas as sustainable development, environmental protection, and environmental responsibility embodied in the concept of "the polluter pays".

The key contents of this Regulation can be summarised as follows:

- the need for companies to establish and implement environmental policies, objectives and programmes, and effective environmental management systems
- to ensure compliance with all relevant regulatory requirements
- to take account of the need to ensure the awareness and training of workers
- the inclusion of environmental auditing procedures to help management assess compliance with the system and the effectiveness of the system supporting the environmental policy
- the public provision of information on the environmental aspects of a company's activities
- that a company's policies, programmes, management systems, audit procedures and environmental statements are examined to verify that they meet all the requirements of the Regulations (e.g. assessment to be conducted by an accredited environmental verifier)

- the provision of an independent and neutral accreditation and supervision of environmental verifiers in order to ensure the credibility of the scheme
- the encouragement of small and medium-sized companies to be involved in the scheme through the establishment and promotion of technical assistance measures and structures aimed at providing the required expertise and support.

The Regulation goes on to define the Eco-Management and Audit Scheme (EMAS) in 21 constituent Articles. The key contents are summarised in Table 15.1.

Table 15 EMAS as set out in EC Council Regulation 1836/93

Article Ref.	Title	Comments
1	The eco-management and audit scheme and its objectives	
2	Definitions	
3	Participation in the scheme	i.e. companies operating a site or sites where an industrial activity is performed
4	Auditing and validation	i.e. defining the basis for the conduct of *internal* environmental auditing
5	Environmental statements	i.e. for publication
6	Accreditation and supervision of environmental verifiers	i.e. establishment of an appropriate national system for the accreditation/supervision of verifiers
7	List of accredited environmental verifiers	i.e. the establishment and maintenance of a list of accredited environmental verifiers in each Member State
8	Registration of sites	i.e. maintenance of a register of those sites which have met all the conditions of the Regulation
9	Publication of the list of registered sites	
10	Statement of participation	i.e. the use of official EU format statements to signify participation in the scheme
11	Costs and fees	Covering the administration of the site registration process and the accreditation of environmental verifiers
12	Relationship with national, European and international standards	Governing the development of suitable standards in support of the Regulation
13	Promotion of companies' participation, in particular of small and medium-sized enterprises	i.e. the development and operation of suitable technical assistance measures and structures aimed at providing such firms with the required expertise and support
14	Inclusion of other sectors	i.e. the potential to extend the provisions of the Regulation to sectors outside industry, for example the distributive trades and public service
15	Information	i.e. each member state shall ensure that companies are informed of the Regulation and that the public are informed of the objectives and principle arrangements
16	Infringements	i.e. the right for member states to take appropriate legal or administrative measures in cases of non-compliance with the Regulation
18	Competent bodies	i.e. the designation, by member states, of the competent body responsible for the registration of sites and the maintenance of associated lists

The EMAS initiative established by this European law is essentially a voluntary scheme introduced in April 1995 and supported by the UK government.[3] The scheme is primarily targeted at industrial sites located within Europe, but in the UK the scheme has been extended to include local authorities. EMAS is supported by standards such as BS7750 in the UK and the emerging ISO14000 series which is currently at the draft stage. The underlying long-term aim of EMAS is to continuously improve environmental performance with benefits accruing for both the organisation and the environment.

Participation in EMAS is site-based, but multi-site organisations can obviously apply the mechanism to all their locations. Organisations seeking involvement in EMAS will need to address each of the following requirements at each site:

1. Establish a company-wide **environmental policy**, which incorporates the environmental priorities, a commitment to continuous improvement and acknowledges compliance with the relevant environmental regulations. Any such policy should be documented and ratified by senior management. In order to maintain its relevance, the policy should periodically be reviewed and modified if necessary—amendments should be officially authorised by senior management.

2. Undertake an **environment review** incorporating an analysis of all inputs, processes and outputs for the site. Use this data to catalogue the environmental impacts and issues for management attention. This stage should be broad-based and take account of such areas as energy, materials, noise control, waste avoidance, waste disposal. It is also crucial to identify any regulations or laws that apply to the site and to confirm that they are being fully complied with.

3. Using the previous two stages as a guide and structural framework, create an **environmental programme** which documents the targets, objectives and goals for the site in question and the measures to be taken in order to achieve them.

4. Develop an **environmental management system** which incorporates the necessary operating procedures and controls to achieve the successful implementation of both the environmental policy and environmental programme. This process is likely to generate changes in operations, procedures, staff responsibilities, etc. The requirements of a standard such as BS7750 (for environmental management systems) can be applied at this stage, or you can opt to develop your own. NB: There is considerable synergy between the requirements of EMAS and the structured approach of BS7750.

5. Having defined and officially documented your environmental policies and practices, it is now necessary to enter the **environmental audit cycle** so that the actual performance is compared to the standards and objectives. This level of environmental audit is an *internal* review and is aimed at identifying any specific changes in order either to confirm compliance with the required practices or to generally improve the efficiency or effectiveness of same. The frequency of the audit cycle at this stage will vary in relation to the underlying levels of risk and the nature of activities; however, such a review

must take place at least every three years. It is possible initially to register the organisation under EMAS at stage 2 (the environmental review) assuming that stage 4 (the environmental management system) is operational, and prior to undertaking the audit review. However, the intended audit process should be described and subsequently carried out.

6. Following the audit review (and every year thereafter) the organisation should prepare an **environmental statement** for each site, which is intended for publication. The aim here is to reassure the public and others that the environmental impacts associated with the site are fully understood and subject to ongoing management attention. Where related plans and objectives have been defined (or previously set), the statement should make reference to the progress achieved.

7. At the end of each cycle, the following elements must be verified by an accredited and independent environmental verifier in a formal validation process:

   - the environment statement produced at stage 6 above
   - the environmental policy (stage 1)
   - the environmental programme (stage 3)
   - the environmental management system (stage 4)
   - the environmental audit procedure (stage 5).

   Of course, if the relevant component systems are certified to BS7750 they will meet the EMAS requirements.

Those organisations that have been successful in achieving (and maintaining) registration under EMAS have the right to use the official scheme symbol in correspondence and company reports.

Within the European Union context, the development of environmental regulations continues. In association with the community-level actions, national governments have followed suit by enacting localised legislation; for example, in the UK there is the Environmental Protection Act (1990), which targets the impact of industrial plants on the environment and permits inspection and authorisation of a company's plans.

BS7750 and ISO14000

BS7750 is a UK standard, published in 1992, which is a specification for environmental management systems. Like its quality system counterpart (BS5750), this was the world's first such standard. BS7750 was deliberately developed to be compatible with the EMAS initiative described above. Although the use of BS7750 is not an obligatory part of EMAS, it is a complementary management system and if a site is registered under BS7750 it will also satisfy the related requirements within EMAS. The principal difference between BS7750 and EMAS is that the latter requires the public reporting of the organisation's achievements.

There is also considerable synergy between BS7750 and BS5750,[4] and although BS5750 is not a prerequisite for the operation of BS7750, it is possible to extend the total quality management (TQM) systems created under BS5750 to accord with the structures required by BS7750. TQM is examined in Chapter17.

It is important to stress that BS7750 does not, in itself, define any specific environmental performance criteria. It is primarily concerned with "the development, implementation and maintenance of an environmental management system aimed at ensuring compliance with stated environmental policy and objectives." "The standard is applicable to any organisation which wishes to: (a) assure itself of compliance with a stated environmental policy; and (b) demonstrate such compliance to others."

Although an organisation may be affected by existing regulations and legislation in respect of environmental standards (i.e. emission levels) and will have to ensure ongoing compliance with such requirements, in the context of BS7750 it sets its own environmental objectives and targets. This is similar in application to the internal determination of quality performance standards under BS5750. In practice this means that the target levels of environment performance can be set as high or as low as the organisation wishes (albeit within the confines of any other applicable legislation).

Key points within the BS7750 standard

Environmental management system:

- the preparation and implementation of documented system procedures and instructions for an **environmental management system** that accord with the standard.

Environmental policy:

- The definition of an **environmental policy** which:

    - is relevant to the organisation's activities, products and services and their environmental effects
    - is understood, implemented and maintained at all levels
    - is publicly available
    - includes a commitment to continuous improvement of environmental performance
    - provides for the setting and publication of environmental objectives.

Organisation and personnel:

- Define and **document the responsibilities, authorities and interrelations of key staff** who manage, perform and verify work affecting the environment.
- Identify **in-house verification requirements** and procedures, provide adequate resources, and assign trained personnel for verification;
- **Allocate management responsibility** for implementing and maintaining the BS7750 standard.
- Set up and maintain procedures to **ensure that employees are aware of**:

- the importance of compliance with the environmental policy and objectives, and the requirements of BS7750
- potential environmental effects of their work activities and the environmental benefits of improved performance
- their roles and responsibilities in achieving compliance with the environmental policy and the objectives of BS7750
- the consequences of departing from the agreed operating procedures.

- **Identify and address training needs**.

Environmental effects:

- Set up and maintain a **register of all legislative, regulatory and other policy requirements** relating to the environmental aspects of activities, products and services.
- Establish and maintain a **procedure for receiving, documenting and responding to communications** concerning environmental effects and management.
- Set up and maintain procedures for examining and assessing the environmental effects and **compile a register of those identified as significant**. This requirement includes consideration of the effects arising from normal operating conditions, abnormal conditions, incidents, accidents, past, current and planned activities.

Environmental objectives and targets:

- Establish and maintain procedures to **specify the organisation's environmental objectives, and consequent targets** at all levels. Considerations here should take into account any regulatory or legal requirements. The objectives and targets should be quantifiable, related to a defined timescale, and consistent with the adopted environmental policy.

Environmental management programme:

- Establish and maintain a **programme for achieving the objectives and targets**. The standard details the type of information required at this stage.

Environmental management manual and documentation:

- **Create and maintain a manual** which addresses and describes:

  - the collation of the environmental policy, objectives, targets and programme
  - the key roles and responsibilities
  - the interaction of system elements
  - the management system and provides information on related documentation
  - the requirements in normal, abnormal, accident and emergency situations.

- Set in place and maintain **procedures for controlling all the documents** required by BS7750, including:

- ensuring that they are periodically reviewed, amended as necessary and approved prior to issue
- ensuring that current versions are available
- the complete removal of obsolete documents.

Operational control:

- Define management responsibility to ensure the co-ordination and performance of control, verification, measurement and testing processes throughout the organisation.
- Identify functions, activities and processes which have an effect on the environment and plan to ensure that they are carried out under controlled conditions. Include:

  - documented work instructions
  - procedures for procurement and contracted activities (i.e. to ensure that suppliers and others are complying with the organisation's policy)
  - monitor and control process characteristics
  - written performance criteria, etc.

- Establish and maintain **procedures for verification of compliance** with specified programme targets, manuals and instructions;
- Allocate responsibility and authority for investigating non-compliance and taking corrective action. In addition, set up and maintain procedures for such investigation and corrective processes.

Environmental management records:

- Establish and maintain a system of records in order to demonstrate compliance with the requirements of the environmental management system and to record the extent to which the planned objectives and targets have been met. (BS7750 goes on to describe the explicit types of records that should be maintained, required data types, and requirements covering the legibility, storage, retention and disposal of such records.)

Environmental management audits:

- Establish and maintain procedures covering the carrying out of audits to determine:

  - whether or not environmental management activities are effectively implemented and conform to the environmental management programme
  - the effectiveness of the environmental management system in fulfilling the environmental policy.

- Establish and maintain an audit plan which addresses the following:

  - the activities and areas to be audited
  - the frequency of audit coverage (related to the nature and environmental importance of the related activity)

- responsibility for auditing each activity or area
- audit personnel requirements (taking account of independence, relevant expertise, access to (either internal or external) support resources)
- the audit methods to be applied in the conduct of the audit (the use of questionnaires, checklists, interviews, and so on)
- procedures for reporting audit findings and the responsibilities for taking timely action on the findings
- (where relevant) procedures for publishing audit findings.

Environmental management reviews:

- Undertake periodic management reviews of the environmental management system to ensure:
  - it satisfies the requirements of BS7750
  - it remains suitable and effective
  - it incorporates assessments of any results emerging from the environmental management audit process described in the previous section.

Refer to a copy of the actual standard, which features, as Annex A, some further general guidance on these summary requirements.

Internal auditors working in organisations applying the BS7750 standard will need to become familiar with both the general requirements of the standard and its specific application within their organisation.

The International Standards Organisation (ISO) is currently developing an international standard for environmental management, under the reference ISO14000. There are currently two sections of this standard available in draft form[5] with others planned:

ISO14001   *Environmental management systems—Specification with guidance for use*

ISO14004   *Environmental management systems—General guidance on principles, systems and supporting techniques.*

The specification of ISO14000 has some synergy with both BS7750 and the EMAS structure, but the current version of ISO standard is not so comprehensive in the areas of assessing environmental effects and the commitment to continuous performance improvements. It is hoped that the final ISO standard in this area will more closely match both BS7750 and EMAS.

LINKING ENVIRONMENTAL ISSUES TO CORPORATE STRATEGY AND SECURING BENEFITS

To address environmental issues effectively, they need to be woven into the business strategy and direction of the organisation. The relative issues cannot be regarded as elements to "bolt on" to the organisation, but they must be treated as fundamental to the day-to-day business. The cynical may say that the marketing and public relations imagery projected by a business entity in relation to the environment need only be skin deep, but here we are more concerned with ingrained, realistic and responsible processes which make an effective contribution to the environment and at the same time generate tangible benefits for the organisation, such as:

- potential for cost savings (e.g. recycling materials, less waste)
- lower costs achieved through improved production processes
- improved usage of energy (i.e. possible reduction in consumption)
- potential savings in packaging, storage and transportation costs
- the creation of new technologies, product lines and/or new markets
- effective marketing exploitation of the current public concerns over the environment
- securing competitive advantages through improved performance
- avoidance of potential environmental liabilities (i.e. fines, clean-up costs and punitive insurance premiums)
- improved relationships with customers, investors, insurers, the media, regulators, and so on.

Before any of the benefits can be achieved, an organisation must accurately determine the current environmental impact of its business as the basis for moving forward and applying effective change and improvements. A structured and methodical approach is therefore required, especially if compliance with the relevant standards is to be achieved.

Of course, when developing a corporate strategy, the environmental issues do not stand alone, but rather sit alongside the principal business considerations (such as financial and operational performance, efficiency, risk implications, and so on). The environmentally aware dimensions may be secondary in nature—for example, the conversion of waste by-product into a useful new product. In addition to both the general business and internally relevant factors which are likely to influence corporate direction, account also needs to be taken of the views of interested external parties (for example, customers, shareholders, local communities).

In establishing a strategy which takes account of environmental matters, the organisation will wish to formalise aspects of its related approach so that all concerned are aware of the objectives and their responsibilities. One process of this output is the development of written environmental policies and/or codes of practice.

ENVIRONMENTAL ASSESSMENT AND AUDITING SYSTEM CONSIDERATIONS

Here we are initially concerned with the operation of an *internal* environment audit system, which in larger organisations is likely to be operated by a specialist function within the organisation as distinct from any internal audit review of the overall environmental approach applied by the business. We also initially exclude here the use of the term *environmental audit* in the context of verification audits conducted by accredited verifiers.

The EMAS framework and the BS7750 standard (as discussed earlier) can be applied as recognised and well-defined models that address the spirit of the relevant EU Directive.

In order to take account of all the possible environmental consequences of the business, management and auditors alike will need to consider the organisation's products and services on a "cradle to grave" or "life cycle" basis. This approach, which can point up those areas of significant environmental concern, assesses the implications at each stage of the product life cycle spanning from creation through to destruction, for instance:

- research and development
- design and performance criteria
- selection and sourcing of raw materials
- methods of production
- waste materials, emissions, discharges, etc. during production
- the use of energy
- product packaging
- methods of distribution
- environmental impacts generated by using or applying the product
- implications for the eventual disposal (or recycling) of the used product.

The nature of the business and its operations will dictate the type(s) of environmental audits that are applied. For example, they may focus on the audit of:

- current (or projected) production methods
- the use of energy
- the extent of any potential liabilities related to either the acquisition or divesture of specific activities
- the determination of safety and/or health risks
- compliance with all the prevailing industry regulations
- the effectiveness of the prevailing environmental management system
- pollution prevention measures
- a particular product or service.

The scale of each audit may also vary—for example, the review may either span the whole organisation, a specific area of activity or particular physical site.

The frequency of audit reviews may represent the last factor in the equation of planned coverage; for instance, a cyclical approach within a total timescale (i.e. annually) may be appropriate, or alternatively circumstances may require a special one-off review to be conducted.

There is some implied synergy between the approach adopted for the development of an environmental assessment/audit strategy and that relevant to the formation of a total quality management (TQM) culture. Both require high levels of employee commitment, effective communication and the encouragement of a culture underpinned by continuous improvement. Furthermore, there are structural similarities between the TQM standards (BS5750/ISO9000) and those applicable to environmental systems (BS7750/ISO14000)—for example, the requirements for verification assessment carried by accredited bodies and the use of similar system management structures.

The development of a corporate approach to environmental management takes time and considerable resources. Given that each business will have unique and specific requirements, it is likely that external expertise may have to be sought during the emergence of the overall strategy and programme.

THE ROLE OF INTERNAL AUDIT

The Institute of Internal Auditors—UK concluded in their Professional Briefing Note (PBN) number 2 on Environmental Auditing: "Environmental auditing is no different to the approach to an internal audit."[6] They go on to say: "Environmental matters should be covered within the scope of work of the internal audit department operating in accordance with the IIA-UK Standards."[7] Where an internal auditing function has responsibility for environmental auditing reviews, this should clearly be defined in the relevant terms of reference or audit charter.

The above mentioned IIA PBN on Environmental Auditing clearly expresses a potential general role for internal audit in this area:

Internal audit should review the ways in which the organisation:

takes account of laws and regulations pertaining to all aspects of the environment;

plans, organises and directs operations so as to comply with environmental aims and objectives;

monitors performance from the information available; and

ensures that the information available is accurate and produced in a timely fashion for use by the appropriate level of management.[8]

It is apparent that the overview internal auditing approach described in the above extract can be generally aligned with some of the key stages of the current BS7750 standard.

The internal conduct of environmental auditing presupposes that adequate and appropriately skilled *auditors* are available, and that they have an accurate awareness of both the plans of the organisation and the practical options for improving environmental performance, etc. Although in some instances the required skilled resources will need to be bought-in from outside the organisation, members of the internal audit function could be trained to perform these duties. Internal auditors should, in any event, maintain a general awareness of the organisation's operations and the factors (such as environmental legislation) that affect them, partly so that they can suitably target and focus their auditing activities on relevant aspects of the entity.

Where the organisation has established a specialist environmental auditing function, the internal auditing function still has a legitimate role to play in:

- "appraising the value of the environmental audit to determine whether it will assist the organisation in attaining the organisation's objectives and goals."[9]
- assessing the separate environmental auditing function as part of the management control system. In doing so, internal audit should consider "whether the creation of a separate function is an effective, economical and efficient way of attaining the objectives of environmental audit."[10]

EXAMPLE PROGRAMME

In this section we have provided an example of a high-level programme for the review of environmental issues within an organisation. The format follows that adopted in earlier chapters and features control objectives and risk/control issues (divided into key issues and detailed issues) in the form of relevant questions. This data can be used within the Standard Audit Programme Guides (SAPGs) looked at in chapter 3. To save space we have not presented the information within the SAPG format.

Control Objectives for Environmental Issues

(a) To provide an authorised and documented policy on environment issues as a framework for responsibly conducting related business activities.

(b) To minimise the impact of the organisation's activities on the environment.

(c) To ensure that the organisation's products are environmentally friendly.

(d) To ensure that waste is minimised and properly disposed of.

(e) To avoid pollution and environmental contamination.

(f) To assess, on an ongoing basis, the environmental impacts of business operations and define the requirements to be adhered to.

(g) To ensure that alternative and potentially environmentally friendly processes and technologies are considered and implemented where justified.

(h) To minimise or avoid the use of scarce materials and non-renewable energy sources.

(i) To ensure that harmful or hazardous materials and waste products are safely and responsibly transported and disposed of.

(j) To ensure that all environmental legislation and regulations are fully complied with.

(k) To avoid adverse impacts on the organisation's reputation and image.

> (l)   To ensure that environmental issues are subject to monitoring and management.

Risk and Control Issues for Environmental Issues

1 Key Issues

1.1   Has an approved and documented environment policy been established which defines the required approach for business operations?

1.2   What measures ensure that the principles of the environmental policy are complied with, and how would non-compliance be promptly detected?

1.3   Have production processes and other business activities been assessed for their environmental impacts (and how is the necessary corrective action evidenced)?

1.4   How does management ensure that all the relevant environmental legislation and regulations are fully complied with, thus avoiding penalties and adverse effects on the organisation's public image?

1.5   How does management ensure that all waste products are correctly and safely treated, discharged or disposed of?

1.6   What measures prevent the pollution and contamination of the environment?

1.7   Are the organisation's products assessed for "environmental friendliness" (e.g. impact during production/use, potential to be recycled, safe disposal at end of product life, restricted use of scarce resources)?

1.8   Has management actively considered alternative and less environmentally harmful production/business processes?

1.9   Are measures in place to ensure that all environmental impacts are identified, monitored and effectively managed (and what is the evidence for this)?

1.10   Has management established a "recycling" policy and if so, how is compliance confirmed?

1.11   Have the full costs of adopting an environmental approach to the business been accurately identified, justified and authorised (and are they subject to monitoring and review)?

2 Detailed Issues

2.1   Is the environmental policy supported by the commitment of senior management and a suitable staff training/awareness programme?

2.2 Are all projects to reduce the impact of business activities on the environment subject to a full feasibility and cost appraisal, before being authorised?

2.3 Is the assessment of environmental impacts kept up to date so that management action is relevant and targeted?

2.4 Where required, have measurements of environmental impact (e.g. water discharge, fume extraction, waste materials) been established (and are they checked for accuracy)?

2.5 How does management make certain that it remains aware of all the relevant environmental legislation and regulations?

2.6 Has a responsibility for environmental management been defined and allocated?

2.7 What measures ensure that all waste products are identified, assessed for their environmental impact, and appropriately treated/processed?

2.8 Are all discharges of waste products subject to monitoring and permitted within the prevailing regulations (and how would non-compliance be detected)?

2.9 How does management ensure that all waste product treatment processes are operating correctly and efficiently?

2.10 Would management be made aware of all accidental and unintentional spillages of potentially harmful materials?

2.11 Are contingency plans and resources in place to deal effectively with the likely range of environmental accidents?

2.12 How does management check that waste disposal sites and operators are appropriately licensed to handle the specific by-products generated by the organisation?

2.13 Whenever necessary, is management considering utilising alternatives to hazardous or scarce materials as a means of reducing the environmental impacts?

2.14 Are the potential long-term environmental liabilities adequately assessed for both newly acquired sites and those being disposed of?

2.15 Are environmental impact audits regularly conducted by appropriately experienced personnel and are their findings and recommendations effectively followed up?

2.16 Does the design and development of new products take into account the potential environmental impact of production, and what measures ensure that such impacts are minimised and contained?

2.17 Are the operating costs of any "recycling" programmes monitored, and are such programmes assessed for their effectiveness?

2.18   How does management verify that the adopted environmental approach is justified (on either cost or company image grounds)?

2.19   Has management reviewed the type of packaging in use as the basis for adopting alternatives with a reduced environmental impact?

2.20   In the event of an environmental problem, are mechanisms in place to deal effectively with media and public relations, so that the reputation of the organisation will be protected?

2.21   How is the accuracy of data input from other systems (e.g. new product development or design) confirmed?

2.22   How is the accuracy of data output to other systems (e.g. industry regulation and compliance) confirmed?

NOTES

1. See Ledgerwood, G., Street, E. and Therivel, R. (1992) *The Environmental Audit and Business Strategy*. Pitman/Financial Times, London. Appendix B has a very comprehensive analysis of the related EU legislation.
2. No. 1836/93 dated 29 June 1993—Published in L168 Volume 36 of the *Official Journal of the European Communities*.
3. Further details of EMAS in the UK can be obtained from Eco-Management & Audit Schemes (EMAS)—see Appendix 1 for address.
4. In Annex B to BS7750 the linkages with BS5750 are explained.
5. Copies of the draft ISO14000 standards are available from the British Standards Institute—see Appendix 1 for address.
6. PBN No. 2—section 3.1, p. 3.
7. PBN No. 2—section 3.1, p. 3.
8. PBN No. 2—section 3.5, p. 5.
9. PBN No. 2—section 5.1, p. 5.
10. PBN No. 2—section 5.2, p. 5.

16

Alternative Views of the Business for Review Purposes

INTRODUCTION

The other chapters in this book have adopted a primarily functionally oriented approach to defining the activities for operational audit review. We shall now turn our attention to some alternative ways of dividing up the audit universe for review purposes.

In the course of examining the various approaches, you should be aware of the practical advantages and disadvantages from the auditor's point of view. We do not necessarily promote or suggest any specific method as the ideal, as the environment and culture of organisations will vary considerably in practice and no one approach can ever be universally appropriate. Auditors will need to assess the risks inherent within their organisations as the primary basis for allocating audit review resources, and accordingly adopt the most suitable review methods for their specific circumstances.

The role played by internal audit within organisations will also vary in practice, and their chosen review basis will need to meet the specific needs of the relevant organisation and adapt to the prevailing management culture while addressing the requirements of professional internal audit practice. The nature of the organisation's operations is likely to have the greatest influence here, and unless the internal audit function can ensure that their review activities are suitably aligned with the corporate approach and objectives, the credibility of the auditing service may be adversely affected.

ALTERNATIVE VIEWS OF THE BUSINESS FOR REVIEW PURPOSES

Up to now we have predominantly focused on the review of the organisation from a functional standpoint. In other words, we have tended to look at the whole organisation as a set of discrete and definable activity areas, such as treasury, production, payroll, etc. This is one traditional and convenient way of approaching audit assignments, but there are some associated drawbacks, which we discuss here.

Function-Oriented Reviews

How do auditors decide upon the most appropriate way to define their universe of audit review projects? There are obviously a number of ways that an organisation can be divided up. One way would be to separate the "productive" or commercial aspects of the business (such as manufacturing or sales) from the support or infrastructure activities (such as accounting, photocopying or security). This type of subdivision is generally geared to the fundamental nature of the business or operations of the organisation and tends to lend a natural priority to those more significant areas of activity.

The simplest (although not necessarily the best) way to define the audit universe is to look at the internal telephone directory. This will identify the discrete departments and may, if viewed alongside any organisation charts, lend a definable form to the company. However, this approach perpetuates the misguided view that such departments operate in isolation of each other within their own orbit.

Two apparent advantages of using this "departmental" or "functional" basis for defining audit reviews are: (1) the area under review is clearly bounded, and (2) reporting lines to responsible management are clear-cut. However, although this may suggest that the audit administration may theoretically be straightforward, this is not necessarily true in practice. It is unlikely that any one department, system or activity will operate in complete isolation, but each will need to interact with other data and systems in order to be fully effective.

At a simple level, such interaction could relate to the input of data from a source system (outside of the department) which is then processed in some way so that some form of enhanced or amended data is generated for output to the next process or department. For example, taking coded transactions from an accounts payable system into the general ledger as the basis for producing management accounts information—all the stages being handled by discrete domains. There is something inherently unnatural and disturbing about self-perpetuating departments/functions that lack points of interconnection with others!

It is often at the point of interaction between systems or departments where controls are critical. This is where the custody of data, etc. changes hands. Auditors should be aware of these points of interaction and satisfy themselves that the data moving between systems is consistent, complete and accurate, so that the subsequent processes are undertaken on a reliable basis.

The way in which defined functions are mapped and interconnected across an organisation will obviously differ considerably between organisations, and may be influenced by best practice, sector-specific practice and the requirements of legislation and regulation. In any event, the auditor will need to establish and communicate the boundary or scope of each review project, partly as a means of ensuring that all concerned are aware of what is being examined (and equally important, what is *not* being included) within the review.

One of the shortcomings of the functional approach to defining the audit universe is that it often fails to identify very significant activities that naturally span departments. For example, the process of launching a new product or service may be extremely significant for a company. This will normally involve the appropriately co-ordinated contributions of a number of functions, including research and development, marketing, production, accounting, legal department, and so on. The auditor is unlikely to find an entry on the internal telephone directory called "product launch", and so it is possible that this critical area would be missed if a purely functional approach to assignment definition was adopted.

Whenever an auditor draws a boundary (or scope) around an audit review project, there will inevitably be loose ends or points of onward interconnection to consider. One way of avoiding this eventuality is to consider the business operations as a series of "cradle to grave" processes or cycles, where a chain of interrelated events or activities is plotted from the origin to the conclusion. We look at this approach in the next section.

Business Cycles as the Basis for Audit Reviews

This approach focuses on a number of related economic events that occur within an organisation that in turn may generate transactions and interactions with systems. It is often referred to as the "business cycle" approach. Its prime aim is to take account of the life cycle of a series of events within the business operations and review them in their entirety across all functional and organisational boundaries.

Before going on to look at this approach in some detail, we should pause for a moment to deal with a matter of basic terminology. The term "cycle" in this context may be potentially confusing as not all the economic activities that form the backbone of this method are truly cyclical in nature. It may be preferable to use the term "business processes".

The following simple definitions can be applied to the five principal cycles or processes.

The Revenue Cycle

Related to those activities that exchange the organisation's products and services for cash, and therefore include (*inter alia*) the following elements:

- credit granting
- processing orders
- delivery and shipping
- billing to customers
- maintaining accurate and reliable inventory records
- the activities associated with accounts receivable
- bad debt (including pursuing debtors and writing off balances)
- reflecting the related transactions correctly in the accounting systems.

The Expenditure Cycle

Those activities/systems that acquire goods, services, labour and property; pay for them; and classify, summarise and report what was acquired and what was paid. For example:

- ensuring that suppliers are stable, reliable and able to provide the appropriate goods/services on time, at the right price and to the required quality

- the requisitioning of goods, services, corporate assets and labour
- receiving, securely storing and correctly accounting for goods
- all the activities associated with accounts payable (e.g. matching orders to suppliers' invoices and confirming the accuracy of pricing, etc.)
- recruiting and correctly paying staff
- ensuring that all taxes due are correctly calculated and disbursed
- ensuring that all the related accounting records are accurate, up to date and complete.

The Production\Conversion Cycle

In this context, the term "conversion" relates to the utilisation and management of various resources (inventory stock, labour, etc.) in the process of creating the goods and service to be marketed by the organisation.

The key issues in this cycle (or process) include accountability for the movement and usage of resources up to the point of supply which is then dealt with in the revenue cycle. Conversion cycle activities include product accounting/costing, manufacturing control, and stock management.

The Treasury Cycle

This cycle is fundamentally concerned with those activities relating to the organisation's capital funds, such as:

- the definition of the cash requirements and cash flow management
- allocation of available cash to the various operations
- investment planning
- the outflow of cash to investors and creditors (i.e. dividends).

The Financial Reporting Cycle

This cycle is *not* based on the basic processing of transactions reflecting economic events, but concentrates upon the crucial consolidation and reporting of results to various interested parties (i.e. management, investors, regulatory and statutory authorities).

The auditor who chooses the business cycle method of defining the scope of reviews is faced with the need to identify all the relevant managers responsible for the inherent activities. This will be necessary in order to ensure that they are duly consulted about the review and so the auditor is clear about the reporting lines for the report and auditor's recommendations.

The main benefit of this approach is that it should encompass all the relevant issues and aim to provide reassurance to management on the effectiveness of the internal control measures in place across the whole process. On the down side, this method requires auditors to plan very carefully how they approach the review assignment and to ensure that the fieldwork is adequately co-ordinated in order to initially identify and consider all the risks and control issues, which will potentially span a number of organisationally separate areas. These considerations will have implications for the general *manageability* of the audit review project.

17

Topical Business/ Management Techniques and their Impact on Control and Audit

INTRODUCTION

In this chapter we will examine selected emerging and contemporary business management approaches in respect of their nature allied to an awareness of their potential impact on the control of operations and internal audit.

The following approaches will be discussed:

- business process re-engineering (BPR)
- total quality management
- delayering
- empowerment
- outsourcing
- control self-assessment
- JIT (just in time management).

BUSINESS PROCESS RE-ENGINEERING

Definition

BPR is normally a strategically driven programme of change which concurrently affects the organisation's structure, human resources, systems and processes. The process is usually both far-reaching in its effects and normally represents a quantum leap in change terms.

It is often a realignment of the business processes to the core organisational strategy of the business because they are regarded as unsound. Frequently it is the strategy itself which is being changed significantly so that the business processes need to be brought in line with the modified strategy.

BPR is not essentially an IT project. It is driven by the business and IT takes its place in the process as an enabling factor along with employees, key business processes, etc. Indeed, one cornerstone of the BPR approach is that it is holistic in nature; in that change and development are viewed across a spectrum of people, processes and technology, with the implications for all being assessed and addressed. Of course, the rapid pace of information technology change has, of itself, offered greater and more flexible opportunities to the business community.

Continuous Improvement

An alternative approach, which is less cataclysmic, is to apply a gradual programme of continuous improvement to operations over a longer time period. In this situation, the affected operations may basically be sound and only require small degrees of change to be applied, and then only to selected elements of the overall process, for example the modification of information technology systems. Continuous improvement is normally a fundamental component of total quality management (which we discuss next). However, there really is no reason why an organisation should not implement a suitable cocktail of different techniques in order to achieve its objectives.

The Radicalism of BPR

Business process re-engineering is the re-engineering of business systems. It has been called a radical change programme which is designed to:

- reduce costs significantly
- make operations significantly more efficient
- find a competitive advantage.

The need for BPR is often driven by acutely unfavourable business circumstances, but even without these a prudent management will consider the competitive advantages which may follow from BPR. It is better to be proactive rather than be forced to respond when a crisis is upon the company.

BPR can be said to be a high risk technique as the aim is to achieve high levels of improvement in a short timescale.

The Driving Force for BPR

The motivations for applying this technique will be varied, but the continuing survival and development of the organisation are normally at the heart of such radical change methods. There may be, on the one hand, the fundamental need to re-focus the strategy of the organisation or alternatively external forces (such as a new competitor in the market or changed economic conditions) may be brought to bear. The following general examples may apply:

- increasing cost burdens squeezing profit margins
- declining income levels from a given product or service, suggesting that additional or improved service is necessary
- inefficient usage of resources possibly linked to funding limitations
- poor productivity and efficiency levels when compared to industry norms
- the need to maintain or improve customer loyalty.

As with the application of any form of strategically driven technique, top management should be seen as the driving force and be responsible for the re-engineering initiative. In order to enhance the possibility of success, the BPR project team should include suitably senior and experienced managers.

Benefits from BPR

Very frequently, post BPR, the business is likely to be more closely aligned with customer needs ("customer focused") than before BPR. All processes become geared to the customer. Staff and management are likely to benefit from increased empowerment. (We examine empowerment later in this chapter.) The IT systems will more closely correspond to need. Business costs will have been reduced through downsizing, better asset management, better supplier relationships and productivity benefits.

How BPR may Affect the Business

Although the results of BPR are intended to be beneficial, the process has risks associated with it. Staff are likely to be resistant to major change and morale may suffer. The efficiency of running existing systems may be impaired as staff resources are diverted to the BPR project. The transition from the old systems to the post-BPR approach can be unsettling and, unless planned with very great care, lead to major breakdowns in business performance. This is especially so as BPR usually involves the redesign of IT systems. Customers may suffer in the short term even though they should notice perceptible improvements after implementation of BPR. In the short term BPR will be expensive as it is likely to entail major investment of time by management and staff, and of capital by the business itself. If consultants are used, the business must be careful to ensure that it does not lose ownership of the programme.

The following 11 general principles for a BPR project are taken from *Business Process Re-Engineering—A Practical Handbook for Executives*, by Stephen Towers:[1]

1. A BPR programme will take strong leadership, substantial time, and real commitment.
2. Begin with a baseline assessment of your processes today.
3. Consultants are extremely useful in moving a BPR programme forward.
4. Define BPR in quantitative terms, and set up a BPR directorate.
5. BPR should be institutionalised through structural changes including "working groups".

6. BPR means revised and revamped technology.
7. Successful BPR begins internally, within an organisation, before it moves out to your business partners and customers.
8. Your organisation's training budget will increase considerably, but it's worth it because BPR rests on the shoulders of your staff.
9. Staff motivation remains the most difficult aspect of BPR to get right.
10. Expect that a percentage of your staff will not be able to measure up.
11. Evaluate your risks, but don't let them deter you.

The Implications for Internal Audit

The more major the change within a business, the greater the risk to effective internal control. BPR is intrinsically linked to major change. It is major change which results in staff being more process or project oriented and less functionally oriented: this very often reduces the extent to which internal control is achieved through segregation of functions and duties—and so alternative ways of achieving satisfactory control must be implemented.

Internal auditors are often rightly asked to participate in the BPR process. When BPR is being designed and implemented, invariably the resources of the internal audit function will be targeted in large measure to the new systems being developed. Internal auditors must understand the BPR process in order to advise on the control quality of the new systems. Internal auditors should also be in a position to review the BPR change process itself and advise whether that process has effective controls built into it. One particular risk is that of escalating costs associated with the BPR project. Internal auditors should be alert to the risk that established controls may not be operated effectively during the BPR project as management and staff resources are diverted to the BPR project itself.

The internal audit function itself may be the object of a BPR project, perhaps as a part of a larger BPR exercise.

TOTAL QUALITY MANAGEMENT

Total quality management (TQM) is:

A way of managing to improve the effectiveness, flexibility, and competitiveness of a business as a whole.[2]

More specifically, TQM is:

A management philosophy embracing all the activities through which the needs and expectations of the customer, the community, and the objectives of the organisation are satisfied in the most efficient and cost effective way by maximising the potential of all employees in a continuing drive for improvement.[3]

A strategy can involve significant changes to an organisation's attitudes, priorities, and controls. It is therefore a decision for management. It is not the responsibility of internal audit. However, internal audit departments will often take charge of the appraisal of the organisation's systems of control to monitor and assess the implementation and operation of the new quality operations.[4]

Quality Systems

Quality assurance systems are systems which set out to demonstrate to customers that a business is committed to quality and able to supply its customers' quality needs. National and international standards[5] for quality systems have been established which place an emphasis on formalising individual systems, procedures and associated quality controls. Considerable emphasis is placed on documenting systems and establishing what the standards of performance are to be.

One criticism of the quality assurance systems movement is that the business seeking registration determines what its own systems will be and what standards of performance will be achieved—these are not externally imposed—they may not be very impressive in terms of quality. But they will be documented and registration is only achieved after they have been appraised by accredited external independent reviewers. Periodic external reviews will be conducted to ascertain whether the established quality systems are being complied with—as a requirement for continued registration. Many customers (such as British Telecommunications plc) insist on using suppliers who are registered for quality systems.

Since registration is dependent upon *external* assessment, internal audit is not in a position to provide this service within their company. They can, however, advise the company on how to set about the process of obtaining registration, and assist the company to meet the requirements for registration. An internal auditing unit may however make arrangements for one or more of its staff to be trained and approved as ISO/BS assessors: they will not be able to act as assessors within their business but the experience of what is involved will be helpful to the business, assisting in avoiding the cost of employing "fee charging assessors over a period of many weeks to analyse the improvements necessary to reach the standards required for ISO/BS certification"[6].

Either the whole business can seek registration covering the organisation as a whole, or sections of the business may do so. Many internal auditing units have gone for registration for a variety of reasons:

- The high level of existing standardisation of internal audit methods often means that an internal auditing unit is well placed to prepare for and seek registration.
- Registration by internal audit sets a good example to the business as a whole.
- Registration by internal audit gives internal audit practical experience of what is involved—which it can then make use of in the advice it gives to the rest of the company.
- Being a service department, registration by internal audit may give its clients, as well as the company's external auditors and regulators, more confidence in the quality of the internal audit unit.
- A registered internal audit unit gains a competitive advantage in several ways, for example, in bidding for outsourced internal audit work, or in recruitment and retention of audit staff.

One familiar element of a TQM programme is promotion of a culture of continuous improvement which is based on the premise that those involved in applying the various processes have the detailed knowledge and are therefore best placed to improve them. Although the initiative for TQM and related continuous improvement programmes will invariably stem from senior management (and be actively endorsed by them), the basic responsibility for improvements lies with employees at the sharp end of the business.

In order to ensure that continuous improvement programmes are successful, staff will need to be supported by suitable training in such relevant techniques as effective team working, brainstorming, problem identification, problem solving, and so on.

As with any rudimentary cultural re-orientation, it will take time to achieve the necessary changes in roles and to generate the anticipated benefits.

The Cost of Quality

Unavoidably there are costs associated with maintaining a quality environment, just as there are financial implications in instances of poor quality. Here we are concerned with categories of quality cost beyond those associated with setting up the TQM environment and accreditation processes. Managers will need to identify quality costs in a number of categories if they are to be in position to quantify the effects of possible improvement and prioritise their improvement efforts in areas which are likely achieve significant savings.

Quality costs may apply in the following example areas:

- in the prevention of defects (i.e. improved design and production techniques/ practices)
- in the monitoring of ongoing quality through inspection and appraisal activities
- the cost of correcting defective products or services *prior* to delivery to the customer (i.e. internal failures)
- the costs associated with correcting defective products/services detected *after* delivery to the customer (i.e. external failures). This may include the cost of refunds, discounts, repairs or replacements.

The last category should be of special concern as the reputation and image of the organisation can be adversely affected and future trading relationships put in jeopardy.

Quality Audits

Quality auditing is established in many businesses that have adopted TQM and/or sought and obtained ISO/BS registration for quality systems. The quality audit process seeks to establish and maintain high standards of TQM and/or quality systems.

Some of the options for approaching quality auditing are:

- address these matters as part of the programme of work of the internal auditing unit

- run a separate quality audit function discrete from the internal audit unit but with a full level of co-ordination between the two so as to avoid duplication of work
- have one audit department divided into two principal sections—one for conventional internal auditing, the other for quality auditing.

ISO/BS standards stipulate the incorporation of self-audit procedures into quality systems. This represents an element of auditing with cost implications.

Quality auditing is not the same as internal auditing. It is an essential part of TQM management philosophy and of a dedication to quality systems. The internal audit approach ideally should be:

- to reassure management and the board that quality auditing is being done effectively, and therefore to conduct internal audits of the quality auditing processes. If internal audit are conducting the quality audits itself, this will have to be done by others.
- to assess the extent to which internal audit can rely on work done by quality audit where it overlaps with the scope of internal audit, thereby avoiding unnecessary duplication.

In concluding this discussion of TQM, we note below a set of control objectives and risk and control issues for the subject, which could be used as the basis for developing an internal audit review programme.

Control Objectives for Quality Management

(a) To ensure that quality management techniques are appropriately considered and utilised in order to improve competitive advantage and the quality of service to customers.

(b) To ensure that the quality management approach is suitably justified, authorised and documented.

(c) To ensure that senior management are committed to the relevant quality strategy.

(d) To ensure that the costs of achieving and maintaining the quality regime are accurately assessed and subject to monitoring.

(e) To ensure that suitable quality and performance criteria are established, which are capable of measurement.

(f) To accurately determine customer requirements for products and services.

(g) To ensure that, whenever justified, nationally or internationally recognised quality standard accreditations are obtained and retained.

(h) To ensure that actual performance against the required quality standards is monitored and managed.

> (i) To ensure that staff are suitably motivated to contribute to the quality programme and provided with the appropriate skills.
>
> (j) To ensure that defined objectives and tangible benefits are actually achieved.
>
> (k) To ensure that the quality management programme is subject to regular monitoring and review, and remains up to date and relevant.

Risk and Control Issues for Quality Management

1 Key Issues

1.1   Has the use of quality management techniques been the subject of adequate research, justification and authorisation (and how is this evidenced)?

1.2   Has the quality management policy/programme been documented?

1.3   Have the objectives of the quality programme been clearly defined (i.e. in terms of potential competitive advantage, improved customer satisfaction, etc.)?

1.4   How has senior management demonstrated its commitment to the quality programme?

1.5   Have all the costs associated with the quality programme been accurately and realistically identified, agreed and authorised?

1.6   Have realistic and measurable quality and performance criteria been defined for all the affected activities, and are the relevant staff aware of the requirements?

1.7   How has the involvement and motivation of staff been signified in the development of the quality programme?

1.8   What steps have management taken to ensure that the appropriate national or international quality standard accreditation will be achieved and maintained?

1.9   How does management ensure that all the relevant staff training requirements have been identified and suitably addressed?

1.10 Are all the quality initiatives subject to ongoing monitoring in order to ensure that targets and objectives are realised?

1.11 How is management to be made aware of performance and quality shortfalls against the defined expectations, and what measures ensure that such problems are adequately followed up?

2 Detailed Issues

2.1   Have all the relevant operational procedures and policies been updated in light of the documentary requirements of the quality management scheme?

2.2   What processes has management applied in order to select the most suitable areas for the quality initiatives?

2.3   What mechanisms prevent unsuitable business operations being targeted with quality initiatives?

2.4   What prevents the implementation and operation of unauthorised or unjustified quality schemes?

2.5   Have customer requirements been accurately identified and taken into consideration?

2.6   How has the quality scheme been justified?

2.7   How does management verify that it has identified all the costs and operational requirements of applying the quality management programme?

2.8   Are the costs associated with the quality programme subject to suitable authorisation (and how is this evidenced)?

2.9   What processes prevent unauthorised expenditure for quality-related activities?

2.10   Are all the costs associated with the quality programme adequately reported and subject to suitable monitoring and reaction?

2.11   Have suitable and justifiable quality control and testing facilities been provided?

2.12   Are quality control defect and rejection rates identified and monitored?

2.13   What action is taken if quality control defect and rejection rates fail to improve as a result of the quality programme?

2.14   How does management ensure that staff are adequately trained to fulfil their quality obligations?

2.15   What mechanisms are in place to identify and promptly resolve quality problems?

2.16   Where applicable, how did management justify the adoption of national or international quality standards?

2.17   Have the costs of obtaining and maintaining recognised quality standards been accurately identified and authorised?

2.18   Have suitably experienced external examiners been appointed to conduct the required reviews of the quality programme?

2.19   How can management be sure that the examiners' fees represent good value for money and are competitive?

2.20   How are shortcomings noted by the external examiners brought to the attention of management, and what measures are in place to ensure adequate follow-up and that action is taken?

2.21 How would the failure to achieve the potential benefits of the quality programme be detected and reported?

2.22 How does management ensure that the quality programme remains relevant, effective and justifiable?

2.23 How does management ensure that serious failures in the quality programme are dealt with?

2.24 Have non-productive or wasteful processes been identified through the quality scheme and what has been done in such instances?

2.25 How does management ensure that external suppliers and agencies are able to contribute effectively to the achievement of the required quality standards adopted by the organisation?

2.26 Are customer satisfaction levels subject to ongoing monitoring so that the success (or otherwise) of the quality initiative can be accurately assessed?

2.27 How are existing customer service concerns identified and effectively addressed?

2.28 How is the accuracy of data input from other systems (e.g. quality control) confirmed?

2.29 How is the data output to other systems (e.g. planning) confirmed?

DELAYERING

Definition

Delayering simply means removing one or more levels of management from the enterprise, or from a part or parts of it.

Potential Implications of Delayering for the Enterprise

Even within very modern organisations where organisation structure is fluid and the structural emphasis is on project organisation or on matrix organisation, you will find a hierarchical organisation structure.

The number of levels of management and staff will vary according to the historical evolution of the business and also according to the type of business it is. Some enterprises, or parts of enterprises, are appropriately very flat. An implication of being flat is that each manager supervises a larger number of subordinates. This is called "the span of control" of the manager—an expression first coined by Henri Fayol [1916].[7] How wide the span of control of a manager can be depends largely on these features:

- the extent to which subordinates are doing similar jobs
- the extent to which subordinates need to be monitored and helped

- the degree to which the supervisory task is streamlined by techniques such as IT-based reporting by exception
- the extent to which the manager has fundamental work to complete which does not involve supervising others
- the extent to which the manager invests time reporting upwards
- the extent to which the manager expends time liaising with collateral associates within the business
- the extent to which the manager has a communication role *external to the business* such as with the media and customers
- the degrees of personal assistance the manager has in performing his or her duties.

The principal underlying theme behind these features is that of *limited cognitive ability*. In business almost everyone suffers from information overload. Managers resort to various devices to handle information overload, which occurs because our minds are unable to process rationally all the information that needs to be processed in order to make optimal decisions. Clearly, the more staff a manager has to supervise, the more information the manager is required to process. The risk is that supervision becomes nominal—that delegation becomes abdication.

Many businesses have little idea how many levels of management and staff they have. They have an even vaguer idea as to how they stack up in this regard compared to their competitors. It is an even more difficult decision to determine how many levels of management and staff the business *should* have.

Removing a layer of management and staff broadens the span of control of the managers involved. It generally therefore leads to greater *empowerment* of those being supervised (see the following section for a discussion of empowerment). Generally it should be associated with the development of modern IT-based systems which make it easier for managers to supervise more subordinates, perhaps through IT-generated *reporting by exception*.

Delayering usually has a dramatic impact on lowering staffing costs. So it is often part of a business process re-engineering project (discussed earlier). It can be one way of achieving productivity gains. It is often made feasible when a factor of production other than staff (such as automation or outsourcing) becomes more economic than investment in staff, which perhaps becomes too costly or unreliable.

Yet its other advantages may be even greater. We have mentioned the greater empowerment inherited by the level of management or staff beneath the level which has been removed. This should ideally lead to greater job satisfaction and to greater work motivation.

Equally dramatic can be the speeded up responsiveness which occurs within the business as a consequence of delayering. Instructions communicated downwards to operating levels have one less layer to filter through. Each layer usually represents a time delay and a potential for distortion of the message which was originally intended to be communicated downwards. Likewise, information communicated upwards about the results of operations, reaches decision-making levels more quickly and with less corruption en route. So a faster-moving, more responsive enterprise is created.

Each unnecessary level of management or staff is a superfluous, unproductive and costly overhead. Delayering simplifies the business. For instance, to mention just one example, a smaller personnel function will be required if there are fewer staff employed.

The Informal Organisation

It is probable that every enterprise has an informal organisation as well as a formal one. Where staff find they need to interact with certain other staff in order to do their job, they will tend to find a way of doing so—even if the formal structure does not provide this opportunity. They may get into the habit of having lunch together, for instance, or a junior executive may bypass a boss to report a matter of concern to a higher level. In turn, the higher level may interact directly with staff several levels more junior, bypassing intermediate levels of management. Some businesses are very formal in defining and applying reporting relationships; others are much more informal. Some businesses have formal codes of business practice and some of these will specify that junior staff may address matters of concern directly to much more senior levels of management (and to internal audit as well) if they perceive a need to do so.

The informal organisation structure is as real as the formal one. Any analysis of structure and of levels of management and staff may need to take both the informal and the formal aspects of organisation structure into account.

In addition to having an informal organisation structure, staff tend to develop informal procedures when the formal laid-down procedures prove to be inadequate.

Internal Audit Implications

Questions for internal audit include:

- How many levels of management and staff does the enterprise have, and how many should it have? This is a question that should be asked during any operational audit.
- Does management have the information it needs to supervise effectively, and *is* management supervising effectively?
- Will a proposed delayering project lead to a loss of control, (a) temporarily while the project is in progress, and (b) after it has been implemented—and what can the auditor recommend to avoid this?
- Are there too many levels of management and staff in the internal auditing department?

EMPOWERMENT

Definition

The delegation of responsibility to and trust of staff for making business decisions, without the need for close, detailed review and approval of those decisions. This approach is based on the premise that employees, at all levels, are responsible for their own actions and should be given the authority to make decisions about their work.

Rationale for Empowerment

Determined cost-cutting (perhaps as one of the objectives of a business process re-engineering project and prompted often by acute competitive pressures) often has the effect of giving more responsibility to most staff. Since there are likely to be fewer staff, it follows that the responsibilities of most are likely to be greater. This will also generally be the effect of greater automation, although we should not overlook that many decisions are now "programmable"—meaning they can be automated so that no member of staff may have the responsibility to make these decisions. Of course, the development of systems for programmed decision making is itself a responsibility that has to be taken very seriously by any business. The operation of programmed decision making should also be monitored by management who have the responsibility to note unsatisfactory programmed outcomes and intervene so as to override them on a timely basis.

So, to some extent "empowerment" is a likely by-product of several of the new approaches to management which we are discussing in this chapter.

But "empowerment" is also an objective in its own right as it is perceived to have many positive outcomes. Herzberg's[8] bipolar analysis of job satisfaction factors divided them into two groups. The *hygiene factors* are to do with the surroundings of the job (such as good working conditions, pleasant colleagues to work with, easy travel to work, etc.) whereas the *motivators* are more closely to do with the job itself (such as job interest, opportunity for achievement, recognition of achievement, advancement). Herzberg maintained that if management attended well to the hygiene factors which related to their staff, then this would only remove negative feelings of dissatisfaction: in themselves the hygiene factors would not positively motivate staff. For positive motivation, the motivators had to be in place. And if staff were motivated to perform well, then outputs would improve—in effect the business would be buying-in to the potential of its people.

Maslow's[9] view of satisfaction was not bipolar: it was uni-polar. He perceived of a hierarchy of needs. At the lowest level people have (a) physiological needs (for food, water, warmth, etc.). At progressively higher levels are (b) security needs, (c) social needs, (d) esteem needs, (e) autonomy needs, and (f) self-actualisation (or self-fulfilment) needs. Maslow found that most people display some degree of dissatisfaction with the extent to which their needs are satisfied. He found that an acute level of dissatisfaction with the extent to which a lower-level need was satisfied would often lead to a major preoccupation by the individual designed to alter things and meanwhile the higher level needs would signify little in that person's consciousness. For instance, a starving person will be preoccupied with the need to find food and will not indulge in concern about their level of self-actualisation. Maslow found that most occupational groups in the developed world have achieved levels of satisfaction which mean that most or all of Maslow's needs are a matter of concern to them.

Autonomy is the need that most closely corresponds to the concept of "empowerment". Autonomy means taking decisions and being able to see the results which follow from those decisions.

If managers and staff are able to obtain more of their lives' needs through their work experiences, they are likely to be motivated to focus on their job so as to fulfil themselves. If their jobs provide inadequate opportunities to fulfil their needs, they will not identify with their work so much and will seek to obtain fulfilment in their leisure activities. The half-hearted focus of such employees on their work will result in much less effective levels of performance. "Empowerment" is seen as an important way of providing staff with the opportunity to fulfil themselves more at work. From the organisation's viewpoint there is likely to be the additional objective of increasing motivation to do the job well (for example, to satisfy customers and participate more fully in the "life" of the organisation).

If empowerment confers the authority to make decisions, it is possible that varying levels of service (i.e. to customers) will result through the differing interpretations applied by individual members of staff. In addition, there may be an attendant lack of clarity, in that it is more difficult to discern who is responsible for what.

We should not overlook the other perspective which suggests that many people do not want responsibility; many people may be happier not to have to make decisions; many people may be happier in a job that enables them to focus on non-work activities, such as hobbies, family, voluntary work, church etc. And a happy employee is better than an unhappy one.

Internal Audit Implications

- Has "empowerment" weakened control by weakening supervision—and, if so, are there effective compensating controls?
- Has "empowerment" removed or weakened *segregation of duties* controls— and, if so, are there effective compensating controls?
- Has "empowerment" increased the potential for employee or management fraud—and, if so, what are the safeguards?
- Has "empowerment" led to excessive dependence on one or a few key members of staff?
- Has "empowerment" led to the motivational and productivity gains expected of it—or are management and staff disillusioned by excessive responsibilities and excessive work loads?

OUTSOURCING

Meaning

Sometimes termed "contracting out", outsourcing occurs when services previously provided by in-house personnel are supplied by an outside contractor. This often takes place after a due process of market testing, which requires that a fully specified tender document is prepared and potential outside contractors are invited to tender for the work against the specification. The in-house personnel who previously provided the services (sometimes known as the direct labour) may be invited to tender for the work in competition with the outside tenderers.

Impact on In-house Personnel

Very often, a condition of tendering imposed on the outside tenderers is that they must agree to take on the direct labour personnel. The drawback for those whose contract of employment transfers in this way from the business to the outside contractor is that their terms and conditions of service and their job security are often not so good with the outside contractor as they were previously, when perhaps they had been insulated from the effect of market forces. Large organisations often end up paying premium employment costs (such as profit-sharing and pension schemes) to peripheral employees for whom they were not originally intended; outsourcing their work can eliminate that premium.

Broadening Scope of Outsourcing

In recent years there has been a general trend to outsourcing non-core activities such as catering, security, office cleaning and, in the case of local authorities, refuse collection. More recently, more fundamental activities such as accounting, computer operations and site maintenance have been seen as candidates for outsourcing. Outsourcing computer operations is normally termed *facilities management* (see Chapter 13).

Cost–benefit Issues

In the public sector, the push towards outsourcing is often initiated to inject a competitive element into the tendering for services. It is believed that this can lead to lower costs of public services as well as higher quality. Management must, however, take great care to ensure that it is not *just* costs that determine the choice of outsourcer—essential standards of service provision must be maintained. An outside contractor is unlikely to provide any service unless it is part of the contract, and the contract must specify the standard of service expected, with penalty clauses for shortfall. Outsourcing also has the effect of reducing the size of (or at least reducing the rate of growth of) the public sector in a national economy, which is perceived as having certain macroeconomic advantages.

Cost Escalation

At first, outsourced services may be provided on favourable terms, but once well established, and as soon as the contractual terms permit, the contractor may raise the price of providing the service. Then, with the in-house provision no longer being available, the organisation may be in a weak position to resist escalating costs of ensuring that the service continues to be provided. Of course, if there is an open market in the provision of these services, the services can be market tested again so that a competitive provider is found.

Contractors may be able to justify low-price tenders as they can often be costed on a marginal cost basis for a while. For instance, firms of public accountants may tender for outsourced internal audit work in anticipation that they will be able to resource that work using staff at a time of the year when they are not heavily engaged with year-end external audit work.

A common practice is to bid for a market-tested service at cost price and, once the contract has been won, to charge at expensive rates for services that the client needs but did not include in the tender document and which are therefore not covered by the contract. Careful specification of the job and careful wording of the contract can reduce this risk.

Re-invigorating a Business through Outsourcing

The cultural implications of outsourcing are considerable. The net effect of a significant amount of outsourcing is to make the organisation smaller and simpler to run. There is a reduced requirement for staff functions such as a large personnel department, so there are these indirect cost savings as well. Many of the popular approaches to contemporary management are designed to achieve this.

Outsourcing can help a business keep or regain its dynamism—its ability to adapt more rapidly. Management have more freedom to make changes without the problem of having to overcome staff who may be resistant to change, or at least have to be managed effectively during times of change. Management are able to focus more single-mindedly on the main issues.

Impact on Human Resource Inventory

By using outside contractors, the reservoir of in-house trained and experienced staff will be reduced and consequently the organisation may become less competent, more vulnerable and perhaps less able to competently handle a future need to change. On the other hand, outsourced activities provide outside contractors with learning experience *on the job*. This may be a potential competitive threat, as in effect the business is developing outsiders who may set up in competition or take their resultant know-how to a rival business for whom they also provide outsourced services.

Outsiders working for the business may also represent a security risk. For example, most businesses take incredible risks with their contract cleaners who may have virtually unrestricted access to premises out of hours.

The Decision to Outsource

How does management decide what and whether to outsource? First, they apply cost-benefit principles to the decision. Secondly, they consider which of their non-core activities might be done better by outsiders who specialise in those activities—in other words, by outsiders for whom those activities *are* core. For example, an automobile manufacturer might not regard its core business as involving machining—it may buy in all its components and merely assemble and market its products. Much of the marketing is also likely to be contracted out.

It is not always immediately apparent what are the core activities of a business—and they may change over time. One way of identifying what is the businesses core activity is to determine what it is that it is consistently able to do at greatest profit in terms of return on capital employed. For instance, a domestic home loan company may develop special expertise in collecting overdue debts—to the extent that it becomes the market leader in collections. In such a case its core business might be regarded as changing from having been a home loans company to having become a collections company, which may tender for the collections work of other home loans and consumer credit companies.

Strategic Implications

The decision to outsource may have strategic implications. Businesses must consider the security of their supplier and distribution lines. Outsourcing may make the organisation more dependent on outside suppliers and distributors and so it might opt for vertical integration instead. Vertical integration is the process whereby a business expands so that it absorbs other businesses in the supply and distribution chain. Since each of these businesses intends to make a profit, gathering them together so that they are all "in-house" ensures that all the profit margins are retained. However, the business may not be so successful at making a profit on non-core activities in which it has relatively low expertise. In any case, if outside contractors are in plentiful supply the strategic risks are fewer, and vertical integration may be neither attractive nor appropriate.

There may be broader issues at stake which militate against outsourcing. For instance, customers and clients of the business might *expect* that certain elements of the service they receive are provided internally and not outsourced.

Implications for Internal Audit

You can see from the above discussion that outsourcing poses control risks of particular interest to the internal auditor. We summarise some of them here:

- Do the tender document and the subsequent contract specify an adequate minimum standard of service, and ensure that unanticipated contingencies will be serviced effectively?
- Are the contracting procedures for outsourcing adequate to ensure the contractor is selected objectively, and are these procedures followed?
- Is it evident that contracted-out services are value for money?
- Has management considered and is management managing the security risk associated with utilisation of outsiders for contracted out work?
- Is contracted-out work periodically market tested to ensure the service is provided competitively?
- Are all services currently performed by in-house personnel considered on an impartial basis for market testing?
- Has the business a clear strategic grasp of what is its core activity and so should not be regarded as a candidate for outsourcing?

- Is partial outsourcing (whereby contract staff work alongside in-house staff) rationally considered as an option wherever it may be applicable?
- Is contracting out leading to excessive dependence on one supplier, and does management regularly consider this risk?
- Does management review the discharge of contracts for outsourced services with a view to learning lessons from cost overruns, etc.?

CONTROL SELF-ASSESSMENT

Responsibility for Control

Management is responsible for control. Control (along with, for instance, planning and leading) has traditionally been seen as one of the functions, or elements, of management. The COSO *Internal Control—Integrated Framework* study makes it clear that monitoring is one of the five interrelated components of internal control:

Internal control systems need to be monitored—a process that assesses the quality of the system's performance over time. This is accomplished through ongoing monitoring activities, separate evaluations or a combination of the two. The scope and frequency of separate evaluations will depend primarily on an assessment of risks and the effectiveness of ongoing monitoring procedures. Internal control deficiencies should be reported upstream, with serious matters reported to top management and the board.[10]

In the UK, for instance, parallel guidance to directors of listed companies also identifies monitoring and corrective action as one of the criteria of internal control.[11]

Since management is responsible for internal control, it follows that management is also responsible for the monitoring component of internal control. Management can exercise this responsibility directly themselves or they can delegate aspects of it to others who report to them, or a combination of both. It has been said that "Internal audit does what management would do, if management had time and knew how".[12]

Many businesses have delegated to internal audit the responsibility of reviewing on management's behalf their systems of internal control. Setting up a specialist function (internal audit) to do this is more likely to ensure that it is not neglected as day-to-day work pressures are likely to deflect line management from standing *back* and reviewing (or monitoring) their systems of internal control. Furthermore, a specialist internal audit function is in a position to develop and maintain specialist skills at a high level in the art of conducting effective, objective reviews of internal control.

The Fashion for Control Self-Assessment

Recently, in some quarters the pendulum has started a tentative swing away from reliance on internal audit towards control self-assessment (CSA) programmes or, as they are sometimes known, control risk self-assessment (CRSA), or simply self-assessment programmes (SAP). (The expression "SAP" makes allowance for the inclusion within the programme of other issues additional to control assessment such as quality and environment issues.) This swing has often been driven by a desire to economise on the cost of internal auditing to the business while not neglecting the rightly perceived need to keep systems of internal control under review—a particular requirement now that directors are reporting formally, publicly and annually on internal control.

Many who have participated in CSA doubt if there are genuine cost savings involved. Reliance on CSA to the exclusion of internal audit overlooks the justification for an internal audit function, which can be summed up as follows:

- Day-to-day work pressures make it difficult for line management to stand back and review their systems of internal control.
- Effective review of internal control benefits from the possession of professional auditing skills which line management cannot be expected to have.
- Senior levels of management and outsiders (such as external auditors and regulators) may be more reassured by internal auditors reviewing internal control, as they are independent of executive management because they have no routine responsibilities for the operations they review.

The Characteristics of Control Self-Assessment

CSA has arrived dressed up in a packaging promoted by management consultants who have associated it with a particular methodology that has to some extent served to confuse managements and internal auditors. Certainly, a formal method is needed if CSA is to be successful and admirable methodologies are on offer from specialist consultants. Terms such as CSA and SAP perhaps have been consciously coined to give the process a sort of brand image rather like other management *isms* of the past (such as O&M or MBO) and present (such as TQM or QA). There is no holy grail or alchemy for control self-assessment. Neither in essence is it in any way a new approach. It is easily understood if it is stripped of the mystique which has become associated with it.

CSA is a structured approach that allows individual staff and line managers to take part in reviewing existing controls to assess their adequacy and, if appropriate, to make recommendations to improve them. Improvement may mean amendment of existing controls, development of additional controls or elimination of unnecessary controls. The review must take account of cost-benefit issues and to do this it will be necessary to apply risk criteria. In addition to reviewing the suitability of the system of internal control, the control self-assessment process includes confirming that the key identified controls are operating effectively.

There is an obvious advantage in control self-assessment in that it makes staff and management more control aware. It is quite similar to the established internal auditing practice of requiring line management to complete internal control questionnaires (for instance, on their PC usage), with the completed questionnaires being reviewed by internal audit. However, it needs to be kept in proportion. Many managers rightly do not see their mission as being to control exposure: rather they have objectives to achieve. Research has shown that control-oriented approaches to management can be dysfunctional (i.e. harmful).[13] CSA programmes need to ensure that management keeps its eye on the ball. Too much preoccupation with control self-assessment may deflect line management from focusing on achieving other objectives.

A control self-assessment programme may be broadened beyond control to include other issues—in particular, it is frequently being broadened to include assessment of quality issues and sometimes environmental issues as well. There is a clear parallel between the control self-assessment approach and the approach taken with "quality circles".

The full "structure" to the control self-assessment approach is provided in several ways:

- A series of formal training sessions will be required before implementation of a process of control self-assessment, as most staff will be unfamiliar with the approach needed. The training sessions will cover:

  - the meaning of internal control and how it is achieved
  - the theory and use of risk criteria
  - an introduction to the process to be followed by the business in completing the control self-assessment and monitoring agreed actions
  - an explanation of the control self-assessment documentation, focusing on its correct completion
  - coverage of any other issues which are to be included in the self-assessment process (such as quality issues).

- The self-assessment documentation is likely to have separate sections on each of the following:

  - financial controls
  - system and process controls
  - IT controls
  - other areas, such as quality, covered by the self-assessment programme.

- Workshop sessions between management and staff to identify and record risks, control weaknesses and opportunities for improvements.
- A formal process to document self-assessments is an essential part of the process and has the purpose of documenting:

  - control weaknesses
  - that risk criteria have been applied
  - the recommended corrective actions
  - suggested target dates for corrective action.

- Action plans and target dates are monitored.
- Each self-assessment is consolidated upwards and formally reviewed at each level of consolidation—at the functional level and ultimately for the entire enterprise where it is reviewed by the audit committee. This can be a valuable approach to equipping the board with the basis for forming its overall view on the quality of internal control within their business, which is both a general duty they have and also a prerequisite for their public reporting on internal control. A practical

difficulty is that excessive time may be taken in performing the control self-assessments and consolidating them upwards: this is particularly so if the process is recommenced as frequently as once a year. An annual cycle is, however, appropriate if the outputs of control self-assessment are to be used in a significant way by the directors in preparing their annual public report on internal control, but it is very demanding to consolidate upwards on a timely basis.

- We have described the full structure of a control self-assessment process. Many businesses find this too demanding on staff and management to be an acceptable proposition. An alternative, minimalist approach followed in some businesses is to dispense with training sessions and workshops in favour of relying on questionnaires completed by management. Thereafter, consolidation upwards, formal agreement to required actions and monitoring implementation may or may not occur. Of course, the minimalist approach makes it much less likely that the programme will achieve so much. In essence this betrays the rationale for internal audit. Management is caught between the devil and the deep blue sea: if it effectively reviews the control arrangements itself, it may neglect other things; if it contains the review within affordable proportions it becomes an ineffective, unpopular, bureaucratic paper-filling exercise. Perhaps control self-assessment has particular value as a one-off or occasional (rather than regular and routine) exercise if and when management can be persuaded that there is a strategic justification in placing special emphasis on control assessment—perhaps during or after periods of major change. It does seem likely that ongoing programmes of control self-assessment will become less effective with time as managers and staff find the repetitiveness de-motivating.

Guides for Management and Staff on Internal Control

In Chapter 3 we discussed the use of Standard Audit Programme Guides as a tool for control self-assessment. See also the internal control Guides for management and staff in Appendices 4 and 5. These are intended to be summary guides to explain to management and staff the basic fundamentals of internal control. The longer version (Appendix 4) gives more explanation, which could be omitted where management requires less detail.

Management Letters of Representation on Internal Control

Another useful mechanism in a programme of control self-assessment can be the Letter of Representation on Internal Control by each key manager within the business. It is convenient to think in terms of "long form" and "short form" letters of representation. The short form letter will cover all of the manager's areas of responsibility in a single, general letter perhaps of one or two pages. An example, without any qualifications, is given as Appendix 10. The long form version addresses each area of the manager's responsibility separately—either in letter form or in questionnaire form. In the latter form, Standard Audit Programme Guides may be these basis for these.

Letters of representation will certainly force chief executives of operating units and companies and other key managers to focus on the most important control matters. There is really no limit to the amount of detail that can be included within a letter of representation. The key is to determine the level of detail that is practical to be followed by management in the context of the company in which it will be used.

It would perhaps be better to avoid the word "letter" if a high level of detail is adopted, which is better addressed using a questionnaire/checklist format. This level of detail would be responded to more readily by some managers if it were computer-based. There are various options for the design of an appropriate format. One option is that these issues are presented in the form of questions with an opportunity for management to insert Yes/No answers and comments only. Another option is a format similar to the format of Standard Audit Programme Guides. Using this approach the subject matter would be distilled into risk/control issues which would be printed in the appropriate column of the SAPG, distinguishing between major and minor issues if appropriate. Either management could be left to decide for themselves what to enter in the *Current Control/ Measure* column or, if procedures are sufficiently standardised, these could be pre-entered by internal audit, leaving management to express their opinion in the *Effective—Yes/No* column. If management went further they could complete further SAPG columns; alternatively these further columns could be omitted or retained for possible internal audit use.

Some forms of drafting permit use only by the head of an operating unit or company reporting to group internal audit. This may be quite valid. There may be a case for letters of representation to be reported upwards through the line management chain starting with junior levels of management in operating units.

Long form letters of representation need to be specially designed for each type of line manager since each addresses specific controls some of which are applicable to one line manager and others to another—and so on.

Design could be given precise linkage to the Cadbury internal control reporting requirement.[14] This could be achieved by classifying the issues being addressed by management according to the components/elements of internal control understood by COSO/Rutteman. There should be reference to timing: UK directors of listed companies are reporting on internal control as it has applied over the period under review by the financial statements.

The example of a short form letter of representation given as Appendix 10 commits the manager both to acknowledging responsibility for internal control and to discharging effectively the most important general aspects of that responsibility. This short form example does not address specific control areas, as would a long form one. It could be expanded to do so, but would then more closely resemble the longer form. This short form example has been designed to be used by any level of manager reporting upwards to more senior management (or in the case of the most senior line management, to the audit committee possibly) or by line management reporting to internal audit.

Role of Internal Audit in Control Self-Assessment

The prudent corporate approach is not to see control self-assessment as an alternative to internal audit, but rather to co-ordinate control self-assessment with the internal audit process. Internal audit can facilitate the control self-assessment process in a number of important ways. A successful control self-assessment programme can also provide valuable reassurance to internal audit.

Internal Audit as a Facilitator of Control Self-Assessment

Internal audit is a respected adviser to management on internal control matters. Management will require from internal audit:

- advice on which parts of organisation should use CSA and which parts are unlikely to benefit from it
- advice on the preparation of the training sessions; involvement beyond an advisory one would constitute a departure from the accepted role of internal audit
- a review of control self-assessment work completed by individual line managers
- guidance on the consolidation upwards of the results of control self-assessments; an active role in making these consolidations would represent a departure from the accepted role of internal audit
- advice to management and to the audit committee as to the effectiveness of the control self-assessment process
- a review of the follow-up of agreed actions to be taken resulting from control self-assessment; responsibility for the follow up process would be beyond the generally accepted scope of internal audit.

Management and administration of the control self-assessment programme by internal audit would represent a conflict of interest for internal audit. Internal auditing Standards require internal audit to be independent of the activities they audit.[15] For executive responsibility to be given to internal audit for the control self-assessment programme would be in conflict in particular with the role that internal audit may have in giving advice to management and to the audit committee as to the effectiveness of the control self-assessment process.

Control Self-Assessment as Reassurance to Internal Audit

The results of the control self-assessment process can be used by internal audit once the head of the internal auditing unit is satisfied that the quality of the control self-assessment work means that it can be relied upon. Internal audit has always had a professional obligation to avoid duplication of audit work where the work of others can be relied upon to meet internal audit objectives at least in part. Involvement of internal audit as an adviser in the control self-assessment process will provide internal audit with the confidence to draw conclusions as to the effectiveness of the control self-assessment process and the extent to which it can be relied upon to meet internal audit objectives.

Avoiding Disillusionment from Line Managers

Beyond the achievement of the first cycle of the CSA programme, it is possible that managers will assume that the exercise is now complete and that there is no further justification for their continued involvement. In any case, they may not see their main mission as being driven by control, but rather to ensure that their (and the organisation's) objectives are achieved.

Management and staff often misguidedly assume that control is the prime domain of the internal auditing function, and they fail to recognise that they have the prime responsibility for control activities and that control is an integral part of their management processes. Therefore, it follows that cost-effective internal control activities are often positive means of achieving the required targets and objectives.

A realistic (and healthy) view of the related risks will need to be developed against which control activities can be set. Line managers should be encouraged to acknowledge ownership of their systems and processes, and to aim to reduce, counter or eradicate the related risks as one mechanism for contributing to improved performance. All parties need to recognise that control activities should be cost-effective and therefore in proportion to the underlying risks.

Among the many stated benefits of CSA are that line managers accept their control responsibilities and are "empowered" to determine such controls and influence how they are applied in practice (rather than being imposed). However, the success (or otherwise) of CSA is heavily dependent on how the concept is "sold" to management, for example:

- what is the agenda? (Cost saving, quality and performance improvements, corporate survival through the achievement of objectives, linkages with other concurrent initiatives, such as quality, etc.)
- the prevailing attitude of senior management and whether they are seen to be committed to the process
- the past and future role of internal auditing within the organisation
- whether the CSA process is, in itself, unduly cumbersome and bureaucratic
- the extent to which line management and their staff are able to influence the process and "have their say" (i.e. a partnership approach)
- the degree of preparation and support provided to managers and their staff (i.e. training workshops and the clear communication of the objectives of the CSA programme).

CSA is an opportunity for management and internal audit to establish a common perception of the organisation through its procedures and control activities. It is fundamentally important to have a clear idea of where the organisation is going (objectives) and the underlying key factors that will influence the way there (i.e. cost containment/reduction, quality achievements, maintaining customer/client relationships, etc.).

Line managers and their staff may view the need to identify and document the controls as an onerous task. However, this initial administrative overhead is reduced in subsequent years as only amendments and refinements need to be documented.

Managers may be concerned that any detected control weaknesses in their domain will be used against them in some way. Unless this perception is corrected, they may be reluctant to be open and honest about control shortcomings. Taking into account the prevailing management ethos, managers may not be inclined to reveal potential control problems within their area in case they are penalised. This negative perception will need to be corrected so that mangers are positively encouraged (perhaps even rewarded) to draw attention to weaknesses in control and to openly contribute their ideas for future improvements.

The CSA process should be forward-looking. Recognising and accepting the need to improve control processes as a success factor, rather than negative reactions to past oversights. Without an open and honest approach to the review and assessment of control, the results are likely to be half-hearted and the opportunity to reap real benefits will be missed.

The CSA process should be built on, promoting a collective responsibility for internal control as a partnership between line management, who are accountable for control as part of their responsibilities, and internal audit, who objectively appraise the effectiveness of controls in place on behalf of senior management.

Where possible, forms of measuring achievements can be devised that enable performance comparisons to be assessed over time, as a means of marking improvements and gains. Internal audit should consider formally reporting the positive aspects of their findings in the context of attaining the strategic and operational goals set for the organisation.

Highlighting Savings and Greater Control Assurance in Departmental Reviews

Applying measurement criteria can facilitate the quantification of potential savings (i.e. cost reductions, performance improvements, meeting quality targets, etc.).

In addition to identifying improvements in control practices, CSA can also reveal redundant or unnecessary processes. These can be dispensed with and there may be related cost savings.

Internal audit reporting on their independent reviews should not solely focus on the negative aspects of their findings (i.e. the "what can go wrong" approach) but strike a positive tone (i.e. "What needs to be done to ensure that management objectives are achieved?"). Where benefits have been achieved by management's application of effective control, these should be acknowledged and reported as such by internal auditors.

Encouragement from the Top

Senior management need to demonstrate commitment to the CSA process and encourage line management to buy-in to the fact that internal controls can support the achievement of corporate goals. Senior management should clearly communicate the motivation and purpose for the CSA process, as a way of focusing personnel towards good practice, etc.

In order to provide the direction and focus for CSA, it will be necessary to identify the strategic and operational objectives for the organisation. These may be linked to other related initiatives, such as TQM, safety or environmental assessments.

Staff taking part in the CSA programme should be well informed about its purpose and provided with training (perhaps through workshops facilitated by internal audit).

Management should aim to engender a positive and contributive environment, where CSA participants can have their say and influence outcomes. This can be reinforced by adopting constructive attitudes, perhaps linked to team building concepts. Using a "team building" approach can emphasise that the CSA process is about assessing "real world issues", and empowering people to take effective action(s).

Managers should be encouraged to reveal potential control weaknesses in their departments without the fear of recriminations. However, they also need to be aware of the related need to suggest effective and justifiable control solutions.

CSA offers unique opportunities for a new and more proactive relationship to be established between line managers and the internal audit function, with all parties focusing their attention on positive achievement through an effective internal control environment. If they haven't already done so, internal auditors should recognise that their service should be tuned to the needs of the business, and co-ordinate their work accordingly.

Internal audit management can, through the auspices of CSA, raise the profile of the internal audit service and help promote the significance of internal control as a device for ensuring corporate success.

Self assessment can be considered as a necessary activity aimed at self preservation. Finding and correcting weaknesses in a company's operations, before such weaknesses cause the business to fail. It is an indicator as to the health and fitness of an organisation and a gauge to its ability to survive and prosper".[16]

JUST-IN-TIME MANAGEMENT (JIT)

The driving objectives of JIT are to eliminate wasteful or non-value-added activities, and by doing so achieve improvements (such as increased quality, reduced work-in-progress stock levels, improved productivity, and reduced costs). The radicalism of the technique will invariably mean the reassessment and/or the casting aside of existing practices, and it is, therefore, important that those involved approach the exercise with open minds.

The conceptual origins of JIT have a connection with the work of Frederick Taylor[17] early in this century and were really brought into wider prominence by Japanese industry as an extension of their struggles to survive after the Second World War. One of the first practical working examples was implemented by Toyota in the early 1960s. What emerged was an integrated approach to managing production which brought together a number of techniques, including JIT.

In 1982, Schonberger[18] listed the 14 concepts associated with a streamlined and focused approach to production, including such elements as quality at the source, automation and robotics, minimised set-up time, quality circles, and just-in-time production. Information technology systems, particularly those which are capable of interfacing with supplier's IT systems, have made the contemporary development and use of JIT feasible.

It is important to understand that JIT manufacturing systems are driven by the principle of being "demand-pulled" through the production process, i.e. production activities are governed (or "pulled") by downstream processes requiring subassemblies from upstream processes. This the reverse of more traditional production systems where the flow is "pushed" through the production chain. Smaller production batches will usually apply in JIT systems and this more readily facilitates other related aspects of the method to be accommodated. For example, the concurrent employee responsibility for ensuring that the required quality criteria are met at the conclusion of each discrete production stage, rather than relying on the more traditional quality control inspection after the final production stage has been completed and when it is more difficult to pinpoint the source of any quality problem. In tandem with the allocation of responsibility for quality matters, employees can also halt the production process if a defect or problem is discovered, thus permitting the (hopefully) prompt resolution of the problem. This approach is referred to as "quality at the source" and is based on the Japanese concept of *Jikoda* which translates to "stop everything when something goes wrong". The aims here are to minimise defects as an important contribution to quality and to coincidently empower employees to identify and solve them.

Co-ordination of the JIT process is clearly critical and this is influenced, in turn, by effective communication along the production chain. A simple system of cards called *Kanbans* is normally used to send signals between production workers. The *Kanban* cards are used to instruct workers either to obtain the parts required for their stage of the process (i.e. using the so-called "move" cards) or to actually produce a number of parts (i.e. utilising the so called "production" cards). Both types of card are attached to (and associated with) standardised containers which physically flow through the production processes, "pulled" by the downstream demands.

So far, we have primarily looked at JIT from a theoretical or concept viewpoint. We should hasten to point out that information technology usually has a vital role to play in the technique, especially in respect of the provision of up-to-date and accurate information about the current state of the production process. Data about the units of production and their progress is not only held on the physical *Kanban* cards but tracked using IT systems which can provide timely interactions with inventory records, accounting systems, planning processes, and so on.

The JIT concept can apply beyond the in-house world of production and have links to suppliers, in which case it is normally referred to as just-in-time-purchasing (JITP). The principal aims of JITP are to reduce and contain stock-holding levels, improve the quality of parts and to minimise all the associated costs (i.e. of storage facilities). JITP has implications for the selection of suitable suppliers who can meet all the demands of the system of supply. Suppliers participating in JITP schemes, will have to become more flexible to enable the call-off of smaller delivery quantities on a swift turnround basis.

Figure 17.1 features a simple example to illustrate the primary advantages and disadvantages of a JIT relationship with a supplier.

An example of JITP

An automobile manufacturer will design deliveries from suppliers so that the correct number and type of components needed for perhaps only today's production arrive just in time and in the right sequence from the component suppliers.

By doing this, the automobile manufacturer achieves the following:

- inventory space and carrying costs are minimised
- in-house inventory management is simplified (for instance, a search for a missing component is a search through a smaller inventory of parts)
- some risks are transferred to suppliers (such as risk of damage to components while in storage, etc.)
- suppliers become more "locked in" to the automobile manufacturer's business
- changes in production schedules and product mix may become easier to make
- there is less risk of redundant, surplus or obsolete stock of components
- less working capital is needed as less is invested in inventory
- JIT contributes to making the business less complex and easier to change (in a similar way to outsourcing)

But the automobile manufacturer risks:

- assembly line stoppages through late arrival of components
- production losses due to industrial disputes at component suppliers or their distributors
- higher component costs to compensate suppliers for their carrying costs.

Figure 17.1 Examples of the advantages and disadvantages associated with a JIT approach to procuring supplies

Applying new techniques, such as JIT, will require that staff and managers adopt a more flexible attitude to their thinking about the processes under review. They may have to reposition their existing concept of the situation and embrace alternative viewpoints so that the revision will be successful. The successful adoption of such philosophies presupposes that the in-house culture is tuned to the same harmonious frequency, where the employees' contributions are also seen as coincidently contributing to their motivation, fulfilment and self-esteem. If so, the organisation can potentially benefit from a more committed and creative workforce. One manifestation of this enlightened attitude is the concept of *bottom-round management*, which is typified by a consensus management stance supported by the participation of workers in the discussion and resolution of problems, which may have been historically viewed as the sole concern of management.

Implications for Internal Auditors

The following are implications of JIT management for internal auditors:

- Auditors must have a suitable understanding of the associated techniques in order that their reviews are both effective and credible. The inclusion of internal auditors in the development of manufacturing systems will go towards helping address this potential shortcoming, but only if the organisation is at the stage of introducing new or revised methods, thus offering the audit function the opportunity of early involvement.
- Auditors should be aware of the cultural implications for the organisation of introducing and using production management methods such as JIT. Unless both management and workforce are adequately prepared to adopt a more contributive and collaborative approach, the successful implementation of such methods can be jeopardised.
- There may be broader control implications associated with the devolution of responsibilities to employees. Unless the wider (environmental) levels of controls are effective, they may easily be overridden (or ignored) by employees empowered to act within the confines of collective initiative (as typified by the concept of bottom-rounded management).
- Consider the cost-accounting implications of a JIT or JITP system. For example, with the emphasis placed on minimising waste and avoiding activities that do not add value, how does management accurately identify the associated costs as the basis for taking appropriate corrective action?
- Auditors will need to co-ordinate their approach to operational reviews of JIT systems so as to take into account such diverse aspects as product planning, cost accounting, process design, related information flows, quality issues, and relationships with suppliers.
- The use of JIT manufacturing systems leads to a reduction in paperwork and this can present problems for auditors when tracking processes along a production chain unless there are compensating points of reference (for example, the use of bar-codes to facilitate the recording of the flow of products, sub-assemblies, etc.). The contrary situation can apply in JITP systems, in that more frequent and smaller order quantities are common and can generate more transaction paperwork to flow between the organisation and the supplier. Electronic data interchange (EDI) between business partners may be used to reduce physical paperwork and speed up the flow of relevant data (see Chapter 13).
- Increased use of automation throughout the production chain theoretically supplants the need for more traditional forms of control. Auditors will,

however, need to ensure that automated processes take due account of any control implications.

NOTES

1. Towers, S. (1994) *Business Process Re-engineering—A Practical Handbook for Executives.* Stanley Thornes, Cheltenham.
2. Department of Trade and Industry, UK (May 1990).
3. British Standard 4778 (Draft) (1990).
4. Total Quality Management: The Implications for Internal Audit Departments, *Professional Briefing Note No. 1*, Institute of Internal Auditors—UK (1992)
5. British Standard 5750 series; ISO Standard 9000 series; both now known in the UK as the ISO/BSEN 9000 series.
6. IIA—UK (1992) *op. cit.*
7. Fayol, H. ([1916] 1949) *General and Industrial Management.* Trs. Constance Storrs. Pitman, London. First published in France as *Administration Industrielle et Générale.*
   Henri Fayol was born in France in 1841 and graduated, aged 19, as a mining engineer to be appointed engineer of the Commentry pits of the Commentry-Fourchambault, from which he retired as managing director in 1918. In his retirement he propounded his Theory of Administration.
8. Herzberg, F. et al. (1959) *The Motivation to Work* (2nd edn). Harper & Row, London.
9. Maslow, A. (1954) *Motivation and Personality.* Harper & Row, London.
10. Committee of Sponsoring Organisations of the Treadway Commission (COSO) (September 1992). *Internal Control—Integrated Framework*, Executive Summary, p. 3. AICPA, New York.
11. Institute of Chartered Accountants (December 1994). *Internal Control and Financial Reporting*, p. 6. ICAEW, London.
12. Attributed to Lawrence B. Sawyer.
13. See, for example, Burns, T. and Stalker, G. M. (1961). *The Management of Innovation.* Tavistock Press, London.
14. The Cadbury Report (December 1992) *Report of the Committee on the Financial Aspects of Corporate Governance.* Gee, London.
15. Institute of Internal Auditors: General Standard 100.
16. Beasley, K. (1994) *Self Assessment—A Tool for Integrated Management.* Stanley Thornes, Cheltenham.
17. Frederick Taylor (1856–1915) was an American engineer who worked for the Midvale Steelworks in Philadelphia. He introduced time-and-motion study to improve output and management. In 1893 he became an independent consultant in what he termed "scientific management". His publications include *Shop Management* (1903) and *The Principles of Scientific Management* (1911).
18. Schonberger, R. J. (1982). *Japanese Manufacturing Techniques—Nine Hidden Lessons in Simplicity.* Free Press, New York.

Appendix 1
Useful Contacts

British-American Chamber of Commerce, 19 Stratford Place, London W1N 9AF. Telephone 0171 491 3361

British Standards Institute (BSI), 389 Chiswick High Road, London, W4 4AL.

Chartered Association of Certified Accountants (ACCA), 29 Lincoln's Inn Fields, London WC2A 3EE. Telephone 0171 242 6855.

Chartered Institute of Management Accountants (CIMA), 63 Portland Place, London W1N 4AB. Telephone 0171 917 9244

Chartered Institute of Public Finance and Accountancy (CIPFA), 3 Robert Street, London WC2N 6BH. Telephone 0171 895 8823.

Chartered Institute of Purchasing and Supply, Easton House, Easton on the Hill, Stamford, PE9 3NZ. Telephone 01780 56777.

Confederation of British Industry, Centre Point, 103 New Oxford Street, London WC1A 1DU. Telephone 0171 379 7400. Fax 0171 240 1578.

Data Protection Registrar, Wycliffe House, Water Lane, Wilmslow, Cheshire, SK9 5AF. Telephone 01625 545700. Fax 01625 524510.

Department of Trade and Industry. Telephone 0171 215 5000

Eco-Management & Audit Scheme (EMAS), Department of the Environment, Room C11/09, 2 Marsham Street, London, SW1P 3EB. Telephone 0171 276 378.

Groundwork National Office, 85–87 Cornwall Street, Birmingham, B3 3BY. Telephone 0121 236 8565. E-mail: info@groundwork.org.uk. [This is a national network of environmental businesses aiming to regenerate degraded environments.]

Health and Safety Executive (HSE), Informaion Centre, Broad Lane, Sheffield S3 7HQ. Infoline: Telephone 0541 545500. Fax 0114 289 2333. HSE Books: telephone 01787 881165.

HMSO Publications Centre, 51 Nine Elms Lane, London, SW8 5DR. Telephone (enquiries) 0171 873 0011; (orders) 0171 873 9090.

Institute of Chartered Accountants in England and Wales (ICAEW), PO Box 433, Chartered Accountants' Hall, Moorgate Place, London EC2P 2BJ. Telephone 0171 920 8100. Fax: 0171 920 0547.

Institute of Chartered Accountants in Ireland (ICAI), 87/89 Pembroke Road, Ballsbridge, Dublin, Irish Republic. Telephone 01 668 0400. Fax 01 668 5685.

Institute of Chartered Accountants of Scotland (ICAS), 27 Queen Street, Edinburgh EH2 1LA. Telephone 0131 225 5673. Fax 0131 225 3813.

Institute of Directors, 116 Pall Mall, London SW1Y 5ED. Telephone 0171 839 1233. Fax 0171 930 1949.

Institute of Internal Auditors—UK (IIA), 13 Abbeyville Mews, 88 Clapham Park Road, London SW4 7BX. Telephone 0171 498 0101. Fax 0171 978 2942.

Institute of Internal Auditors Inc. (IIA), 249 Maitland Avenue, Altamonte Springs, FL 32701-4201, Florida, USA. Telephone (001) 407 830 7600. Fax (001) 407 831 5171.

Institute of Personnel and Development, IPD House, 35 Camp Road, London SW19 4UX. Telephone 0181 971 9000. Fax 0181 263 3333.

International Chamber of Commerce (ICC), 14–15 Belgrave Square, London SW1X 8PG. Telephone 0171 823 2811. Fax 0171 235 5447.

Management Audit Ltd, The Water Mill, Moat Lane, Old Bolingbroke, Spilsby, Lincolnshire, PE23 4EU. Telephone 01790 763350. Fax 01790 763253. E-mail: 100713.2663@compuserve.com.

Appendix 2
Relevant Standards, Guidelines, Directives, etc.

BRITISH/ISO STANDARDS[1]

BS5750 *Quality Systems*
BS7750 *Specification for Environmental Management Systems* (1992)
BS7799 *Code of Practice for Information Security Management* (1995)
ISO14001 *Environmental Management Systems—Specification with Guidance for Use*
ISO14004 *Environmental Management Systems—General Guidelines on Principles, Systems and Supporting Techniques*

INTERNAL AUDITING STANDARDS (AND PROFESSIONAL GUIDANCE MATERIALS)[2]

Standards and Guidelines for the Professional Practice of Internal Auditing (1994).
Professional Briefing Notes (selected titles as below with publication dates).

No. 1 *Total Quality Management—The implications for internal audit departments* (1992)
No. 2 *Environmental Audit* (1993)
No. 3 *Contracting Out, Market Testing and Outsourcing* (1993)
No. 6 *Internal Control* (1994)
No. 7 *Control Self Assessment and Internal Audit* (1995)
No. 8 *Reporting on Internal Control* (1995)

EU DIRECTIVES AND REGULATIONS[3]

L13 Volume 20 Directives 77/62/EEC (21 December 1976) co-ordinating procedures for the award of public supply contracts, and *77/63/EEC* (21 December 1976) amending *Directive 71/306/EEC* setting up an Advisory Committee for Public Contracts.
L127 Volume 31 Directive 88/295/EEC (22 March 1988) amending *Directive 77/62/EEC* relating to the co-ordination of procedures on the award of public supply contracts and repealing certain provisions of *Directive 80/767/EEC*.
L168 Volume 36 Council Regulation 1836/93 (29 June 1993) allowing voluntary participation by companies in the industrial sector in a Community eco-management and audit scheme.

L209 Volume 35 Directive 92/50/EEC (18 June 1992) relating to the co-ordination of procedures for the award of public service contracts.

L210 Volume 32 Directive 89/440/EEC (18 July 1989) concerning co-ordination of procedures for the award of public works contracts.

L215 Volume 23 Directive 80/767/EEC (22 July 1980) adapting and supplementing in respect of certain contracting authorities *Directive 77/62/EEC* co-ordinating procedures for the award of public supply contracts.

L297 Volume 33 Directive 90/531/EEC (17 September 1990) on the procurement procedures of entities operating in the water, energy, transport and telecommunications sectors.

NOTES

1. Available from BSI—see Appendix 1 for address.
2. Available from the Institute of Internal Auditors—UK—see Appendix 1 for address.
3. Available from HMSO—see Appendix 1 for address.

Appendix 3
Abbreviations

Noted below are selected abbreviations and terms used both throughout this book and generally in operational auditing, IT auditing and business contexts.

AICPA	American Institute of Certified Public Accountants
ASCII	American Standard Code for Information Interchange
ASQS	American Society of Quality Control
AVC	additional voluntary contributions
BACS	Bankers Automated Clearing Services (Ltd)
BATNEEC	best available techniques not entailing excessive costs
BCS	British Computer Society
BPEO	best practicable environmental option
BPR	business process re-engineering
BSI	British Standards Institute
CAAT	computer-aided [or assisted] audit techniques
CAD	computer-aided design
CAE	computer-aided engineering
CAM	computer-aided manufacturing
CAPM	capital asset pricing module
CASE	computer-aided [or assisted] software [or systems] engineering
CCAB	Consultative Committee of Accountancy Bodies
CEO	chief executive officer
CIA	chief internal auditor
CIM	computer-integrated manufacturing
CIMA	Chartered Institute of Management Accountants
CIPFA	Chartered Institute of Public Finance and Accountancy
COSHH	Control of Substances Hazardous to Health [Act 1994]
COSO	Committee of Sponsoring Organisations [of the Treadway Commission]
CPM	critical path method
CPU	central processing unit
CRSA	control risk self-assessment
CSA	control self-assessment
DBMS	database management system
DCF	discounted cash flow
DD	data dictionary
DDP	distributed data processing
DES	Data Encryption Standard (National Bureau of Standards, USA)
DoE	Department of the Environment
DOS	Disk Operating System

DP	data processing
DPA	Data Protection Act [1984]
DTI	Department of Trade and Industry
DTP	desktop publishing
EC	European Community [became European Union on 1 November 1993]
EDI	electronic data interchange
EDIA	Electronic Data Interchange Association
EDICON	electronic data interchange in construction
EDIFACT	electronic data interchange for administration, commerce and trade
EDP	electronic data processing
EDPAA	EDP Auditors Association
EFT	electronic funds transfer
EFTPOS	electronic funds transfer at point of sale
EMAS	Eco-Management and Audit Scheme
EU	European Union [from 1 November 1993; prior to this it was known as the European Community]
FD	finance [or financial] director
FIFO	first in first out
FM	facilities management
FMS	flexible manufacturing systems
GB	gigabyte
GII	global information infrastructure
HMSO	Her Majesty's Stationery Office
HRD	human resources department
HRM	human resource management
IAD	internal audit department
IASC	International Accounting Standards Committee
ICAEW	Institute of Chartered Accountants in England and Wales
ICAI	Institute of Chartered Accountants in Ireland
ICAS	Institute of Chartered Accountants of Scotland
ICC	International Chamber of Commerce
ICQ	internal control questionnaire
ICSA	Institute of Chartered Secretaries and Administrators
IFIP	International Federation for Information Processing
IIA	Institute of Internal Auditors
IPC	integrated pollution control
IPD	Institute of Personnel and Development
IPM	Institute of Personnel Management [now IPD—Institute of Personnel and Development]
IPSE	integrated project support environment
ISDN	integrated services digital network
ISO	International Standards Organisation
IT	information technology
JCL	job control language
JIT	just-in-time [management]
JITP	just-in-time purchasing
KB	kilobyte
LAN	local area network
LIFO	last in first out
MAN	metropolitan area network
MBO	management by objectives

MD	managing director
MIPS	millions of instructions per second
MIS	management information system
MPCS	manufacturing planning and control systems
MPS	master production schedule
MOD	Ministry of Defence
MRP	material requirements planning
MS-DOS	Microsoft Disk Operating System
NCC	National Computing Centre
NII	national information infrastructure
NPV	net present value
O & M	organisation and methods
OA	office automation
OCR	optical character recognition
PC	personal computer
PDN	public data network
PIN	personal identification number
PRP	profit related pay
PSS	packet switchstream
PSTN	public switched telephone network
PV	present value
QA	quality assurance
QBE	query by example
QM	quality management
R&D	research and development
RACF	resource access control facility
RJE	remote job entry
ROCE	return on capital employed
SAP	self-assessment programmes
SAPG	Standard Audit Programme Guide
SCL	system control language
SCM	supply chain management
SCEEMAS	Small Company Environmental and Energy Management Assistance Scheme
SIAS	Statement on Internal Auditing Standards
SSADM	structured systems analysis and design method
TQM	total quality management
UPS	uninterruptable power supply
VADS	value-added and data services
VAN	value-added network
VAT	value-added tax
VFM	value for money
WAN	wide area network
ZBB	zero-based budgeting

Appendix 4
Internal Control—
A Guide for Management
and Staff (Long Version)

This is the longer version of the Guide. The shorter version is given as Appendix 5. In its longer form it is more suitable for use as reference by those who need to develop similar guides for their organisations. In its shorter form it is more suitable for issue to management and staff. The key control issues are identical in both versions and are repeated in the interests of completeness in each case.

1. WHY INTERNAL CONTROL?

Fraud is definitely on the increase and it involves people right at the top. They do it because of greed and the lack of proper controls. It's extraordinary how large companies don't have even the most basic controls to prevent it.[1]

- Four out of five organisations in the UK suffered a breakdown in their IT systems during 1992/93, at an annual cost of £1.2 bn and increasing. A quarter of the incidents led to serious losses. Fire is the threat most feared, but viruses, power failures and computer failures are more common.[2]
- In September 1995 the operations of Age Concern, the UK's leading charity for the elderly, ground to a halt following the theft of computer chips worth £100 000 from 150 PCs.[3]
- In the weeks before its collapse on 24 February 1995 after 233 years as the UK's oldest merchant bank, Barings transferred from London to Singapore £800 m—outstripping its entire consolidated capital of £540 m. This was to cover margin calls on open futures and options trading positions largely taken by employee Nick Leeson. When he joined Barings, he had two outstanding County Court judgments against him totalling £3000. Because of his record, Barings had failed to get Leeson a trading licence in the UK, but they had not disclosed his record to the Singaporean authorities. An ignored internal audit report in August 1994 had concluded that there was "a significant general risk that the controls could be over-ridden by Nick Leeson as he is the key manager in the front and the back office". The internal audit report recommended that he should be stripped "immediately" of specific managerial functions—including supervision of the back office team. Leeson was not only trading but was supervising the trading function (i.e. the "front room") as well. In addition he supervised the "back room" where the

accounting for and settlement of trades was done. So he was able to conceal the true impact of his conduct and build up an enviable but unwarranted trading reputation within Barings and outside it. For 1994 he had been in line for a bonus of £450 000 (£100 000 bonus for 1993) as he had been able to declare a $50 m profit for Barings' trading operations, but this concealed a $80 m deficit held in an "error account" unknown to the Barings directors. This deficit was to grow—£386 m was added to it on the day that Leeson fled. In December 1995 it was being alleged that shortly after the bank's collapse key documents had been shredded and records of telephone conversations between London and Singapore had been removed—possibly in breach of City rules.[4] The report of the Bank of England's Board of Banking Supervision had this to say:

> A material failure in the management, financial and operating controls of Barings enabled massive unauthorised positions on exchanges to be established without detection . . . until it was too late to save Barings . . .

> Our conclusions, in summary, are:

> (a)   the losses were incurred by reason of unauthorised and concealed trading activities within BFS;
> (b)   the true position was not noticed earlier by reason of a serious failure of controls and managerial confusion within Barings;
> (c)   the true position had not been detected prior to the collapse by the external auditors, supervisors or regulators of Barings.[5]

- On 26 September 1995, criminal complaints were filed against a rogue trader, Mr Iguchi, for running up £700 m losses over 11 years in the New York trading arm of Daiwa Bank (Japan's tenth biggest commercial bank), through unauthorised trading of American Treasury bonds and falsification of the bank's books and records to conceal the losses. Mr Iguchi had been in charge of front and back office operations.[6]

The achievement of business objectives is risked by unwanted events—such as fraud. At least half of large companies are victims of fraud more than once a year, and in over 70% of cases an employee is involved.[7] Fraud is only one example of avoidable loss due to an inadequate system of internal control, or a failure to comply with it. Other avoidable losses due to internal control breakdown may be at least as damaging: they include accidental errors or omissions, malicious damage and so-called "acts of God" such as fire or flood.

Yet internal control is not just negative: it is not designed and followed just to prevent these sorts of unwanted consequences from occurring. No business achieves its objectives merely by avoiding unwanted outcomes. Even more importantly, internal control, properly designed and observed, provides reasonable assurance of the achievement of the objectives and plans of the business. It provides *reasonable assurance*, not an *absolute guarantee* of the achievement of objectives, as a business may be thrown off course by external events. But we can be sure that without effective internal control no enterprise is likely to achieve its objectives. So effective internal control is a key responsibility of management and staff at all levels.

Looked at in this light, internal control should not be regarded as a costly overhead. It will be too costly *not* to have control.

2. WHAT IS INTERNAL CONTROL?

External control is control by the stakeholders over the board and management. In essence, *internal control* is control by management of what happens within the business. It is the same thing as *management control*.

The standard definition of internal control is now:

Internal control is broadly defined as a process, effected by the entity's board of directors, management and other personnel, designed to provide reasonable assurance regarding the achievement of objectives in the following categories:

- Effectiveness and efficiency of operations.
- Reliability of financial reporting.
- Compliance with applicable laws and regulations."[8]

Within this definition, "effectiveness and efficiency of operations" includes the safeguarding of assets, that is:

. . . the prevention or timely detection of unauthorised acquisition, use or disposition of the entity's assets . . ."[9]

The "reliability of financial reporting" should be interpreted as relating both to "financial information used within the business" and that "for publication."[10]

Internal control is much more than internal check. Internal check can best be understood as being internal cross check, which is certainly an important element of most effective systems of internal control. The system of internal control is the totality of methods and measures that management has introduced to provide reasonable assurance of the achievement of objectives and the avoidance of unwanted outcomes. As such, internal control is the essence of good management. The classic view of management is that it comprises effective planning, organising, staffing, directing and controlling. Each of these must be done well if there is to be effective internal control.[11]

There are many ways of classifying internal control into types. One is to distinguish between (a) *preventive controls*, designed to avoid the non-achievement of objectives or to avoid the occurrence of unwanted outcomes, and (b) *detective controls*,[12] to inform management and others when things have gone wrong. Of course, detective controls are best when they are prompt—and the more prompt they are, the harder it is to distinguish between them and preventative controls.

3. PRACTICAL ADVICE ON INTERNAL CONTROL

Internal control should assist and never impede management and staff from achieving their objectives. It follows that management's objectives need to be clearly understood when an internal control framework is established or modified. There is no such thing as 100% effective control. There comes a point when the allocation of additional resources to improve control would have inadequate marginal benefit. Where that point is becomes a matter of management judgement in the light of:

- the importance of the objectives, and the degree of risk of not achieving them
- the seriousness of the potential exposures, and the degree of risk of them occurring
- the cost, if any, of additional control measures.

So control must be cost-effective—tailored to a *realistic* assessment of need and should be appropriate for the purpose. For instance, some assets are more liquid, or more portable, than other assets and therefore need to be controlled appropriately.

Control will be more cost-effective and acceptable if, wherever possible:

- complex control procedures are rejected in favour of simple ones which have the same control effect

- redundant controls[13] are jettisoned. Resist the temptation of continuing with a procedure which has outlived any constructive purpose
- compensating controls[14] are identified and eliminated where practical
- where control depends upon a check (for instance, to deter invalid claims), that this check is made on an adequate sample of transactions only (say 10% or 20%).

Internal control measures are not necessarily costly: much can be arranged to be done in a well-controlled way with no additional use of resources. For instance, dividing work between two members of staff, who thus act as an automatic cross-check on each other, will not necessarily cost anything while reducing the likelihood of additional investment to, if possible, rectify a situation that has become out of control.

Where there is choice, it is preferable to place control as early as possible within the system. Until control has been established there is a greater possibility of error or loss (accidental or deliberate) and that it may be undetected. For instance, control should be established over incoming cash as soon after it enters the enterprise as possible: once control over cash has been established it is less likely that cash will be diverted or that incorrect handling of cash will remain undetected and uncorrected on a timely basis.

Where control depends on a comparison or reconciliation of figures it is preferable to arrange things so that the generation of the figures which need to be compared is the responsibility of different people, and that the reconciliation is performed or supervised by someone who is both competent and independent of the generation of any of the figures which are to be reconciled.

Where control depends on supervision it is important that this is taken seriously and that the work of subordinates is not left to trust. Delegation is an important and valid management approach, but it is not *abdication*. Authority is delegated but responsibility is never delegated. Of course, those to whom authority has been delegated (to perform particular tasks and to make particular decisions) assume their own responsibilities for their performance. But the delegator retains overall, undiminished responsibility and must place him or herself in the position to know that this responsibility is being discharged properly by those to whom authority has been delegated.

Control must be taken seriously. A well-designed system of internal control is worse than worthless unless it is complied with, since the semblance of control will be likely to convey a false sense of assurance. Controls are there to be kept, not avoided. For instance, exception reports should be followed up. Senior management should set a good example with regard to control compliance. For instance, physical access restrictions to secure areas should be observed equally by senior management as by junior personnel.

While control serves a much broader purpose than the prevention and detection of fraud, this is nevertheless one aspect which is important. You should not assume that a well-designed system of internal control deals with the risk of fraud. Fraud often involves the circumvention or violation of controls through deception, collusion[15] and/or concealment. The best control systems are often vulnerable to breakdown if there is collusion. So, beyond the formal control procedures, management and staff should be encouraged to watch out for tell-tale signs[16] (of both fraud and error) and to follow up accordingly.

Broadly, a 25%–50%–25% rule applies to staff. Perhaps 25% will be honest in all circumstances whatever the temptation; 25% may be dishonest whenever the circumstances permit it; and the 50% in the middle are easily swayed one way or the other. Few will be able to resist the temptation to perpetrate fraud if most of these ingredients are present:

- They have a financial problem which is perceived as being unsharable.
- There is the opportunity.
- There is thought to be very little risk of detection.
- The consequences upon detection are thought to be very modest.

We should take a lot of trouble to recruit trustworthy staff. But thereafter, wherever possible we should not trust them—in the sense that our systems of internal control should be designed and operated so as to confirm that our staff are working in a trustworthy way. This is in the interests of the staff themselves—otherwise the finger of suspicion is likely to start pointing at them and they will be unable to exonerate themselves. A good system of internal control reduces the opportunity for fraud and makes detection more likely. It has been said that the best form of prevention (of fraud) is detection; but it is important that firm action is known to follow detection so that it acts as a deterrent.

4. KEY CONTROLS WHICH SHOULD BE IN PLACE

It is now accepted internationally that there are five necessary components of a system of internal control[17]:

Control environment:

- Commitment to competence and integrity (leadership by example, employment criteria etc).
- Communication of ethical values and control consciousness (codes of conduct, performance appraisal, etc.).
- Appropriate organisational structure.
- Appropriate delegation of authority with accountability.

Risk assessment[18] *:*

- Identification of key business risks in a timely manner.
- Consideration of the likelihood of risks crystallising and their likely impact.
- Prioritising allocation of resources for control.

Control activities[19]*:*

- Procedures to ensure completeness and accuracy of transactions, accounting, data processing and information reports.
- Appropriate authorisation limits.
- Controls to limit exposure to loss of assets or to fraud (e.g. physical controls, segregation of duties etc.).
- Procedures to ensure compliance with laws and regulations.

Information and communication:

- Performance indicators to monitor activities, risks and progress in meeting objectives, and to identify developments which require intervention.
- Systems which provide (and communicate appropriately) relevant, reliable and up-to-date information—both internal and external.

Monitoring[20]*:*

- A monitoring process which provides reasonable assurance to the board and to senior management that there are appropriate control procedures in place, which are being followed.
- Identification of change in the business and its environment which may require modification of the system of internal control.

- Formal procedures for reporting weaknesses and for ensuring appropriate corrective action.

More specifically, Figure A4.1 is a checklist of some of key control issues likely to be relevant in most contexts.

		Yes	No
1.	Is there shared responsibility for all important parts of the accounting system—so that absolute and independent control by any one person is avoided?		
2.	Have you avoided giving any one person custody or control of (a) assets (such as cash or stock), or (b) operations (such as purchasing)—where that person *also* has involvement in accounting for those assets or operations?		
.1	If this is unavoidable, is there frequent, independent review of the accounting records?		
3.	Is authorisation of (a) the acquisition, use or disposal of an asset, or (b) the initiation of any operation or programme—segregated from those who have custodial or operational responsibilities for these matters?		
4.	Do two people always work together when handling significant quantities of cash and other attractive assets?		
5.	Where control depends upon a reconciliation of accounting and other data, is it always conducted by someone independent of the generation of any of the data being reconciled?		
6.	Have you avoided situations where a single person or department inappropriately is allowed to handle all or several phases of a transaction or operation?		
7.	Wherever possible is the work of one employee complementary to (i.e. serves as a check upon) that of another so that a continuous audit is made of the details of the business?		
8.	Do staff who have been assigned to segregated duties also use adequately segregated office facilities (such as office, telephone, filing cabinet, E-mail)?		
9.	Do you successfully avoid staff standing in for other staff when their respective duties are meant to be segregated for control purposes?		
10.	Are authorisation limits and methods of authorisation (sole, dual, by committee, etc.) appropriate to the risks involved in every case?		
.1	Is "third level" authorisation applied where risks of collusion are greatest?		
.2	Is "after the event" authorisation applied where prior authorisation may not be effective?[21]		
11.	Is full use made of the potential of exception reports, and are these reports followed up?		
12.	Are physical security controls applied wherever necessary and are they satisfactory in the light of the risks involved?		
13.	Do personnel controls maximise the opportunities for recruiting and retaining trustworthy staff?		
.1	Are procedures upon dismissal adequate to minimise the security risks associated with terminated staff?		

		Yes	No
14.	Are all managers capable of supervising effectively the number of staff for which they are directly responsible?		
.1	Is the supervision of contractors, suppliers etc. similarly effective?		
15.	Are adequate records created and retained in accessible form for a sufficient period of time?		
16.	Is all information necessary for management control available promptly (e.g. no later than one-third of the way through the next period so that timely corrective action is possible)?		
17.	Is there satisfactory control over who can add, delete, amend and interrogate computer-based corporate data?		
18.	Where appropriate, as a last resort to achieve satisfactory internal control, is certain knowledge segregated on a need to know basis?		
19.	Are there effective procedures to ensure the validity of payments?		
20.	Is there effective physical and accounting control over returns from customers, and over the payment of refunds?		
21.	Is there effective custody and control (including accurate accounting for) all promotional vouchers (and other "accountable documents" with potential value)?		
22.	Is the control over non-standard transactions effective?		
23.	Are all staff required to take their holidays?		
.1	Do all staff take at least one holiday of at least two weeks' duration each year?		
.2	Are duties re-assigned to other staff when staff are on holiday?		
24.	Is excessive dependence upon key members of staff avoided?		
.1	In every case are there substitute staff ready to step in promptly to perform competently the duties of staff who become unavailable?		
25.	Are duties rotated where appropriate?		
26.	Is original documentation (such as expenses vouchers) required to support claims—to avoid the risk of multiple presentation?		
27.	Is all documentation stamped appropriately—e.g. with "Date Received" or with a cancellation stamp?		
28.	Are there adequate arrangements to protect corporate data and data processing?		
.1	Where appropriate are they tested?		
29.	Are there effective arrangements to ensure business continuity?		
.1	Where appropriate, are they tested?		
30.	Are all important procedures fully documented?		
.1	Are the procedures known to those who apply them?		
.2	Is the documentation of procedures kept up to date?		
31.	Is there an effective internal audit with unrestricted scope and unrestricted rights of access?		

Figure A4.1 Key control issues

5. CONTROL SELF-ASSESSMENT

Many contemporary management approaches[22] may place effective internal control at risk. For instance, delayering broadens the span of supervisory control of remaining management layers and empowers staff to make more decisions on their own authority. Replacing hierarchical management by project-based management may have the effect of increasing individual authority and weakening reporting.

A necessary part of any process of business re-engineering is to preserve the essential internal control framework which is at risk both during the process of re-engineering (when the attention of staff to internal control matters may be diverted) and after processes have been re-engineered (when essential controls may have been superseded inadvertently).

In an environment of empowered staff it is appropriate that management and staff should assume more responsibility for identifying risks and improving internal control. An annual, formal process of control risk self-assessment by management and staff is called for, especially where delegation of this to internal audit results in only incomplete coverage on an annual basis.

6. INTERNAL CONTROL FOR THE SMALLER OPERATING UNIT

In a small business there is less opportunity to rely on forms of segregation (e.g. of activities and staff) so as to achieve internal control at minimal or no cost. On the other hand, the greater closeness to operations of the small unit's senior management means that they may be more sensitive to control problems as they develop. Where control cannot be achieved by segregation it has to be achieved by supervision. Parts of the supervisory control process may be automated using the computer.

It is the control risk rather than the number of staff employed which should determine the controls that are appropriate even for the operating unit which employs few people—as is illustrated by the collapse of Barings (see Section 1 above) following (a) a lack of segregation of duties, and (b) ill-defined authorisation controls in their small Singapore office.

NOTES

1. Chris Dickson, Assistant Director with the SFO (Serious Fraud Office) quoted in *The Sunday Times*, 4 June 1995.
2. 1995 report co-sponsored by ICL and the National Computing Centre.
3. *Computer Weekly*, 28 September 1995.
4. *The Times*, 22 December 1995, p. 19.
5. *Report of the Board of Banking Supervision Inquiry into the Circumstances of the Collapse of Barings*. London, HMSO, 18 July 1995, pp. 119 and 232.
6. *The Times*, 27 September 1995, p. 1.
7. Mori survey, commissioned by *Security Gazette and Control Risks*, reported in *The Sunday Times*, 4 June 1995.
8. COSO (September 1992) *Internal Control—Integrated Framework*. New York.
9. COSO, *op. cit., Addendum* (May 1994).
10. ICAEW (1994) *Internal Control and Financial Reporting—Guidance for Directors of Listed Companies Registered in the UK*, p. 1.
11. For instance: effective planning involves the design of appropriate procedures, which are essential for effective internal control; an inappropriate organisation structure will weaken internal control; disloyal, incompetent or inadequate staff may contribute to the breakdown of internal control; poor directing may weaken control, and so on.

12. Sometimes called "after the event controls", or "*ex ante* controls".

13. That is, those which at one time, but no longer, served a justifiable purpose.

14. A compensating control is one that serves a control purpose which is also adequately served by another control. Where both of these controls serve no other useful purpose, one of them should be superseded.

15. Collusion may be between:

    - "collateral associates" working on tasks which are intended to be segregated from each other in the interests of control
    - a boss and his or her subordinate(s)
    - a category of staff (such as delivery van drivers in collusion with each other and with customer goods inward personnel).

16. Tell-tale signs of employee fraud might include appearance of being under pressure on the job, unclear explanations for work events, changed attitudes, altered life style, conspicuous expenditure, excessive leave from work which is not satisfactorily explained; failure to take holidays, etc.

17. While COSO (US) calls these "components", Rutteman (UK) calls them "criteria for assessing internal control effectiveness".

18. In the UK, this is called "Identification and evaluation of risks and control objectives" (*Internal Control and Financial Reporting—Guidance for Directors of Listed Companies Registered in the UK*. ICAEW, December 1994).

19. In the UK, this is called "Control procedures" (*Internal Control and Financial Reporting—Guidance for Directors of Listed Companies Registered in the UK*, ICAEW, December 1994).

20. In the UK, this is called "Monitoring and corrective action" (*Internal Control and Financial Reporting—Guidance for Directors of Listed Companies Registered in the UK*, ICAEW, December 1994).

21. For instance, changes to computer-based customer credit limits may require prior authorisation; but additionally it may be helpful for a changed credit limit *not* to be applied by the computer until an appropriate manager has had it displayed on his or her screen and has approved the new value. This acts as an additional safeguard against unauthorised or invalid computer input.

22. For example: downsizing, empowerment, delayering, participative management, business process re-engineering, etc.

Appendix 5
Internal Control—A Guide for Management and Staff (Short Version)

This is the shorter version of the Guide. The longer version is given as Appendix 4. In its shorter form it is more suitable for issue to management and staff. In its longer form it is more suitable for use as reference by those who need to develop similar guides for their organisations. The key control issues are identical in both versions and are repeated in the interests of completeness in each case.

1. WHY INTERNAL CONTROL?

- Four out of five organisations in the UK have suffered a breakdown in their IT systems during 1992/93 at an annual cost of £1.2 bn and increasing. A quarter of the incidents led to serious losses.
- Age Concern, the UK's leading charity for the elderly, ground to a halt after theft of computer chips.
- In February 1995 the UK's oldest merchant bank, Barings, collapsed. When Leeson joined Barings, he had two outstanding County Court judgments against him. Because of this record, Barings had failed to get Leeson a trading licence in the UK, but they had not disclosed his record to the Singaporean authorities. An ignored internal audit report in August 1994 had concluded that there was "a significant general risk that the controls could be over-ridden by Nick Leeson as he is the key manager in the front and the back office". He was also not only trading but was supervising the trading function (i.e. the "front room") as well.
- On 26 September 1995, criminal complaints were filed against a rogue trader, Mr Iguchi, for running up £700 m losses over 11 years in the New York trading arm of Daiwa Bank (Japan's tenth biggest commercial bank), through unauthorised trading of American Treasury bonds and falsification of the bank's books and records to conceal the losses. Mr Iguchi had been in charge of front and back office operations.

At least half of large companies are victims of fraud more than once a year, and in most cases an employee is involved. Fraud is avoidable loss due to an inadequate system of internal control. Other avoidable losses, including accidental errors or omissions, may be even more damaging.

Internal control is not designed just to prevent these sorts of unwanted consequences. Internal control, properly designed and observed, provides *reasonable assurance* of the achievement of objectives—not an *absolute guarantee*, as a business may be thrown off course by external events. Without effective internal control no enterprise is likely to achieve its objectives.

2. WHAT IS INTERNAL CONTROL?

Internal control is control by management of what happens within the business. It is *management control:*

Internal control is broadly defined as a process, effected by the entity's board of directors, management and other personnel, designed to provide reasonable assurance regarding the achievement of objectives in the following categories:

- Effectiveness and efficiency of operations.
- Reliability of financial reporting.
- Compliance with applicable laws and regulations.[1]

"Effectiveness and efficiency of operations" includes the safeguarding of assets, that is the prevention or timely detection of unauthorised acquisition, use or disposition of the entity's assets.

Internal control is much more than internal (cross) check. It is the totality of methods that management has introduced to provide reasonable assurance of the achievement of objectives and the avoidance of unwanted outcomes. As such, internal control is the essence of good management. The classic view of management is that it comprises effective planning, organising, staffing, directing and controlling. Each of these must be done well if there is to be effective internal control.

We can distinguish between (a) *preventive controls*, designed to avoid the non-achievement of objectives or to avoid the occurrence of unwanted outcomes, and (b) *detective controls*, to inform management and others when things have gone wrong.

3. PRACTICAL ADVICE ON INTERNAL CONTROL

Internal control should assist management to achieve its objectives. These objectives must be clear when an internal control framework is established.

There is no such thing as 100% effective control. The allocation of additional resources to improve control may have inadequate marginal benefit. Whether that is so is a matter of management judgement in the light of:

- the importance of the objectives, and the degree of risk of not achieving them
- the seriousness of the potential exposures, and the degree of risk of them occurring
- the cost, if any, of additional control measures.

Control must be cost-effective—tailored to a *realistic* assessment of need and appropriate for the purpose. Control will be more cost-effective if:

- complex controls are rejected in favour of simple ones which have the same control effect

- redundant controls are jettisoned
- compensating controls are rationalised
- checks are performed on samples where appropriate.

Much can be done in a well-controlled way with no additional use of resources. For instance, dividing work between two members of staff will not necessarily be costly.

It is best to place control as early as possible within the system. Until control has been established there is a greater possibility of error or loss which may go undetected.

Where control depends on a reconciliation of figures, the reconciliation should be performed or supervised by someone who is both competent and independent of the generation of any of the figures which are to be reconciled.

Where control depends on supervision it is important that this is taken seriously. Delegation is an important and valid management approach, but it should not be abdication. Authority is delegated but responsibility is not.

A well-designed system of internal control is worse than worthless unless it is complied with, since the semblance of control may lead to a false assurance. Senior management should set a good example with regard to control compliance.

While control serves a much broader purpose than the prevention and detection of fraud, this is nevertheless an important aspect. But fraud often involves the circumvention of controls through deception and/or collusion. Management and staff must be encouraged to watch out for tell-tale signs of both fraud and error.

Broadly, a 25%–50%–25% rule applies: 25% will be honest in all circumstances, 25% dishonest whenever circumstances permit, and 50% are easily swayed. Few will be able to resist the temptation to defraud if: they have an unsharable financial problem, there is opportunity and very little risk of detection, and the consequences on detection would be modest.

We should take a lot of trouble to recruit trustworthy staff. But thereafter systems of internal control should confirm they are working in a trustworthy way. This is in the interests of staff themselves—otherwise the finger of suspicion is likely to start pointing at them. A good system of internal control reduces the opportunity for fraud and makes detection more likely. It has been said that the best form of prevention (of fraud) is detection.

4. KEY CONTROLS WHICH SHOULD BE IN PLACE

There are five necessary components of a system of internal control:

Control environment:

- Commitment to competence and integrity.
- Communication of ethical values and control consciousness.
- Appropriate organisational structure.
- Appropriate delegation of authority with accountability.

Risk assessment:

- Identification of key business risks in a timely manner.
- Consideration of the likelihood of risks crystallising and their likely impact.
- Prioritising allocation of resources for control.

Control activities:

- Procedures to ensure completeness and accuracy of transactions, accounting, data processing and information reports.
- Appropriate authorisation limits.
- Controls to limit exposure to loss of assets or to fraud.
- Procedures to ensure compliance with laws and regulations.

Information and communication:

- Performance indicators to monitor activities, risks and progress in meeting objectives.
- Systems which communicate relevant, reliable and up-to-date information.

Monitoring:

- A monitoring process to give reasonable assurance to the board of appropriate control procedures in place.
- Identification of business change which may require modification of the system of internal control.
- Formal procedures for reporting weaknesses and for ensuring appropriate corrective action.

Figure A5.1 is a checklist of some of key control issues likely to be relevant in most contexts.

5. CONTROL SELF-ASSESSMENT

Contemporary management approaches risk effective internal control. Delayering broadens the span of supervisory control of remaining management layers and empowers staff to make more decisions; replacing hierarchical management by project-based management may have the effect of increasing individual authority and weakening reporting.

Any process of business re-engineering must preserve the essential internal control framework both during the process of re-engineering (when the attention of staff to internal control matters may be diverted) and after processes have been re-engineered (when essential controls may have been superseded inadvertently).

In an environment of empowered staff, both management and staff may assume more responsibility for identifying risks and improving internal control—through a process of control risk self-assessment—especially where delegation of this to internal audit results in only incomplete coverage on an annual basis.

6. INTERNAL CONTROL FOR THE SMALLER OPERATING UNIT

In a small business there is less opportunity to rely on forms of segregation to achieve internal control at minimal or no cost. On the other hand, the closeness to operations of the small unit's senior management means that they may be more sensitive to control problems as they develop. Where control cannot be achieved by segregation it has to be achieved by supervision. Parts of the supervisory control process may be automated using the computer.

It is the control risk rather than the number of staff employed that should determine the controls which are appropriate even for the operating unit employing few people.

		Yes	No
1.	Is there shared responsibility for all important parts of the accounting system—so that absolute and independent control by any one person is avoided?		
2.	Have you avoided giving any one person custody or control of (a) assets (such as cash or stock), or (b) operations (such as purchasing)—where that person *also* has involvement in accounting for those assets or operations?		
.1	If this is unavoidable, is there frequent, independent review of the accounting records?		
3.	Is authorisation of (a) the acquisition, use or disposal of an asset, or (b) the initiation of any operation or programme—segregated from those who have custodial or operational responsibilities for these matters?		
4.	Do two people always work together when handling significant quantities of cash and other attractive assets?		
5.	Where control depends upon a reconciliation of accounting and other data, is it always conducted by someone independent of the generation of any of the data being reconciled?		
6.	Have you avoided situations where a single person or department inappropriately is allowed to handle all or several phases of a transaction or operation?		
7.	Wherever possible is the work of one employee complementary to (i.e. serves as a check upon) that of another so that a continuous audit is made of the details of the business?		
8.	Do staff who have been assigned to segregated duties also use adequately segregated office facilities (such as office, telephone, filing cabinet, E-mail)?		
9.	Do you successfully avoid staff standing in for other staff when their respective duties are meant to be segregated for control purposes?		
10.	Are authorisation limits and methods of authorisation (sole, dual, by committee, etc.) appropriate to the risks involved in every case?		
.1	Is "third level" authorisation applied where risks of collusion are greatest?		
.2	Is "after the event" authorisation applied where prior authorisation may not be effective?[2]		
11.	Is full use made of the potential of exception reports, and are these reports followed up?		
12.	Are physical security controls applied wherever necessary and are they satisfactory in the light of the risks involved?		
13.	Do personnel controls maximise the opportunities for recruiting and retaining trustworthy staff?		
.1	Are procedures upon dismissal adequate to minimise the security risks associated with terminated staff?		

		Yes	No
14.	Are all managers capable of supervising effectively the number of staff for which they are directly responsible?		
.1	Is the supervision of contractors, suppliers etc. similarly effective?		
15.	Are adequate records created and retained in accessible form for a sufficient period of time?		
16.	Is all information necessary for management control available promptly (e.g. no later than one-third of the way through the next period so that timely corrective action is possible)?		
17.	Is there satisfactory control over who can add, delete, amend and interrogate computer-based corporate data?		
18.	Where appropriate, as a last resort to achieve satisfactory internal control, is certain knowledge segregated on a need to know basis?		
19.	Are there effective procedures to ensure the validity of payments?		
20.	Is there effective physical and accounting control over returns from customers, and over the payment of refunds?		
21.	Is there effective custody and control (including accurate accounting for) all promotional vouchers (and other ''accountable documents'' with potential value)?		
22.	Is the control over non-standard transactions effective?		
23.	Are all staff required to take their holidays?		
.1	Do all staff take at least one holiday of at least two weeks' duration each year?		
.2	Are duties re-assigned to other staff when staff are on holiday?		
24.	Is excessive dependence upon key members of staff avoided?		
.1	In every case are there substitute staff ready to step in promptly to perform competently the duties of staff who become unavailable?		
25.	Are duties rotated where appropriate?		
26.	Is original documentation (such as expenses vouchers) required to support claims—to avoid the risk of multiple presentation?		
27.	Is all documentation stamped appropriately—e.g. with ''Date Received'' or with a cancellation stamp?		
28.	Are there adequate arrangements to protect corporate data and data processing?		
.1	Where appropriate are they tested?		
29.	Are there effective arrangements to ensure business continuity?		
.1	Where appropriate, are they tested?		
30.	Are all important procedures fully documented?		
.1	Are the procedures known to those who apply them?		
.2	Is the documentation of procedures kept up to date?		
31.	Is there an effective internal audit with unrestricted scope and unrestricted rights of access?		

Figure A5.1   Key control issues

NOTES

1. COSO (September 1992) Internal Control—Integrated Framework. AICPA, New York.
2. For instance, changes to computer-based customer credit limits may require prior authorisation; but additionally it may be helpful for a changed credit limit *not* to be applied by the computer until an appropriate manager has had it displayed on his or her screen and has approved the new value. This acts as an additional safeguard against unauthorised or invalid computer input.

Appendix 6
Board Policy Statement on Fraud

The XYZ Group will deal with fraud within the framework of its Statement on Business Ethics, and its Security Policy, which require a secure working environment to protect people, capital information and the assets from the risk of deliberate harm, damage or loss.

In particular:

- We require all employees to act honestly and in the best interests of the company at all times, and to ensure that XYZ acts with integrity in its dealings with third parties.
- We will ensure that effective controls and procedures are in place for preventing, detecting and dealing with fraud.
- We will ensure that all employees are aware of their responsibility to report details immediately to their line manager (or next most senior person) if they suspect that a fraud has been committed or see any suspicious acts or events.
- We will ensure that the controller is advised of any significant fraud or attempted fraud.
- We require management to investigate any allegations or evidence of fraud in consultation with the relevant security adviser and internal audit manager.
- We require employees to assist in investigations by making available all relevant information and by co-operating in interviews.
- In appropriate cases, and after proper investigation, we will dismiss without notice employees who are found to be defrauding the company and, where appropriate, press for criminal prosecution and to seek financial recovery through civil proceedings.

All businesses and subsidiaries shall establish, and audit, procedures to ensure that this Policy is fully implemented.

Appendix 7
Example Statement of Corporate Principles

XYZ

XYZ London Limited
150 River Walk
London WC2 3XD

[Chairman's name]
Chairman

[Date]

STATEMENT OF CORPORATE PRINCIPLES

This policy Statement addresses the general principles of our corporate life. Our separate Code of Business Conduct sets out the rules which govern our application of these principles. Our Code of Ethical Conduct applies our policy principles to scientific and environmental issues in particular. You will find some wording in common between the Statement and the two Codes where similar principles and practices are set out.

Copies of these three documents are available to all staff—from regional and country managers, and from divisional and business unit heads. They are also available from Environmental Affairs staff or through Internal Audit locally or at Group level, from whom guidance on interpretation and application may be sought.

XYZ operates responsibly and with integrity, avoiding even the suggestion of impropriety. There should be no risk to our reputation if any details about our affairs became public knowledge. It is our policy to operate worldwide in a manner which protects the environment and the health of our employees and of those in the communities where we have an impact. We conduct our business honestly, scrupulously and free of deception or fraud. We observe applicable laws and regulations. We endeavour to ensure that equivalent standards are followed in companies in which XYZ has an interest but does not have control and also in those businesses with whom XYZ has contractual relationships.

The board of XYZ regards it as the duty of every individual employed by or acting for XYZ to observe the principles set out here. Any individual has a right to raise concerns about apparent breaches of these principles directly with senior management or with the Group Director of Internal Audit.

Conflicts of Interest

XYZ's staff are to avoid any real or apparent conflict between their personal interests and those of XYZ. XYZ's assets and other resources are for use in XYZ's business only.

Business Gifts, Favours and Entertainment

XYZ does not encourage the practice of giving or receiving gifts, even of nominal value. This also applies to gifts etc. made *indirectly* by another on XYZ's behalf. We believe that commercial criteria, rather than the influence of gifts, etc., best serve XYZ's interests. When gifts etc. are made they should be lawful and ethical, necessary and appropriate, of nominal or moderate value, capable of reciprocation, and properly authorised and recorded. They should *not* be interpretable as an improper inducement, nor be extravagant or too frequent.

Confidentiality

XYZ's information is handled with discretion. It is not to be misused nor disclosed so as to place XYZ at a potential or actual commercial disadvantage, or for the benefit of another who is not entitled to receive it. Rights and responsibilities under privacy and other data legislation are to be observed.

Internal Control

XYZ acknowledges its duty to maintain an effective system of internal control which provides reasonable assurance of the achievement of business objectives, of the reliability of information used for reporting, of the safeguarding of resources, and of compliance with laws and regulations.

Operational and Accounting Records

It is company policy (a) that the operational records and accounts of the business are to be reliable, truthful, accurate, complete, up to date and in compliance with prescribed standards and regulations, and (b) that there shall be no falsification. There are to be no secret or unrecorded activities, bank accounts, funds of money or other assets; no liabilities are to go knowingly unrecorded or unprovided for; and there are to be no off-books transactions.

Relationships with Suppliers

The viability of our suppliers is a key concern of XYZ. We set out to observe the terms of purchase orders and contracts—including the payment of suppliers according to agreed payment terms. We give weight to the quality of past service to XYZ while ensuring that transactions are justified on commercial grounds, and while actively considering alternative sources of supply. We avoid excessive dependence upon particular sources of supply when possible.

Political Activities and Contributions

XYZ companies are authorised to make political donations in the countries where they operate in so far as the objective is to facilitate a healthy political process and to the extent that the contributions are lawful and meet our other criteria relating to purpose, amount, transparency and authorisation.

We have an interest in communicating relevant, reliable and responsible information and views on issues of public concern which impact upon our business.

XYZ strives to be a good employer with regard to individual staff who are actively involved in politics as private individuals.

Conduct Towards Employees

XYZ is committed to its employees. We seek to maximise the extent to which employees achieve their personal potential through their work with XYZ. We do this in part through appropriate commercial policies so that employees share in the company's success, and in part through policies which relate to health and safety. We believe in the inalienable right of every person to their personal dignity and do not allow practices which infringe upon this. All XYZ employees have equal opportunity in their employment. Staff are recruited for their relevant aptitudes, skills, experience and ability. Discrimination or harassment on grounds of race, colour, marital status, religion, sex, sexual orientation, ethnic or national origin, or legal political activity is not permitted. Treatment at all times shall be fair in terms of compensation, job security, work experiences, recognition of achievement and opportunities for advancement.

Conduct in the Community, and Charitable Contributions

Our business is dedicated to the well-being of individuals. We have a duty to avoid conduct prejudicial to the communities where we do business and to enhance community life where practical. Our community support is targeted to improve economic or social well-being.

Customer Relations and Product Quality

We strive to ensure that our products and services meet or exceed customer and statutory requirements at economical price; that our product information is reliable, and that we are responsive to customers' enquiries.

Please use your best endeavours to bring this *Statement* to the attention of all personnel and to any with whom we are associated or do business.

[Chairman's photograph]

[Chairman's signature]

Appendix 8
Example Code of Business Conduct

XYZ

XYZ London Limited
150 River Walk
London WC2 3XD

[Chairman's name]
Chairman

[Date]

CODE OF BUSINESS CONDUCT

XYZ is a major multinational corporation whose business partners range from governments and multinationals through to small suppliers, and whose ultimate customers are the many individuals who rely on the quality of our products for their well-being. So it is appropriate that we are seen to operate responsibly and with ethical integrity in our business conduct and in our corporate governance—to a standard which would usually be associated with the major public, listed companies who are so often our competitors—and we should avoid even the suggestion of impropriety. This should be so even when the law is permissive. In principle, there should be no risk to our local or international reputation if any details about our business affairs were to become public knowledge. At all times our business must be conducted honestly and scrupulously, free of deception and fraud.

To these ends, this Code provides detailed guidance on the application to issues of business conduct of the policies outlined in XYZ's Statement of Corporate Principles. A separate Code of Ethical Conduct applies those policies to scientific and environmental issues in particular. You will find some wording in common between the Statement and the two Codes where similar principles and practices are set out.

Copies of the three documents are available at all locations to all staff—from regional and country managers, and from divisional and business unit heads. They are also available from Environmental Affairs staff or through Internal Audit locally or at Group level, from whom guidance on interpretation and application may be sought by staff.

This document has been approved by the Executive Committee and adopted by the Board of XYZ. The Executive Committee reviews annually the Code's appropriateness and effectiveness, and advises the Board accordingly. As part of this review, line managers annually are required to formally monitor their and their staff's performance in observing the requirements of this Code within their areas of responsibility and, where judged appropriate, to develop initiatives to provide reasonable assurance of future compliance.

The board places particular importance on timely actions to be taken whenever necessary to identify, contain and eliminate illegal acts.

A fundamental principle of the way XYZ conducts its business affairs is that applicable laws and regulations are to be scrupulously observed at all times. Practical difficulties may arise in many cases, such as when there are conflicts between the law of different countries, when local business custom and practice is inconsistent with local law or when there is ambiguity as to the legal position. Any case of actual or prospective non-compliance with law should be raised urgently with management and, if material, with the Group Chief Executive.

The XYZ person responsible should endeavour to ensure that equivalent standards to those set out in this Code are followed in companies in which XYZ has an interest but does not have control and also in those businesses with whom XYZ has contractual relationships. Where they are not, the XYZ person responsible should refer the matter upwards within XYZ.

The Board of XYZ regards it as the duty of every individual employed by or acting for XYZ to follow all the requirements of this Code. Any proposed action which appears to be in breach of any requirement of this Code should not be progressed without full disclosure to and prior approval of the Group Chief Executive or as delegated to the Group Financial Controller or the Group Director of Internal Audit. Appropriate behaviour by individuals which is in compliance with this Code and also specifically approved departures from this Code will be supported by the company under the principle of collective responsibility.

Your duty to comply with this Code includes a duty both to yourself and to XYZ to raise any concerns you may have on any matter of business conduct which appears to be a violation of this Code and in which you are actively involved. In addition you have a right to raise similar concerns about the conduct of others even where you are not directly involved. Usually you should first raise a matter of concern with your line manager and you should do so at the earliest opportunity. At your discretion you may raise your concerns directly with senior management, with local internal audit or with the Group Director of Internal Audit and you should do so where an issue remains unresolved to your satisfaction after you have consulted your immediate management about it.

Conflicts of Interest

Directors and employees of XYZ are responsible to avoid any real or apparent conflict between their own personal interests and those of XYZ. This may be at risk with respect to:

- Dealings with suppliers, customers and other parties doing, or seeking to do, business with XYZ.
- Transactions in securities of XYZ or of any company with whom XYZ has or is likely to have a business relationship.
- Acceptance of outside positions whether or not for a fee.

In appropriate circumstances XYZ encourages its directors and staff to be active outside the company.

XYZ's assets and other resources should not be used for any purpose other than for XYZ's business. They are not to be used for personal gain. These resources include but are not limited to staff time, materials, property, plant, equipment, cash, software, trade secrets and confidential information.

In cases of doubt, an employee should discuss the matter with his or her manager.

Business Gifts, Favours and Entertainment

XYZ operates in many host countries of the world with widely differing laws, regulations, customs and business practices. As a multinational XYZ is expected by its host in each case to conform to local societal norms and values whether enshrined in their laws, regulations, customs or business practices. Ethical dilemmas abound and have to be managed in harmony with the requirements of this Code.

By way of illustration these may be some of the dilemmas:

- Inconsistency between different applicable laws within one country.
- Inconsistency between the laws of different countries involved in a transaction.
- Inconsistency between law on the one hand and customs and practice on the other hand.
- An opportunity to achieve a considerable social good (such as by successfully marketing an effective product) but only at an ethical cost (such as by making a facilitating payment).
- The difficulty of distinguishing convincingly between on the one hand *facilitating payments* which may in some circumstances be permissible (to facilitate a legal right which might otherwise be withheld or delayed) and *bribes* which should not be permissible even when legal (to influence a business decision or gain an unfair commercial advantage which is not a right).
- At what level a payment becomes extravagant.

As a general rule XYZ does not encourage the practice of giving or receiving gifts, even those of nominal value. Employees should use their best endeavours to ensure so far as is possible that commercial criteria, rather than the influence of gifts, favours or entertainment, best serve XYZ's business interests and their ongoing maintenance.

In determining whether any given or received business gift, favour and/or entertainment is permissible under this Code each occurrence (and all connected ones taken together) are required to pass all of the following tests unless a requirement is specifically waived by the Group Chief Executive or his or her delegatee. These tests should also be applied equally to gifts etc. made *indirectly* by another party such as by an agent using funds which could be construed as having originated in XYZ.

The tests:

- It could not be interpreted reasonably as an improper inducement.
- It is necessary.
- It would be considered nominal or moderate, and neither extravagant nor too frequent.
- It would be considered appropriate to the business responsibilities of the individual concerned.
- In the case of a gift etc. received, it would be capable of reciprocation as a normal business expense.
- Unless of nominal value, there is appropriate prior specific approval usually of regional management.
- It is properly recorded, whether given or received.

- The Group Financial Controller and the Group Director of Internal Audit have both been made fully aware of it beforehand.
- It is lawful and ethical.

Confidentiality

All of XYZ's employees and contractors have a general duty to ensure that all XYZ's data and information which they encounter is handled with discretion.

XYZ personnel are not permitted to use confidential price-sensitive information or to engage in other ways with competitors or others to fix the market price for products.

XYZ's information (whether technical, commercial, financial, personnel or other) must not be disclosed so as to place XYZ at a potential or actual commercial disadvantage, or for the benefit of another party who is not entitled to receive it.

Employees and contractors must ensure they act so as not to jeopardise (a) the rights of staff and others under privacy legislation and (b) the responsibilities and restrictions which apply to XYZ under data protection and other legislation.

Internal Control

All businesses and projects owned, managed or controlled by XYZ must maintain an adequate system of internal control which is in accordance with XYZ's control policies. Management and staff are responsible to ensure that, within their respective areas of responsibility, necessary arrangements at acceptable cost are in place and are complied with to give reasonable assurance that the objectives of internal control are met. These objectives include:

- the achievement of business objectives efficiently and economically
- the reliability of information used internally and for external reporting
- the safeguarding of corporate resources
- compliance with laws, regulations and policies of the company.

The necessary arrangements comprise proper attention to the following:

- the control environment
- information and communication
- risk analysis
- control activities or procedures
- monitoring.

All incidents involving a breakdown of control leading to any actual or potential losses should be reported upwards immediately to management and to internal audit. For companies in which XYZ has an interest but does not have control, the XYZ person responsible should endeavour to ensure that equivalent standards are applied and should refer the matter upwards within XYZ when they are not.

Operational and Accounting Records

Responsible staff must ensure that all the operational records and books of account of the business represent a reliable, truthful, accurate, complete and up-to-date picture in compliance with prescribed corporate procedures and external standards and regulations;

and that they are suitable to be a basis for informed management decisions. The prompt recording and proper description of operations and of accounting transactions is a duty of responsible staff. Falsification of records and books is strictly prohibited.

No secret or unrecorded bank accounts, funds of money or other assets are to be established or maintained; no liabilities should knowingly go unrecorded or unprovided for; and there should be no off-books transactions.

Relationships with Suppliers

It is as important for XYZ to secure satisfactorily its sources of supply as it is for XYZ to achieve and maintain market penetration. To this end, the viability and well-being of XYZ's suppliers must be a key concern of XYZ's management and staff. Employees have a duty to ensure that XYZ observes the terms of purchase orders and contracts—including the payment of suppliers according to agreed payment terms.

While it is appropriate that due weight be given to the quality of past service to XYZ rendered by a supplier, the placing of an order for goods or services should always be demonstrably defensible on commercial grounds, and as a general principle XYZ's employees should be active in seeking new sources of supply. Excessive dependence upon particular sources of supply should be avoided whenever possible.

Political Activities and Contributions

XYZ recognises that a healthy political climate is, in the long term, an essential attribute of a prosperous and stable society as well as a key ingredient for the long-term success of XYZ whose mission is to improve the quality of life of ordinary people through the responsible application of its expertise. XYZ acknowledges that a healthy political climate depends in part upon adequate funding of the political process, upon there being active participation by many in the political process, and upon open and well-informed debate on societal issues.

XYZ Group companies are authorised to make political donations in the countries where they operate in so far as the objective is to facilitate a healthy political process by contributing to the adequacy of funding, by raising the level of participation or by enhancing the quality of informed debate on issues related to the XYZ business—but only to the extent that such contributions are:

- entirely lawful
- in the public domain
- modest in amount and not disproportionate in size to local conditions and to XYZ's public profile
- not designed to prejudice political or commercial outcomes
- properly recorded in the accounting records
- authorised in advance by the appropriate managing director.

XYZ has an enlightened self-interest in communicating information and views on issues of public concern which have an important impact upon the XYZ business: management should be active in looking for appropriate opportunities to do so. The information and views so communicated must be relevant, reliable and responsible.

XYZ strives to be a good employer with regard to individual staff who are actively involved in politics. Accordingly XYZ management should facilitate and not unnecessarily impede the process when individual XYZ staff exercise their legal rights to become actively involved in local or national politics. In turn, staff who are politically active, or minded to become so, should be candid with their XYZ management so that management are best able to be co-operative and difficulties are more likely to be avoided. Staff so involved have an obligation to XYZ to weigh carefully their obligations to XYZ when actual or potential conflicts of interest arise—in their use of time, in campaigning of issues of relevance to the XYZ business, and so on. Employees engaging in political activity do so as private individuals and not as representatives of XYZ.

Conduct Towards Employees

XYZ is committed to its employees. An underlying principle is to maximise the extent to which all employees have the opportunity to achieve their personal potential through their work with XYZ. XYZ believes that it succeeds through the dedication of all its employees. Their motivated involvement, work satisfaction and security are high priorities. In part this depends upon the implementation of appropriate commercial policies so that employees share in the company's success; in part upon policies which relate to health and safety. Apart from the inalienable right of every person to their personal dignity, practices which intentionally or unintendedly infringe upon personal dignity are likely to interfere with an individual's work performance.

In the conduct of his or her business responsibilities every XYZ employee is expected to apply the principle of equal opportunity in employment. No member of staff shall discriminate so that another member of staff (or a member of staff of a contractor, supplier or customer) is victimised or less favourably treated than another on grounds of race, colour, marital status, religion, sex, sexual orientation, ethnic or national origin, or legal political activity. Treatment shall at all times be fair in terms of compensation, job security, work experiences, recognition of achievement and opportunities for advancement.

Staff shall be recruited for their relevant aptitudes, skills, experience and ability; and their advancement shall be on the same grounds according to the opportunities available within XYZ. Employment practices including recruitment practices, contract terms and working conditions shall be sensitive to the culture of the country concerned so as to ensure that company conduct does not contribute to unacceptable social tensions or malaise. At the same time, care must always be taken to ensure so far as is reasonably possible (a) that no harm occurs to those whose services the company employs while they are engaged in work-related activity, and (b) that the equal opportunity principles outlined in the preceding two paragraphs are applied.

XYZ seeks to ensure that employees have and exhibit mutual respect for each other at all times—both at work and also at business-related functions. XYZ staff are expected to behave in this way towards other employees, contractors, suppliers and customers. Harassment is unacceptable. Discrimination—in action, writing or through remarks—is a form of harassment. Unwelcome verbal and physical advances and derogatory remarks are other forms of harassment. It is a duty of all XYZ employees to ensure that their behaviour at no time contributes towards the creation of an intimidating, offensive or hostile work environment.

For staff to identify with XYZ and for XYZ to benefit most from the potential within its staff, the approach to their staff of XYZ's managers and supervisors must be as open and candid as possible. Staff also must be made to feel that they can communicate upwards without formality, rebuff, rancour or victimisation. While not abdicating their personal responsibility, managers should delegate downwards to as great an extent as possible so as to empower and develop their staff. Rigid hierarchical styles of management should be discouraged and staff may address any issues directly above the level of their immediate supervisor if they judge this to be appropriate.

Conduct by People Acting on XYZ's Behalf

In the introduction to this Code I indicated that the XYZ person responsible should endeavour to ensure that equivalent standards to those set out in this Code are followed in companies in which XYZ has an interest but does not have control, and also in those businesses with whom XYZ has contractual relationships. I also stated that it is the policy of the board of XYZ that those employed by or acting for XYZ should follow all the requirements of this Code. For instance, contractors working on behalf of XYZ must ensure they act in accordance with this Code with respect to confidentiality, conflicts of interest, the making and receiving of gifts and with respect to their and their employees' conduct towards XYZ's employees and towards those whom the contractors employ on XYZ's business.

It is not accepted that management and staff of XYZ circumvent their obligations under this Code by deputing unacceptable practices to intermediaries acting directly or indirectly on XYZ's behalf so that XYZ may achieve a desired end while endeavouring to avoid any opprobrium.

Conduct in the Community and Charitable Contributions

XYZ accepts that it has community obligations where it does business. We have a general duty to avoid conduct prejudicial to the best interests of the communities where we do business. We have a positive duty as well as a self-interest, as corporate citizens committed within our business to improving the well-being of individuals, to use our best endeavours to enhance community life. Apart from altruistic motivations which are important, we believe that a positive approach to our community relations is in the best long-term interests of our company, of those who work within it, and of our present and future customers.

Staff are asked to assist XYZ to be proactive in searching out appropriate opportunities to contribute positively to community affairs and staff will be encouraged by XYZ to do likewise as individuals. Our contributions may be in leadership by initiating or steering community projects; they may be supportive in terms of donations of facilities, equipment, materials, time or cash.

To avoid waste, our community support should be targeted to improving economic or social well-being in demonstrable ways with a particular emphasis upon improving the quality of life of ordinary people. In nature and scale our support should be appropriate in each community while bearing favourable comparison with other companies of similar standing. Our support should be consistent with XYZ's business interests and corporate image, and should have a clear potential to enhance both of these.

Customer Relations and Product Quality

XYZ has no future unless it continues to satisfy customer needs in a competitive environment characterised by rapid technological advances. The company acknowledges the primacy of the following business principles which it expects its staff, as of duty, to apply consistently in practice and to encourage those who supply our ultimate customers to do likewise:

- We strive to ensure that the specifications of our products meet or exceed customer requirements at economical price.
- We strive to provide services which are excellent value for money and are delivered courteously and with sensitivity to our clients' requirements.
- We endeavour in all circumstances to ensure that all information about our products and services is reliable and a sufficient basis for fully informed customer decision making and customer use.
- We will be truthful and not misleading in our public relations, marketing and advertising.
- We are committed to satisfying enquiries, complaints and suggestions thoroughly and promptly.
- We are committed to meeting or exceeding all statutory requirements with regard to our products and services as well as to their marketing, sale, distribution and subsequent after-sales support.

Grievance Procedures

Every XYZ operating unit must have in place and comply with suitable procedures to ensure that the concerns of staff on any issue related to this Code are considered promptly and thoroughly, and that remedial action is taken where appropriate.

Please use your best endeavours to bring this Code appropriately to the attention of all personnel, to all new employees, to our business partners and contractors as well as their staff and to any others with whom we are associated or do business.

[Chairman's photograph]

[Chairman's signature]

Appendix 9
Example Code of Ethical Conduct on Scientific and Environmental Matters

XYZ

XYZ London Limited
150 River Walk
London WC2 3XD

[Chairman's name]
Chairman

[Date]

CODE OF ETHICAL CONDUCT ON SCIENTIFIC AND ENVIRONMENTAL MATTERS

XYZ is a major multinational corporation operating in many countries, impacting upon the environment in many ways, employing many people and whose ultimate customers are the many individuals who rely on the quality of our products for their well-being. So it is appropriate that we are seen to operate responsibly and with ethical integrity in our scientific conduct and our environmental responsibility.

Our guiding principle is that we should endeavour at all times to maximise community benefit while never doing any harm. We should avoid even the suggestion of impropriety. This should be so even when the law is permissive. There should be no risk to our local or international reputation if any details about our affairs were to become public knowledge. We should aim to adopt the highest available scientific and environmental standards. At all times our business must be conducted honestly and scrupulously, free of deception.

To these ends, this Code provides detailed guidance on the application to issues of scientific and environmental responsibility of the policies outlined in XYZ's Statement of Corporate Principles. A separate Code of Business Conduct applies those policies to commercial issues in particular. You will find some wording in common between the Statement and the two Codes where similar principles and required practices are set out.

Copies of the three documents are available at all locations to all staff—from regional and country managers, from divisional and business unit heads. They are also available from Environmental Affairs staff or through Internal Audit locally or at Group level, from whom guidance on interpretation and application may be sought by staff.

This document has been approved by the Executive Committee and adopted by the board of XYZ. The Executive Committee reviews annually the Code's appropriateness and effectiveness and advises the board accordingly. As part of this review, line managers annually are required to formally monitor their and their staff's performance in observing the requirements of this Code within their areas of responsibility and, where judged appropriate, to develop initiatives to provide reasonable assurance of future compliance. Line managers are responsible to foster a sense of responsibility for the environment among employees at all levels. The board places particular importance upon timely actions to be taken whenever necessary to identify, contain and eliminate irresponsible or illegal acts—especially having regard to changes in technology, industrial practices, product design and trends in legislation.

A fundamental principle of the way XYZ conducts its affairs is that applicable laws and regulations are to be scrupulously observed at all times. Practical difficulties may arise in many cases, such as when there are conflicts between the law of different countries, when local business custom and practice is inconsistent with local law or when there is ambiguity as to the legal position. Any case of actual or prospective non-compliance with law should be raised urgently with management and, if material, with the Group Chief Executive.

The XYZ person responsible should endeavour to ensure that equivalent standards to those set out in this Code are followed in companies in which XYZ has an interest but does not have control and also in those businesses with whom XYZ has contractual relationships. Where they are not, the XYZ person responsible should refer the matter upwards within XYZ.

The Board of XYZ regards it as the duty of every individual employed by or acting for XYZ to follow all the requirements of this Code. Any proposed action which appears to be in breach of any requirement of this Code should not be progressed without full disclosure to and prior approval of the Group Chief Executive or the Group Head of Environmental Affairs. Appropriate behaviour by individuals which is in compliance with this Code and also specifically approved departures from this Code will be supported by the company under its principle of collective responsibility.

Your duty to comply with this Code includes a duty both to yourself and to XYZ to raise any concerns you may have on any matter of scientific or environmental conduct which appears to be a violation of this *Code* and in which you are actively involved. In addition you have a right to raise similar concerns about the conduct of others even where you are not directly involved. Usually you should first raise a matter of concern with your line manager and you should do so at the earliest opportunity. At your discretion you may raise your concerns directly with senior management, with local internal audit or with the Group Head of Environmental Affairs and you should do so where an issue remains unresolved to your satisfaction after you have consulted your immediate management about it.

Conduct in the Community

XYZ accepts that it has community obligations wherever XYZ sources its supplies, conducts its business and where its products are used. We have a general duty to avoid conduct prejudicial to the best interests of these communities. We have a positive duty as well as a self-interest, as corporate citizens committed within our business to improving the well-being of individuals, to use our best endeavours to enhance community life. Apart from altruistic motivations which are important, we believe that a positive approach to our community relations is in the best long-term interests of our company, of those who work within it, and of our present and future customers and users of our products.

Staff are asked to assist XYZ to be proactive in searching out appropriate opportunities to contribute positively to community affairs and staff will be encouraged by XYZ to do likewise as individuals. Our contributions may be in leadership—by initiating or steering community projects; they may be supportive—in terms of responsible donations of facilities, equipment, materials, time or cash.

To avoid waste, our community support should be targeted to improving economic or social well-being in demonstrable ways with a particular emphasis upon improving the quality of life of ordinary people. In nature and scale our support should be appropriate in each community while bearing favourable comparison with other companies of similar standing. Our support should be consistent with XYZ's business interests and corporate image, and should have a clear potential to enhance both of these.

XYZ has an enlightened self-interest in communicating information and views on scientific and environmental issues which should be of public concern which have an important impact upon the XYZ business: management should be active in looking for appropriate opportunities to do so. The information and views so communicated must be relevant, reliable and responsible. We should seek to cooperate with official bodies and technical organisations in the formulation of standards and the means of complying with them.

XYZ strives to be a good employer with regard to individual staff who are actively involved in community life, including involvement in politics. Accordingly, XYZ management should facilitate and not unnecessarily impede the process when individual XYZ staff exercise their legal rights to become actively involved in local or national affairs and politics. In turn, staff who are so active, or minded to become so, should be candid with their XYZ management so that management are best able to be co-operative and difficulties are more likely to be avoided. Staff so involved have an obligation to XYZ to weigh carefully their obligations to XYZ when actual or potential conflicts of interest arise—in their use of time, in campaigning on issues of relevance to the XYZ business, and so on. Employees engaging in political activity do so as private individuals and not as representatives of XYZ.

Business and Product Development

The environmental impact and potential health effects of all new corporate activities, acquisitions, projects, processes, products and services shall be assessed in advance by responsible staff. XYZ accepts a responsibility to evaluate the "cradle-to-grave" impacts of our products and services. All investment decisions are to take account of environmental and health considerations. There is an *a priori* assumption that clean technologies shall be chosen. The environmental impact of facilities shall be assessed with regard *inter alia* to site appearance, effect on local and remote ecological systems, and storage safety and access.

XYZ's transport strategy shall be determined having due regard to its environmental soundness.

Conduct towards Employees

XYZ is committed to its employees. An underlying principle is to maximise the extent to which all employees have the opportunity to achieve their personal potential through their work and in the rest of their lives. XYZ believes that it succeeds through the dedication of all its employees. Their work satisfaction, security and safety are high priorities. In part this depends upon the implementation of appropriate policies which relate to health and safety.

Employment practices including recruitment practices, contract terms and working conditions shall be sensitive to the culture of the country concerned so as to ensure that company conduct does not contribute to unacceptable social tensions or malaise. At the same time, care must always be taken to ensure so far as is reasonably possible that no harm occurs to those whose services the company employs while they are engaged in work-related activity.

For staff to identify with XYZ and for XYZ to benefit most from the potential within its staff, the approach to their staff of XYZ's managers and supervisors must be as open and candid as possible. Staff also must be made to feel that they can communicate upwards without formality, rebuff, rancour or victimisation. While not abdicating their personal responsibility for scientific and environmental matters, managers should delegate downwards to as great an extent as possible so as to empower and develop their staff. Rigid hierarchical styles of management should be discouraged and staff may address any issues directly above the level of their immediate supervisor if they judge this to be appropriate.

Supply

XYZ is concerned about the sources and methods of production of the raw materials and components it acquires, and the environmental conditions of service providers. XYZ subscribes to the principle of sustainable development—development which meets the needs of the present without compromising the abilities of future generations to meet their own needs. Wherever possible we use renewable, recycled and recyclable materials and components. Responsible XYZ staff should enquire so as to ascertain the extent to which elements of XYZ's suppliers' environments, products and services are hazardous, toxic, over-packed, non-renewable or not re-usable.

Production and Administration

In designing and operating production and administrative processes, XYZ staff shall endeavour to maximise efficiency by minimising or eliminating waste in all parts of the business with respect to materials, supplies, energy and other inputs and processes. Excess production is to be avoided. Where available "waste free" processes and business practices shall be chosen in preference to others. Wherever possible XYZ reuses and recycles by-products of production. Hazardous substances, discharges, emissions, activities, practices and equipment are formally identified and necessary measures (including satisfactory plant maintenance and quality control) introduced and followed to prevent unwanted outcomes.

Product Quality and Customer Relations

XYZ aims to provide eminently usable products which function for users efficiently and reliably and without harmful effects. They are, where possible and appropriate, to be reusable and repairable. At the time of production there must be sufficient opportunities to ensure ultimate safe and environmentally friendly disposal of our products and their parts including packaging; and wherever practical our products and their components shall be recyclable.

Appropriate advice shall be provided to customers on all relevant environmental aspects of the handling, use and disposal of the products made or distributed by the company.

XYZ has no future unless it continues to satisfy customer needs in a competitive environment characterised by rapid technological advances. The company acknowledges the primacy of the following environmental and technical principles which it expects its staff, as of duty, to apply consistently in practice and to encourage those who supply our ultimate customers to do likewise:

- We strive to maximise the operational efficiency and reliability of all products we supply.
- We strive to eliminate all possible hazards arising from the use of the products we supply.
- Wherever possible we intend to provide products which are environmentally friendly through their reliability, reparability, reusability and recyclability.
- We ensure that our products and packagings can be disposed of safely;
- We endeavour in all circumstances to ensure that all information about our products and services is reliable and a sufficient basis for fully informed customer decision making and customer use.
- We are committed to satisfying enquiries, complaints and suggestions thoroughly and promptly.
- We are committed to meeting or exceeding all statutory requirements with regard to our products and services as well as to their marketing, sale, distribution and subsequent after-sales support.

Internal Control

All businesses and projects owned, managed or controlled by XYZ must maintain an adequate system of internal control which is in accordance with XYZ's control policies. Management and staff are responsible to ensure that, within their respective areas of responsibility, necessary arrangements at acceptable cost are in place and are complied with to give reasonable assurance that the objectives of internal control are met. These objectives include:

- the achievement of business objectives efficiently and economically
- the reliability of information used internally and for external reporting
- the safeguarding of corporate resources
- compliance with laws, regulations and policies of the company.

The necessary arrangements comprise proper attention to the following:

- the control environment
- information and communication
- risk analysis
- control activities or procedures
- monitoring.

All incidents involving a breakdown of control leading to any actual or potential breaches of the Code should be reported upwards immediately to management and to internal audit. For companies in which XYZ has an interest but does not have control, the XYZ person responsible should endeavour to ensure that equivalent standards are applied and should refer the matter upwards within XYZ when they are not.

Records

Responsible staff must ensure that all the operational records of the business represent a reliable, truthful, accurate, complete and up-to-date picture in compliance with prescribed corporate procedures and external standards and regulations; and that they are suitable to be a basis for informed management decisions. The prompt recording and proper description of operations is a duty of responsible staff. Falsification of records is strictly prohibited.

No secret or unrecorded scientific activities are to be established or maintained.

Conduct by People Acting on XYZ's Behalf

In the introduction to this Code I indicated that the XYZ person responsible should endeavour to ensure that equivalent standards to those set out in this Code are followed in companies in which XYZ has an interest but does not have control, and also in those businesses with whom XYZ has contractual relationships. I also stated that it is the policy of the Board of XYZ that those employed by or acting for XYZ should follow all the requirements of this Code. For instance, contractors working on behalf of XYZ must ensure they act in accordance with this Code.

It is not accepted that management and staff of XYZ circumvent their obligations under this Code by deputing unacceptable practices to intermediaries acting directly or indirectly on XYZ's behalf so that XYZ may achieve a desired end while endeavouring to avoid any opprobrium.

Grievance Procedures

Every XYZ operating unit must have in place and comply with suitable procedures to ensure that the concerns of staff on any issue related to this Code are considered promptly and thoroughly, and that remedial action is taken where appropriate.

Please use your best endeavours to bring this Code appropriately to the attention of all personnel, to all new employees, to our business partners and contractors as well as their staff and to any others with whom we are associated or do business.

[Chairman's photograph]

[Chairman's Signature]

Appendix 10
Example Letter of Representation on Internal Control

(This letter is suitable for use from a line manager to more senior management, the audit committee, or to internal audit. It is sometimes known as "comfort letter". A related concept is the "Accounting Declaration".)

"SHORT FORM" EXAMPLE[1,2]

From: A Line Manager

To: Internal Audit

or to:

Line Manager immediately senior (copy Internal Audit)

or to:

The Audit Committee (copy Internal Audit) in the case of the most senior executive management

Re: Representations on internal control

Date:

I confirm that the objectives I am responsible for achieving are clearly defined and understood. I acknowledge that the development and maintenance of effective internal control to provide reasonable assurance of the achievement of these objectives are among my key managerial responsibilities. I am confident I understand what this entails and have been given the necessary authority to achieve these outcomes.

Having monitored achievement of my objectives and the functioning of the internal control arrangements in place within my area of responsibilities, I consider that throughout 19XX internal control has been adequate to provide reasonable assurance of effective and efficient operations, of internal financial control, and of compliance with laws and regulations; and that these arrangements have been complied with in all material respects throughout this period.

I have communicated to my staff the essential elements of an effective system of internal control and have ensured that: (a) they are aware of their responsibilities especially in areas of potential critical risk, and (b) they have been empowered to operate appropriate control procedures effectively.

All staff within my area of responsibility, at all levels, have been appraised of their duty to report upwards unresolved matters of concern about internal control and to deal expeditiously and effectively with such matters reported to them. In reporting upwards, staff have been empowered, without risk of victimisation, to bypass intermediate levels of management where they consider this to be necessary. I have taken appropriate steps to confirm that no matters remain unresolved as a result of this process. All such matters drawn to my personal attention by staff have been dealt with to my satisfaction.

No findings or recommendations relating to internal control made by internal or external audit or by others remain outstanding.

I have considered whether significant changes have been made to business practices in my area of responsibility which may have weakened internal control, and believe that this is not the case. Furthermore our plans for future change have been appraised in the context of their internal control impact and I believe these issues have been addressed satisfactorily.

I am unaware of any weaknesses in control or irregularities in accounting practice which should be drawn to your attention.

NOTES

1. While this is described as a "short form" letter, it does force the correspondent to *conclude* in general managerial terms with respect to his/her responsibilities for internal control and the quality of internal control. It does *not* address specific controls.
2. Drafted as an example of an unqualified letter of representation. Departures and exceptions should be incorporated by the correspondent.

Appendix 11
High-level Consideration of Risk and Control Issues for a Range of IT Related Activities with Illustrative Controls

We provide here an an example of a Standard Audit Programme Guide (SAPG) in truncated format which addresses the subject of information technology within an organisation at a summary level. This Appendix should be used in conjunction with Chapter 13. This type of review, which examines a broad range of related activities at a top level, may be applicable where either (a) it is necessary to gather an overall impression of the information technology environment in a restricted timescale, or (b) where the audit function is undertaking an initial review in order to gather data so that subsequent full-scale reviews can be appropriately targeted.

A typical information processing facility is explored through a selection of the previously identified discrete IT activity areas. The data implies a mixed platform IT environment with mainframe equipment, networks and personal computers all in evidence.

Each IT topic is addressed by the inclusion of a number of essential (or key) control and risk issues. Additionally, each issue is complemented by illustrative controls and measures.

The scenario depicted by the issue and control data is intended to be neither definitive nor comprehensive, but rather to provide some general guidance as to the nature of controls that could be found in practice.

CONTROL AND RISK ISSUES

Seq.	Risk/Control Issues	Example Control(s)/Measure(s)
	IT Strategic Planning (Issues 1.1 to 1.4)	
1.1	How does management ensure that the provision of all IT hardware, software, methods and resources remains in step with the strategic direction of the business and the achievement of competitive advantage, etc.?	• *IT strategic planning exercise conducted in accordance with a proven methodology.* • *IT requirements and action plans documented and authorised by the board.* • *All acquisitions of hardware and software are verified against the agreed plan.*
1.2	What measures ensure that only authorised and appropriate IT systems and facilities are provided?	• *All IT projects have to be formally assessed, justified and authorised against the strategic plan.* • *IT steering committee signifies approval to proceed in their minutes.*
1.3	How does management ensure that the information needs of the business are adequately served?	• *A data model has been established for the organisation and all new and amended systems have to comply with the model structure.* • *Requests to amend the data structure are assessed and authorised where necessary.* • *Corporate information flow has been mapped and reporting requirements established.*
1.4	What measures ensure that the existing IT facilities remain appropriate to the underlying business needs?	• *Business objectives are re-assessed periodically and mapped against the current and planned IT facilities. Any perceived change require-ments for IT have to be justified and authorised.* • *Performance and operational criteria are monitored for the key IT systems and facilities. Shortcomings are highlighted and addressed in relation to the underlying business requirements.*
	IT Organisation (Issues 1.5 to 1.9)	
1.5	Has management adequately defined the organisational structure and responsibilities of the IT function (and how is this kept up to date and relevant)?	• *Formal terms of reference have been defined for the IT division.* • *IT action plans generated by the strategic plan define the resource, skill and procedural requirements.* • *Manpower planning exercise undertaken for the IT division.* • *Organisational structure reflects the logical association of activities and lines of communication. Conflicts of interest and the potential for malpractice are minimised by the defined segregation of duties.*

Seq.	Risk/Control Issues	Example Control(s)/Measure(s)
		• *Organisational structure is formally reviewed every year against the updated business objectives.*
1.6	How is management assured that sufficient levels of IT resource (including suitably skilled staff) are provided to support the current and future needs of the business?	• *Manpower and skill planning exercise undertaken for the IT division.* • *Specific or specialist recruitment requirements are identified and addressed in tandem with the human resources dept.*
1.7	What steps does management take to ensure that the skills of the IT staff remain relevant (and what specific measures are in place to ensure the maintenance of a minimum skill level)?	• *Existing staff are continuously monitored for their skills against the requirements for the current and planned environments. Training and development needs are identified and addressed.* • *Each member of staff has a job specification which incorporates their specific minimum skill requirements.*

1.8	Has management provided an adequate framework of operating standards and policies as a means of ensuring secure and reliable IT related activities?	• *Authorised and documented standards and policies have been implemented for the following areas:*
		  • *operations dept.*
		  • *system development methodology*
		  • *data control procedures*
		  • *programming standards including testing requirements*
		  • *safety standards*
		  • *access control and logical security policy*
		  • *data back-up and media handling procedures*
		  • *disaster and contingency plan*
		  • *data protection policy*

1.9	How does management prevent potential staff fraud or malpractice in the operation of key systems?	• *Key duties are strictly segregated as a means of reducing the opportunity for malpractice without a high degree of collusion (i.e. operations and programming functions are separated in order to prevent unauthorised program amendments being applied to the live environment).*
	IT Sites *(Issues 1.10 to 1.16)*	
1.10	How does management ensure that all IT sites are secure and adequately protected from unauthorised access?	• *Main building entrance manned by security personnel who check staff and visitors.* • *Access beyond reception is controlled by key-card system. The key-cards are programmed in relation to activity zones and allocated on a "needs" basis.*

Seq.	Risk/Control Issues	Example Control(s)/Measure(s)
		• *Intruder alarms are installed and regularly tested and serviced.* • *Access to the central computer room is restricted to key personnel only via programmed key-card.*
1.11	What specific measures control the access of visitors, delivery staff, etc. and what prevents unauthorised access to the main computer room)?	*See responses to 1.10 above.* • *All visitors are registered upon arrival and escorted while in the building.*
1.12	Have adequate physical security and fire prevention systems been installed, and how does management ensure that they remain operational and effective?	• *Intruder alarms are installed and regularly tested and serviced.* • *Main computer room covered by CCTV system monitored by security staff.* • *Premises are patrolled after normal working hours.* • *Fire detection and alarm system installed and linked to fire station—regularly tested and serviced.* • *Main computer room is protected by an ozone friendly gas smothering system.*
1.13	Are regular emergency and fire drills conducted as a means of evaluating the effectiveness of the prevailing measures?	• *Building evacuation drills are regularly conducted and assessed for their effectiveness.*
1.14	What measures are in place to both prevent and detect the unauthorised removal of IT equipment?	• *Goods moving in or out of the premises are inspected for the relevant written authorities.* • *All corporate hardware is identified with a non-removable label.* • *Personal computers are securely fixed to desks with flexible metal cords.*
1.15	How does management ensure that staff are sufficiently aware of their responsibilities in respect of fire prevention and emergency evacuation drills?	• *All health and safety requirements are contained in the relevant procedures manual given to all employees.* • *Building evacuation drills are regularly conducted and assessed for their effectiveness.*
1.16	How is management assured that adequate and appropriate levels of insurance cover are in place for the IT facilities?	• *Legal department undertake an annual review of insurance cover based on a formal risk assessment and the events in the past year.*
	Processing Operations (Issues 1.17 to 1.35)	
1.17	What general measures ensure that processing activity is valid, accurate and authorised?	• *Only valid, tested and authorised program versions are available in the production environment.*

Seq.	Risk/Control Issues	Example Control(s)/Measure(s)
		• *All runs are authorised prior to operation.* • *JCL ensures that correct files, data and programs are called during processing.* • *System access controls prevent unauthorised access to data and mainframe facilities.* • *Data preparation is reconciled to source documents.* • *Data is validated for errors.*
1.18	What specific measures prevent unauthorised transactions and/or system amendments being applied?	• *System access controls prevent unauthorised access to data and mainframe facilities.* • *Production program files are read only and cannot be amended directly.* • *Production and development program libraries are separated and subject to strict program movement authorities and processes.*
1.19	How does management ensure that data is accurate, complete, authorised and reliable?	*See responses in sections 1.17 and 1.18 above.*
1.20	How is commercially sensitive or confidential data protected from unauthorised access or leakage?	• *System and data "owners" define the access rights to their data and these definitions are reflected in the access control system.* • *Access controls in place which give each user a defined range of access to systems and data, and prevent access to all other systems.* • *Especially sensitive data is further protected in that it is only accessible from a restricted number of securely located terminals.* • *All confidential output is routed to the laser printer and shrink wrapped.*
1.21	What measures ensure that only authorised and tested versions of programs are utilised?	• *Production and development program libraries are separated and subject to strict program movement authorities and processes.* • *Following development and comprehensive testing, development programs are moved to the production library on the authority of the operations manager and end users.* • *The production program library contains only current and approved versions. The contents are regularly independently checked against an approved schedule of programs.* • *Access to the production library is restricted and in live use is controlled by the JCL or SCL.*

Seq.	Risk/Control Issues	Example Control(s)/Measure(s)
1.22	What specific steps would prevent the loading and use of unauthorised or untested programs or system amendments?	• *Production and development program libraries are separated and subject to strict program movement authorities and processes.* • *Access to the production library is restricted and in live use is controlled by the JCL or SCL.* • *Unauthorised programs located in the production library would be detected during the regular verification of the contents.*
1.23	Would management promptly be made aware of any abnormal processing activities?	• *Job runs are controlled by authorised JCL or SCL. The ability to introduce unauthorised JCL is prevented by access control measures.* • *All activity is logged and exception reports highlighting defined categories of activity are produced and sent to management for review, investigation and sign-off.*
1.24	What steps are in place to prevent development staff directly accessing the live production environment?	• *Access to the production facilities is restricted to privilege users only and augmented by password control.*
1.25	How is management assured that the skills of the operating and technical support staff are kept up to date and relevant?	• *Existing staff are continuously monitored for their skills against the requirements for the current and planned environments. Training and development needs are identified and addressed.* • *Each member of staff has a job specification which incorporates their specific minimum skill requirements.*
1.26	How does management verify that the mainframe and distributed systems are operated at optimum efficiency (and that facility overloads are prevented)?	• *Job scheduling is planned in advance for mainstream production tasks.* • *Loading requirements are based on historical evidence of resource requirements and run times.* • *On-line resource usage monitoring is applied on all key systems and warning signals activated if defined parameters are exceeded.* • *Operations and technical support staff are on call to affect schedule amendments and activate reserve capacity if necessary.* • *Performance statistics are generated and reviewed by management.*
1.27	What measures prevent unauthorised usage of mainframe facilities?	• *Access to mainframe facilities is restricted by user ID and password.* • *Runs are controlled by authorised JCL and generating JCL requires specific skills.* • *All non-standard jobs are reported on the system logs and reported to management for sign-off or investigation.*

Seq.	Risk/Control Issues	Example Control(s)/Measure(s)
1.28	How does management ensure that the operating system is efficiently configured and that adequately skilled staff are available to maintain and/or rebuild the system in the event of a major failure?	• *Performance statistics are generated and reviewed by management.* • *Manufacturer's recommended configurations are taken into account when the system is set up.* • *Experienced technical support staff are employed and supported by ongoing training and development.* • *Regular exercises are conducted to simulate system failure and environment rebuilds. These are evaluated for their effectiveness.*
1.29	Have adequate steps been taken to ensure that all key hardware is regularly and appropriately maintained in order to avoid unnecessary disruption of services, etc.?	• *All mainframe equipment is subject to regular preventive maintenance by the supplier.* • *Fault diagnostic software is used to highlight potential problems.* • *Contingency plans are in place to counter the effects of any disruption to services.*
1.30	Is access to the job control language (JCL) or system control language (SCL) facilities adequately restricted?	• *Access to JCL and SCL facilities is restricted to experienced personnel outwith the operations department.*
1.31	What measures ensure that the use of JCL and SCL is optimised and that inefficient or inappropriate tasks are not loaded?	• *All JCL and SCL is tested prior to use and authorised prior to transfer into the production environment.*
1.32	How does management ensure that access to and use of utility programs is valid, appropriate and trailed?	• *Utilities are not held on-line and their use (and loading) is subject to written authorisation.* • *Utility program usage features on the management review log of system activity and has to be checked against the written authorities.*
1.33	What steps ensure that only authorised, accurate and appropriate data is loaded for access by users?	• *System controls (including JCL parameters) confirm that the correct data and system files are accessed during processing.* • *System access and validation controls contribute to the accuracy and reliability of data.*
1.34	Has management defined the required service provision levels and what measures ensure that such performance is adequately monitored and reacted to?	• *Job scheduling and prioritisation contributes to meeting the defined service levels.* • *On-line performance and job progress monitoring is in place and subject to review.* • *Delays or problems are detected and promptly reacted to.*
1.35	What measures prevent unauthorised access to confidential data output, and how is such data securely distributed to authorised users?	• *All confidential and sensitive output is routed to the laser printer and shrinkwrapped prior to distribution.*

Seq.	Risk/Control Issues	Example Control(s)/Measure(s)
		• *Alternatively, confidential data can only be accessed and displayed on nominated securely located terminals.*
	Back-up *(Issues 1.36 to 1.47)*	
1.36	How does management ensure that all key systems and data are protected in the event of a failure or breakdown?	• *Back-up policy and procedures are in place as the basis for effective data protection.* • *Each system has an agreed back-up schedule and timetable. Mainframe systems automatically back up as part of the control procedures.* • *Separate PC procedures are in place.* • *Regular confirmatory checks are conducted to ensure that the requirements are being complied with.*
1.37	How can management confirm that the prescribed data back-up routines are being applied in practice?	• *Contents of back-up store are checked regularly to ensure that the required files are available.* • *Regular confirmatory checks are conducted to ensure that the requirements are being complied with.*
1.38	What measures ensure that all data and system back-ups are securely stored and adequately protected from damage, deterioration or loss?	• *Secure and remote back-up store is provided and all back-up media are moved out to the store on a daily basis.* • *Store is adequately protected by alarms and out-of-hours patrol.* • *Store is air-conditioned and the environmental conditions are monitored and controlled to ensure the optimum conditions for the media.*
1.39	How can management be assured that end-users are applying adequate data back-up routines in order to protect their PC-based activities?	• *Guideline and procedures are circulated to all end-users.* • *Regular visits are conducted by the user support staff to verify if users are applying sufficient back-up to their systems and data.*
1.40	What measures ensure that all key data and system back-ups can be accurately and promptly identified and traced?	• *Physical and magnetic labelling standards are in place as a means of identifying specific media.* • *Mainframe media is tracked using a library control system which identifies each item of media. The storage location is recorded for each item.*
1.41	Does management ensure that all key back-ups are regularly accounted for?	• *Mainframe media store contents are reconciled on a monthly basis.*

Seq.	Risk/Control Issues	Example Control(s)/Measure(s)
1.42	How can management be certain that organisation is correctly complying with all the relevant data retention legislation?	• *The retention periods for key corporate data (i.e. accounting records) are defined in accordance with any prevailing legislation.* • *Destruction dates for media are established which comply with the regulations.*
1.43	What measures ensure that long-term back-up media remains readable and usable?	• *Key system back-up media are checked periodically to ensure that the contents remain readable. Secondary copies are provided for crucial systems in the event that the prime copy fails to read.*
1.44	What specific measures prevent the premature erasure or reuse of back-up media?	• *Write protect devices activated.* • *Usage of media items is controlled by the library system and the incorrect loading of media would be detected by the JCL or SCL parameters.*
1.45	How is the disposal of outdated or unwanted media controlled so that valid items are not destroyed or overwritten?	• *Usage of media items is controlled by the library system.*
1.46	What measures are in place to prevent and detect virus infection of media?	• *All external media is checked for virus infection before use.* • *PC users are required to run all external media through virus software located on a free-standing machine before loading on to their systems.*
1.47	How is management sure that virus infections would be promptly detected, contained and effectively dealt with?	• *All external media is checked for virus infection before use.* • *All PCs have virus detection software loaded which runs on boot-up. Any virus infections have to be reported immediately to technical support dept. for corrective action.*
	Systems/Operating Software (Issues 1.48 to 1.62)	
1.48	What measures ensure that only recognised, reliable and correctly configured operating systems are used?	• *Only tested and approved operating software is used.* • *Operating software is configured (in accordance with the supplier's recommendations) to ensure maximum efficiency and appropriate functionality.*
1.49	Does management ensure that adequate and appropriately skilled staff are available to maintain operating and systems software?	• *Experienced technical support staff are employed. Relevant training is provided so that their skills are maintained at the required level.*

Seq.	Risk/Control Issues	Example Control(s)/Measure(s)
1.50	What measures prevent the inappropriate or disruptive configuration of operating/systems software?	• *Configuration amendments are only applied by the technical support staff.* • *All amendments are subject to prior management authority.* • *All potential amendments are subject to rigorous prior testing outside the production environment.*
1.51	What measures prevent unauthorised access to and amendment of operating systems?	• *Access is restricted via the access control system which only permits access by authorised technical support staff. Specialist knowledge requirements also have the effect of reducing the opportunity for unauthorised access.*
1.52	Are all system software upgrades and fixes adequately assessed, tested and authorised prior to application to the live environment?	• *All potential amendments are subject to rigorous prior testing outside the production environment.* • *Test results are reviewed by management prior to the granting of update authority.*
1.53	Are systems and operating software facilities effectively configured so that unauthorised access to data and systems is prevented?	• *The access control system operates in tandem with the operating system to ensure that access is controlled on a "needs" basis.* • *The mainframe system is further protected by runs being controlled via the JCL or SCL which defines those systems and files to be accessed during the job.*
1.54	How does management make sure that the efficiency and performance of the operating system is optimised?	• *Operating software is configured (in accordance with the supplier's recommendations) to ensure maximum efficiency and appropriate functionality.*
1.55	How is management assured that full recovery from a major systems failure can be promptly achieved?	• *All the necessary recovery journals are maintained. Recovery is regularly tested.* • *Rebuilding of the operating environment is tested as part of the disaster recovery plan tests.*
1.56	Are abnormal or unauthorised events promptly and independently brought to the attention of management?	• *Attempted access violations are logged and circulated for review.* • *All errors and non-standard runs are reported to management for review and sign-off.*
1.57	Is access to "privilege user" facilities adequately restricted and trailed?	• *Access control system permits access to the high level facilities for named users with double password access control.* • *Amendments applied to configuration files are logged and reported to management.*
1.58	Is access to utility and diagnostic facilities suitably restricted and trailed?	*Identical to methods described in 1.57 above.*

Seq.	Risk/Control Issues	Example Control(s)/Measure(s)
1.59	Has management established adequate and appropriate levels of operating system journals in order to maintain an awareness of system usage and operating efficiency?	• *All standard journals are generated.* • *In addition, specific journals and logs have been established to highlight the application of sensitive or wide-ranging amendments. Such reports are circulated to management for action.*
1.60	How does management ensure that all personal computers throughout the organisation are appropriately and consistently configured?	• *Operating systems are initially loaded and configured by technical support staff in accord with the supplier's recommendations and operational requirements of the company.* • *Regular checks are conducted by technical support to ensure that the machines retain their original and authorised configurations.*
1.61	What specific measures prevent the use of unauthorised or unreliable PC operating systems?	• *Regular checks are conducted by technical support to ensure that only authorised operating systems are present on company PCs.*
1.62	What measures prevent users from applying unauthorised or inappropriate amendments to PC configurations?	• *Regular checks are conducted by technical support to ensure that the machines retain their original and authorised configurations.*
	System Access Control *(Issues 1.63 to 1.71)*	
1.63	Has management established a policy of system and data ownership whereby users take responsibility for their systems and data?	• *All data and systems are allocated to users.* • *Users grant access rights and these are reflected in the database administration system.*
1.64	What measures are in place to ensure that data and systems are effectively protected from unauthorised access and/or amendments?	• *Access control system is in place which supports the access rights granted by the users/owners (as defined in the DBMS).* • *Access control system operates on a user-id and password basis. Each user-id has a range of access permissions defined.* • *Access is not permitted to systems or data where rights have not been granted and set up on the system.*
1.65	What measures ensure that the access control arrangements are kept up to date and relevant to the underlying business needs?	• *Managers are periodically provided with departmental summaries of users and required to confirm that the details are correct.* • *Access usage is monitored and redundant user-ids highlighted for removal.* • *System level access rights are granted on a "needs" basis in accord with defined standard patterns of access.*

Seq.	Risk/Control Issues	Example Control(s)/Measure(s)
1.66	Who controls the granting of access rights and does management ensure that this operation is correctly conducted?	• *The granting of rights is related to the current policy.* • *The data administrator is held responsible for maintaining the access control system in accord with the policy and the wishes of system owners.* • *Managers are periodically provided with departmental summaries of users and required to confirm that the details are correct.*
1.67	Will attempted security breaches or violations be promptly detected and effectively reported to management?	• *The system allows only three unsuccessful log-on attempts before reporting the events to the data administrator for follow-up investigation.*
1.68	What additional measures are in place to ensure that high-level or privilege access rights are effectively controlled and that relevant actions are trailed?	• *Use of high level facilities is protected by two levels of access control and two passwords.* • *All usage of utilities and privilege facilities are logged and reported to management for sign-off.*
1.69	How does management ascertain that staff are fully aware of their responsibilities with regard to data and system security?	• *The system security and access policy is given to all employees and is augmented by documented procedures which specify responsibilities for data and system security measures.* • *Spot checks are conducted by the technical support team to verify that the prescribed procedures are being complied with.*
1.70	What measures are in place to ensure that user access passwords are effective, and are protected from leakage and misuse?	• *The system enforces password changes every six weeks and prevents the re-use of previous passwords.* • *The system enforces a minimum password length and rejects blank passwords and selected words.* • *Procedures define action to be taken if user suspects a breach of password confidentiality.*
1.71	What measures prevent the casual use of terminals left switched on and unattended?	• *Unattended and inactive terminals are automatically logged-off after a fixed time period. Re-entry of the user-id and password are required to re-activate the system.* • *Personal computers require the entry of a password to reactivate after a period of inactivity.*
	***Personal Computers** (Issues 1.72 to 1.85)*	
1.72	How does management ensure that PC facilities are justified and contribute to business efficiency?	• *PC acquisitions have to be justified against the business requirements and also conform with the IT strategic plan.* • *All purchase requests have to be authorised.*

Seq.	Risk/Control Issues	Example Control(s)/Measure(s)
1.73	How does management ensure that suitable personal computers are obtained from reliable suppliers and that they meet the relevant performance and facility requirements?	• *Only industry standard PC hardware is permitted and specification guidelines have been established.* • *All authorised purchase requests are checked against the defined standard criteria and preferred supplier lists.* • *Preferred suppliers are assessed as to their reliability and stability before any trading relationship is established.* • *Underlying user requirements and performance criteria are established as the basis for acquisition.*
1.74	Does management take steps to ensure that PC hardware is of an appropriate type and quality, and is capable of suitable future expansion?	• *Only industry standard PC hardware is permitted and specification guidelines have been established.* • *Expansion capabilities are assessed as part of the review of preferred suppliers.*
1.75	What steps does management take to protect PC hardware from theft, damage or misuse?	• *Personal computers are fixed to desks with lockable flexible steel cables.* • *All PC hardware is identified with a non-removable label bearing a unique fixed assets register number.* • *Hardware can be removed from the premises only if accompanied by a written authority. Security staff challenge all persons removing equipment and check for the required authority documentation.*
1.76	How is unauthorised and inappropriate software prevented from being loaded on to personal computers (and what specifically prevents users from loading their own software files)?	• *Only established and proven software packages are obtained.* • *A register of licensed copies and their locations is maintained as the basis for regular spot checks on PC hard disk contents.* • *Staff are not permitted to load their own or unlicensed software. All official software is loaded and configured by members of the technical support team, who undertake regular software audits.* • *In selected instances, users' PCs have the floppy drive disabled with a lock to prevent the loading of unauthorised software and data.*
1.77	What measures prevent users from applying unauthorised or inappropriate configuration amendments which could affect performance and reliability?	• *All official software is loaded and configured by members of the technical support team, who undertake regular software and configuration audits.* • *Access to specific configuration facilities is restricted by the use of a password issued only to technical support staff.*

Seq.	Risk/Control Issues	Example Control(s)/Measure(s)
1.78	How is the unauthorised use of personal computers and the relevant data prevented?	• *The system boot-up process is augmented by the use of an access control system requiring the correct entry of a user-ID and password.* • *On-line systems have additional access controls in place which aim to support the access rights granted by the system owners.*
1.79	How does management make sure that staff are adequately trained in the correct and efficient use of PC facilities?	• *General training materials are available to support the efficient and controlled use of PC facilities.* • *Specific application and software package training courses and materials are made available as part of the introduction of new or amended systems.* • *Users have access to the technical and user support teams to assist them with day-to-day problems.*
1.80	Are all hardware and software upgrades applied only by suitably trained and authorised staff (and how is this confirmed)?	• *All hardware and software upgrades are applied by the technical support team.*
1.81	What steps does management take to ensure that the requirements of the prevailing data protection legislation are fully complied with?	• *A data protection policy is in place and reinforced by specific procedures and practices. Training is provided for relevant staff.* • *System access controls and validation measures contribute to the accuracy and relevance of data.* • *Data security and circulation procedures contribute to the protection of data and the prevention of unauthorised disclosure.*
1.82	What steps are in place to prevent undue disruption in the event of hardware failure?	• *Preventive maintenance contracts are in place with suppliers for PC and related hardware.* • *Faults are reported and dealt with on a "same day" basis.* • *Limited numbers of reserve and standby hardware are available in the event of prolonged fault and resolution.*
1.83	What measures protect personal computers from virus infection?	• *All incoming media have to be scanned on a free-standing machine designated for that purpose, before being loaded on to company machines.* • *All PCs have virus detection software installed, which is automatically run on boot-up.* • *Staff are obliged to report all potential virus infections to the technical support team for investigation, isolation and corrective action.*

Seq.	Risk/Control Issues	Example Control(s)/Measure(s)
1.84	What measures prevent users from making unauthorised copies of licensed software and sensitive data files?	• *Unless justified by management, floppy disk drives are locked and therefore unavailable to staff.* • *Original source system diskettes are held by the technical support team.*
1.85	What measures prevent users from circumventing access and operating system controls?	• *Disk drive locks prevent users from booting their PCs via a system disk in the floppy drive.*
	Software Maintenance (Issues 1.86 to 1.92)	
1.86	Are all key systems adequately documented so as to ensure that they can be maintained effectively?	• *All corporate application systems are documented to a defined standard.* • *The details of all authorised program amendments are updated on the system documentation as a trail for subsequent use.*
1.87	What steps ensure that all software amendments are justified, authorised and fully tested before being applied to live use?	• *All system amendments are subject to specification by users and assessment and justification processes. Formal authorisation is required from the IT steering committee.* • *Development and programming standards are in place which define the minimum testing standards.* • *Management and users have to signify their acceptance of the amendment and the test results before transfer to the production environment is permitted.*
1.88	How does management ensure that all software amendments are appropriately coded and are valid for the purpose?	• *Development and programming standards are in place which define the minimum testing standards.* • *Users are required to sign off the testing results and signify their confirmation that the amendment fulfils the specified purpose.*
1.89	What specific measures prevent the unauthorised application of invalid software amendments?	• *Strict version control is exercised over program amendments. The introduction of an unauthorised amendment would require simultaneous amendments to the relevant JCL/ SCL and written authority to permit the transfer from the development environment to the production library.* • *Direct update access to the production library is not permitted. All amendments have to be generated in the development environment and then authorised prior to update in the production area.*

Seq.	Risk/Control Issues	Example Control(s)/Measure(s)
1.90	How can management be assured that only authorised and current versions of programs are utilised in the live production environment?	• *The program contents of the production library are periodically verified against the register of authorised program versions. This check is independently carried out in order to circumvent any possible collusion between operations and development staff.*
1.91	Are all software amendments adequately specified and documented?	• *The details of all authorised program amendments are updated on the system documentation as a trail for subsequent use.* • *Program amendments have to conform to the prescribed documentation standards.*
1.92	What specific arrangements are in place to ensure that only authorised and valid software amendments are applied to personal computers?	• *All application software updates are handled by the technical support team in a consistent manner.* • *Staff are not permitted to introduce their own or unofficial software amendments. Any such unauthorised software would be detected by the technical support team during their regular software audits.*
	Local Area Networks (Issues 1.93 to 1.99)	
1.93	How does management ensure that LAN requirements are fully assessed, justified, and fit in with future expansion requirements?	• *Assessment of current and future LAN requirements was undertaken as part of the strategic planning exercise.* • *Future expansion flexibility taken into account when designing and installing LANs.*
1.94	Are performance and service availability requirements identified as the basis for determining the optimum networking solution?	• *Critical performance and response criteria were identified and incorporated into the LAN requirements specification.* • *Various LAN solutions were fully assessed and costed as the basis for selection.*
1.95	What steps prevent unauthorised access to the networked facilities and protect user systems and data from invalid access?	• *User-id and password system in place to control access to systems and data on a "needs" basis.*
1.96	How does management ensure the integrity of the network system software and its contribution to general data and system security?	• *Only industry standard hardware and network software are utilised.* • *All the appropriate access and facility control mechanisms are enabled.*
1.97	How are file and system servers adequately protected from unauthorised access?	• *File servers, gateway PCs and PCs used for overnight back-up are located in a separate lockable area.* • *File server keyboards are disabled by locks.*

Seq.	Risk/Control Issues	Example Control(s)/Measure(s)
1.98	How is the usage of supervisor and high-level facilities protected from unauthorised usage?	• *Such facilities only accessible via the file server keyboard, which is disabled by a lock.* • *Supervisor facilities are subject to enhanced access controls using double passwords.*
1.99	Has management made adequate arrangements to provide suitable skills for the maintenance and amendment of the network facilities?	• *Suitably experienced staff have been engaged.* • *Additional training is provided when necessary.*
	Database *(Issues 1.100 to 1.111)*	
1.100	How does management ensure that the data needs of the organisation are accurately identified and reflected in current systems and databases?	• *A data modelling exercise was conducted as part of the IT strategic planning review.* • *A corporate data model has been developed and accepted by senior management as the basis for future business requirements.* • *All new and amended systems are required to comply with the agreed data structure.*
1.101	How does management ensure that appropriate, secure, reliable, and flexible database management systems are in place and maintained?	• *Selection of DBMS was subject to formal software evaluation and selection methodology.* • *Stability and reliability of DBMS supplier fully assessed prior to purchase being approved.*
1.102	How does management ensure that appropriate control is exercised over data ownership and the determination of access rights?	• *All systems and associated data are allocated to key users as "owners". The owners determine and agree the access rights of all others.* • *The database administrator is responsible for ensuring that the agreed access rights are reflected in the database system.* • *The access arrangements established to the database are subject to periodic review and agreement by "owners".*
1.103	How is data protected from unauthorised access and amendments, and how is management assured of the accuracy of corporate data?	• *Partly through the application of the access system described in section 1.102 above.* • *Data is subject to various validation and range checks during input. Additionally, data exception reports are generated by the relevant applications for management review and action.*
1.104	How is management assured of the accuracy and relevance of database set-up in support of the business?	• *All new database systems are subject to a planned implementation including the loading of new or set-up data. Such data is reconciled to source and tested for integrity prior to live operation.*
1.105	How is the initial and ongoing integrity of the database structure and records assured?	*See 1.104 above.* • *DBMS has integral integrity checking facilities, i.e. valid pointers, block sums, etc.*

Seq.	Risk/Control Issues	Example Control(s)/Measure(s)
1.106	Has management made adequate arrangements for the ongoing maintenance and operation of the database?	• *The data administrator is responsible for ensuring that adequate day-to-day procedures are in place covering the updating and maintenance of the system.* • *Performance is monitored against agreed service levels and problems are promptly reported and followed up.*
1.107	Are all subsequent amendments to the database structure and contents subject to authorisation, and what measures prevent unauthorised structural amendments?	• *All subsequent database structure amendments are authorised in writing and only applied and thoroughly tested by the data administrator, who then provides confirmation that the appropriate action has been taken.* • *High-level access control is exercised over database amendments and all are reported on activity reports.*
1.108	What specific measures ensure that the database can be promptly and accurately rebuilt in the event of major failure?	• *DBMS incorporates effective tracking of all transactions with before and after images to enable recovery to a defined point in time.* • *DBMS rebuilds are regularly tested in the development environment as part of the contingency plan tests.*
1.109	How does management verify that adequate and effective database back-up precautions are taken?	• *DBMS incorporates effective tracking of all transactions with before and after images to enable recovery to a defined point in time.* • *Back-up is daily. Data is retained in secure back-up store.*
1.110	How would management be made aware of any attempts to violate access arrangements or other unusual database activities?	• *All accesses are logged.* • *Unsuccessful or invalid log-on attempts are restricted to three. All attempted violations are logged and reported to the data administrator and access system manager for follow-up.*
1.111	What measures are in place to ensure that query languages are efficiently and appropriately used (and that enquiries are neither excessive nor over-demanding on system resources)?	• *User training has been provided for the DBMS query language.* • *Overnight batch processing of extensive query language runs to minimise disruption.* • *Query language runs greater than X minutes are switched into background mode to avoid degradation of services*
	Data Protection Law *(Issues 1.112 to 1.117)*	
1.112	What steps has management taken to ensure that all affected staff are made aware of their responsibilities under the prevailing data protection legislation?	• *All new staff receive training in data protection.* • *Data protection principles are incorporated into corporate procedures and instructions.*

Seq.	Risk/Control Issues	Example Control(s)/Measure(s)
1.113	How does management ensure that all the data protection requirements are cost effectively complied with?	• *Data protection principles are incorporated into corporate procedures and instructions.* • *The data protection co-ordinator is responsible for monitoring compliance and following up procedural shortcomings, etc.*
1.114	What measures ensure that the organisation's registration details remain accurate and up to date (e.g. for new systems and business activities)?	• *Registration is periodically reviewed in order to ensure that it remains up to date and accurate.* • *All new activities and systems are reviewed for potential data protection implications.*
1.115	What steps ensure that data protection implications are considered for all systems under development (or where significant amendments are being applied)?	• *The system development methodology incorporates a module for assessing the data protection implications of new systems.* • *All new activities and systems are reviewed for potential data protection implications.*
1.116	What systems are in place to deal effectively with enquiries from data subjects?	• *Each data subject enquiry is logged by the data protection coordinator and referred to the responsible system manager for action.* • *Each enquiry is investigated and assessed—a decision is reached and the enquirer informed of the proposed action.*
1.117	What processes ensure that data errors are promptly corrected?	• *Any detected data errors (or those arising from a data subject enquiry) are corrected or erased as appropriate, and the action is confirmed by the data protection co-ordinator.*
	Facilities Management (Issues 1.118 to 1.126)	
1.118	Where necessary, how does management justify the use of external facilities management services?	• *Current and proposed IT facilities were subject to full cost-benefit assessment.* • *The requirements of the IT strategic plan were taken into account and the approval of the board sought.*
1.119	How does management ensure that the required levels of service provision and cost saving are being achieved?	• *The contractual relationship with the FM supplier incorporates minimum service level requirements. These are monitored and reacted to.* • *Anticipated cost savings were calculated and actual costs are monitored to ensure that predicted benefits are being achieved.*
1.120	How does management ensure that the optimum facilities management solution is selected, taking into account service quality, reliability, and cost?	• *Quality, service and operational criteria were established for the full assessment of all the possible options.* • *The determination of the type of FM service was subject to justification as part of the strategic planning exercise.*

Seq.	Risk/Control Issues	Example Control(s)/Measure(s)
1.121	What processes ensure that all the required responsibilities, rights and liabilities are identified and appropriately allocated between the parties?	• *A comprehensive contract has been established which defines rights, responsibilities, performance requirements and liabilities.* • *Ongoing performance and achievement monitoring is applied to ensure that targets are attained.*
1.122	How is management assured that adequate and effective security will be exercised over company data?	• *Third-party facilities and security arrangements were subject to a full review by the company auditors.*
1.123	Has management clearly established the ownership of hardware, general software and specific company systems?	• *Ownership of all elements has been clearly defined in the contract.*
1.124	Are actual costs and performance measures monitored against defined targets, and what action is taken in the event of service disruption, poor performance or general failure?	• *Ongoing performance and achievement monitoring is applied to ensure that targets are attained.* • *Actual costs are monitored to ensure that predicted benefits are being achieved.* • *Shortfalls and problems are highlighted for management follow-up and action.*
1.125	Has management confirmed that adequate and regularly tested contingency plans are in place to protect ongoing processing and service provision?	• *The third-party supplier has confirmed that documented contingency plans are in place and are regularly tested.* • *Company auditors have attended contingency testing exercises and confirmed that they are satisfied with the arrangements.*
1.126	Are steps in place to ensure that all new systems or process amendments are agreed and fully tested prior to live usage?	• *All amendments to existing programs are justified, agreed, documented, tested and signed off by the users before live usage.*
	System Development (Issues 1.127 to 1.128)	
1.127	How is management assured that all system developments are conducted to a required standard and are appropriately secure?	• *A recognised systems development methodology has been established which incorporates best practice.* • *All aspects of the development are addressed in the methodology including documenting systems, testing, etc.*
1.128	Does management ensure that all new systems are fully tested to the satisfaction of users prior to live usage (and how is this evidenced)?	• *All system developments are subject to formal testing to a prescribed standard.* • *Users are involved in the testing process and are required to sign off the system as meeting their requirements*

Seq.	Risk/Control Issues	Example Control(s)/Measure(s)
	Software Selection (Issues 1.129 to 1.136)	
1.129	How does management ensure that only reliable, proven and secure software products are acquired?	• *Software package evaluation procedures are in place.* • *Products are fully assessed against requirements. Existing users are contacted and their opinions obtained on quality, performance and user support facilities.*
1.130	What steps does management take to confirm the reliability and stability of software suppliers?	• *Only established software suppliers are used.* • *Existing users are contacted and their opinions obtained on supplier performance and reliability.*
1.131	Are all the impacts, costs and implications of software acquisition assessed and is the purchase subject to formal testing and authorisation procedures?	• *All costs are identified (i.e. customising, maintenance, training, implementation, etc.).* • *All purchases have to conform with the documented standards and requirements. Authorisation to purchase is obtained from the IT steering committee.*
1.132	How does management ensure that the software supplier is capable of providing initial and ongoing support?	• *Support services are assessed. The frequency and costs of upgrades are assessed for reasonableness.* • *The opinion of existing users is sought.*
1.133	How does management ensure that the optimum software solution is selected (and are all possible solutions examined)?	• *The formal evaluation of possible solutions should take in the market leaders. All are subject to full assessment as the basis for an informed selection.*
1.134	Does management ensure that software products have a demonstrable upgrade path and are capable of meeting user requirements?	• *The potential for future flexibility and expansion is taken into account during the assessment process. All facilities are reviewed against the requirements specification agreed with users.*
1.135	Does management ensure that adequate user support facilities (including documentation and training) are provided in order to maximise the benefits of the system?	• *Support services are assessed.* • *Adequate user and technical documentation has to be supplied—the quality of this will be reviewed prior to purchase. The supplier will be expected to address any shortcomings.* • *Training needs will be identified during the assessment process. Training proposals and associated costs will, whenever necessary, be incorporated in the proposed solution.*
1.136	What measures ensure that the implementation of new software is planned for and that adequate resources are made available?	• *All implementation impacts are identified and addressed. An implementation plan is produced and resource requirements determined.*

Seq.	Risk/Control Issues	Example Control(s)/Measure(s)
	Contingency Planning (Issues 1.137 to 1.139)	
1.137	What procedures have management provided to ensure that any emergency or major failure can promptly and effectively be rectified?	• *A full risk assessment was conducted and a documented contingency and recovery plan has been developed, agreed and introduced.* • *All possible recovery options were examined and the optimum solution selected.*
1.138	How does management ensure that the prevailing contingency arrangements remain up to date, appropriate and effective?	• *All systems and IT facility changes are assessed for their impact on the contingency and recovery plan, which is accordingly updated.*
1.139	How can management be certain that the current contingency arrangements are the most appropriate and cost-effective in the circumstances?	• *All possible recovery options were examined and costed.* • *The arrangements are reviewed every year in order to ensure that they remain appropriate.*
	User Support (Issues 1.140 to 1.143)	
1.140	Has management taken steps to ensure that adequate and appropriate user support facilities are provided, as a means to ensure the consistent and secure use of corporate IT facilities?	• *Help desk and user support team established. Appropriate skills and facilities provided to address support needs of users throughout the company.* • *Use of IT is supported by documented procedures, policies and guidelines.*
1.141	Have reporting lines been established for both hardware and software faults, and how can management be assured that such problems are promptly and effectively addressed?	• *All faults are initially reported to the help desk, where the details are logged and action is initiated.* • *Call and rectification progress is monitored by the help desk supervisor. Problems are escalated in accord with an agreed timetable.* • *The service provided by external engineers and suppliers is subject to monitoring against the contractual service levels. Problems and delays are escalated.*
1.142	What measures prevent end-users taking unauthorised action to investigate and rectify faults?	• *Standing instructions prohibit users tampering with computer equipment. They could be held liable for any damage.*
1.143	Have service level requirements been established for the user support function, and how is management assured that such levels are being achieved in order to minimise disruption?	• *All calls are logged and subsequent corrective progress is timed against established service level requirements.* • *Failures to meet the established deadlines are reported and escalated for further action. Overall performance statistics are maintained and reviewed by management.*

Seq.	Risk/Control Issues	Example Control(s)/Measure(s)
	IT Accounting *(Issues 1.144 to 1.147)*	
1.144	Has management agreed, circulated and established an accounting policy for the IT function?	• *User management participated in the development of an agreed IT accounting policy incorporating charge-out rates for IT services.* • *Procedures are in place governing the flow of IT accounting information and the process for challenging charges.*
1.145	Have budgets been established and are they subject to effective monitoring and follow-up?	• *Monthly budget and actual reports circulated to all key user managers.*
1.146	Have end-users been allocated responsibility for their IT-related costs?	• *Users are made aware of the basis for incurring IT charges based on service provision and transaction levels.* • *Usage of query systems and report generators is in hands of users. Estimated costs are displayed at the end of the appropriate processing session.* • *Costs can be broken down to individual user-ids if required.*
1.147	What measures have management taken to ensure that IT usage costs are fairly, accurately and completely accounted for and charged out to users where necessary?	• *Users have been involved in the determination of the charge-out basis.* • *System statistics can be supplied in support of queried charges if required*

Bibliography

American Institute of Certified Public Accountants, *Internal Control—Integrated Framework*, Committee of Sponsoring Organisations of the Treadway Commission, AICPA, September 1992.

Atkinson, H., Hamburg, J. and Ittner, C. (1994) *Linking Quality to Profits; Quality-Based Cost Management*. ASQC Press, Milwaukee.

Barden, R. A. (1987) *DP Back-up Procedures*. NCC Publications, Manchester.

Barefield, R. M. and Young, S. M. (1988) *Internal Auditing in a Just-in-Time Manufacturing Environment*. The Institute of Internal Auditors Research Foundation, IIA Inc., Florida.

Baston, J. and Brown, A. (1991) "Spreadsheet Modelling Best Practice". *Accountants Digest 273*. ICAEW, London.

Beasley, K. (1994) *Self Assessment—A Tool for Integrated Management*. Stanley Thornes, Cheltenham.

British Standards Institute (1995) *Code of Practice for Information Security Management—BS7799*. BSI, London.

British Standards Institute (1989) *Recommendations for the Accommodation and Operating Environment of Computer Equipment—BS7083*. BSI, London.

British Standards Institute/International Standards Organization/IEC (1993) *Information Technology Vocabulary and Fundamental Terms*. BS/ISO/IEC2382 & 2382-1.

Burns, T. and Stalker, G. M. (1961) *The Management of Innovation*. Tavistock Press, London.

Buttery, R., Hurford, C. and Simpson, R. K. (1993) *Audit in the Public Sector*. ICSA, London.

Casler, D. J. and Crockett, J. R. (1982) *Operational Auditing: An Introduction*. IIA, Altmonte Springs, Florida.

Chambers, A. D. (1992) *Effective Internal Audits*. Pitman, London.

Chambers, A. D. and Court, J. M. (1991) *Computer Auditing*. Third edition, Pitman, London.

Chambers, A. D. and Rand, G. V. (1994) *Auditing Contracts*. Pitman, London.

Chambers, A. D. and Rand, G. V. (1994) *Auditing the IT Environment*. Pitman, London.

Chambers, A. D. and Rand, G. V. (1995) *IT-Based Risk Analysis*. ICAEW, London.

Chambers, A. D., Selim, G. M. and Vinten, G. (1987) *Internal Auditing*. Second edition, Pitman, London.

Chartered Institute of Public Finance and Accountancy (1989) *A Guide to the Financial Management and Audit of Contracts*. CIPFA, London.

Chartered Institute of Public Finance and Accountancy (1981) *Audit Occasional Paper No. 3: An Approach to the Measurement of the Performance of Internal Audit.* CIPFA, London.

Chartered Institute of Public Finance and Accountancy (1992) *BACS Guidance Note.* Third edition, CIPFA, London.

Chartered Institute of Public Finance and Accountancy (1992) *Contract Audit—JCT Guidance Notes.* CIPFA, London.

Chartered Institute of Public Finance and Accountancy (1984) *Contract Audit (Site Visits) Guidance Notes.* CIPFA, London.

Chartered Institute of Public Finance and Accountancy (1983) *Contract Audit Guidance Notes (ICE Conditions—Fifth Edition).* CIPFA, London.

Chartered Institute of Public Finance and Accountancy (1992) *Measuring the Performance of Internal Audit.* CIPFA, London.

Chartered Institute of Public Finance and Accountancy (1991) *Value for Money Auditing— The Investigation of Economy, Efficiency and Effectiveness.* CIPFA, London.

Court, J. M. (Ed.) (1984) *Audit and Control in a Complex Computer Environment.* ICAEW, London.

Court, J. M. (Ed.) (1988) *Audit and Control in a Microcomputer Environment.* ICAEW, London.

Department of Trade and Industry (the Commercial IT Security Group) (April 1992) *Dealing with Computer Misuse.* HMSO, London.

Devargas, M. (1992) *Local Area Networks.* Second edition, NCC Blackwell, Oxford.

Devargas, M. (1993) *Network Security.* NCC Blackwell, Oxford.

Doswell, R. and Simons, G. L. (1986) *Fraud and Abuse of IT Systems.* NCC Blackwell, Oxford.

Douglas, I. J. (1982) *Audit and Control of Minicomputers.* NCC Publications, Oxford.

Douglas, I. (1995) *Computer Audit and Control Handbook.* Butterworth-Heinemann, Oxford.

Elbra, R. A. (1990) *A Practical Guide to the Computer Misuse Act 1990.* NCC Blackwell, Oxford.

Elbra, R. A. (1986) *Security Review Manual.* NCC Publications, Manchester.

Ellison, J. R. and Pritchard, J. A. T. (1987) *Security in Office Systems.* NCC Blackwell, Oxford.

Hagen, J. T. (Ed.) (1986) *Principles of Quality Costs.* Quality Cost Committee, American Society of Quality Control, ASQC Press, Milwaukee.

HMSO (1990) *Computer Misuse Act.* HMSO, London

HMSO (1984) *Data Protection Act.* HMSO, London.

Hertz, D. and Thomas, H. (1984) *Practical Risk Analysis—An Approach through Case Studies.* John Wiley, Chichester.

Hook, C. (1989) *Data Protection Implications for Systems Design.* NCC Publications, Manchester.

Impey, K. W. (1993) *Operational Review.* Butterworths, Oxford.

Insight Consulting (1995) "Security on the Internet", *Insight on Risk*, Vol. 1, Issue 2, August. Insight Consulting, Walton on Thames.

Institute of Chartered Accountants in England and Wales (Faculty of Information Technology) (1995) *An Approach to the Audit of Less Complex Computerised Accounting Systems.* The Faculty of Information Technology of ICAEW, London.

Institute of Chartered Accountants in England and Wales (Faculty of Information Technology) (1994) *Business Process Redesign*. NCC Blackwell and The Faculty of Information Technology of ICAEW, Oxford.

Institute of Chartered Accountants in England and Wales (1987) *Countering Computer Fraud*. ICAEW, London.

Institute of Chartered Accountants in England and Wales (1994) *Internal Control and Financial Reporting*. ICAEW, London.

Institute of Internal Auditors Inc. (1994) *Systems Auditability and Control*. IIA, Florida.

Institute of Internal Auditors Inc. (1993) *The Role of Internal Auditors in Environmental Issues*. Institute of Internal Auditors Research Foundation, Altamonte Springs, Florida.

Institute of Internal Auditors—UK (1993) *A Quality System Manual for Internal Audit*. IIA-UK, London.

International Chamber of Commerce (ICC) (1989) *Environmental Auditing*. ICC Publishing S.A., Paris.

Jones, L. G. (1990) *Internal Audit Involvement in the Joint-Venture Process*. Institute of Internal Auditors Research Foundation, IIA Inc., Florida.

Koontz, H., O'Donnell, C. and Weihrich, H. (1976) *Management*. Eighth edition, McGraw-Hill, Singapore.

Ledgerwood, G. Street, E. and Therivel, R. (1992) *The Environmental Audit and Business Strategy*. Pitman, London.

List, W. and Melville, R. (1994) *Integrity in Information Systems*. City University Business School, Working Paper, October 1994; and International Federation for Information Processing (IFIP) Working Group 11.5.

Mair, W. C., Wood, D. R. and Davis, K. W. (1978) *Computer Control and Audit*. Revised edition, Institute of Internal Auditors Inc. Florida.

Ministry of Defence (1994) *Security in Open Systems TDP: Generic Security Principles*. TDP/S/94/01, 14 March 1994, MOD Procurement Executive, London.

Nugus, S. and Harris, S. (1992) *PC Data Recovery and Disaster Prevention*. NCC Blackwell, Oxford.

O'Shea, G. (1991) *Security in Computer Operating Systems*. NCC Blackwell, Oxford.

Parfett, M. (1992) *What is EDI?* NCC Blackwell, Oxford.

Remenyi, D. S. J. (1991) *Introducing Strategic Information Systems Planning (SISP)*. NCC Blackwell, Oxford.

Remenyi, D. S. J. (1990) *Strategic Information Systems*. NCC Blackwell, Oxford.

Renger, M. (1992) *Environmental Audit*. ICAEW, London.

Report of the Committee on the Financial Aspects of Corporate Governance ("The Cadbury Report") (December 1992). Gee, London.

Report of the Committee on the Financial Aspects of Corporate Governance—Compliance with the Code of Best Practice (1995). Gee, London.

Robb, A. F. (1992) *The Management Guide to the Selection and Implementation of Computer Systems*. NCC Blackwell, Oxford.

Roberts, D. W. (1990) *Computer Security: Policy Planning and Practice*. NCC Blackwell, Oxford.

Tibor, T. and Feldman, I. (1995) *ISO 14000 A Guide to the New Environmental Management Standards*. Irwin Professional Publishing, Burr Ridge, Illinois.

Towers, S. (1994) *Business Process Re-Engineering—A Practical Handbook for Executives*. Stanley Thornes, Cheltenham.

Velasquez, M. G. (1992) *Business Ethics. Concepts and Cases*. Prentice-Hall.

Walden, I. and Braganza, A. (Eds) (1993) *EDI, Audit and Control*. NCC Blackwell, Oxford.

Index

Page numbers in **bold italics** refer to example programmes of Control Objectives and Risk/Control Issues.